We Are a People

We Are a People

Narrative and Multiplicity in Constructing Ethnic Identity

EDITED BY

Paul Spickard and W. Jeffrey Burroughs

TEMPLE UNIVERSITY PRESS

PHILADELPHIA

Temple University Press, Philadelphia 19122
Copyright © 2000 by Temple University
All rights reserved
Published 2000
Printed in the United States of America

Library of Congress Cataloging-in-Publication Data

We are a people: narrative and multiplicity in constructing ethnic identity / edited
    by Paul Spickard and W. Jeffrey Burroughs.
        p.   cm.
    Includes bibliographical references.
    ISBN 1-56639-722-7 (alk. paper). — ISBN 1-56639-723-5 (pbk.: alk. paper)
    1. Ethnicity.   2. Indigenous peoples.   3. Immigrants—Ethnic identity.
4. Multiculturalism.   I. Spickard, Paul R., 1950– .   II. Burroughs, W. Jeffrey.
GN495.6.W4   1999
305.8–DC21   99-14398

To Lonia Burroughs and Jim Spickard

Contents

Acknowledgments   ix

1.   WE ARE A PEOPLE   1
      Paul Spickard and W. Jeffrey Burroughs

Part I: The Indeterminacy of Ethnic Categories: The Problem and a Solution

2.   MULTIPLE ETHNICITIES AND IDENTITY IN THE UNITED STATES   23
      Mary C. Waters

3.   THAT'S THE STORY OF OUR LIFE   41
      Stephen Cornell

Part II: Construction of Ethnic Narratives: Migrant Ethnicities

4.   BLACK IMMIGRANTS IN THE UNITED STATES   57
      Violet M. Johnson

5.   THE CHILDREN OF SAMOAN MIGRANTS IN NEW ZEALAND   70
      Cluny Macpherson and La'avasa Macpherson

Part III: Ethnicities of Dominated Indigenous Peoples

6.   NARRATING TO THE CENTER OF POWER IN THE MARSHALL ISLANDS   85
      Phillip H. McArthur

7. DISCOVERED IDENTITIES AND AMERICAN INDIAN SUPRATRIBALISM 98
   Stephen Cornell

8. THE ANATOMY OF SCIENTIFIC RACISM: RACIALIST RESPONSES TO BLACK ATHLETIC ACHIEVEMENT 124
   Patrick B. Miller

9. I'M NOT A CHILENO! RAPA NUI IDENTITY 142
   Max E. Stanton

Part IV: Emerging Multiethnic Narratives

10. MULTIRACIAL IDENTITY IN BRAZIL AND THE UNITED STATES 153
    G. Reginald Daniel

11. MIXED LAUGHTER 179
    Darby Li Po Price

12. PUNJABI MEXICAN AMERICAN EXPERIENCES OF MULTIETHNICITY 192
    Karen Leonard

Part V: Theoretical Reflections

13. RETHINKING RACIAL IDENTITY DEVELOPMENT 205
    Maria P. P. Root

14. THE CONTINUING SIGNIFICANCE OF RACE 221
    Lori Pierce

15. WHAT ARE THE FUNCTIONS OF ETHNIC IDENTITY? 229
    Cookie White Stephan and Walter G. Stephan

16. ETHNICITY, MULTIPLICITY, AND NARRATIVE: PROBLEMS AND POSSIBILITIES 244
    W. Jeffrey Burroughs and Paul Spickard

Contributors 255

Acknowledgments

This book began with a conference held in the stimulating intellectual and intercultural climate of Brigham Young University–Hawai'i, funded by that institution's Division of Social Sciences and the Institute for Polynesian Studies. We are grateful to President Eric Shumway, Vice-President Olani Durrant, and Director of Continuing Education Theresa Bigbie, all at BYUH, to President Lester Moore of the neighboring Polynesian Cultural Center, and to their excellent colleagues for their generosity and hospitality. The BYUH Division of Social Sciences and the University of California–Santa Barbara Asian American Studies Department have supported the subsequent editing of the manuscript. Janet Francendese of Temple University Press has been a rigorous and supportive guide throughout the editing and production stages. Lynne Frost (Berliner Inc.) and Jennifer French (Temple University Press) shepherded this project to completion with efficiency and grace.

Among the participants in that original conference whose ideas and *mana* helped shape this book, but whose words we were not able to include in the final volume, are: Melani Anae, Arthe Anthony, Margaret Baker, Jeff Belnap, David Bertelson, Wurlig Borchigud, Dan Boylan, Maria Brave Heart-Jordan, Cy Bridges, David Chappell, Allen Chun, Chad Compton, Patricia Delaney, Yen Le Espiritu, Rowena Fong, Xuanning Fu, Inoke Funaki, Dru Gladney, Theo Gonzalves, Karina Kahananui Green, Henry Gutierrez, Marilyn Halter, Marie Hara, Tim Heaton, Mark Helbling, Debbie Hippolite Wright, Ann-Marie Horvath, Alan Howard, Ron Jackson, Cardell Jacobson, Larry Jensen, Jon Jonassen, Kelly Kautz, Nora Keller, David Knowlton, Roberta Lang, Greg Mark, Tony Marsella, Davianna McGregor, Arapata Meha, Laurie Mengel, Taima Moeke-Pickering, Sandra Morrison, Sue Nance, Dorri Nautu, Ann Ngatai, Linda Nikora, Jonathan Osorio, Barbara Peterson, Jan Rensel, Linda Revilla, Keith Roberts, Dale Robertson, Malka Shabtay, Tom Svensson, Monique Taylor, William Kauaiwiulaokalani Wallace III, Gale Ward, Kathleen Ward, Hillary Weaver, and Vernice Wineera. We are grateful to them all.

We Are a People

Paul Spickard and W. Jeffrey Burroughs

---

1 We Are a People

Miskito Indian leader Steadman Fagoth was asked in 1985 what he thought about the policy of Nicaragua's Sandinista government toward his "ethnic group." "Ethnic group!" he snorted. "We're not an ethnic group. Ethnic groups have restaurants. We are a *people*!"[1]

One may quibble that "ethnic group" means "people" (after all, *ethnos* is the Greek word for "a people"). But Fagoth's point is a good one. Ethnicity is not trivial. It is not just having a Polish last name, going to a Chinese restaurant, or wearing a button that says, "Kiss me, I'm Irish." Ethnicity—that powerful bond of peoplehood—is one of the most important forces organizing individual understandings of reality and the grouping and dividing of peoples in the world today. It organizes and gives meaning, as groups, to the Basques in Spain, Byelorussians in the former Soviet Union, Kurds in Iraq and Turkey, Uygurs in China, and Whites in America.[2]

It has been ever thus. England was formed out of the mixing and battling ethnic consciousnesses of Angle and Celt, Saxon and Norman. South Africa's history is defined by the confrontation of Boer and Briton and Zulu and Xhosa. India was built by Dravidians dominated by Aryans and conquered in turn by Turko-Afghans and then by English people. Yugoslavia was built out of Croat and Serb, Slovene and Macedonian, Muslim and Montenegrin—and then it fell apart on those same ethnic lines. Ethnicity is one of the primary organizing principles of human history.

Having said that, it is also true that no one seems to understand very well how ethnicity works. There is at present no satisfactory theory that unites the field.[3] There is not even a common definition of what ethnicity is, or exactly how it relates to other, contiguous concepts such as "race" and "nation." Some students have interpreted ethnicity as a naturalistic phenomenon, with emphasis on biology or ancestry. Others have pursued social scientific explanations that emphasize the factors—such as group interests, culture, and institutions—that have shaped the creation, maintenance, and change of ethnicity in groups. Psychologists and humanists have delved into ethnicity as individual experience and expression.

The tasks of this collection of essays are to try to sort out some of the confusion surrounding ethnicity; to explore the linkages between naturalistic, social scientific, and humanistic ways of understanding ethnicity; and to move toward some common theoretical understandings of ethnic phenomena. In particular, the authors whose work comes together in this volume are concerned with narrative and multiethnicity as key issues in understanding ethnic questions.

Naturalistic Explanations of Ethnicity

The first thing to be said about an ethnic group is that it is an arrangement of people who see themselves as biologically and historically connected with each other, and who are seen by others as being so connected. Whether the biological connection is true or not is less important than that the people in question and others around them believe it to be true. It may be that many east European Jews were not in fact biological descendants of the ancient Israelites—they perhaps did not issue from the loins of Abraham. Rather, they may in fact have been the descendants of Central Asian Khazar tribes who converted to Judaism in the Middle Ages.[4] Nonetheless, they believed themselves to be descended from Abraham, Isaac, and Jacob, and non-Jews believed it, too. That sense of shared ancestry and the thousands of years of shared history that went with it form the basis of Jewish ethnic identity.[5]

Race vs. Ethnicity

Beyond that common understanding of ethnicity as shared ancestry, there is plenty of confusion surrounding the subject. There is confusion, for instance, about the nature of the relationship between ethnicity and race. There was a time when most Americans, Europeans, and others who had imbibed Western education—at least those who thought about ethnicity—would divide the human population conceptually first into discrete races: red, yellow, black, brown, and white. These "races," supposedly based in biology, were simply a bottom-level extension of the system of classification of all living things, first constructed in the eighteenth century by Linnaeus, the Swedish botanist and taxonomist, and extended to human "races" by nineteenth-century pseudoscientific racists such as Blumenbach and Gobineau. According to such a system, an individual from sub-Saharan Africa would be a member of the kingdom Animalia, the phylum Chordata, the class Mammalia, the order Primates, the family Hominidae, the genus *Homo,* the species *Homo sapiens,* and the race *africanus.*[6] The rationale for putting certain people in one race and others in another derived from geography and observed physical differences.

Ethnic groups, according to such thinking, were simply subdivisions of these larger phenotypic categories called "races." Thus, a person whose ancestors came from Bavaria belonged to the German ethnic group and the Caucasian race, while a person from Kyoto was seen as a member of the Japanese ethnic group and the Mongolian race. These, then, were the ideas of Gobineau and Blumenbach, a century ago and more.

Even today, in talking about ethnic issues, many people intuitively divide humankind up into large groups that they call "races" and smaller subgroups that they call "ethnic groups." According to that way of thinking, a partial listing of racial and ethnic groups might look like the schema in Figure 1.

Species	Homo sapiens								
Race	White			Black			Yellow		
Ethnic Group	English	German	Italian	Ibo	Zulu	Fon	Korean	Chinese	Japanese

FIGURE 1.   Pseudoscientific racists divided the human species conceptually into big "races" and smaller "ethnic groups."

There are at least three problems with this way of thinking about race and ethnicity. In the first place, although this purports to be a biological classification system, "race" as defined here has only a tiny basis in biology. It is, in fact, primarily a social construct (with obvious economic and political motives and implications), as are the ethnic groups that are supposed to be subdivisions of races in this schema. James C. King, a prominent U.S. geneticist of racial matters, contends: "Both what constitutes a race and how one recognizes a racial difference are culturally determined. Whether two individuals regard themselves as of the same or of different races depends not on the degree of similarity of their genetic material but on whether history, tradition, and personal training and experiences have brought them to regard themselves as belonging to the same group or to different groups. . . . [T]here are no objective boundaries to set off one subspecies [his term for 'race'] from another."[7]

The process of racial labelling starts with geography, culture, and family ties and runs through politics and economics to biology, not the other way around. That is, a group is defined by an observer according to its location, its cultural practices, or its social connectedness. Then, on looking at physical markers or genetic makeup, the observer may find that this group shares certain items with greater frequency than do other populations that are also socially defined. But even in such cases, there is tremendous overlap between racial categories with regard to biological features. As Yale psychologist Edmund Gordon writes: "The problem of reliably identifying biological subgroups of human beings is intractable. . . . [T]here are [quoting A. K. Appiah] 'few genetic characteristics to be found in the population of England that are not found in similar proportions in Zaire or China, and few too (though more) that are found in Zaire but not in similar proportions in China and England.' . . . [T]he differences within so-called races are more significant than the differences between them. Nonetheless, race designations have been arbitrarily assigned based almost solely on a few physical differences such as skin color, hair curl, and eye-fold. . . . [T]he colloquial designation of a group as a race is thus not a function of significant biological or genetic differences."[8]

The second problem with thinking of "ethnic groups" as subdivisions of "races" is that the manifestations of these supposed racial categories are not clearly distinct. Races do divide people into groups that are, *on the average,* physically different from each other. For example, Black people do, on the average, have darker skin, longer limbs, and more wiry hair than do White people, on the average. And Asians do, on the average, have shorter limbs and darker hair than do Caucasians, on the average. But those averages disguise a great deal of overlap.

Let us take just one marker that is supposed to divide races biologically: skin color. Suppose people can be arranged along a continuum according to the color of their skin, from darkest to lightest. The people we call Black would nearly all fall on the darker end of the continuum, while the people we call White would nearly all fall on the lighter end. On the *average,* the White and Black populations would differ from each other in skin color. But a very large number of the individuals classified as White would have darker skin than some people classified as Black, and vice versa. This situation inevitably leads one to the suspicion that so-called "races" are not biological categories at all, but primarily social divisions that rely only partly on physical markers such as skin color to identify group membership.

Sometimes, skin color and social definitions run counter to one another. Take the case of Walter White and Poppy Cannon. In the 1930s and 1940s, White was one of the most prominent African Americans. An author and activist, he served for twenty years as the executive secretary of the National Association for the Advancement of Colored People (NAACP). Physically, White was short, slim, sandy haired, and blue-eyed. On the street he would not have been taken for an African American by anyone who did not know his identity. But he had been raised in the South in a family of very light-skinned Blacks, and he was socially defined as Black, both by others and by himself. He dedicated his life and career to serving Black Americans. In 1949, White divorced his African American wife of many years' standing and married Cannon, a White journalist and businesswoman. Although Cannon was a Caucasian socially and ancestrally, her hair, eyes, and skin were several shades darker than her new husband's. If a person were shown pictures of the couple and told that one partner was Caucasian and the other Black, without doubt that person would select Cannon as the Afro-American. Yet, immediately upon White's divorce, the Black press erupted in protest. White was accused of having sold out his race for a piece of White flesh, and Cannon, of having seduced one of Black America's most beloved leaders. White segregationists took the occasion to crow that this was what Black advocates of civil rights really wanted: access to White women. This was because White was socially Black and Cannon was socially White; biology—at least physical appearance—had nothing to do with it.[9]

Despite the idea of "race" having little biological basis, it has been used as if it had such a foundation, to the detriment of a lot of people. The ideas about race described here—as the bottom layer in an orderly, enduring, nested hierarchy of groups and subgroups, based on biological criteria—were picked up by pseudoscientific racists in the late nineteenth and early twentieth centuries and put to vicious use. Such racists arranged the "races" hierarchically, with northwestern Europeans at the top and a rough hierarchy of color descending. Differences between peoples were deemed to be immutable, the inevitable product of their gene pools. Such ideas provided much of the justification for the U.S. anti-immigrant movement of the first quarter of the twentieth century.[10] The most prominent recent published example of peudoscientific racism is *The Bell Curve,* by Richard Herrnstein and Charles Murray, which purports to find genetic differences at the root of such a phenomenon as ethnic variation in school performance.[11]

The third problem with the notion of large "races" and smaller "ethnic groups" as subdivisions is that "races," so defined, do not classify very much that is important. According to this way of thinking, Vietnamese and Koreans are supposed to be of the same race. If one grants that they may look a bit similar to outsiders (they certainly do not to insiders), in what other ways are they similar? In what other ways is grouping them in one "race" significant? Do they act alike? Do they worship in the same way? Are their governments or family systems similar? Are they more like each other in action, thought, worship, and political behavior than either is like Swedes or Jews? Insofar as they may in fact be similar, is it because of their biology, or is it because of centuries of contact and sharing Chinese imperial culture?

All of this is not to argue that "race" does not matter. It is, on the contrary, very important: people kill people over "race." The argument here is merely that "race," like "ethnic group," is primarily a social and political, not a biological, means of classifying people. It does not mean that "race" is not an important category in human relationships, only that what are often called "races" are for analytical purposes varieties of what we here are calling "ethnic groups".[12] The mechanisms that divide races from each other are the same mechanisms that divide ethnic groups from one another. The processes that bind a race together are the same processes that bind an ethnic group together. For the purposes of the essays by the editors of this volume, we use "ethnic group" as the generic term.[13]

Racialization

There is another school of opinion on this question, and it is represented within this volume as well. Scholars of the racialization school are active opponents of racism yet adopt the terminology, hence the oppressive categories, of the pseudoscientific racists. They contest racism but not racial thinking. As one of their most outspoken advocates, Roger Sanjek, puts it, their use of "race focuses on the present and future of the *contemporary* racial order."[14] That is, they note that "race," while it is an artificial social and political construction, lies at the heart of the current social hierarchy. They are preoccupied with fighting oppression within that social hierarchy, and they choose to use the categories of the racists to fight racism.

For racializationists, "race" means a variety of "ethnicity" where one group uses power negatively against another, and where there is emphasis on the body. The emphasis on the physicality of "race," a holdover from the pseudoscientific racists, is only a minor key for the racializationists. For writers of this school, "ethnic group" is the generic term for a group of people who share common descent and culture; they become a "race," according to this kind of thinking, when someone does something bad to them on account of their ethnicity. "Race," so understood, entered the world as a key support for a system of "racism," part of the intellectual apparatus created by Europeans and North Americans to justify the capitalist colonial (later neocolonial) system of exploitation that began to emerge in the fifteenth century and came to dominate world affairs and oppress colonized peoples most mightily in the nineteenth and twentieth centuries. Such authors speak of "racialization": when ethnic groups are oppressed, they become racialized. The locus of causality is placed in biology, rather than in human relationships.[15]

April Henderson locates the value of the racialization approach in its usefulness as a tool for organizing resistance: "oppression serves as rationale enough to organize.... [T]he connection between oppression and race is then made; because the politics of oppression are so often cast in terms of the politics of race, the politics of resistance have also been imbued with racialized language."[16] Michele Dominy notes that White lesbians and Maori women activists in Aotearoa (i.e., New Zealand) both use the word "Black" to describe themselves, "as an oppositional marker rather than as a biological category."[17] Henderson notes that this equation of Blackness (and we may extend her analysis to include the idea of race itself) not with racial typology but with the experience of oppression "provides an alternative framework for discussing blackness at a time when scientific typologies are for the most part denounced and rejected. Stripped of its shaky biological underpinnings, race becomes a state of existence, even a state of mind."[18]

Consideration of ethnic situations outside the U.S. context makes obvious the limitations of the racialization model for ethnic analysis. The twentieth-century actions of Turks murdering Armenians and Germans exterminating Jews both fit the racializationists' criteria for "racial" encounters: domination based on ancestral identity that is supposedly grounded in biological differences. Yet the racializationists' model of big races and little ethnic subgroups would force Turks and Armenians, Germans and Jews, all into the White or Caucasoid race. It would seem important to examine the oppressive qualities of these ethnic interactions as well.

The racialization model does not sufficiently illuminate ethnic interaction in Asia and the Pacific, either. In those regions, ethnic processes happen mightily and with immense negative force, but terms like "race" make little sense. In Fiji, for example, ethnic Fijians (mixed Melanesians and Polynesians, a little less than half the population) complain of economic discrimination at the hands of ethnic Indians (a little less than half the population), who complain that ethnic Fijians have disenfranchised them and monopolized the political system. Both charges are more or less true, and both groups see their identities as ethnically based, but no one talks of race. In the People's Republic, Han Chinese are the worst sort of colonial oppressors of Tibetans and Uygurs, yet they are all Asians, and "race" is the term of almost no one's analysis.[19]

Because this book has an international focus, we are searching for terminology that works in many contexts around the globe. We think "ethnicity" fills that bill. We do not wish to have this preference of ours for using "ethnicity" as the generic term overshadow other aspects of this book or this essay. It is really just a minor terminological quibble. We hold no particular brief for the term "ethnicity" and welcome proposals for another term.[20]

Perhaps which term is most appropriate may depend on a scholar's main purpose in a particular piece of work. In using "race," the focus is either on the body (a minor key) or on political action. People who speak of "racialization" use the term as a starting point for pursuing an antiracist political project. One can make a distinction between "race" and "ethnic group" and still work at understanding group processes, but for that purpose the racializationist approach is ultimately confusing. By the same token, antiracist political action is possible using "ethnicity," no less than with the racializationist choice, although we must admit that calling someone an "ethnist" lacks the punch of calling someone a "racist." The danger with the racializationist position is that one may easily slide over into speaking of "racializing" other sorts of difference, such as gender and class, making "race" an amorphous synonym for "oppressed." To adopt the rhetorical posture of our racializationist colleagues is, in the larger scheme of things, to give in to the pseudoscientific racists. It tends to grant the implication of legitimacy to the racists' use of genetic markers to explain social and political behavior, and to acquiesce in the popular notion of big races and smaller ethnic subunits. We cannot help feeling that adopting the language of the oppressor (and thereby the analytical categories of the oppressor) is a poor platform from which to fight oppression.

On the other hand, use of the term "ethnicity" may be most appropriate when the focus is on understanding group processes, as in the present volume. Some contend that to use "ethnicity" is to try to make universal or normative the experiences of White European immigrant groups to the United States. While that may have been an intellectual (or even a political) project for Robert Ezra Park or Nathan Glazer, we emphatically reject that use of the term.[21] Our intent in this volume is to provide a common platform for students of ethnic processes in many cultures to examine the dynamics of those processes. The strength of our approach is that it gives us a single language for understanding ethnic groups and their processes around the globe.

So, while we share the political convictions of the racializationists, the task of this book is not to advance our antiracist political agenda so much as it is to understand ethnic processes of cohesion and identity as they affect individuals and groups, and we choose "ethnicity" as the generic term. Nonetheless, though we quibble over language, we think the racializationist approach important enough that we have solicited a specific response to this terminological issue from a racializationist perspective. It appears as chapter 14, "The Continuing Significance of Race," by Lori Pierce. We view Pierce's essay and this one as cooperative, rather than competitive for the reader's allegiance.

Social Scientific Explanations of Ethnicity

The task of this book is to understand what makes ethnic groups work—what kinds of things hold ethnic groups together and what may cause them to fall apart. Ethnic groups are not primordial units of human relationship. They are social groupings that form, change their shape and the glue that holds them together, and sometimes fall apart. Many writers who treat only the U.S. ethnic scene seem to think otherwise. They echo the sentiments of Hector St. John de Crèvecoeur: "What then is this American, this new man? ... *He* is an American, who, leaving behind him all his ancient prejudices and manners, receives new ones from the new mode of life he has embraced, the new government he obeys, and the new rank he holds. He becomes an American by being received into the broad lap of our great *Alma Mater*. Here individuals are melted into a new race of men."[22] Thus, Richard Alba writes of Italian Americans (and, indeed, of *all* American ethnic groups) marching inexorably "into the twilight of ethnicity." He depicts them as putting off their primordial identities, losing the salient aspects of ethnic ties, and, keeping the labels but none of the content of those ancient identities, becoming "assimilated" into a single, nearly undifferentiable, nonethnic mass.[23]

Such an interpretation seems short-sighted. Alba's Italian Americans may in fact dissolve and cease to function as an ethnic group. But that does not mean that the people who have Italian ancestors lack ethnicity, only that their ethnicity has changed from Italian American to Catholic American or White American or simply American.[24]

For purposes of the discussion in this book, these are all ethnic identities. Here we shall see ethnic groups being formed; we shall see them changing their boundaries and the bases that hold them together; and we shall see some come close to disappearing.

In the twentieth century, most systematic thinking about ethnicity has been done by social scientists. Beyond the commonsense understanding of ethnicity as shared ancestry, as kinship writ large, a survey of social scientific writing identifies three forces that shape the creation, sustenance, dissolution, and re-formation of ethnic groups.[25] These are shared interests, shared institutions, and shared culture. All three are important. No one of them is more fundamental than the others to the nature of an ethnic group. Each has a role to play in shaping group consciousness and action at various times in the history of the ethnic group. Most theorists have been inclined to see one of the three as fundamental and the others as superstructural. It is not true.

Shared interests, political or economic, are usually what pulls an ethnic group together in the first place. That is, if a set of people perceive themselves to share a common heritage and also have concrete economic or political reasons for affiliating with each other, they may begin to form an ethnic group. Much of the recent writing about ethnicity, from Abner Cohen on south central African copper miners to William Julius Wilson on African Americans, has centered around ethnicity as shared interests.[26]

One example of this type of group formation is occurring among Latinos in the United States today. Latinos, or "Hispanics," as some call them, are not a single group. The three largest groups—Mexicans, Puerto Ricans, and Cubans—have very little in common. Mexican Americans live throughout the country but are concentrated in the Southwest, exhibit an ancestral mixture of Spanish and Indian, are concentrated in the lower and middle classes, and vote heavily for the Democratic Party. Some have been in what is now the United States since before the American Revolution, while others arrived yesterday. Puerto Rican Americans are concentrated mainly in the industrial cities of the Northeast, mix Black ancestry with Spanish and Indian, are heavily working class, and generally vote Democratic. Cuban Americans are concentrated in Florida, are visibly lighter of skin on the average than the other two groups, have many more members of the upper middle class, and usually vote for the Republican Party. Each of these groups came to the United States at a different time and for very different reasons. Each spoke a different variety of Spanish, and each pursued a subtly different variety of Catholic Christianity.[27]

All share certain cultural similarities, but there is not strong cultural uniformity. What all three groups have most in common is an *interest.* Independently, none of the groups is large enough to attract much attention from the U.S. government or the public at large outside the locale of its highest concentration. But together they can muster millions of voters. Thus, Mexican, Cuban, and Puerto Rican Americans have a political *interest* in banding together as "Hispanics." In time, we may see Hispanics forming shared institutions and creating shared culture that will sustain their group.

A similar situation obtained for Italian immigrants and Jews. Both these groups highlight the role that ascription by outsiders frequently plays in defining ethnic boundaries. Italy was hardly a nation when Italians began emigrating in large numbers to the United States in the 1880s. People from very different regions, cultures, and social strata were lumped together because they all held Italian documents, even if they had little or no connection or fellow feeling. The meaning of "Italian" in San Francisco was a Torino or Milano; in New York it was a Siciliano. The two groups migrated from very different parts of Italy for very different reasons, brought with them very different aspirations and cultures, and in fact have never mixed. Joe DiMaggio shared almost nothing with Lucky Luciano. Yet they were both seen as Italians.[28]

Similarly, many different sorts of people were lumped together as "east European Jews." In 1890, the entity "east European Jew" did not exist save in the minds of people outside both Judaism and eastern Europe. Instead, there were Litvaks and Galitsianers and Ukrainian Jews. They had a sense of commonality with other Jewish immigrants, but in their personal lives they identified themselves as natives of their own region and *shtetl*. They joined pan-Jewish synagogues and labor unions, but their strongest ties were with the *landsmanshaftn,* benevolent associations organized by geographical origin. Sometimes regional acrimony was intense. In New York at the turn of the century, Russian and Galician Jews were known to shout at each other on the streets and at work, defaming each other as unfit to live because of their regional origin. The research of one of this essay's authors uncovered Litvak families who sat *shivah* for their sons because they married the daughters of Galitsianer families; he found very little Jewish marriage across lines of national origin in the first generation.[29]

Yet in the United States, people who brought with them many different regional or local identities found themselves treated as one with people with whom they would not have associated in the Old World, and they began to think of themselves as east European Jews, and then, in later generations, simply as Jews. Note that such a change in ethnic identity is not an example of melting-pot assimilation, but rather the creation of a new, superordinate, but still distinct, ethnic group.

In like manner, Asian Americans may currently be in the process of becoming an ethnic group on the basis of shared interests. A generation ago, Japanese and Chinese and Filipino Americans saw themselves as three distinct groups, and they did not like each other very much. But the late 1960s saw the rise of a pan–Asian American movement with an explicit ideology of mixing, or at least of connecting. The rationale for coming together was that they shared related elements of historical oppression, and White Americans could not tell Asians apart, so the various Asian groups might as well band together, especially since none was populous enough to command much attention by itself.[30] In the 1980s and 1990s, partly in response to government census labeling, partly in solidarity with otherwise unconnected ethnic groups, and partly in the interest of gathering yet a larger constituency, some Asian activists have been trying to add Pacific Islanders to their number. A prominent textbook on Asian Americans has a chapter on Pacific Islanders as Asian Americans, a situation that mystifies many Samoans and Tongans and offends some, who do not see themselves as any kind of Asian.[31] In just the past few years, Japanese community newspapers have taken to referring to their ethnic group as "Asian Pacific Americans."[32]

While interests may bring a group together initially, interests change easily—they are external to the group and largely determined by others. Hispanics are becoming a single ethnic group in the United States not because of any substantial natural commonality among them, but because there is a major tangible advantage to be gained by acting as a single group. Yet interests are only a short-term basis for group cohesion.

If an ethnic group endures, it is usually because it forms shared institutions and builds up shared culture.

Shared institutions are the ways people within the ethnic group organize themselves to achieve their interests, practice their culture, and maintain their group identity.[33] There are any number of examples of ethnic institutions. The United Farm Workers are a Mexican American ethnic institution that expresses and protects the interests of laboring Chicanos. Cumberland Presbyterian Church in San Francisco is an ethnic institution where Chinese Americans come together to worship and to socialize. Hadassah is an ethnic institution where Jewish women gather to connect with each other, reinforce their Jewishness, and serve their ethnic community. The Daughters of the American Revolution is an Anglo-American ethnic institution that seeks to celebrate and maintain the elite position of the dominant group in U.S. society. The NAACP is an ethnic institution that acts to create and defend the rights of African Americans. The family is the most powerful ethnic institution of all, a place where people of one ethnic group come together for many purposes, among them to pass on their group's understandings of the world from one generation to the next.

Ethnic institutions are the places where members of a group come together to pursue group interests—the United Negro College Fund is an example, as is the Anti-Defamation League of B'nai B'rith. But ethnic institutions are also places where *shared culture* is created and maintained. It is in Chinese churches, Chinese families, and Chinese neighborhoods that the Chinese language—an item of culture—is spoken and the ability to speak passed on. The culture is not just what people do in institutions, however. It is, on its own, an important binding agent that keeps group identity alive. Ethnicity-as-culture is an old view of these things, associated with people like Robert Ezra Park and E. Franklin Frazier.[34] But it has a lot to recommend it. What do an Israeli farmer, a New York journalist, and a London businessman have in common? Nothing at all, in terms of interests or institutions. Yet once a year they all say the same words at a Passover seder, and that ritual act—that piece of culture—binds them tightly together. Because they share culture, they all see themselves as Jews and as fundamentally related, indeed as essential to each other.[35]

Shared culture may be outward and apparent to the noninvolved observer. Italian food, Polish language, and Vietnamese Buddhism are examples. Or shared culture may be inward and more or less invisible. It can have to do with shared values, orientations, ways of framing issues or seeing the world. A trivial example will illustrate. Most Americans flip a switch and say they "turned on the light." But most Chinese Americans, down to the third generation, including those who speak no Chinese at all, on performing the same act say they "opened the light." Most U.S.-born Chinese do not even realize that their expression derives from the Chinese-language term, which connotes opening a gate to allow a current to flow. This is inward shared culture, albeit of a relatively inconsequential sort. Aspects of inward shared culture include patterns of child-rearing, facial affect, talking with one's hands, and a host of other items.

To summarize, we see the forces of shared interests, institutions, and culture interacting in a dynamic way to provide the glue that holds together ethnic consciousness. Most ethnic groups form, in the beginning, on the basis of some tangible shared interest, as Hispanics seem to be doing today. They create ethnic institutions by which they organize themselves to pursue their common interests. As people come together in those institutions, they interact and create shared culture—rituals, habitual turns of phrase, behaviors, and understandings that bind them together. Institutions and culture are much longer lived than are interests. They enable ethnic groups to survive changing circumstances. After an initially shared interest changes or disappears, culture and institutions may even hold the group together long enough for a new set of interests to emerge.

This was the situation for many Native American peoples earlier in this century. Under the impact of fragmenting social forces, urbanization, and the relentless pressure of White Americans and the U.S. government, the numbers of almost every Native American tribe dwindled steadily for eighty years after the Dawes Act of 1887. People gave up the land they had been allotted and left the reservation. Many were of mixed parentage, and they took on the White or Black part of their identity and became more or less merged into other streams of U.S. society.

Still, a remnant remained on most reservations, filling tribal leadership roles, maintaining with varying degrees of success relations with the Bureau of Indian Affairs, and keeping as best they could to the old tribal ways. Some herded sheep on the Navajo reservation in New Mexico. Others built sweat lodges and danced the Sun Dance on the Rosebud and Yankton reservations in South Dakota.

In the 1960s and 1970s, the remnants of many tribes were able to wrest from the U.S. government substantial new benefits—housing and education programs, even land and fishing rights. Alaskan natives reaped huge sums from oil leases, and some tribes cut lucrative deals with mining companies. Simultaneously, the rise of ethnic chic meant that minority ethnic identity became less of a drawback in majority social circles. This coincidence of a renewed *interest*—economic advantage—and social cachet meant that individuals who formerly asserted no Indian connection now flooded back to many reservations or at least proclaimed and connected themselves with their Indianness. Between the 1970 and the 1980 censuses, the number of people who called themselves Native Americans went *up* significantly for the first time in U.S. history, and the number rose again in 1990. In the cases of many native peoples, the remnant had kept Indian culture alive and Indian institutions functioning—albeit in changing ways—until a new interest gave power to tribal ethnicity once again.[36]

A Field Theory of Ethnic Group Development

One can imagine a number of situations in which ethnic groups might find themselves with regard to these three factors—interests, institutions, and culture. One might view these factors in ethnic group development schematically as three continua (see Figure 2) from low to high salience.[37] At any given point in the history of an ethnic group, one ought to be able to locate that group on the continuum with respect to each factor in ethnic group saliency. Some ethnic groups—African Americans today, for example— are high on all three indices. Although there is tremendous regional and class variety, there is also a good quantum of shared culture among Black Americans, from dialect to food to affective behavior. There are shared interests, insofar as Blacks as a group still suffer systematic social and economic disabilities, and insofar as they may also all

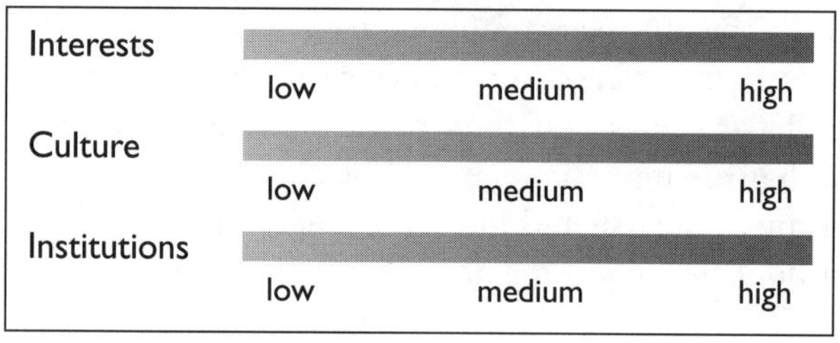

FIGURE 2.   At a point in time, an ethnic group may range from low to high salience in interests, culture, and institutions.

potentially benefit from, for example, affirmative action. And there is a web of shared institutions, from the NAACP to First A.M.E. Zion Church. African American ethnicity seems to be quite high.

There are also groups that are high on only one or two of the three indices. Latinos today, for example, are a group that may be high in certain sorts of interests and elements of shared culture, but quite low in institutions. Yet they are even now creating shared institutions such as the various Hispanic or Latino caucuses in government and professional circles. In time, they may build up a good deal more shared culture—language and religion are similar enough to provide a basis for some of that. Much will depend on whether or not they function historically as a group from here on out.

The Coloureds, or mixed racial population, of South Africa constitute another group that was created not out of culture or institutions but out of interests. Over the course of the nineteenth century, as slavery ended and the formerly fuzzy line between White and Black was being sharply redrawn to enhance White domination, people who were products of earlier racial mixing found themselves consigned to a third group. Culturally, most spoke Afrikaans. Institutionally, most worshiped in Dutch Reformed churches. But first socially and then legally, they found themselves pushed by Whites into a separate and limited status. Since that time they have developed their own institutions (for example, their own branches of the Dutch Reformed and Anglican churches) and their own webs of culture.[38]

Other groups are high on culture yet low on institutions and interests. There is a tremendous amount of shared religious, intellectual, and emotional culture among U.S. Jews—at the same time that Jews are arrayed across the class spectrum, anti-Semitism is at an unusually low point (not gone, just low), and perhaps a third of the Jewish population has not been inside a synagogue or community meeting in over a year. Interests are fairly low, institutional connectedness is not much higher, but certain aspects of culture (not necessarily including formal religious observance) are fairly high. Ethnicity remains.

The Hui people in China are a group that may be in the process of being formed primarily out of shared culture. They are not a historic ethnic minority nationality like the Mongols, Tibetans, or Uygurs. They are simply Muslims, from any of a dozen different ethnic derivations. Because of a tremendous amount of interregional migration in China over the past two decades, these disparate peoples find themselves in eastern Chinese cities far from their ethnic homes. They have no single shared culture in the sense of lan-guage, food, or family style. And no overarching national Islamic institution brings them together. But they do tend to wear some distinctively Muslim items of clothing even in non-Muslim cities, and they seek out coreligionists so they can get steady supplies of properly prepared lamb to eat. They have begun to group themselves in Muslim—Hui—neighborhoods, to build common mosques, and to worship together insofar as the Chi-nese government will let them. They have coalesced to the point that they are now rec-ognized as an ethnic minority by the Chinese government, although unlike all the other national minorities they have no ethnic home and no common ethnic history.[39]

Manchus in China are an ethnic group that seems to be quite low on all three fac-tors—interests, institutions, and culture. Most Han, or majority Chinese, do not even recognize the Manchus' separate existence. Although Manchus are a minority nation-ality officially noted by the Chinese government, almost no one speaks Manchu any-more, no one practices ancestral festivals or shamanistic religion. One would be extremely hard-pressed to find a "Manchu leader." Manchus are concentrated in the northeastern provinces of China, but even there they are a tiny numerical minority unrecognized by the general public. They are almost completely assimilated into the Han majority, to the point where one of the authors of this essay has been in a room with thirty Chinese college students who knew each other well and has heard the majority assert that there were only Han people present, while he knew that two of the group were in fact Manchus. One may reasonably predict that Manchu ethnicity is on the brink of extinction.[40]

Other ethnic groups are in similar situations. Richard Alba thinks that Italian Amer-ican ethnicity is a near-dead issue. Intermarriage is high, no one speaks Italian, specif-ically Italian Catholic parishes are being replaced by multiethnic parishes as city Ital-ians have moved to the suburbs. Even the Mafia is an interethnic organization, and it is in any case being replaced by crime organizations dominated by other ethnic groups.[41] Herbert Gans would call this "symbolic ethnicity," where ethnic oblivion has nearly been reached.[42] The ethnic label remains but is essentially trivial. The ethnic group does not organize anything important about one's life. But as with Basques in Spain, what appears at one point to be a dying ethnic group may simply be a group that is enter-ing a state of latency—with temporarily low interests, low culture, and low institu-tions.[43] Like Basques, Italians and Manchus may one day develop a cultural revival or a compelling set of interests that makes their ethnicity live again. Something of this sort has occurred in the past few years among several of the peoples of the former Soviet Union and various parts of Eastern Europe.[44]

Such, one might argue, has been the case with Hawaiians. Consigned to oblivion and tourist trivialities a generation ago, Hawaiian ethnicity is alive and well today. Inter-ests are being pursued with a vengeance, from Hawaiian studies at the University of Hawai'i and Brigham Young University–Hawai'i to what are asserted to be Hawaiian ethnic claims on the part of the islands' major land baron, the Bishop Estate. Culture is being reasserted—there has been a renaissance of genuinely Hawaiian music and group life during the last fifteen years. And fragmented institutions are gradually coalescing—for example, Hui Na'au'ao and the Office of Hawaiian Affairs on a large scale, and several Big Island communities at the local level.[45]

Toward a New Look in the Representation of Ethnicity

Scholarly study of ethnicity has come unglued—unglued from the influence of a single discipline, sociology, that has traditionally structured thinking in the field toward issues of classification and demographics. The rise of multidisciplinary modes of understanding has caused the question "But is it sociology?" to matter not much any more. Economists write history, theologians write criticism, historians write sociology, and an amorphous field called "cultural studies" has taken a central place in intellectual life.[46]

The field has also come unglued from primary attention toward a single set of ethnic relations—those between African Americans and European Americans—in a single country, the United States. In place of this myopic vision of ethnicity is an understanding of the world that reflects increasing multiplicity. Since George Bush announced in his 1988 U.S. presidential inaugural address that the United States was but one player in a multipolar world, the simple, bipolar view of international relations that dominated the cold-war era has been swept away. Migration is no longer viewed as a one-way trip from the old country to the new, but rather as a complex whirl of peoples about the globe.[47] In these last years of the twentieth century, it is increasingly clear that few nations are ethnically homogeneous. Places like the United States and Brazil have long been conscious of the heterogeneity of their peoples; in this era Britain, Germany, Scandinavia, Fiji, even Japan have begun to see themselves as ethnically plural societies.

Finally, ethnic studies has come unglued from a vision of ethnicity that emphasizes distinction and has come increasingly to recognize mixedness. New and increasing patterns of social relationships between groups, to the point of intergroup mating and marriage in the United States and elsewhere, have contributed to the sense of intergroup connectedness and of multiethnicity.[48]

International examples of ethnic relations swirl around us while researchers working at many different levels of analysis seek to bring order to the diversity that is ethnicity. The changes described here impel the editors of this volume to seek a unifying framework that can both accommodate the richness that the field has to offer and allow for generalizations between diverse cases. In short, we wish to prescribe some glue that may add coherence to the field. To anticipate the contribution of Stephen Cornell among the essays that follow, we submit that *narrative* is a key concept for understanding ethnicity.

Narrative provides the ground for individual identity when the story that is told presents and retains in memory important events in the life of the individual. As Stephen Cornell points out in chapter 3, such a narrative describes a subject, represents some action in which the subject engaged, and attaches some value to the subject by virtue of that action. The sum of a number of action accounts organizes an individual's life experiences into a narrative that provides a sense of self. Humanists have long understood narrative as a powerful means of expressing identity. Writers in the social sciences have recently come to emphasize the organizing quality of narratives of identity, and to point to narrative as a metatheoretical framework for self and personality.[49]

Narratives of identity also apply to collectives. Theories developed at the individual level of analysis often have parallels at the group level.[50] The development and use of narratives to achieve and maintain identities has been documented for families, for particular social classes, and for genders.[51] However, little research has been directed at narratives developed by ethnic groups. Stephen Cornell here remedies this situation and provides a theoretical context for further discussion; several of the other authors then take up the theme.

Organization of *We Are a People*

This book uses the concept of narrative as an organizing principle. Nearly all the papers that follow demonstrate the power of the narrative formulation. With the narrative construct it is possible to encompass great diversity of example—our intent is to move toward a conceptual system that can flexibly integrate the endless diversity that ethnic formations and interactions display worldwide. The papers we present range from an account of the experiences of Samoan migrants in New Zealand to an analysis of ethnic formations in Brazil. The narrative formulation allows us to comprehend together a wide variety of ethnic experiences.

We first present what we see as a central problem in the study of ethnicity: the limits of existing systems of ethnic categorization. The authors in this section variously use demographic data, interview results, and ethnographic analysis to demonstrate the limitations of traditional social scientific approaches to ethnicity in an age when migration and multiplicity upset neat, stable understandings of ethnic categories.

An important paper by Stephen Cornell points the way to a significant advance in the discourse on ethnicity: conceptualizing ethnicity as a collective narrative.

The next three parts of the book present a series of concrete examples of narrative construction under different social and cultural circumstances. Part II focuses on collective narratives created by groups of ethnically distinct migrants as they have moved into complex host societies. Part III analyzes the narratives created by indigenous peoples who have been dominated by colonial or internal colonial cultures. Part IV examines the emerging phenomenon of multiethnicity in several diverse contexts.

In Part V, the papers offer theoretical reflections on issues ranging from individual psychology to group politics.

Notes

1. Private communication with James V. Spickard, 1990.

2. On White ethnicity, see, for example, David R. Roediger, *The Wages of Whiteness* (London: Verso, 1991); Theodore W. Allen, *The Invention of the White Race* (London: Verso, 1994); Noel Ignatiev, *How the Irish Became White* (New York: Routledge, 1995).

3. Theoretical treatments include: J. Milton Yinger, *Ethnicity* (Albany: SUNY Press, 1994); John Rex, *Race Relations in Sociological Theory*, 2d ed. (London: Routledge and Kegan Paul, 1983); John Rex and David Mason, eds., *Theories of Race and Ethnic Relations* (Cambridge, UK: Cambridge University Press, 1986); John Hutchinson and Anthony D. Smith, eds., *Ethnicity* (New York: Oxford University Press, 1996); Michael Banton, *The Idea of Race* (London: Tavistock, 1977), *Racial and Ethnic Competition* (Cambridge, UK: Cambridge University Press,

1983), and *Racial Theories* (Cambridge, UK: Cambridge University Press, 1987); Michael Omi and Howard Winant, *Racial Formation in the United States: From the 1960s to the 1990s,* 2d ed. (New York: Routledge, 1994); E. K. Francis, *Interethnic Relations* (New York: Elsevier, 1976).

4. Raphael Patai and Jennifer Patai, *The Myth of the Jewish Race,* rev. ed. (Detroit: Wayne State University Press, 1989).

5. For ethnicity as shared ancestry, see Max Weber, "Ethnic Groups," in Weber, *Economy and Society* (Berkeley: University of California Press, 1979), 385–98; and R. A. Schermerhorn, *Comparative Ethnic Relations* (Chicago: University of Chicago Press, 1970). G. Carter Bentley offers an imaginative but, we think, not entirely persuasive explanation for this initial identification as a group sharing ancestry; see Bentley, "Ethnicity and Practice," *Comparative Studies in Society and History* 28 (1987): 24–55; Kevin A. Yelvington, "Ethnicity as Practice? A Comment on Bentley," *Comparative Studies in Society and History* 33 (1991): 158–68; and Bentley, "Response to Yelvington," *Comparative Studies in Society and History* 33 (1991): 169–75.

6. Some of the ideas in this section appear in somewhat different form in Paul R. Spickard, "The Illogic of American Racial Categories," in Maria P. P. Root, ed., *Racially Mixed People in America* (Newbury Park, Calif.: Sage, 1992), 12–23; and in Paul R. Spickard, *Japanese Americans* (New York: Twayne, 1996), chap. 1. See also Johann Friedrich Blumenbach, *The Anthropological Treatises of Johann Friedrich Blumenbach* (Boston: Milford House, 1973; orig. 1865); Joseph Arthur, comte de Gobineau, *The Inequality of Races* (1915; reprint, New York: H. Fertig, 1967; Carolus Linnaeus, *Systema Naturae* (1758).

7. James C. King, *The Biology of Race,* 2d ed. (Berkeley: University of California Press, 1981), 156–57.

8. Edmund W. Gordon, "Putting Them in Their Place," *Readings,* March 1995, 12. See also Jonathan Marks, *Human Biodiversity* (New York: Aldyne DeGruyter, 1995).

9. Poppy Cannon, *A Gentle Knight* (New York: Rinehart, 1952).

10. See, for example, Madison Grant, *The Passing of the Great Race* (1918; New York: Arno, 1970); John Higham, *Strangers in the Land: Patterns of American Nativism, 1860–1925* (New York: Atheneum, 1969).

11. Richard Herrnstein and Charles Murray, *The Bell Curve: Intelligence and Class Structure in American Life* (New York: Free Press, 1994). Another pseudoscientific racist exposition is J. Philippe Rushton, *Race, Evolution, and Behavior* (New Brunswick, N.J.: Transaction, 1995). Broad, balanced correctives can be found in Steven Fraser, ed., *The Bell Curve Wars: Race, Intelligence, and the Future of America* (New York: Basic Books, 1995); and William H. Tucker, *The Science and Politics of Racial Research* (Urbana: University of Illinois Press, 1994).

12. Werner Sollors, *Beyond Ethnicity* (New York: Oxford University Press, 1986), 36.

13. We are obliged to note that this is the position of the editors of this volume, and of some, but not all, contributors. Only a few social scientists argue that "race" is a separate concept, and their arguments generally are self-contradictory (see, for example, Joe R. Feagin, *Racial and Ethnic Relations,* 3d ed. [Englewood Cliffs, N.J.: Prentice-Hall, 1989]). More observers, particularly those who look at ethnicity outside the United States, use the generic term "ethnic group"; see, e.g., Hutchinson and Smith, *Ethnicity;* Montserrat Guibernau and John Rex, eds., *The Ethnicity Reader: Nationalism, Multiculturalism, and Migration* (Cambridge, UK: Blackwell, 1997); Fredrik Barth, ed., *Ethnic Groups and Boundaries* (Boston: Little, Brown, 1969); George DeVos and Lola Romanucci-Ross, eds., *Ethnic Identity* (Chicago: University of Chicago Press, 1982); Francis, *Interethnic Relations;* Nathan Glazer and Daniel Patrick Moynihan, eds., *Ethnicity* (Cambridge, Mass.: Harvard University Press, 1975); Charles F. Keyes, ed., *Ethnic Change* (Seattle: University of Washington Press, 1981); Anya Peterson Royce, *Ethnic Identity* (Bloomington: Indiana University Press, 1982). One thoughtful proponent of the larger-

races–smaller-ethnic-groups view is David A. Hollinger, "Postethnic America," *Contention* 2 (1992): 79–96.

14. Roger Sanjek, "The Enduring Inequalities of Race," in Steven Gregory and Roger Sanjek, eds., *Race* (New Brunswick, N.J.: Rutgers University Press, 1994), 11 (italics added).

15. The most thorough treatment of this theme is Omi and Winant, *Racial Formation*. We fully credit the insight that, while "race" is not real, racism surely is, and it must be resisted. We believe our antiracist commitments are as strong as those of our colleagues from the racialization school. Antiracism is the passion of our lives. For that very reason, we eschew the use of the term "race" insofar as possible. There is no long-term good to be served by maintaining false and oppressive categories such as "race." Letting the bad guys define the territory is giving them an advantage from the start.

16. April K. Henderson, "Black Like Who? On Racialized Language and the Struggles against Oppression," Department of American Studies, University of Hawai'i, March 1997.

17. Michele D. Dominy, "Maori Sovereignty: A Feminist Invention of Tradition," in *Cultural Identity and Ethnicity in the Pacific*, ed. Jocelyn Linnekin and Lin Poyer (Honolulu: University of Hawai'i Press, 1990), 249.

18. Henderson, "Black Like Who?"

19. See Rowena Fong and Paul R. Spickard, "Ethnic Relations in the People's Republic of China," *Journal of Northeast Asian Studies* 13, 1 (Fall 1994): 26–48.

20. Still, we suspect that even some racializationists sense that "ethnicity" is a broader term of suitable usefulness. Some of them work in, even preside over, departs of *ethnic* (not racial) studies, even though the subjects of study in those departments are what they would call *racial* groups—African, Latino, Native, and Asian Americans—and the power and cultural relations between them and the dominant society.

21. For a fairly stereotypical indictment of that use by Park, Glazer, and others, see Omi and Winant, *Racial Formation*.

22. Hector St. John [Michel-Guillaume Jean] de Crèvecoeur, *Letters from an American Farmer* (London, 1782), quoted in William Petersen, Michael Novak, and Philip Gleason, *Concepts of Ethnicity* (Cambridge, Mass.: Harvard University Press, 1982), 64.

23. Richard D. Alba, *Italian Americans: Into the Twilight of Ethnicity* (Englewood Cliffs, N.J.: Prentice-Hall, 1985). Others who have an essentially straight-line, assimilationist view of ethnic processes include Milton Gordon, *Assimilation in American Life* (New York: Oxford University Press, 1964); Robert E. Park, *Race and Culture* (New York: Free Press, 1950); Marcus Lee Hansen, *The Immigrant in American History* (New York: Harper, 1940); and Oscar Handlin, *The Uprooted*, 2d ed. (Boston: Atlantic-Little Brown, 1973).

24. See Mary C. Waters, *Ethnic Options* (Berkeley: University of California Press, 1992).

25. We owe to Stephen Cornell this conceptual division of ethnicity into essentially three different kinds of processes with three different kinds of ethnic glue. See his article, "The Variable Ties That Bind: Content and Circumstance in Ethnic Processes," *Ethnic and Racial Studies* 19 (1996): 265–89.

26. Abner Cohen, "The Lesson of Ethnicity," in Cohen, ed., *Urban Ethnicity* (London: Tavistock, 1974), ix–xxiv; June Teufel Dreyer, *China's Forty Millions: Minority Nationalities and National Integration* (Cambridge, Mass.: Harvard University Press, 1976); Guibernau and Rex, *Ethnicity Reader*; Nathan Glazer and Daniel P. Moynihan, *Beyond the Melting Pot* (Cambridge, Mass.: MIT Press, 1963); William Kornblum, *Blue Collar Community* (Chicago: University of Chicago Press, 1974); Joseph Rothschild, *Ethnopolitics* (New York: Columbia University Press, 1981); William Julius Wilson, *The Declining Significance of Race*, 2d ed. (Chicago: University of Chicago Press, 1980). The writings of the racialization school also exemplify thinking in this ethnicity-as-interests mode (see notes 14–15).

27. Alejandro Portes, "'Hispanic' Proves to Be a False Term," *Chicago Tribune*, November 2, 1989.

28. Paola Sesia, "White Ethnicity in America: The Italian Experience," *Berkeley History Review* 2 (1982): 18–32.

29. Paul R. Spickard, *Mixed Blood: Intermarriage and Ethnic Identity in Twentieth-Century America* (Madison: University of Wisconsin Press, 1989), 211–16; Moses Rischin, *The Promised City* (Cambridge, Mass.: Harvard University Press, 1962), 95–111; Irving M. Engel, memoir (American Jewish Archives, Cincinnati, n.d.); Isaac Bashevis Singer, *Crown of Feathers* (New York: Farrar, Straus and Giroux, 1973), 299–319; Julius Drachsler, *Intermarriage in New York City* (New York: Columbia University, 1921), 134–40; Egon Mayer, *Love and Tradition: Marriage between Jews and Christians* (New York: Plenum, 1985); Jonathan Sarna, "From Immigrants to Ethnics: Toward a Theory of 'Ethnicization'," *Ethnicity* 5 (1978): 370–78.

30. William Wei, *The Asian American Movement* (Philadelphia: Temple University Press, 1992); Yen Le Espiritu, *Asian American Panethnicity* (Philadelphia: Temple University Press, 1993).

31. Harry H. L. Kitano and Roger Daniels, *Asian Americans* (Englewood Cliffs, N.J.: Prentice-Hall, 1990).

32. One can see this usage in almost any issue of the San Francisco Japanese community newspaper, *Hokubei Mainichi,* or of the Asian American studies publication, *Amerasia Journal*. See Sucheng Chan, "Asian American–Pacific American Relations: The Asian American Perspective" (paper presented to the Association for Asian/Pacific American Studies, 1982), for dissent from this usage.

33. Alba, *Italian Americans;* Gordon, *Assimilation;* William Yancey, Eugene P. Ericksen, and Richard N. Juliani, "Emergent Ethnicity," *American Sociological Review* 41 (1976): 391–403.

34. Park, *Race and Culture;* E. Franklin Frazier, *Race and Culture Contacts in the Modern World* (New York: Knopf, 1957); Stephen Steinberg, *The Ethnic Myth* (Boston: Beacon, 1981).

35. A. L. Epstein, *Ethos and Identity* (London: Tavistock, 1978).

36. Stephen Cornell, *The Return of the Native: American Indian Political Resurgence* (New York: Oxford University Press, 1988).

37. This is a refinement of the two-category analytical schema of Stephen Cornell in "Variable Ties That Bind." This analysis is carried through the history of one ethnic group in Paul R. Spickard, *Japanese Americans: The Formation and Transformations of an Ethnic Group* (New York: Twayne, 1996).

38. George M. Fredrickson, *White Supremacy: A Comparative Study in American and South African History* (New York: Oxford University Press, 1981), 131–35.

39. Fong and Spickard, "Ethnic Relations in China"; Dru Gladney, *Muslim Chinese: Ethnic Nationalism in the People's Republic* (Cambridge, Mass.: Harvard Council on East Asian Studies, 1991); Dreyer, *China's Forty Millions;* Stevan Harrell, "Ethnicity, Local Interests, and the State: Yi Communities in Southwest China," *Comparative Studies in Society and History* 32 (1990): 515–48; Thomas Heberer, *China and Its National Minorities* (Armonk, N.Y.: M. E. Sharpe, 1989). Although it is possible to imagine an ethnic group that would be low on interests and culture but high on institutions, we cannot think of a good example.

40. Fong and Spickard, "Ethnic Relations in China."

41. Alba, *Italian Americans*.

42. Herbert Gans, "Symbolic Ethnicity," *Ethnic and Racial Studies* 2 (1979): 1–20.

43. Robert P. Clark, *The Basques* (Reno: University of Nevada Press, 1979); Davydd H. Greenwood, "Castilians, Basques, and Andalusians: An Historical Comparison of Nationalism, 'True' Ethnicity, and 'False' Ethnicity," in Paul Brass, ed., *Ethnic Groups and the State* (Totowa,

N.J.: Barnes and Noble, 1985), 204–27; Ken Medhurst, "Basques and Basque Nationalism," in Colin H. Williams, ed., *National Separatism* (Cardiff: University of Wales Press, 1982), 235–61.

44. *Journal of Soviet Nationalities* vol. 1–2 (1990–91); George Schoepflin, "National Identity in the Soviet Union and East Central Europe," *Ethnic and Racial Studies* 14 (1991): 3–14; Alexander J. Motyl, ed., *The Post-Soviet Nations* (New York: Columbia University Press, 1992); Kumar Rupesinghe, Peter King, and Olga Vorkunova, eds., *Ethnicity and Conflict in a Post-Communist World* (New York: St. Martin's, 1992); Hugh Poulton, *The Balkans: Minorities and States in Conflict* (London: Minority Rights Publications, 1991); Sabrina P. Ramet, *Nationalism and Federalism in Yugoslavia, 1962–1991*, 2d ed. (Bloomington: Indiana University Press, 1992); Mark Thompson, *A Paper House: The Ending of Yugoslavia* (New York: Pantheon, 1992).

45. Haunani-Kay Trask, *From a Native Daughter* (Monroe, Me.: Common Courage, 1993); Lilikala Kame'eleihiwa, *Native Lands and Foreign Desires* (Honolulu: Bishop Museum, 1992); Jocelyn Linnekin, "Defining Tradition: Variations on the Hawaiian Identity," *American Ethnologist* 10 (1983): 241–52; George Kanahele, *Ku Kanaka: Stand Tall* (Honolulu: University of Hawai'i Press, 1986).

46. See, for example: bell hooks, *Outlaw Culture* (New York: Routledge, 1994); Homi K. Bhaba, ed., *Nation and Narration* (New York: Routledge, 1990); Lawrence Grossberg, Cary Nelson, and Paula A. Treichler, eds., *Cultural Studies* (New York: Routledge, 1992); Henry Giroux, *Border Crossings: Cultural Workers and the Politics of Education* (New York: Routledge, 1992); David Trend, *Cultural Pedagogy* (New York: Bergin and Garvey, 1992); Henry Giroux and Peter McLaren, eds., *Between Borders: Pedagogy and the Politics of Cultural Studies* (New York: Routledge, 1994).

47. See, for example, Elliott Robert Barkan, *Asian and Pacific Islander Migration to the United States: A Model of New Global Patterns* (Westport, Conn.: Greenwood, 1992); Bharati Mukherjee, *The Middleman and Other Stories* (New York: Grove, 1988); Sau-ling C. Wong, "Denationalization Reconsidered: Asian American Cultural Criticism at a Theoretical Crossroads," *Amerasia Journal* 21 (1995): 1–28; Paul Gilroy, *The Black Atlantic* (Cambridge, Mass.: Harvard University Press, 1993); and Anthony King, ed., *Culture Globalization and the World-System* (London: Macmillan, 1991). See also the journals *Diaspora* (1991–94) and *Public Culture* (1988–).

48. Spickard, *Mixed Blood;* Barbara Tizard and Ann Phoenix, *Black, White, or Mixed Race?* (London: Routledge, 1993); Maria P. P. Root, ed., *Racially Mixed People in America* (Newbury Park, Calif.: Sage, 1992), and *The Multiethnic Experience* (Newbury Park, Calif.: Sage, 1995).

49. Dan P. McAdams, *The Stories We Live By* (New York: Morrow, 1993); Dan P. McAdams and Richard L. Ochberg, eds., *Psychobiography and Life Narratives* (Durham, N.C.: Duke University Press, 1988).

50. George Kelly, *The Psychology of Personal Constructs* (New York: Norton, 1955).

51. See Elizabeth Stone, *Black Sheep and Kissing Cousins: How Our Families' Stories Shape Us* (New York: Times Books, 1988); George Steinmetz, "Reflection on the Role of Social Narrative in Working-class Formation: Narrative Theory in the Social Sciences," *Social Science History* 16 (1992): 489–516; Margaret Somers, "Narrativity, Narrative Identity, and Social Action: Rethinking English Working-Class Formation," *Social Science History* 16 (1992): 591–630; Personal Narratives Group, *Interpreting Women's Lives: Feminist Theory and Personal Narratives* (Bloomington: Indiana University Press, 1989).

Part I

The Indeterminacy of Ethnic Categories: The Problem and a Solution

Mary C. Waters

---

2   Multiple Ethnicities and Identity in the United States

Most students begin my course in race and ethnic relations believing that race and ethnic groups are biologically derived. They believe, like most Americans, that ancestry determines racial or ethnic identities, that such identities are fixed at birth and reflect ancient cultural differences, and that all ethnic groups in the United States can be summed up by four or five racial categories. My task in the course is to expose them to a very different way of thinking. Current social science theory and research on the concepts of ethnicity and race recognize both as "social constructs." This means that categories vary across time and place, that new categories come into existence over time and others cease to have meaning for people. This also means that the construction of race and ethnic categories reflects shared social meanings in society, and that those shared social meanings in turn reflect differences in power relations. Finally, the social construction of race and ethnicity means that rather than being immutable, racial and ethnic identities at the individual level are subject to a great deal of flux—both intergenerationally, over the life course, and situationally.

Last year the experiences of one of my students brought home both the truth of the social construction approach and the limits to this approach in everyday life. After class one day, a young freshman came up to see me and asked if I could help her to determine her identity. She is from a small town in the rural South, and her mother had told her that she is an American Indian, but that they were not real American Indians because they were mixed with Blacks. In addition she knew she was part Irish and Scottish. She applied to many universities, and she checked various boxes on the applications, depending on the instructions. She preferred to check all boxes that applied to her identity. After she arrived at Harvard she began getting mail from the Black Students Association, and she was getting pressure from other Black students about not hanging around with Blacks. So she assumed that Harvard had assigned her to be Black. She has an identical twin sister, however, who is also at Harvard, and who checked the same boxes she did. Her sister is receiving mail from the Native American Students Association and is being lobbied to attend their meetings on campus.

My student wanted three things from me. First, she wanted my aid in navigating the university's bureaucracy to find out what identity the university thought she was, and how they decided that. Second, she wanted to know what sociological principle could justify what she perceived as an absurd situation—she and her identical twin sister having different racial identities. Third, she wanted to know whether either she or her sister would be allowed by the university to change their identity.

If there was any story that fit with my analysis of ethnicity and race as social constructions, this one did. Here were two genetically identical twins attending the same university, yet assigned to different races and already feeling some social consequences (in the form of peer pressure and political lobbying by student organizations) because of that classification. The story also shows some of the limits of a social constructionist approach—this situation was deeply disturbing to this young woman and her sister, it caused some consternation in the university administration when I investigated it, and it is understood by most people who hear about the story as an aberration. It is seen as an absurd problem to be rectified, not a reflection of the reality that multiple ancestries exist among a large proportion of the population in the United States, and that people often choose or are forced into a single category for purposes of administrative classification or counting schemes. The story is a confirmation of the socially constructed nature of race, and at the same time it warrants telling because it is an exception in a world where we assume that race and ethnicity are fixed characteristics, that individuals have only one socially meaningful identity, and that if we know a person's ancestry or genetic makeup we can determine their race and ethnicity.

In this chapter I explore the paradox my student's experience lays bare—the recognition that races are socially constructed and the everyday assumption that they are real—through an examination of how the federal government measures race and ethnicity and the challenges to that measurement posed by multiracial and multiethnic people and by intermarriage, and I suggest some possible results of this rapid social change.

How We Measure Race and Ethnicity

In the United States the vast bulk of our demographic data comes from the decennial census and from government administrative records. The federal government attempted to standardize its data collection on race and ethnicity in 1978 when the Office of Management and Budget (OMB) issued a federal directive (Number 15) designating the standards for reporting race and ethnic data. This directive established five federal reporting categories: American Indian or Alaska Native, Asian or Pacific Islander, Black, Hispanic, and White. Since then, federal administrative agencies that collect data on race and ethnic identity may collect those data with more detail than these five categories, but the data must be able to aggregate to these standard categories. This directive organized all federal statistics into the same standard categories, ending much confusion that had resulted from different agencies collecting data with categories that often did not match. Yet these five categories quickly became so standard that Americans came to believe they represented anthropological or biological categories that reflected "true races."

The federal standards laid out by Directive 15 have recently been reviewed, and several controversial aspects of the directive have been studied and changed. In October

1997 it was announced that the Asian and Pacific Islander category would be separated into two categories—"Asian," and "Native Hawaiian or Other Pacific Islander." In addition the OMB made the historic decision to allow people to self identify with more than one racial/ethnic category. The OMB rejected proposals to establish a separate category for Arab Americans, to establish a separate "multiracial category," and to move native Hawaiians to the American Indian category.[1] While all of these proposals and decisions are highly charged politically, perhaps the most politically controversial issue has been a proposal to add a multiracial ategory.[2]

Decisions about standards for collecting information about racial and ethnic identities involve struggling with two issues. First, there is the technical issue of dealing with the growing complexity of racial and ethnic identity as we become a more diverse society. This requires careful attention to how we can best design categories that are mutually exclusive and exhaustive. For public policy and administrative purposes, the goal should be agreed-upon categories that can be used to classify the entire population. The second issue, however, is the disjuncture between what has come to be perceived as a "right to self identification" and the need to gather information on a very finite number of categories to meet legislative and public policy needs. In the past few decades, many Americans have come to expect that when they fill out a census or a government form they are publicly declaring an identity and having that identity recognized by their society. Many Americans now believe that they have a right to racial and ethnic self-identification. Recognizing this function of the census and other forms would require allowing as much complexity and as many overlapping categories as possible, since we all know that human beings interbreed across socially defined racial and ethnic identities, and many if not most of us have complex ancestries. This tension between legislative needs and self-identification has been handled by assuming that "races" are mutually exclusive, but allowing ancestry and ethnicity to be more complex. The multiracial movement is a direct challenge to this distinction in data collection.

While all federal agencies collect data that can be put in the five OMB categories, the census is by far the most detailed federal data collection effort and in many ways the most visible and politically charged. There are currently three questions on the census that collect the bulk of the demographic data on race and ethnicity in the United States: the race question, the Spanish origin question, and the ancestry question (see Figure 1). The race question was a closed-ended one whose possible responses included the categories White, Black or Negro, Indian Amer. (with a blank space for the person to fill in the name of their tribe), Eskimo, Aleut, Chinese, Filipino, Hawaiian, Korean, Vietnamese, Japanese, Asian Indian, Samoan, Guamanian, Other Asian or Pacific Islander (with a blank space to fill in the specifics), and Other race (also with a blank space). The question was labeled Race in 1990 and 1970; in 1980 it had no label. The race question specifically told respondents that they were not to give two answers, but to only choose one response. The October 1997 decision of OMB suggests that the year 2000 census will allow people to check more than one race category. It has not yet been decided how these race results will be tabulated.

The Hispanic origin question also presented the respondents with fixed response categories, which included No (not Spanish, Hispanic); Yes, Puerto Rican; Yes, Cuban; and Yes, Other Spanish/Hispanic, with a space to write in the specific response.

4. **Race**
Fill ONE circle for the race that the person considers himself/herself to be.

- ○ White
- ○ Black or Negro
- ○ Indian (Amer.) (Print the name of the enrolled or principal tribe.) ↓

If **Indian (Amer.)**, print the name of the enrolled or principal tribe. _____ ▶

- ○ Eskimo
- ○ Aleut

Asian or Pacific Islander (API)

○ Chinese	○ Japanese
○ Filipino	○ Asian Indian
○ Hawaiian	○ Samoan
○ Korean	○ Guamanian
○ Vietnamese	○ Other API ↓

If **Other Asian or Pacific Islander (API)**, print one group, for example: Hmong, Fijian, Laotian, Thai, Tongan, Pakistani, Cambodian, and so on. _____ ▶

If Other race, print race. _____ ▶

- ○ Other race (Print race) ↑

7. **Is this person of Spanish/Hispanic origin?**
Fill ONE circle for each person.

- ○ No (not Spanish/Hispanic)
- ○ Yes, Mexican, Mexican-Am., Chicano
- ○ Yes, Puerto Rican
- ○ Yes, Cuban
- ○ Yes, other Spanish/Hispanic
  (Print one group, for example: Argentinean, Colombian, Dominican, Nicaraguan, Salvadoran, Spaniard, and so on.) ↓

If **Yes, other Spanish/Hispanic**, print one group. _____ ▶

13. **What is this person's ancestry or ethnic origin?** ↓
(See instruction guide for further information.)

(For example: German, Italian, Afro-Amer., Croatian, Cape Verdean, Dominican, Ecuadoran, Haitian, Cajun, French Canadian, Jamaican, Korean, Lebanese, Mexican, Nigerian, Irish, Polish, Slovak, Taiwanese, Thai, Ukrainian, etc.)

FIGURE I.   1990 Census Questions on Race, Hispanic Origin, and Ancestry.

Finally, the ancestry question was a "fill in the blank" question, which asked "What is this person's ancestry or ethnic origin?" Under the blank line a number of possible responses were given. The ancestry question allowed people to identify with more than one group. The instructions read, "Persons who have more than one origin and cannot identify with a single group may report two ancestry groups." In 1980 the census coded up to three of the write-in responses; in 1990, up to two. In 1990, among those reporting at least one specific ancestry, 28 percent reported at least a second ancestry as well.

The census categories in all three of these questions reflect political decisions about representation, rather than any social scientific rules of measurement or survey design. The list of categories under the designation "race," for instance, includes Black Americans, who have been identified as a racial group in the United States for a very long time, but not West Indians, an "ethnic group" within the Black racial category. Yet it does not include an overall "Asian" category but does include a number of Asian national origin groups, such as Japanese and Chinese. The Hispanic categories include a separate category for Cubans but not for Dominicans, although the numbers of Dominicans immigrating to the United States have been very large recently. "Hispanic" is defined as an ethnic category, and a person of Hispanic origin can say they are of any "race." These categories reflect international power relations as much as domestic ones. In 1930 "Mexican" was listed as a separate race on the census form, and the Mexican government officially protested to the U.S. government that Mexicans were not a separate race, because they were White.[3]

These census measurement decisions also reflect two other factors. First, they reflect the fact that Americans are much more likely to socially recognize multiple ethnic identities than multiple racial ones. The ancestry question allows people to list different groups, but the race question and the Hispanic question do not allow people to check more than one category. Puerto Ricans, who are an ethnic group, can claim another racial identity. But Japanese, who are a racial group, cannot simultaneously be Korean. Second, these decisions reflect the fact that the racial and Hispanic origin questions are used to assign people to mutually exclusive categories for legislative reasons—to comply with the Voting Rights Act and to determine eligibility for government programs awarded by ethnicity.

Yet the division between racial and ethnic groups and the assumption that ethnic groups involve more personal choice than racial ones are not self-evidently true. Groups we think of as "ethnic groups" were seen in earlier times as "racial groups." In the nineteenth century the Irish were seen as a "race" apart from other European groups. Stereotyped for their criminality, lack of education, and poor family values, they were often portrayed as apes in cartoons of the time and referred to as "niggers turned inside out." In the mid–nineteenth century Negroes were referred to as "smoked Irish."[4] If those debating immigration restriction in the early part of the twentieth century had made population projections that accounted for the "race suicide" they felt new immigrants were causing, they would have predicted that the immigrating southern and central Europeans and Irish would make White Protestants a minority by some date in the far off future. Such predictions would have failed to factor in the declining relevance of the boundaries separating European groups from one another. Groups such as Italians and Poles and Greeks then seen as "unassimilable" and racially distinct now intermarry to such a great extent with other White European groups that they are virtually indistinguishable. These groups have reached equality with White Protestants in education, income, occupational specialization, and residential distribution.

Pagnini and Morgan note that, at the turn of the century, "endogamy was castelike for new ethnics from eastern and southern Europe."[5] Since then, social and cultural changes have interacted with ethnic intermarriage to produce an ethnic fluidity that then would have been unthinkable. As Alba reports, "In 1990 census data, more than half

(56 percent) of whites have spouses whose ethnic backgrounds do not overlap with their own at all. Only one fifth have spouses with identical backgrounds."[6]

As a result of this intermarriage, ethnic identity is increasingly a matter of choice for Whites in the United States. An American of Italian, Irish, and Scottish ancestry, for example, can "choose" to identify with one or more of their ethnic ancestries and discard or "forget" others.[7] Hout and Goldstein show that if scholars had done population projections of the Irish at the beginning of the century, they would have seriously underestimated the numbers of Irish Americans; 4.5 million Irish immigrants to the United States resulted in 40 million Irish Americans in the 1980 census partly because the Irish had high rates of intermarriage with other White groups and because the offspring of those marriages differentially chose "Irish" as the identity they kept.[8] This fluidity of White ethnic categories stands in contrast to the seeming essentialism of race. But this is partially the result of the primacy of racial questions in U.S. history, which required unambiguous classifications, first for discrimination and now for affirmative action.

Rates of intermarriage have been growing since 1960 for all groups, even for those defined as "racial" groups. While it is still the case that only a small proportion of marriages by non-Hispanic Whites are with non-Whites and Hispanics, the rate of increase in recent decades has been dramatic; "in 1960 there were about 150,000 interracial couples in the United States. This number grew rapidly to more than 1.0 million in 1990. When marriages with Hispanics are added the intergroup marriages totaled about 1.6 million in 1990."[9] While more than 93 percent of Whites and of Blacks intermarry within their own groups, 70 percent of Asians and of Hispanics and only 33 percent of American Indians do. Although Black-White intermarriages are still the least prevalent, among younger people there is evidence of considerable change. Alba reports that "10 percent of 25- to 34-year-old black men have intermarried, most with White women."[10]

Classifying Multiracial People

While self-identification is the basic means for collecting data on racial and ethnic origins, when it comes to reporting race and Hispanic origin, the Census Bureau cannot allow people to self identify simultaneously with two different groups. The OMB issued a directive advising that in the case of people who are of mixed origins, "The category which most closely reflects the individual's recognition in his community should be used for purposes of reporting."[11] However, since the Census Bureau does not have information on how individuals are recognized in their communities, the procedure is to assign a single race to an interracial child if the parents disobeyed the instructions and checked two boxes or wrote something like "multiracial" as a response. If an unacceptable response was given to the race question, the bureau assigned the child to the mother's race, if the mother was in the household. When the mother's race was unknown, multiracial individuals were assigned the first race that they reported (the first box checked on the form). This represents a change in policy, because in 1970 when persons with parents of different races were in doubt as to their classification, they were assigned to their father's race.

How will the growing numbers of interracial people identify themselves in the future, and how will this affect the size and composition of our existing racial and ethnic groups? I review here three sources of information—patterns of choices about identity made on census forms by intermarried parents of interracial children, information we have on the patterns of how people with multiple ancestries change their identities over time, and evidence from tests of a multiracial question in national sample surveys by the Census Bureau.

Parents Labeling Children

While it is impossible to tell from the census what percentage of adults are themselves of multiple racial origins, it is possible to look at intermarried couples and the decisions they are forced to make about their children's identities because of the design of the census. The ethnic or racial identities reported in the census by parents in the household and the identities reported for their children show various patterns. William Alonso and I have explored the choices parents made for children in answering the 1980 census, and we developed a method for simulating future population change that takes into account the pattern of these identity choices as well as levels of intermarriage.[12] The results show that the flux in race and ethnicity stemming from such changes could have significant effects on the future composition of the U.S. population that a straight population projection would miss.

To examine these choice patterns we drew a sample of the Public Use Microdata Sample (PUMS) 5 percent 1980 individual level census data, restricting the sample to married couple parents, both spouses in their first marriage, with no more children present in the household than the mother reported giving birth to. This was done to control as much as possible for blended families, stepchildren, and adoptions.

Tables 1 and 2 provide basic information on the choices of identity for children in these intermarried households for 1980. When the mother is White and the father is some other race (Table 1), compared to all the other groups, families with Black fathers are much more likely to label their children Black—69.1 percent of the children are Black. Another 8.5 percent are reported as "Other," and 22 percent are reported as White. In contrast, 50 percent of the offspring with Native American fathers are reported to be White, 43 percent of Japanese-White children, 35 percent of Chinese-White children, and 58 percent of Korean-White children. In sharp contrast, when the father is Asian Indian and the mother is White, only 20 percent of the children stay Asian Indian; 74 percent are White. A much lower percentage of children of Japanese, Chinese, and Filipino fathers married to White mothers remain identified with their father's Asian origins. Although these Asian groups do show a large proportion of the children as "Other" race (11.56 percent for children of Japanese fathers, 15.25 percent for children of Chinese fathers, and 10.53 percent for children of Korean fathers), even if one ignores those high percentages, there still are far more children identifying with their mother's White race.

Table 2 reflects the labeling of children in families where the father is White and the mother is non-White. The differences here for the Asian groups are even more striking. For instance, where the mother is Asian Indian, 93 percent of the children are labeled

TABLE 1. Parents' Choice of Children's Identity (White Mothers), 1980

	Race of Children				
Dad's Race	Percent "White"	Percent Dad's Race	Percent "Other Race"[1]	Percent "All Other Races"[2]	TOTAL[3]
Black	21.92	69.10	8.51	0.47	55,020.
Chinese	34.96	48.73	15.25	1.06	9,440.
Japanese	42.58	43.93	11.56	1.93	10,380.
Hawaiian	42.89	53.95	2.89	0.27	7,600.
Vietnamese	45.71	48.57	2.86	2.86	700.
Filipino	54.25	39.23	4.64	1.88	18,100.
Other Asian	55.46	36.24	6.11	2.19	4,580.
Korean	57.89	31.58	10.53	0	2,280.
Native American	60.99	48.21	0.65	0.15	85,020.
Asian Indian	74.13	20.22	3.48	2.17	9,200.

Source: Calculated from the 1980 United States Census Public Use Data Sample A, 5% sample, selecting for interracially married parents: White mothers and non-White fathers.

[1] Includes children whose parents selected "Other Race" from among the options given them by the Census Bureau. Includes "Other Asian" except where Dad's Race is "Other Asian."

[2] A residual category including all children whose parents chose a specific race not the same as the father's race, the mother's race, or the category "Other Race." These children were given one of the other specific races recognized by the Census Bureau.

[3] Total number of children. 1980 data are restricted to families where parents are both in their first marriages and there are no more children in the home than the mother reported giving birth to. 1990 data include parents who have been married more than once. Totals are therefore not comparable across the two censuses.

TABLE 2. Parents' Choice of Children's Identity (White Fathers), 1980

	Race of Children				
Mom's Race	Percent "White"	Percent Mom's Race	Percent "Other Race"[1]	Percent "All Other Races"[2]	TOTAL[3]
Black	21.89	70.82	6.04	1.25	15,900.
Native American	51.27	47.48	0.73	0.52	88,000.
Hawaiian	56.06	42.86	1.08	0	9,240.
Chinese	61.53	26.43	9.54	2.5	13,620.
Filipino	63.04	32.62	2.73	1.61	37,340.
Other Asian	63.92	32.66	3.42	0	12,860.
Vietnamese	64.44	29.78	5.33	0.45	9,000.
Japanese	67.19	24.87	6.68	1.26	38,040.
Korean	73.64	21.33	4.45	0.58	24,280.
Asian Indian	93.31	5.20	0.74	0.75	5,380.

Source: Calculated from the 1980 United States Census Public Use Data Sample A, 5% sample, selecting for interracially married parents: White fathers and non-White mothers.

[1] Includes children whose parents selected "Other Race" from among the options given them by the Census Bureau. Includes "Other Asian" except where Mom's Race is "Other Asian."

[2] A residual category including all children whose parents chose a specific race not the same as the father's race, the mother's race, or the category "Other Race." These children were given one of the other specific races recognized by the Census Bureau.

[3] Total number of children. 1980 data are restricted to families where parents are both in their first marriages and there are no more children in the home than the mother reported giving birth to. 1990 data include parents who have been married more than once. Totals are therefore not comparable across the two censuses.

White; where the mother is Japanese, 67 percent of the children are so labeled; where the mother is Chinese, 61 percent.[13]

In 1990, as Tables 3 and 4 indicate, the patterns are very similar. In general, children with one White parent are predominantly classified as White by their parents. The exceptions are children with White mothers and Chinese fathers, with White fathers and Native American mothers, or with one Black parent. Those with one Black parent are far more likely to be described as Black than as White. Historically in the United States, the offspring of Black-White unions have been forced to identify as Black through the "one-drop rule"—one drop of Black blood makes you Black. The offspring of other races married to Whites, such as Native Americans and Asians, have generally been classified as non-White, but with far less vigilance and certitude.[14] These data show that parents are still most likely to identify their part-Black children as Black, but perhaps the most remarkable finding is that 40–45 percent of these children are labeled not Black, but White or Other.

Thus parents' labeling of their mixed-race children's identities shows that no single rule governs their choices. There is some evidence that some parents try to choose neither parent's identity by checking "Other." Parents do not choose entirely on the basis of the maternal or paternal identity, and some parents choose "majority White" identities and some choose "minority non-White identities."

Alonso and I combined the results of the patterns of the 1980 choices with levels of intermarriage to simulate the changing composition of the population over five generations, roughly 125 years. We used 1980 census data on race and Hispanic origin for each member of the household to examine the effect of intermarriage and ethnic identity choices on the future population. The simulation does not take into account immigration, which is of course the largest element affecting the future size and composition of America's minority population. It also does not take into account differential fertility, or the reproductive behavior or choices of people who are unmarried or not in their first marriage. Thus the exercise is not a projection but a simulation designed to show the effects intermarriage can have on ethnic change, and the pitfalls of population projections that assume no intermarriage. Since the simulation models a stationary population (one without growth due to fertility or immigration), the simulated changes are entirely the result of patterns of intermarriage and heritability of group identities.

The pattern of changes in groups is quite variable. Overall, Whites increase by only 2 percent, and Blacks by 3.6 percent. American Indians decline by 5.8 percent. Cubans decline by 39.3 percent, due to a relatively high degree of outmarriage and a propensity for those outmarried couples to state that the child is White non-Hispanic. Mexicans and Puerto Ricans grow by 51.2 percent and 21.3 percent respectively. Overall, Hispanics as a whole grow by more than 25 percent, while all Asian groups decline. These changes result from relatively high levels of intermarriage, from a substantial number of inter-married couples of different Asian groups who state that their children are not Asian, and from intermarried Hispanic parents absorbing their multiethnic children as Hispanic. While immigration of Asians into the United States will no doubt dwarf this underlying trend in aggregate statistics, nevertheless there is a trend of considerable movement by individuals across the Asian/White boundary. For a group such as the Japanese who

TABLE 3. Parents' Choice of Children's Identity (White Mothers), 1990

| | Race of Children | | | | |
Dad's Race	Percent "White"	Percent Dad's Race	Percent "Other Race"[1]	Percent "All Other Races"[2]	TOTAL[3]
Black	26.82	60.82	11.95	0.41	170,609.
Chinese	36.54	48.63	14.42	0.41	19,910.
Hawaiian	44.09	52.05	2.86	0.99	12,401.
Vietnamese	48.06	31.87	39.71	0	4,076.
Japanese	50.48	43.57	5.57	0.37	26,370.
Native American	51.84	47.52	0.45	0.19	146,887.
Filipino	52.46	43.43	3.49	0.62	27,734.
Korean	54.93	33.63	10.64	0.8	4,127.
Other Asian	59.21	38.94	0.77	1.08	19,151.
Asian Indian	74.02	20.73	4.25	1	15,333.

Source: Calculated from the 1990 United States Census Public Use Data Sample A, 5% sample, selecting for interracially married parents: White mothers and non-White fathers.

[1] Includes children whose parents selected "Other Race" from among the options given them by the Census Bureau. Includes "Other Asian" except where Dad's Race is "Other Asian".

[2] This is a residual category including all children whose parents chose a specific race which was not the same as the father's race, the mother's race or the category "Other Race". These children were given one of the other specific races recognized by the Census Bureau.

[3] Total number of children. 1980 data are restricted to families where parents are both in their first marriages and there are no more children in the home than the mother reported giving birth to. 1990 data include parents who have been married more than once. Totals are therefore not comparable across the two censuses.

TABLE 4. Parents' Choice of Children's Identity (White Fathers), 1990

| | Race of Children | | | | |
Mom's Race	Percent "White"	Percent Mom's Race	Percent "Other Race"[1]	Percent "All Other Races"[2]	TOTAL[3]
Black	30.99	56.06	12.77	0.18	47,299.
Native American	49.06	50.08	0.5	0.36	155,849.
Hawaiian	54.41	43.8	0.41	1.38	12,167.
Chinese	57.16	25.65	16.81	0.38	32,254.
Japanese	57.99	32.23	9.3	0.49	45,301.
Other Asian	65.42	32.63	1.24	0.71	28,387.
Vietnamese	65.65	20.19	14.16	0	11,825.
Filipino	65.9	29.37	4.49	0.24	77,232.
Korean	70.83	18.16	10.91	0.09	44,862.
Asian Indian	74.16	17.59	7.06	1.17	5,604.

Source: Calculated from the 1990 United States Census Public Use Data Sample A, 5% sample, selecting for interracially married parents: White fathers and non-White mothers.

[1] Includes children whose parents selected "Other Race" from among the options given them by the Census Bureau. Includes "Other Asian" except where Mom's Race is "Other Asian".

[2] This is a residual category including all children whose parents chose a specific race which was not the same as the father's race, the mother's race or the category "Other Race." These children were given one of the other specific races recognized by the Census Bureau.

[3] Total number of children. 1980 data are restricted to families where parents are both in their first marriages and there are no more children in the home than the mother reported giving birth to. 1990 data include parents who have been married more than once. Totals are therefore not comparable across the two censuses.

currently have very small numbers of immigrants coming into the United States, this overall trend in intermarriage and heritability could lead to a real decline in relative size.[15]

The number of simplifying assumptions in this simulation means that this is not what will happen to the future population of the United States. This exercise does demonstrate, however, that standard demographic population projection methods can seriously overestimate the stability of socially constructed categories of race and ethnicity, even without a multiracial category. We can now see with hindsight that population projections from the turn of the nineteenth century would have seriously erred because of the social changes in the meanings of ethnic and racial boundaries that have occurred since. As Paul Spickard notes, "Almost no White American extended family exists today without at least one member who has married across what two generations ago would have been thought an unbridgeable gap."[16] This circumstance has changed both the nature of the categories we use for classifying the population and the raw counts of people within each category.

Patterns among People with Multiethnic Ancestry

While we do not know whether these interracial children will repeat their parents' patterns of choices for themselves, the patterns of choices made by people with multiple ethnic ancestries may be suggestive.

The census ancestry question allowed multiple responses, and 1980 and 1990 data have been analyzed by a number of scholars.[17] One clear finding is that more education is positively linked to reporting a multiple ancestry. Less educated people tend to report fewer identities.[18] It is also true that interracial marriages occur at higher rates among the highly educated. Together these two facts suggest that both the pool of multiracial people and those among them who choose to identify with all of their possible identities will be relatively highly educated.

There is also a clear pattern of simplifying or dropping ethnicities over the life course and across generations among people with multiple ancestries. There are three identifiable points where people simplify complex and multiple ancestries to single ancestries: when parents describe the ancestries of their children; when young adults reach maturity, leave home, and begin reporting their identity on forms themselves; and when people marry.

Lieberson and Waters found that parents simplify their children's ancestries in filling out the census form. For instance, in situations where one parent reports a single White ethnic origin (X) and the other parent reports a different single White ethnic origin (Y), about 40 percent of the children are not described as the combination of parental ancestries (XY) but as having the ancestry of only one of the parents.[19] The net discontinuities in the census between the ethnicity parents report for themselves and for their children lead to numbers that range from 14 to 17 percent less than would be expected if they gave their children their exact ancestries. This is also linked to gender. Males are more likely to have their ancestries simplified by their parents and in turn are more likely to simplify their own when they fill out the forms themselves.

In terms of age, much simpler ethnicities are reported by people in their late teens and early twenties compared to younger ages. A comparison of young adults living at home with those living away from home found that the greatest dropoff in complexity occurs for those living away from home.[20]

When people marry they sometimes change their ancestry to match that of their spouse.[21] For instance, a woman who was Italian and Polish who married an Italian man would probably drop the Polish ancestry, and both spouses would report the ancestry that "matched"—in this case, Italian. Lieberson and Waters suggest that standard demographic studies of intermarriage that ask whether ethnicity affects choice of marriage partner might actually be measuring the opposite question—whether choice of marriage partner affects ethnic identity choice—and that religious intermarriage studies might provide a model for dealing with this confusion.[22] It has long been recognized that religious conversion at the time of marriage would bias estimates of religious intermarriage downward if the only consideration were the current religion of both spouses. As a result, studies use two variables to measure religious intermarriage—religion at age sixteen and current religion. Perhaps variables such as current ethnicity and ethnicity at age sixteen will be necessary to measure ethnic intermarriage in a time of mixed ethnicities and changing identifications.

What are the implications of these findings for multiracial reporting? First, to the extent that lobbying groups pressing for a multiracial category or the right to check an unlimited number of racial categories are composed of interracially married parents who do not want to choose a single race for their children, such a category would not necessarily guarantee that those children will choose to report all of those races when they leave home. Parents report more detail on their children's ancestries than the children do themselves as they age, especially after they leave home.

Second, the desire to report a multiracial identity may be associated with age and thus may change as people grow older. Since we know that ethnic and racial self-identity can change over the life course and is related to age and cohort experiences, one hypothesis is that young adults of college age may be vocal about maintaining a multiracial identity, as the number of organizations of multiracial people at universities around the country testifies. But what will happen to some of these students in a few years, when they marry and have children of their own? Will they maintain a multiracial identity for the rest of their lives? Or will they develop one dominant racial or ethnic identity in response to marriage, societal definitions, or the aging process? This is a difficult question to answer, because the movement of self-identified multiracial people is so new, and because rising intermarriage rates mean that most multiracial people are very young. It is still unclear whether these young people are the beginning of a new category or are just going through a phase of identity development. (Such an age/period/cohort problem is notoriously difficult to solve without longitudinal data that follow people over time and monitor how they identify.)

Tests of a Multiracial Question

There is a much larger potential multiracial population than the number of people who currently try to identify as multiracial. Rates of intermarriage have been rising and will continue to rise. The National Academy of Sciences report on revising Directive 15 pointed out that as more people who are Asian or Hispanic are born or raised in the United States, more intermarriages are likely. In the 1990 census, 5 percent of the U.S.

population reported an ancestry that differed from their primary race or Hispanic identification. By race, 4 percent of Whites and 5 percent of Blacks report multiple ancestries. More than 25 percent of those reporting their race as American Indian report a non–American Indian ancestry, and about 10 percent of Asian and Hispanic respondents report a non-Asian or non-Hispanic ancestry, respectively.[23] These people are all "potential multiracials"—people who choose one race in the census but feel strongly enough about their other ancestries to report them on the ancestry question.

There is a strong group now pressing for a multiracial category or for the chance to identify with more than one race. The most vocal are the committed multiracial people, who are extremely unhappy answering the race question the way it is now and who would refuse to answer a race or Hispanic origin question that forced them to choose. In 1990 the Census Bureau reported that 249,119 people wrote in a multiracial response to the question about race. Many more, however, either refused to answer the question or put themselves in the "Other Race" category. Indeed the category "Other Race" grew from 6.8 million in 1980 to 9.8 million in 1990, a growth rate of 45 percent.[24]

We do not know how these committed multiracial people would respond to a question that asks them to choose. In other words, would they be satisfied with saying they are multiracial and then placing themselves in the federal categories? Or would they only be satisfied with giving a multiracial response alone? If committed multiracial people would like to tell the world that they are multiracial but then are willing to put themselves into one of the five OMB categories for administrative purposes, this might allow a reconciliation of the "right to self identify" with the public policy need to classify each person by a single race. If this group is opposed to choosing a single race, however, their stance has a different set of consequences for question design. As the National Academy of Sciences report stated: "If self identification is taken as a basic principle, there are no grounds for recoding a multirace person to a single race. It is difficult to imagine any logical recoding algorithim for people who decline to provide a single race affiliation."[25]

A second group of people who are likely to answer a multirace question affirmatively are the "opportunistically" multiracial—people with two races in their backgrounds who are comfortable identifying with only one, both in their daily lives and on census forms, but who would tell you that they are multiracial given the choice. For instance, imagine a person with a White grandmother and three Black grandparents who is socially identified as a Black American, and who is viewed as a Black American by others in U.S. society; such a person might check "Multiracial" but would be just as happy checking "Black" if the choice "Multiracial" was not available. This is perhaps the most interesting group from a political perspective, because its size and characteristics will shape the changes in the race counts that would result if a multiracial option is provided.

The Census Bureau has conducted three tests of a multiracial question in sample surveys in preparation for the year 2000 census: the May 1995 Current Population Survey, the 1996 National Content Survey, and the 1996 Race and Ethnic Targeted Test. All found that the number of people choosing "Multiracial" in some designs, or checking all races that apply in other designs, was between 1 and 2 percent.[26] Based on these three surveys, then, the committed multiracials and the "opportunistically" multiracials are statistically small—1 to 2 percent. Of course, for some racial and ethnic groups— American Indians and Alaska Natives and Asian and Pacific Islanders—the proportions of people answering "Multiracial" are relatively large and can affect the size of these small groups. The national population figures are relatively unaffected because the overall numbers are so small.

The third group who might use the multiracial response might be an artifact of a change in the overall race and Hispanic origin questions. If the race and Hispanic origin questions are combined, people who think of themselves as, say, Cuban and Black, or Puerto Rican and White, will all of a sudden become multiracial. This is because they will have to choose between declaring their race and their Hispanic identities. The 1996 Race and Ethnic Targeted Sample test of the Census Bureau found this to be the case. When the race and Hispanic origin questions were combined, 17 to 19 percent of responses included both a Hispanic origin and one of the four major race categories.[27]

The fourth group who might use the multiracial response would include people from groups that are themselves multiracial, such as Dominicans, Puerto Ricans, Michifs, Metis, and other American Indians, and Cape Verdeans. Yet we do not know whether the category "Multiracial" will appeal to these self-identified groups or whether they will continue to identify with their specific groups.

Clearly there is a growing pool of people who could potentially identify as multiracial. That pool is much larger than the 1 to 2 percent of the population who have answered "Multiracial" on the test surveys conducted by the Census Bureau, but much smaller than the numbers of people who have multiple races somewhere in their family backgrounds.

Future Scenarios

The political debate over a multiracial question tends to focus on Black/White interracials and on the implications of an interracial category for the long-run political and social fortunes of African Americans. This reflects the enormous importance of the Black/White color line in U.S. society and the legacy of slavery. Yet if there is a multiracial category it will affect much more strongly the Asian, American Indian, and—if Hispanics are included in this racial category—Hispanic populations. This is because of the much higher rates of intermarriage of these groups, and because of their much smaller numbers. Statistically these are the groups that will change the most both now and in the future.

Many Blacks have White ancestors—yet many of these unions of Black slaves and White slave owners were coerced and socially unrecognized. Thus many Black Americans know they are part White, but for a very long time this knowledge has been divorced from meaningful links to White ancestors.[28] Slavery also gave us the one-drop rule for classifying the children of both coerced and voluntary unions. Many, if not most, Black Americans thus technically are "potential multiracials," but because of the unique history of Black/White race relations, they are unlikely to claim a multiracial identity. Young children now born to the rising numbers of voluntary Black/White marriages may choose to claim a multiracial identity in the future. Yet in the three tests of a multiracial question run by the Census Bureau, the number of Black Americans who switched to a multiracial identity was small enough that it did not statistically affect the Black population.

Politically, however, the loaded issues of Black/White race relations will mean that even the potential of Black Americans to become multiracial will get the most attention among politicians and in the media. Indeed, the National Association for the Advancement of Colored People has testified strongly against a multiracial category in congressional hearings on this subject.

Meanwhile, groups that have high intermarriage and relatively small populations will be most affected by a multiracial category. American Indians are already very influenced by large numbers of people who are "part Indian." Indeed, much of the growth in the American Indian population in recent decades has been due to "potential" American Indians claiming a racial identity as American Indian. In order to be an enrolled member of a tribe or to receive government benefits such as treatment at the Indian health service, Indians have had to "prove" their identity—either through blood quantum certification or tribal enrollment in a federally recognized tribe. Self-identification as an Indian is not enough. This is an extreme model of what might happen in the future if intermarriage and identity choices become very high and unstable across racial groups and if the government continues to allocate some resources to individuals because of their racial and ethnic identities. Yet a comparison of people identified as American Indian by race in the census and those who are American Indian by ancestry turns up real differences between the groups. Racially identified American Indians are poorer, more concentrated on reservations, and more likely to report only one identity.[29] Any study of changing income patterns among American Indians must be careful about which questions are used to identify the population and also mindful that changes in socioeconomic status could be due to new, more affluent people identifying as Indian. The addition of a multiracial category will not only affect the size of groups but their measurable characteristics as well, as the case of American Indians makes clear. This has important implications for researchers using these data. Eschbach finds that a simple study of migration of American Indians in the United States is impossible without taking into account changing identifications. He finds that "[a]lmost all of the apparent redistribution of the Indian population between prior censuses and the 1980 census is attributed to changes in identification rather than to migration."[30]

The census and federal forms can create categories that have meaning for people. Creating a multiracial category rather than allowing people to "check all races that apply to them" will create a category with some social meaning that may actually become an ethnic or racial group. The fact that this group does not exist now except as a statistical artifact and a loose coalition of people lobbying the federal government does not mean that it cannot come into existence and begin to have social meaning for people over time.

Now that the federal government has decided to allow people to report that they have more than one race in their ancestries, we should recognize that there are long-run implications of allowing a multiracial category versus allowing people to check all races that apply. Today there is no socially meaningful group called "multiracial" with a culture, a phenotype, a residential or occupational profile, or even a history of being subject to discrimination. A person who is part Asian Indian, part Japanese American has little to nothing in common with a part White, part Black American in terms of ancestry or identity. The only thing they do now have in common is that they may belong to a group who has come together for purposes of lobbying the federal government that they do not want to deny one aspect of their identity. It may be that our government wants to create a new group of people who have nothing in common ancestrally other than parents who come from different socially defined ancestry groups. Indeed, some may argue that this is a good definition of an American—that we are all products of the "melting pot." Yet this should be a conscious decision. If a multiracial category is created, it will have social consequences: people will begin to report statistical findings on the group—their incomes, occupations, and so on, will be presented in tables alongside those of Blacks, Whites, Hispanics, and Asians.

We have experience of this in our country with the creation of panethnicities—groups such as Asian Americans or Hispanic Americans that often combine people whose ancestors would be aghast at the idea that they were members of the same groups.[31] The creation of a statistical category will take on an everyday permanence that will make it a comfortable category for people. Eventually people could come to see "multiracial" as a separate group. Alternatively, the individuals classed as multiracial may decide that they do not share the same experiences, and those who are half Asian might form their own groups, and those who are half Black might form their own groups, and you might have people lobbying for specific categories for these groups. (There are separate multiracial groups and half-Asian groups at my own university.)

Since the civil rights movement in the 1960s, the government has become increasingly involved in counting the population by race and ethnicity in order to monitor enforcement of antidiscrimination laws. Such enforcement involves classifying the population into mutually exclusive categories. The paradox of course is that the more successful the society is in reducing barriers between groups, the more likely it is that relationships will form across these racial and ethnic boundaries and thus make it more difficult to count the population.

This is a paradox we have not faced directly in a political sense. In fact, in the current political climate it is likely to be conservatives who advocate eradicating governmental classification of race and ethnicity and taking up a race-neutral approach to social problems. Often it is minority group members and organizations as well as liberal political forces who argue most strongly for continued monitoring, which means continued classification by rigid rules into race and Hispanic origin categories. The rhetoric of race-neutral language, once the province of integrationists such as Martin Luther King, has been appropriated by conservatives who argue that race-conscious policies are at odds with a race-neutral state. Those who care about the future of America's minority populations are so busy fighting for continued vigilance in enforcement, the very rhetoric of a race-neutral society has been lost to them. At the same time, the success of the racial intermixing of our society is creating ever more complex problems for measurement.

To return to the example of my student who is Black, American Indian, Scottish, and Irish, one can see the many forces shaping her identity. The one-drop rule of racial classification for Blacks in the United States is definitely undergoing change and challenges currently. My student did not automatically place herself in the Black category. The pressure she feels from the Black student association to "reaffiliate" and the administrative rules that require the university to place her in one category are currently at odds with her and her sister's desire to identify with all of their backgrounds. Her uneasiness with the university's decision to assign her and her sister to separate races shows the enormous emotional importance people assign to their identities and to what has come to be perceived as a right of self-identification. The paradox, I believe, is that the strong pressure on the university to classify and report on its minority student enrollment is very much responsible for her being at the university in the first place; at the same time, that pressure is "racializing" the student body in a way that does not allow what could be a natural evolution toward multiethnicity and blurred boundaries to proceed smoothly. This dilemma will become increasingly apparent in coming years, and solving it will require recognizing both the political and the social scientific aspects of measuring a changing and fascinating phenomenon.

Notes

Acknowledgment: An earlier version of this paper was presented at the conference entitled "American Diversity: A Demographic Challenge for the Twenty First Century," Center for Social and Demographic Analysis, State University of New York at Albany, April 15–16, 1994. I am grateful to Monica McDermott, Yu Xie, and Karl Eschbach for research assistance; Nancy Williamson and Cheri Minton for programming assistance; and Lynne Farnum for assistance in preparing the final manuscript. I am grateful to Paul Spickard and Jeff Burroughs for comments on an earlier draft and for patience in waiting for this draft.

1. U.S. Office of Management and Budget, "Revisions to the Standards for the Classification of Federal Data on Race and Ethnicity," *Federal Register* 62.210 (October 30, 1997): 58782–90.

2. Barry Edmonston, Joshua Goldstein and Tamayo Lott, *Spotlight on Heterogeneity: The Federal Standards for Racial and Ethnic Classification* (Washington: National Academy Press, 1996).

3. Margo Anderson, *The American Census: A Social History* (New Haven, Conn.: Yale University Press, 1988).

4. Noel Ignatiev, *How the Irish Became White* (New York: Routledge, 1995).

5. Deanna L Pagnini and S. Philip Morgan, "Intermarriage and Social Distance among U.S. Immigrants at the Turn of the Century," *American Journal of Sociology* 96 (1990): 405–32.

6. Richard D. Alba, "Assimilation's Quiet Tide," *Public Interest* 119 (Spring 1995): 3–18.

7. Mary C. Waters, *Ethnic Options: Choosing Identities in America* (Berkeley: University of California Press, 1990); Richard D. Alba, *Ethnic Identity: The Transformation of White America* (New Haven, Conn.: Yale University Press, 1990).

8. Michael Hout and Joshua Goldstein, "How 4.5 Million Irish Immigrants Became 40 Million Irish Americans: Demographic and Subjective Aspects of the Ethnic Composition of White Americans," *American Sociological Review* 59 (1994): 64–82.

9. Roderick Harrison and Claudette Bennett, "Racial and Ethnic Diversity," in *State of the Union: America in the 1990's*, vol. 2, *Social Trends*, ed. Reynolds Farley (New York: Russell Sage Foundation, 1995), 165.

10. Alba, "Assimilation's Quiet Tide," 17.

11. U.S. Office of Management and Budget, "Statistical Directive No. 15: Race and Ethnic Standards for Federal Agencies and Administrative Reporting," *Federal Register* 43 (May 4, 1978):19269–70.

12. William Alonso and Mary C. Waters, "The Future Composition of the American Population: An Illustrative Projection." Paper presented at the 1993 winter meetings of the American

Statistical Association, Fort Lauderdale, Florida. The analysis that follows is part of a larger collaborative research project with William Alonso on the implications of mixed-race children's identities for the future ethnic and racial composition of the United States.

13. Of course, at this level of aggregation, it is not possible to determine whether some of these parents are of mixed Asian heritage, or whether mixed Asian parents are themselves more or less likely to report their children as being Asian. In other words, we do not know whether parents reporting themselves as Japanese or Chinese are themselves the offspring of intermarriage.

14. Paul R. Spickard, *Mixed Blood* (Madison: University of Wisconsin Press, 1989); F. James Davis, *Who Is Black?: One Nation's Definition* (University Park: Pennsylvania State University Press, 1991); Virginia R. Dominguez, *White by Definition: Social Classification in Creole Louisiana* (New Brunswick, N.J.: Rutgers University Press, 1986).

15. The groups vary greatly in size so that these relative increases and decreases translate into quite different sizes of absolute change. Altogether, the share of Whites in the total population increases by 0.097 percent; Blacks' share increases by 0.140 percent.

16. Paul Spickard and Rowena Fong, "Pacific Islander Americans and Multiethnicity: A Vision of America's Future?" *Social Forces* 73 (June 1995): 1365–83.

17. Reynolds Farley, "The New Census Question about Ancestry: What Did It Tell Us?" *Demography* 28 (August 1991): 411–30; Stanley Lieberson and Mary C. Waters, "Ethnic Groups in Flux: The Changing Ethnic Responses of American Whites," *Annals of the American Academy of Political and Social Science* 487 (September 1986): 79–91.

18. Alba, *Ethnic Identity;* Farley, "The New Census Question about Ancestry"; Lieberson and Waters, "Ethnic Groups in Flux."

19. Stanley Lieberson and Mary C. Waters, "The Ethnic Responses of Whites: What Causes Their Instability, Simplification and Inconsistency?" *Social Forces* 72 (December 1993): 421–51.

20. Waters, *Ethnic Options*, 42.

21. Stanley Lieberson and Mary C. Waters, *From Many Strands: Ethnic and Racial Groups in Contemporary America* (New York: Russell Sage Foundation, 1988); Lieberson and Waters, "Ethnic Responses of Whites."

22. Lieberson and Waters, "Ethnic Responses of Whites."

23. Edmonston, Goldstein, and Lott, *Spotlight on Heterogeneity,* 32.

24. Nampeo McKenney and Arthur Cresce, "Measurement of Ethnicity in the United States: Experiences of the U.S. Census Bureau," in *Challenges of Measuring an Ethnic World: Science, Politics, and Reality.* Statistics Canada and U.S. Bureau of the Census (Washington: Government Printing Office), 207.

25. Edmonston, Goldstein and Lott, *Spotlight on Heterogeneity,* 38.

26. U.S. Bureau of the Census, "Results of the 1996 Race and Ethnic Targeted Test," Population Division Working Paper No. 18 (Washington: U.S. Bureau of the Census, 1997).

27. Ibid., 1–9.

28. Mary C. Waters, "The Role of Lineage in Identity Formation among Black Americans," *Qualitative Sociology* 14 (Spring 1991): 57–76.

29. Matthew Snipp, *American Indians: The First of This Land* (New York: Russell Sage Foundation, 1989).

30. Karl Eschbach, "Changing Identification among American Indians and Alaska Natives," *Demography* 30 (November 1993): 644–45.

31. Yen Le Espiritu, *Asian American Panethnicity: Bridging Institutions and Identities* (Philadelphia: Temple University Press, 1992).

Stephen Cornell

3   That's the Story of Our Life

Several years ago, in the course of extended research on economic development on American Indian reservations, a colleague and I had an introductory appointment with the senior executive of an Indian nation that we hoped to add to our field sample. We were ushered into his office and explained why we were there and what we were doing. We told him what we wanted to know about: the economic strategies his nation was pursuing, the role that tribal government had played in those strategies, the problems and the successes they had encountered as they tried to take greater control of their economic future. When we were done he was quiet for a few moments. Then, without preamble, he sat forward, looked at us intently, and proceeded to relate to us a history of his people. The heart of his account was some key events that had shaped his nation, and more generally the nation's treatment at the hands of the United States. Very little of what he said had to do with the specific things we wanted to know, although all of it had to do with how this particular people had descended into the poverty and powerlessness from which they were trying to rise. He did not take long—a few minutes. His account was pithy and laconic. When he had finished, there was another pause while he looked at us. We were silent, unsure how to respond to this capsule saga. After a moment he sat back, relaxed, and said, "So: economic development," and launched into a discussion of the topics we had introduced.

It was only later that it occurred to me what the purpose of his historical digression had been. It was not merely informational. He was not telling us the history of his people because he thought we would be interested. It was not even a digression. He had wanted to be sure, before we began to talk about the issues that had brought us there— issues of critical importance to the future of his nation—that we understood *who his people were*. And the best way for him to tell us who they were was to tell us *what they had done* and *what had happened to them*. The unspoken subtext of his soliloquy was: Do you know who we are? Let me tell you the story of our life. We are the people who experienced these things. Now you know our story. Now you know who we are. Now we can talk.

This unspoken subtext is key to the argument of this paper. In what follows, I wish to make three points. The first is that narrative lies at the heart of many ethnic identities;

that is, that many such identities often take a narrative form.[1] The second point is that the narrative form of ethnicity becomes most salient in periods of rupture, when the taken-for-grantedness that characterizes most collective identities is disturbed. The third point is that the narrativization of ethnicity is intimately bound up in power relations, albeit in particular ways. Finally, the paper includes some reflections on narrative and multiplicity.

Ethnicity and Narrative

Like most students of ethnicity in recent years, I approach the topic from a constructionist perspective, which emphasizes contingency. Ethnic identities are not given, fixed, or unchanging, but are continually evolving products of material and social circumstances and of the actions of groups themselves, wrestling with, interpreting, and responding to those circumstances, building or transforming identities in the process.[2] This perspective, supported by a vast array of case materials, has greatly improved our understanding of the dynamics of ethnic identity, but it raises a question. When we construct an ethnic identity, what exactly is being built?[3]

At one level, ethnic identities are labels that we claim or assign, ways of classifying ourselves or others. It may be tempting to say they are "simply" labels, but it is seldom simple. Identities have consequences and capabilities. In distributing persons among categories, societies also, inevitably, distribute things among persons: honor or recognition or power or opportunity or disadvantage. Such distributions also may arouse those persons to action; one need only think of ethnic or racial epithets and their capacity to provoke.

Both the distributional and the provocative implications of ethnic labels depend to a large degree on what those labels signify. Most ethnic labels have meanings attached to them that lend them power as organizers of relationships, resources, experience, and action. But where do those meanings come from?

When people take on, create, or assign an ethnic identity, part of what they do—intentionally or not—is to take on, create, or assign a story, a narrative of some sort that captures central understandings about what it means to be a member of the group. It is a story that can be told in many ways, but ultimately it can be reduced to something along the lines of "we are the people who . . ." (alternatively: "they are the people who . . ."), in which the lacuna becomes a tale of some sort, a record of events. The story has a subject (the group in question), it has action (what happened or will happen), and it has value: it attaches a value to its subject. It makes group members feel good or bad or guilty or self-righteous or superior or justified or something else. Its primary idiom is events: the things the group does or did or will do or had done to it. These need not be major events, although they typically are; they could be accumulations of minor, eminently forgettable episodes. The point is that the narrative is an event-centered conception of the group. The label group members carry or assign to others is a referent or symbol, in effect a condensation of that narrative. When a group claims an ethnic identity or assigns one to others, it is claiming that narrative as its story, or as its version of someone else's story. Constructing an ethnic identity involves, among other things, a gradual layering on and connecting of events and meanings, the construction of a collective narrative.

This process of narrativization typically involves three steps (which may occur in any order): selection, plotting, and interpretation. *Selection* refers to the selection of events themselves, to choosing from unlimited amounts of past, anticipated, or imagined experience a limited number of happenings that constitute the episodic components of the narrative. *Plotting* refers to the linking of these events to each other in causal, sequential, associational, or other ways, and the linking of the group in question to those events, an assigning of roles. *Interpretation* refers to the making of claims about what the events and plot signify, and to the making of claims about the degree to which that particular plot and its constituent events define the group as subjects.

For example, these components emerge, unnamed, in Michael Arlen's book *Passage to Ararat*, which traces the evolution of his understanding of his Armenian identity and in the process reveals central components of that identity. Confronted, as a mature adult, with his own partly Armenian descent, something he had only barely acknowledged, he sets out to discover what being Armenian means. His expedition to then-Soviet Armenia is a journey through which he unearths—partly through his own efforts, partly through the intense effort and encouragement of his Armenian guide—an Armenian identity narrative. It embraces selected events—central among them the Turkish genocide directed against Armenians in the early part of the twentieth century—as keys to Armenian experience and therefore identity. It links these events to each other and through them links Armenians to other groups and to the surrounding world. Through these events and the relationships among them it puts forward a moral understanding of suffering and survival that is central to Armenian peoplehood. It assigns those events a central place in Armenian identity and takes from them certain meanings that are held to capture the essence of "what it is to be an Armenian."[4]

This narrative not only emerges from archives and histories but is elaborated in conversations and fierce assertions and made concrete in physical monuments and sacred space. As Arlen pieces the story together, he has the profound sense of discovering, in Armenians' sense of themselves, a missing part of his own sense of self. Armenians become for him the people who did these things, or to whom these things happened, and by virtue of the putative blood connection of ethnic descent, their story becomes in part his story, part of the meaning of his own Armenianness—fundamentally, part of his identity.

This Armenian narrative, while filled with tragedy, is a morally positive one: it exalts Armenians for what they have been through. Not all identity narratives are similarly positive. Some are negative. Of course many groups interpret the things done by others in negative terms, but they may also adopt a negative interpretation of their own life stories. Gordon Nakagawa, for example, shows how some Japanese American narratives about internment during World War II not only detail social control practices taking place under internment but reveal "the historical self-understanding of the Nikkei community," a self-understanding deeply affected by the experience of being turned into "docile and deformed subject[s]."[5]

What makes all of these narratives—positive or negative—ethnic is the principle that governs the three steps involved. Particular narratives play a role in ethnic identity insofar as an ethnic identity or boundary is the "key organizing principle"—I take the phrase from Steinmetz's discussion of narrative and social class[6]—of the narrative. To the extent that selection, plotting, and interpretation take ethnic boundaries into account and use them as central organizing principles, the result is an ethnic identity narrative, the story of a particular ethnic "us" or "them."

The events such narratives include vary substantially. Identity narratives may combine fact and fiction in varying proportions. Some focus on life-shattering or history-making events—migration, genocide, slavery, the Holocaust—while others focus on quotidian behavior. Some are rich with detail; others are barely compositions or narratives at all. Ultimately, what matters is not the events they include but the claims they make about those events, the sources of those events, and their attendant meanings. What matters is not the validity of representations but their effects: the degree to which the narrative and its component parts are understood—by group members or by outsiders—as illustrative or exemplary, as capturing something essential about the group in question.

Of course such understandings may vary across both groups and time. Different groups may see the same events differently or see different events as similarly emblematic of a single group's identity. Furthermore, as groups' understandings of themselves and others change, so do the narratives in which those understandings are encapsulated and through which they are given substance. Selection, plotting, interpretation—all or any may change over time. For some European-descent ethnic groups in the United States, for example, identity narratives have thinned in recent years as the distance from key events in them—departure from the old country, immigration, the experiences of transition and adjustment—increases. The events chronicled in those narratives are fewer now, the detail less, the links among events less clear, their meanings more vague. For some members of those groups, such narratives are being replaced by a more general European identity narrative or a narrative of Whiteness, neither one as richly detailed as the older stories that gave many European immigrants to the United States part of their sense of themselves.[7]

The power of narrative as a source or representation of identity comes from its sense-making properties. "The problem of identity," says Dan McAdams, "is the problem of arriving at a life story that makes sense—provides unity and purpose—within a sociohistorial matrix that embodies a much larger story."[8] Although McAdams is writing about individual identities, we can say much the same of collective identities. The problem of collective identity is the problem of creating an account of who "we" (or "they") are that makes sense of the larger matrix of social relations in which the group finds itself and of its place within that matrix and its experience of those relations. Narrative—the relational ordering and framing of event and experience—is peculiarly suited to these sense-making tasks. Anthony Kerby goes so far as to call it "the privileged medium for understanding human experience."[9] It situates groups among events and situates events in larger matrices of relations. Not only does it give coherence and meaning to what might otherwise seem isolated episodes; it places the group at the center of the tale. It specifies the group's relationship to those events, and in so doing it not only makes sense of events; it makes sense of the group itself.

Not every person with an ethnic identity has an ethnically constructing story to tell. For some, such as the Indian official who prefaced his discussion of economic development with the story of his people, it may be a prominent part of consciousness. For others, it may be a skeletal tale recalled only with difficulty. Narrative may not lie at the heart of ethnic identity as that identity is felt and experienced. But it lies at the heart of the ethnic category. Ultimately that category can be reduced to a statement that follows narrative lines. The category consists of the people who—so the story goes—came from there, did that, experienced this particular history, and so on. Ethnic categories are categories of collective life stories.

Narrative and Rupture

By linking narrative and ethnic identity, I do not mean to suggest that narrative is necessarily a salient part of all ethnicities or of individual ethnic consciousness. The narrative aspect of most ethnicities lies hidden for the most part beneath the taken-for-grantedness that characterizes collective identities generally. But at certain times, in certain circumstances, it breaks the surface, becoming more explicit and apparent.

Jerome Bruner argues that individuals turn to narrative as a means of making sense of situations of breakdown or deviation from expectations, when things are not "as they should be." In search of meaning, they narrate the unexpected or disturbing, creating a sense of order—a sense that things make sense after all—through the imposed order of narrative.[10]

Something similar seems to be the case with ethnically based collective identities. They, too, respond to crisis with a search for order. What we might call periods of rupture—not in the identity but in its taken-for-granted quality—prompt the narrative process, and for similar reasons.

By periods of rupture I mean those periods when identities, for one reason or another, are questioned by those who carry them, are called into question by others, or are severely tested by events. At these times identities lose their taken-for-granted quality. Such periods commonly result from significant changes in group or individual situations, as through, among other things, migration, abrupt changes in group political or economic fortunes, political mobilization, or rapidly rising rates of ethnic intermarriage. At those moments old assumptions or understandings may be challenged, calling for a new or reconfirmed definition of the situation—a new sense of things. New events have to be taken into account or dismissed; new relationships among events proposed; new interpretations made. In short, such situations call for a renarration of group identity.

Of course, sense making may not be the only purpose served. Narrative also can be used to make common cause against both human and nonhuman threats, against both the acts of oppressors or usurpers and the impacts of social change. To claim that "my" story and "your" story are essentially the same is to propose a common bond between us, a reason for us to join together in the face of rupture in the world we have known. To make a particular sense of events can be a way to make common cause as well.

The narrative process comes to the foreground in situations of rupture as groups try to make sense of new problems or opportunities, defend or assert claims, reframe identities, mobilize members for political action, or otherwise rethink who they or others are. The group's story is told or retold at such moments—in new or old forms—as this sense- and cause-making process goes forward, integrating new experiences or concerns with old understandings.

Liisa Malkki provides an example of this reconstruction through narrative in her study of Hutu refugees from Burundi, victims of Hutu-Tutsi conflict in the early 1970s, living in camps in Tanzania. These refugees, writes Malkki, "were intensively and continually engaged in a kind of historical ordering and reordering of their past." It was a process that seemed to involve virtually everyone in the camps and that fused personal and collective experience, as refugees, in talking about their lives, "regularly slipped from the domain of personal life history into the wider field of the collective history" of the group. Much of this effort took the form of narrating the Hutu past, from the colonial history of Burundi through ethnic warfare to the present period of exile. Hutus continually revisited past and present events, incorporating them into an evolving narrative, and in the process reinterpreted those events. The result was what Malkki calls a "mythico-history," replete with recurrent themes and pivotal episodes that added up to a highly standardized, collective Hutu narrative "which heroizes them as a distinct people with a historical trajectory setting them apart from other peoples." It is a narrative in which the Hutus "are the principal actors" and through which they recast historical events in moral terms. Narration is part of the way they deal with loss, with refugee status, with exile, and with discrimination at the hands of the Tanzanians, and it is how they construct themselves as a people. The Hutu label has not changed, but the identity it represents has been narratively reconstructed.[11]

In his study of Afrikaner civil religion in South Africa, Dunbar Moodie describes how, in the early decades of this century, Afrikaners consciously attempted to construct and disseminate within the Afrikaner ethnic population a heroic narrative of Afrikanerdom sufficiently compelling to sustain group solidarity in the face of British domination and the threat of anglicization, emergent class divisions as a result of urbanization and industrialization, and eventually the resistance waged by the vast population of oppressed Black Africans. By selecting particular events (for example, the Great Trek into the interior of the country in 1838, the battle with the Zulus at Blood River, concentration camp experiences in the Boer War), linking them to each other in a narrative of testing, suffering, and heroic survival, and investing them with elements of the sacred, they sought to revivify Afrikaner identity and to overcome emergent, alternative bases of action.[12]

Periods of rupture may be long or short. For some groups they are typically brief and inconsequential; for others, rupture is normal: life is struggle and collective life stories are the currency of daily interaction, retold again and again as continual reminders of "who we are" and why the struggle matters. But as periods of rupture come to an end, as identity issues become less contested, as group conditions—positive or negative—regain some certainty, the narrative process tends to attenuate. Either the newly established narrative becomes the new, taken-for-granted version of collective identity, understood but seldom presented, or narrative itself moves into the background of group consciousness. It retreats again behind the group label, a label that carries ample meaning but now retains few explicit connections to events.

Narrative and Power

Both identity narratives and their production are bound up in power relations. This is apparent in at least two ways.

The first issue has to do with *who gets to narrate whom* and with *whose version of an identity narrative gains currency where.* The same identity may have attached to it very different narratives, some composed by insiders narrating their own identity, some by outsiders narrating the identity of others. The narratives insiders and outsiders construct may be radically different from each other. Members of an ethnic group may discover that the dominant narrative underlying their identity—the one that prevails in the common conception of the group within the society and even, perhaps, among many group members—is not the story they wish to tell at all but is a story composed by nonmembers, reflecting the experience, imagination, and interests of others.

For a long time, the prevailing African American narrative in the society at large was told largely by outsiders; it was someone else's story about African Americans. In the 1960s and 1970s many Blacks waged an aggressive campaign to tell their own story in their own way, and to give that story prominence in the society at large. The selection and interpretation of events—from slave revolts to raising families—were a crucial part of that effort, aided both by new media representations such as the book and television saga *Roots* and by a flowering of new scholarship, both Black and White, that provided new raw material for narrative construction. In time a new narrative of resistance, resourcefulness, and endurance began to replace the older narrative of victimization, passivity, and incapacity.[13] This new narrative gained increasing currency in the wider society as Blacks struggled to make it known and claim it as their own. They struggled not only against those who carried or defended an older account but against that account's inertial power, a product of its embeddedness in popular culture, educational practice, and even in the minds of some Blacks.

As this example suggests, narrative construction is often a contested process, shaped by power differentials. Some groups have greater resources for storytelling than others do; some have greater access to the public arena than others do. "Our" version of your story may prevail in the public arena over "your" version because our group controls access to that arena, or because we have more of the positional or other resources through which one or another version of an identity narrative can be promoted.

This is not only an intergroup issue—whether it will be our story about you or your story about you that gains currency in the public arena, being supported in schools, media, political discourse, and elsewhere. It is also at times an intragroup issue. Conflict over narrative can occur among insiders, where there may be major differences over what should be in or out of "our" story, what the story means, and how it should be told. Different insiders may tell radically different versions of their own story, and one subgroup may have sufficient resources to dominate the storytelling and control the more public narrative. Much of the dynamic of both inter- and intragroup relations is a contest for whose version of a particular identity narrative will prevail.

Such conflict surrounded a 1991 Smithsonian Institution exhibit in Washington, D.C., titled "The West as America: Reinterpreting Images of the Frontier, 1820–1920."[14] While the identity at stake in this exhibit and the responses to it may not match the conventional conception of ethnic, the parallels are acute. The European or Euro-American exploration of the West, the displacement of the indigenous population, and the process of White settlement together have long constituted one of the defining events in U.S. history and, therefore, identity—classically narrated as a triumph of the resourceful, courageous, and pioneering American spirit, a colossal exercise in nation building and the spread of civilization.[15] The Smithsonian exhibit presented many of the classic paintings, photographs, and other icons of that story but recast their meaning, emphasizing as well or—particularly in the wall texts in the exhibit—instead the less triumphant side of the story: the destruction of Native American societies, the exploitation of the labor of other groups, the aggressive seizure of lands, environmental damage, and so forth, as well as the commercial motives behind much of the enterprise.

This renarrating of the West immediately thrust the exhibit deep into controversy, involving not only ordinary museum goers—some of whom praised the exhibit, some of whom condemned it—but also angry members of the U.S. Senate.[16] At stake was the issue of whose version of the American story would remain dominant. Americans were arrayed on either side, struggling to place their own interpretations on events. It was, in effect, a conflict over *who we are*.

Conflict may occur in any or all of the processes involved in the construction of identity narratives: selection, plotting, and interpretation. It is apparent in all of these in the Smithsonian controversy: over which events in the potentially vast story of the West should be highlighted and narrated; over how those events are linked to each other and to the larger American idea; over what those events and the relationships among them mean. Of course not all narrative constructions are conflictual. Some involve little more than the efforts by groups of persons to come to terms with and understand their situations and to establish a clearer sense of who they are—a complex task, to be sure, but not necessarily a contested one.

The second way in which narratives are bound up in power relations has to do with *what an identity narrative claims*. Particular interpretations of events may undergird moral or legal claims to power. A key element in Native American identity narratives, for example, for both Indians and non-Indians, is the history of native land dispossession at the hands first of Europeans and later of Euro-Americans. That history is not only about power relations and the changing distribution of power between Indian nations on the one hand and European colonies and the United States on the other. It also can be used to construct a narrative that in turn asserts moral claims. The narrative may "tell" Indian dispossession in a way that asserts the moral claims of the dispossessors, as in the idea that hunting societies' failure to cultivate the land denies them a moral claim to it. Or it may "tell" dispossession in such a way that it adds moral force to the claims of the group, as in the Indian claim that specific acts of duplicity and violence were the primary methods of dispossession (see chapter 7). Power, in other words, is latent in the narrative itself, in the implicit or explicit claims the story makes and in the asserted bases of those claims. This power is conditional; it may not be manifest unless the group in question has the ability to give currency to the narrative in which it is embedded. But it may be enough to give the narrative currency among the group's own members, where it may arouse the otherwise apathetic or hopeless to action.

Patricia Ewick and Susan Silbey, whose concern is not with identity but with the sociology of narrative itself, distinguish between what they call "hegemonic" and "subversive" narratives: on the one hand, those "that reproduce existing relations of power and inequity," and, on the other, those that reveal "the connections between particular lives and social organization."[17] Certainly this distinction is apparent in ethnic identity narratives,[18] which often help either to reproduce or to challenge the power relations in which the group itself is situated—and can do so from either the superior or the subordinate position.

Narrative and Multiplicity

Among the narratives that challenge existing social arrangements in the United States are the emerging narratives of multiplicity. The idea of the United States as a multi-ethnic and multiracial society is long established, but attached to that idea have been certain assumptions about the nature of that multiplicity. One such assumption has been that the boundaries among groups—and among racial groups in particular—are readily identifiable and nonoverlapping. Racial identities, both in government policy and classification and in a great deal of public discourse, supposedly are singular identities. You only have one. You're either this or that but not both (or more).

This social convention depended on another social convention: the idea that race, when used as a discriminator among human beings, is an essentially biological phenomenon, rooted in consistent, substantial, and identifiable biological difference. Both ideas were nothing but agreed-upon myths, but they nonetheless exercised—and continue to exercise—extraordinary power in American life.

The first of these conventions is the one of interest here—the idea of unmixed races. Although this assumption frequently departed dramatically from the facts, until recently neither the institutions that collect or use data on racial identities nor many individuals whose backgrounds are significantly more complex than this convention allows paid much attention to the discrepancy. African Americans, for example, most of whom are of variously mixed African, native American, and European descent, generally have been thought of by most persons in the United States as monoracial and have tended, largely in response to that assumption and to the stark realities of powerlessness in the United States, to adopt much the same stance as a basis of organization and action.

In recent years, however, new narratives of multiplicity have been emerging, particularly as marriage across racial boundaries has increased and both the partners and their offspring have resisted the idea that those who mix racial or ethnic heritages should have to choose among them when it comes to classification or, for that matter, identity. These new narratives not only underline and, increasingly, celebrate some of the new versions of multiplicity that have come with changing patterns of immigration to the United States; they also have drawn attention to the very substantial degree of multiplicity hidden historically behind official conceptions of race. For example, Itabari Njeri opens her study of multiplicity, identity, and conflict with the following statement: "I am your ordinary, everyday, walking-around Brooklyn Negro. That is to say, I am African, East Indian, French, English, Arawak, and more I don't know about. In other words, I am a typical New World Black."[19]

One of the striking aspects of Njeri's statement is the number of very different stories it brings together in one person's genealogy. There are the English who came to the

New World, fought a revolution, and founded a new society; the Arawaks who were already in that New World but lost their lands and their lives to European force of arms and disease; the Africans whom Europeans dragged across an ocean and forced into brutal labor to build that new society; and so on. An array of identity narratives potentially comes together in Njeri. The word "potentially" is essential, however, for some of those narratives are effectively denied her by the encompassing society. It is not easy for someone of color who is also of mixed racial or ethnic heritage to claim the English or French or White narrative as in any sense her own, for each is jealously guarded by others. The implied trope in ethnicity narratives—"We are the people who ..."—has an implied counterpart: "and you're not." The insistence on monoracial categories supports a social arrangement based on exclusion.

Narratives of multiplicity, whether revealing the complexities within established categories or the overlaps among them, challenge this social arrangement. At the very least, they argue that "we are the people who do not fit the established categories." More ambitiously, they deny some of the assumptions that underlie exclusion. They suggest that identity tales are many-layered and that those who dig deeply will find their stories growing increasingly complex and less exclusive. Indeed, as far as identity narratives are concerned, along with the distinction between hegemonic and subversive narratives we might distinguish between segregating and integrating ones. One of the ways in which narratives of multiplicity are subversive lies in their tendency to be integrative. They are narratives of connection, focused not on boundaries—on what separates peoples—but on connection, on the intertwined patterns of descent that muddy boundaries, fuzz differences, and create shared narrative spaces.[20]

Those spaces are by no means uncontested, however. Those who carry multiple racial or ethnic identities may struggle not only against the dominant group's insistence on clear boundaries and unitary classifications, but against the similar insistence on the part of subordinate groups. A student of mine once pointed this out in her own account of her ethnicity. She is the daughter of an African American father and a German mother who met while her father was serving with the U.S. military in Europe. Her parents raised her to value both of her ancestries, and she gladly claims for herself both African American and German American identities. She is the first to admit that these identities are very different. One is largely symbolic, a matter of food, music, the occasional trip to Germany to visit relatives, and the stories her mother has told her over the years. The narrative attached to that identity is a modest one. The other, however, looms large, not least because its narrative is an elaborate, contentious, and heavily weighted one in U.S. society, and because her African American identity carries with it significant consequences that are apparent both in her daily experience and in her socioeconomic fortunes. Because she looks Black, that identity is the one that organizes much of her life; it is other people's narratives of Blackness that she most often encounters and that shape much of their interaction with her.

But something else is involved. To some of her African American friends, she reported, her insistence on being not only African American but German American presents a challenge. They want from her a wholehearted commitment to Blackness and a concomitant rejection of the European ancestry she also carries. These two sources of pressure have the same result: in the face of their joint rejection, her German

American identity is slipping away. Neither the dominant White society nor her African American friends will allow her the complexity she sees and values in herself and her heritage. Both deny her a genuine choice, including the option that says "I am both."

Thus not only the society at large demands simplification, a choice to be one thing only. Sometimes the identities that come together in individuals make similar demands. To be multiethnic or multiracial is not only to defy the conventions of the social order; on occasion it also is to defy the pressures attached to one or more of the component identities.

These pressures can make narratives of multiplicity tenuous and fragile, the spinning of a story that few other people want to hear. It is often a complicated story to begin with, a piecing together of disparate histories and understandings. Many of the events in such narratives have no obvious linkage other than the moment of union when lines of descent converge, precipitating a lineage that fits no standard category but claims for itself the distinctive events to which several categories refer and struggles to attach meaning of some sort to them all. The connections are there. The task in narrating multiplicity is to give them meaning and to establish for that narrative some currency in the world at large.

Now We Can Talk

In the struggle to construct ethnic narratives, to assert authorship, to control selection, plot, and meaning, and to give narrative currency or dominance in the group's conception of itself and in wider conceptions of the group, much is at stake, and not only power, although surely that is sufficient. Identity itself is at issue. "In the end," says Moraes Zogoiby, the narrator of Salman Rushdie's novel *The Moor's Last Sigh,* "stories are what's left of us."[21] They are a large portion of what the world knows about us.

But they also are what we start with. For ethnic groups, at least, the "we" begins with stories, with the events and interpretations that tell us that "we" are a people and what kind of people "we" are. Sometimes those stories are ours, and for that reason, perhaps, we believe them; sometimes they are the work of others, and for that reason, perhaps, or because they fit our needs or interests, or because we don't know any other stories, we believe them. Even if we don't believe them, they constitute a version of ourselves that we may celebrate or reject, struggle against or struggle to change.

To narrate an identity is to argue: it is to make an assertion about the scope or nature or meaning of that identity. It is a claim to a particular significance. As the official of the Indian nation seemed to suggest: *Now you know who we are. Now we can talk.*

Notes

Acknowledgment: I am grateful to Maura Grogan, Joseph Gusfield, Jeffrey Haydu, Kathy Mooney, Joane Nagel, Paul Spickard, Mary Waters, and Kathryn Woolard for helpful comments and suggestions.

1. The idea that identity and narrative are closely linked is hardly new. In recent years narrative has been treated as a core element in many forms of identity, both individual and collective. See, for example: Dan P. McAdams, *Power, Intimacy, and the Life Story: Personological Inquiries into Identity* (Homewood, Ill.: Dorsey, 1985); Jerome Bruner, *Acts of Meaning* (Cambridge, Mass.: Harvard University Press, 1990); Anthony Paul Kerby, *Narrative and the Self* (Bloomington: Indiana University Press, 1991); George Steinmetz, "Reflections on the Role of Social Narratives in Working-Class Formation: Narrative Theory in the Social Sciences," *Social Science History,* 16 (Fall, 1992): 489–516; Adrian Coyle, "'My Own Special Creation'? The Construction of Gay Identity," in *Social Psychology of Identity and the Self Concept,* ed. Glynis M. Breakwell (London: Surrey University Press, 1992), 187–220; Margaret R. Somers and Gloria D. Gibson, "Reclaiming the Epistemological 'Other': Narrative and the Social Constitution of Identity," in *Social Theory and the Politics of Identity,* ed. Craig Calhoun (Oxford: Blackwell, 1994), 37–99. However, while some beginnings have been made (e.g., Brent O. Peterson, *Popular Narratives and Ethnic Identity* [Ithaca, N.Y.: Cornell University Press, 1991]), the place of narrative in ethnic identities has yet to be worked out systematically. The present paper is an effort to contribute to this working-out process.

2. See, among many others, William Yancey, Eugene P. Ericksen, and Richard N. Juliani, "Emergent Ethnicity: A Review and Reformulation," *American Sociological Review* 41 (1976): 391–403; Elizabeth Tonkin, Maryon McDonald, and Malcolm Chapman, eds., *History and Ethnicity* (London: Routledge, 1989); Kathleen N. Conzen, David A. Gerber, Eva Morawska, George E. Pozzetta, and Rudolph J. Vecoli, "The Invention of Ethnicity: A Perspective from the U.S.A." *Journal of American Ethnic History* 12 (1992): 3–41; Joane Nagel, "The Political Construction of Ethnicity," in *Competitive Ethnic Relations,* ed. Susan Olzak and Joane Nagel (Orlando, Fla.: Academic, 1986), 93–112; Joane Nagel, *American Indian Ethnic Renewal* (New York: Oxford University Press, 1996); Stephen Cornell and Douglas Hartmann, *Ethnicity and Race* (Thousand Oaks, Calif.: Pine Forge, 1998).

3. I treat ethnicity as a form of identification distinguished by an at least implicit claim to shared bonds of kinship (real or assumed) or their approximation (e.g., descent from a common homeland) and by a claimed history or present of shared culture and experience. Ethnic identities may be either asserted or assigned. Racial identities, in contrast, typically are assigned on the basis of selected physical differences. A racial group becomes an ethnic group when it asserts its own distinctive identity on the basis of common descent and present or historical shared culture and experience. Race thus is not a subcategory of ethnicity but a different basis of identification. Some racial groups are at one and the same time ethnic groups; others are not. References to ethnicity in this paper therefore include, by implication, those racial groups involved in their own construction as groups. For relevant definitional discussions, see Stephen Cornell, "The Variable Ties that Bind: Content and Circumstance in Ethnic Processes," *Ethnic and Racial Studies* 19 (April 1996): 265–89; Cornell and Hartmann, *Ethnicity and Race;* and Stuart Hall, "New Ethnicities," in *"Race," Culture, and Difference,* ed. James Donald and Ali Rattansi (London: Sage, 1992), 252–59.

4. Michael Arlen, *Passage to Ararat* (New York: Farrar, Straus, and Giroux, 1975), 72.

5. Gordon Nakagawa, "Deformed Subjects, Docile Bodies: Disciplinary Practices and Subject-Constitution in Stories of Japanese-American Internment," in *Narrative and Social Control,* ed. Dennis K. Mumby (Newbury Park, Calif.: Sage, 1993), 161.

6. Steinmetz, "Reflections on the Role of Social Narratives."

7. Whiteness may be an increasingly important identity for many Euro-Americans, but, as Ruth Frankenberg argues, it remains for many of them assumed, unnamed, and undefined (*White Women: Race Matters: The Social Construction of Whiteness* [Minneapolis: University of Minnesota Press, 1993]). There may be a narrative of Whiteness, but for many Whites it is an

unarticulated one. Of course narratives of Whiteness are hardly a White monopoly. Non-White groups often have their own well-articulated narratives of Whiteness. See, for example, Keith H. Basso, *Portraits of "The Whiteman": Linguistic Play and Cultural Symbols among the Western Apache* (Cambridge, UK: Cambridge University Press, 1979), and John Langston Gwaltney, *Drylongso: A Self-Portrait of Black America* (New York: Vintage, 1981).

8. McAdams, *Power, Intimacy, and the Life Story,* 18.

9. Kerby, *Narrative and the Self,* 4.

10. Bruner, *Acts of Meaning,* 39–40.

11. Liisa Malkki, "Context and Consciousness: Local Conditions for the Production of Historical and National Thought among Hutu Refugees in Tanzania," in *Nationalist Ideologies and the Production of National Cultures,* ed. Richard G. Fox (Washington: American Anthropological Association, 1990), 37, 34.

12. T. Dunbar Moodie, *The Rise of Afrikanerdom: Power, Apartheid, and the Afrikaner Civil Religion* (Berkeley: University of California Press, 1975). See also Hermann Giliomee, "The Growth of Afrikaner Identity," in *Ethnic Power Mobilized: Can South Africa Survive?* ed. Heribert Adam and Hermann Giliomee (New Haven, Conn.: Yale University Press, 1979), 83–127; Leonard Thompson, *The Political Mythology of Apartheid* (New Haven, Conn.: Yale University Press, 1985); Gerhard Schutte, "Afrikaner Historiography and the Decline of Apartheid: Ethnic Self-Construction in Times of Crisis," in *History and Ethnicity,* ed. Tonkin et al., 216–31.

13. E.g., Alex Haley, *Roots* (New York: Doubleday, 1976); Eugene Genovese, *Roll, Jordan, Roll: The World the Slaves Made* (New York: Vintage, 1976); V. P. Franklin, *Black Self-Determination: A Cultural History of the Faith of the Fathers* (Westport, Conn.: Lawrence Hill, 1984); and the discussion in Peter Novick, *That Noble Dream: The "Objectivity Question" and the American Historical Profession* (Cambridge, UK: Cambridge University Press, 1988), chap. 14.

14. A book published by the Smithsonian on the occasion of the exhibit includes much of the material, along with extended essays and commentary. See William H. Truettner, ed. *The West as America: Reinterpreting Images of the Frontier, 1820–1920* (Washington: Smithsonian Institution Press, 1991).

15. See the discussion in Patricia Hills, "Picturing Progress in the Era of Westward Expansion," in *The West as America,* ed. Truettner, 97–147.

16. John Fiske, *Power Plays, Power Works* (London: Verso, 1993), 162–72; Dell Hymes, "Indian Identities: What It Was and Is to Be a Native North American," *Times Literary Supplement,* August 7, 1992, pp. 3–4.

17. Patricia Ewick and Susan S. Silbey, "Subversive Stories and Hegemonic Tales: Toward a Sociology of Narrative," *Law and Society Review* 29 (1995):197–226.

18. See, for example, George Lipsitz, *Time Passages: Collective Memory and American Popular Culture* (Minneapolis: University of Minnesota Press, 1990), chap. 10.

19. Itabari Njeri, *The Last Plantation: Color, Conflict, and Identity: Reflections of a New World Black* (Boston: Houghton Mifflin, 1997), 1.

20. See Paul R. Spickard and Rowena Fong, "Pacific Islander Americans and Multiethnicity: A Vision of America's Future?" *Social Forces* 73 (1995): 1365–83.

21. Salman Rushdie, *The Moor's Last Sigh* (New York: Pantheon, 1996), 110.

Part II

Construction of Ethnic Narratives: Migrant Ethnicities

Violet M. Johnson

4   Black Immigrants in the United States

In December 1993, a Black gunman went on a rampage in a Long Island commuter train, killing six people and injuring several others. The media reported, in the days following the incident, that the gunman's actions were prompted by racial rage. Several handwritten notes allegedly from Colin Fergusson, the gunman, were made public. In these, the writer rambled on about his frustration and anger over how Blacks in the United States are treated and how several segments of the Black population had sold out. It was also revealed that Fergusson was not a U.S. citizen, but an immigrant from Jamaica. His act elicited reactions across the country about mental instability and crime. In some circles the focus was also on Fergusson's status as a foreigner.

While an obviously mentally disturbed Colin Fergusson (at his trial he denied shooting the victims, claiming a White man did it) is not representative of Black foreigners, the questions prompted by his case are pertinent to them. How do Black foreigners perceive themselves in the United States—as immigrants first and Black Americans second, or vice versa? How are they affected by race and racism in the United States? How much of their frustration can be traced to their premigration experiences?[1]

It often takes an unusual incident or situation to draw attention to Black immigrants as having identities and feelings separate from those of the larger African American population. Double invisibility is one of the fundamental experiences of Black foreigners in the United States.[2] They suffer on the national level from one kind of invisibility, along with the native Black population. They also find themselves lumped with U.S.-born Blacks in an artificial, monolithic minority designated Negro, Colored, Black, or African American, for a second kind of invisibility. But native-born Blacks in the United States are of course variegated, and an even more variegated foreign-born Black population consists of Africans (among them Nigerians, Ghanaians, Kenyans, Ethiopians, Somalis, and Gambians), West Indians (including Jamaicans, Trinidadians, Haitians, and Martiniquans), and South Americans (for instance, Brazilians). Furthermore, most Black immigrants in the United States come from societies in which they constitute the numerical majority and in which they are not apt to regard themselves first and foremost as Black.[3]

Although premigration identities do not remain static, they are viable, and they help determine some strategies of adjustment and adaptation. Until the 1970s, much of the research on Black foreigners acknowledged the vitality of premigration identities and experiences but used them primarily to compare foreign- and native-born Blacks. For decades, writers pointed to these immigrants to show that, given the right group characteristics, Blacks did extremely well in the United States.[4] Such approaches, while acknowledging the importance of the foreign identity of this segment of the Black population, fail to explain many crucial aspects of that identity. Fortunately for Black immigration historiography, some recent studies of Black immigrants do not primarily compare them with U.S.-born Blacks but analyze their multifaceted experience as foreigners and Blacks in the United States.[5]

An inquiry into the histories of various Black immigrant groups in this country would reveal some common features regarding identity, along with individual cases nuanced by factors such as place of origin, time and circumstances of emigration, place of residence in the United States, and patterns of responses to the challenges of adjustment and adaptation. A case in point: Blacks who immigrated from the English-speaking West Indies to settle in Boston during the first half of the twentieth century.

The West Indian Community in Boston, 1915–1950

Although West Indians began immigrating to Boston in the last quarter of the nineteenth century, the first major influx came with World War I. The war raised the demand for manufactured goods and also prevented the safe travel of European immigrant workers. Employers started looking to territories of the Western Hemisphere for replacement labor. This was particularly timely for the British West Indians, who were facing stricter immigration laws enacted by the governments of Panama, Cuba, Venezuela, and Costa Rica. West Indian migration to Boston continued steadily until 1924, when the restrictive Johnson-Reed Act reduced their numbers. The immigration reforms of the early 1950s dealt a heavier blow, imposing a ceiling of only 100 immigrants a year from all British colonial possessions.

According to census records, in 1910, Boston's West Indians numbered 566, 5 percent of the city's total Black population. In 1920, the number had risen to 2,877, and by 1950, when the first two major waves ended, the West Indian population was estimated at 5,000, 12 percent of the city's Blacks.

The migrants came mainly from three islands—Jamaica, Barbados, and Montserrat—with only a sprinkling from St. Vincent, Antigua, Guyana, Trinidad, and the Virgin Islands.[6] Following a general Caribbean migration pattern during that period, more men than women emigrated, in a ratio of about three to one.[7] The overwhelming majority were single or in common-law, flexible marriages, which reflected the social structure of their homelands. Between the ages of eighteen and thirty, most had at least one child before emigrating. The children did not usually emigrate with their parents but remained with relatives at home for six months to two or three years, when their parents were settled enough to send for them. Oral histories suggest that few conjugal partners were reunited in the United States, instead forming new, mostly endogamous, unions with other West Indians, usually in Western/Christian marriages.

When the West Indians arrived in Boston, each major ethnic immigrant group was establishing itself in a specific area of the city and claiming this section as its territory. In the nineteenth century, most of the European arrivals congregated in the North End and West End. By 1920, the North End's inhabitants were 90 percent Italian; other Italian enclaves evolved in East Boston. The Irish had by then carved out enclaves in South Boston, Charlestown, and sections of Roxbury and Dorchester. The Jews, like the Irish, had by 1920 moved from the North End and West End, establishing new enclaves in Roxbury and Mattapan.[8]

Although Boston grew significantly during the first half of the twentieth century, the Black population remained comparatively small (less than 5 percent), even in 1950, when its numbers almost doubled.[9] Like the Caucasian majority, more than three-quarters of Boston's Black population was not native to Boston, with two Black migrations occurring simultaneously: the bigger, more noticeable migration of U.S. Blacks from the South, and the less visible arrival of West Indian Blacks.[10]

Blacks had begun to move into new neighborhoods when the West Indians arrived. For much of the nineteenth century, Boston's Blacks had clustered along the western slope of Beacon Hill in the West End. But at the turn of the century, overwhelmed by the influx of European immigrants in that section of the city, they began to move to the South End. Between 1900 and 1950, a new "Black section" evolved, with three main subsections: the South End, where most of the Black entertainment establishments were located; the in-town section, made up of Lower Roxbury and the outer South End, which contained most of the Black service businesses (undertakers, barber shops, beauty salons, and restaurants); and the Hill, made up of areas in Upper Roxbury and Dorchester. This third section did not become a Black neighborhood until the 1930s, when Blacks began to rent and buy the large Victorian houses being vacated by the Jews who were now moving into suburbs like Milton and Randolph.

Thus, West Indian immigrants moved into a clearly defined structure of neighborhoods carved along racial and ethnic lines. Through chain migration, by 1930 hundreds of English-speaking West Indians had settled among Boston-born and Southern migrant Blacks in Black neighborhoods in Cambridge, the South End, and Roxbury. The pull of chain migration notwithstanding, the favorite pockets of West Indian concentration in the Black neighborhoods did not evolve into visible, easily identifiable West Indian enclaves. Today, West Indian restaurants and grocery stores dot some areas of Roxbury, Dorchester, and Mattapan, indicating a strong West Indian presence, but before 1960 such establishments were rare. Without a clearly visible ethnic enclave, for most practical purposes West Indians were integrated into the African American residential turf of Boston.

Occupational experiences constituted another key area in which the Black immigrants' fortunes were closely tied to those of their native-born counterparts. By 1900, most U.S. cities had developed a pattern in which ethnic groups concentrated in and were associated with specific occupations.[11] But while European immigrants could find established occupational niches among their fellow Irish, Italians, Greeks, and so on, the West Indians' occupational niche translated into jobs done by the Black population at large, mostly menial, unskilled, and low paying—the then-traditional Negro jobs.[12] This was especially the case for skilled jobs in industries such as construction. The West Indian–owned *Boston Chronicle* and the other Black weekly, the *Boston Guardian,* frequently reported on the refusal of White foremen to hire Blacks instead of their fellow White, immigrant workers or for fear of encountering the wrath of the White workers, who were known to resist working alongside "colored people."

Most West Indian men worked as laborers, especially on the docks, where they hauled cargo to and from the very sugar and banana boats that had transported them to Boston. A small number were able to secure skilled jobs, especially in the navy yard in Charlestown. But even there, according to the *Boston Chronicle* of September 16, 1939, most of the West Indian and U.S-born Blacks were able to acquire positions only as replacement workers for Whites who had gone off to war.

Although West Indian women had a better experience than the men, they were not immune to the effects of occupational closure. Before 1950, most of them, like the U.S.-born Black women of Boston, seldom found employment as sales clerks in retail stores. They could not enter the European-dominated candy, textile, and shoe factories. Even the accomplished seamstresses among them could not get work in the dressmaking shops in the garment industry. Domestic service was where they found their niche. The majority of West Indian women worked as maids, cooks, and general housekeepers in private homes throughout the greater Boston area, particularly in White, Jewish neighborhoods in Roxbury, Dorchester, Mattapan, and Newton. Entry into that occupational sphere was relatively easy for West Indian women, who had two main advantages in their favor: domestic service had already been established as a traditional Black occupation,[13] and they could communicate in English with their employers, as their non-English-speaking female European immigrant competitors could not.

Adjustment Strategies: Developing and Managing Multiethnic Identities

Even as they adapted to different dynamics of work, relationship structures, status criteria, even climate and food, Boston's West Indian immigrants came to realize that the larger society perceived them differently than they perceived themselves; in time, their own perceptions would change.

In the Caribbean, centuries of conquest, slavery, colonialism, and migration had built a stratified society based on race and color. The British West Indian colonies contained distinct racial groups—Whites, Mulattoes, Asians, and Blacks, who formed the majority in all the colonies. Race and color dictated socioeconomic mobility, with Whites and their Mulatto offspring occupying the highest strata. Marcus Garvey, Jamaican activist and 1916 founder of the Universal Negro Improvement Association (UNIA), the first mass Black movement in the United States, described the society in this way:

> If you were to go into all the offices throughout Jamaica you would not find one percent of Black clerks employed. You will find nearly all White and Coloured [Mulatto] persons . . . ; for proof please go through our post office, government offices and stores in

Kingston, and you will see only White and Coloured men in positions of importance and trust and you will find Black men and women as store-men, messengers, attendants and common servants. In the country parts you will find the same order of things. On the estates and plantations, you will find the Black man and woman as labourer, the Coloured man as clerk and sometimes owner and the White man generally as master.[14]

Blacks, however, might improve their status through "whitening," a process that enabled Blacks who had attained higher education, a profession, a home, or a stable, salaried government job, to join the ranks of the privileged Whites and Mulattoes. In his work *Not by Sun Alone,* novelist George Mikes portrays a Black Jamaican professor waiting in vain in the faculty lounge for a friend whom the Black college porter had refused to admit because he was a Black man. The professor said, "But then why do you let me in?" and the porter replied, "You are not a Black man, sir, you are a professor."[15] A popular West Indian saying of the early twentieth century was "Every rich Negro is a Mulatto, every poor Mulatto is a Negro."[16]

The success of a few Blacks among the other racial groups served to stifle the growth of race consciousness, as the thinking of Garvey in 1916 reflects:

Jamaica is unlike the United States where the race question is concerned. We have no open race prejudice here, and we do not openly antagonize one another. The extremes here are not between White and Black, hence we have never had a case of lynching or anything so desperate.... Unlike the American Negro, the Jamaican never thought of race ideals, much to his detriment, as instead [of] progressing generally, he has become a serf in the bulk, and a gentleman in the few.[17]

Although some West Indian Blacks, including Garvey himself, recognized the racial implications of the islands' uneven socioeconomics, most thought of themselves not as Blacks but as, for instance, Jamaicans or Barbadians. Although emancipation in 1834 had set off a pattern of interisland migration and a move toward a larger West Indian identity, the bigger, more prosperous colonies had protected their economies in part by nurturing competition among the island regions.

West Indians who came to Boston in the 1930s with the conviction, for example, that they were "plain and simple Bajan,"[18] found that most Whites saw them and other West Indians as Black people, period. Whites who bothered to acknowledge their foreign status at best saw them as West Indians or, less perceptively, as Jamaicans, without caring to know whether they were from Jamaica or not.

What concerned the immigrants most was being lumped with the general U.S. Black population, a historically subjugated racial group. Being locked out of most occupations reinforced their awareness of the disadvantages of this mistaken affiliation and, to combat it, West Indians tried to preserve their island identities, upholding and projecting their foreignness while building new identities based in their U.S. experiences. They eventually projected four main ethnic identities: their island/national identity; a pan–West Indian identity; a British identity; and, in many cases reluctantly, a Black American identity.

The West Indian identity grew out of a combination of physical and vocal mannerisms, community institutions, church membership, associations, holiday celebrations, and recreational choices.

Many West Indians, especially in the first few years after migration, deliberately dressed "tropically," especially in the spring and summer months. The men wore flannel pants, silk shirts, white shoes, and straw hats. The women wore silk skirts and light-colored blouses.[19] The *Boston Chronicle* of March 17, 1945, described the distinctive dress of West Indian arrivals to New Bedford, Massachusetts: "Over two hundred Jamaican men were brought in to work in the Firestone Textiles. Although they were given winter clothing, supplied by the government, they prefer to wear their own. This way the residents of the city easily distinguished the Jamaicans by their straw hats, white duck trousers and brown or white shoes."

Sounding different was another way to distinguish themselves. Although most West Indians who migrated during this period understood, spoke,and even wrote English, they spoke pidgin English. Although Americans, especially Blacks, made fun of their patois, many West Indians deliberately maintained their accent, claiming that they spoke "finer English," especially compared to that of the southern Blacks who made up most of Boston's Black population. With pride, some first-generation West Indians tell of times when their accent immediately set them apart from other Black people in a group.[20]

Glaring as such physical and vocal signs were, the more profound creators and indicators of identity were the West Indian community institutions that both tied the immigrants together and set them apart. Perhaps the most fundamental of these was the family. Closely following premigration patterns, their flexible family structure turned unrelated countrymen and women into kin. Like most immigrants, West Indian parents and other adults of the extended family wanted not only to retain their cultural identity, but to pass it on to the children. A second-generation Barbadian recalled this aspect of his cultural upbringing:

> To this day, I will hear my mother, my father, and my two aunts saying, "Back home we respect older people; back home we were taught to work hard for money, but we still cherished human life and good relations over material things." It was always back home, back home. You know what they were trying to do? They wanted me to see what Barbados had, but America lacked. And thank God they did, because it is the balancing of the two that made me what I am today.[21]

Many West Indian families were involved in churches in the Black neighborhoods in which they lived—St. Martin, St. Mark's Congregational, and the Twelfth Baptist Church. A "West Indian church," St. Cyprian's Episcopal on Tremont Street in Lower Roxbury, began in the home of a Jamaican immigrant in 1911 when the small group of black foreigners did not feel welcome in the white Episcopalian churches like St. Paul's Cathedral, or comfortable in one of the churches run by African Americans. When the congregation grew too big for the house, it moved to a White church on Sunday afternoons. But after the White members of this church began fumigating the church after the Black worshipers left, the West Indians built St. Cyprian's in 1924.[22]

St. Cyprian's became the center of West Indian socioreligious activities. The registered members, or communicants, were predominantly Barbadians and Jamaicans, but other West Indians who continued to worship elsewhere maintained strong links with St. Cyprian's. Many West Indians met their spouses in services or other events at the church. Even second-generation children met partners from island families whom they eventually married.

The cornerstones of the West Indian subculture were the West Indian associations that both provided practical support and served as forums to articulate identities. Between 1915 and 1950, there were three main island/national associations—Jamaica Associates, Barbados Union, Inc., and the Montserratian Progressive Association. The two significant pan–West Indian associations were the West India Aid Society and the Boston branch of Marcus Garvey's Universal Negro Improvement Association.[23] These groups regularly organized debates and lectures on issues pertaining to their homeland, events designed not only to keep the immigrants abreast of developments at home but also to nurture their foreign identity. Association fundraisers publicized in the February 15, 1936, *Boston Chronicle* asked West Indians, for example, to "Be a good Jamaican and help your country" or assured them, "Your country, Barbados, needs you."

Besides mirroring immigrants' identities as Jamaican, Barbadian, or Montserratian, the associations also reinforced West Indian and British identities. Parades and tea parties celebrated emancipation in the West Indies and British holidays like Empire Day and Coronation Day. A British identity was considered an even more viable foreign affiliation than a West Indian one, which was still a Black identity in a predominately white Boston. In fact, in the reasoning of most West Indians, a British identity was more than a match for the White American status quo, for they had been taught that everything British was superior. The West Indians' pride in their affiliation with the British crown was clearly demonstrated, for example, in 1943, as the British West Indies was engulfed in a movement for self-government and independence: the *Boston Chronicle* for May 10 reported that part of Boston's West Indian community was extending an invitation to the Duke and Duchess of Windsor for a visit they were convinced would underscore their status as British subjects. The Sons and Daughters of the Associates, an organization for the children of Jamaican immigrants and "other interested children of West Indian parentage," had as one of its main objectives the development of a Jamaican/British identity among the children.

Perhaps no other element reflected this British identity more than cricket. During the colonial era, although cricket was the national sport of the West Indian islands, it was a somewhat esoteric pastime, fully accessible only to the privileged—Whites, Mulattoes, and highly educated Blacks.[24] In Boston, where those race and class obstacles did not exist, the sport was modified so that all Blacks and members of all socioeconomic strata could participate. Cricket sports clubs, most symbolic of West Indian leisure, were crucial to the community. In fact, cricket clubs like the Windsors, West India A, West India B, Standards, and Wanderers were formed earlier than were the national associations. By the 1920s, Boston's West Indians regularly played cricket matches at Franklin Field on the border of Dorchester and Mattapan. The sport was one of the main indices of the immigrants' foreign identity. A non-American British sport, it not only underscored their identity as foreigners, but also importantly affirmed their British affiliation.

But no number of community institutions could fully protect Boston's West Indian immigrants from a confrontation with racist discrimination.

West Indian Responses to Racial Prejudice

West Indian immigrants' first exposure to racism, U.S. style, may have occurred during the journey from the islands. The United Fruit Company, whose steamers provided the primary means of transportation between Boston and the West Indian ports, was frequently accused of the "worst kind of discrimination on the basis of skin color."[25] Yet most new arrivals believed that they could escape the adverse effects of racism by projecting a foreign identity.

They entered a Black community that frequently complained about blatant segregation in both public and private enterprises. Although by the 1920s, most Blacks were satisfied with patronizing businesses and entertainment spots in their own enclave in the South End, the *Boston Chronicle* of May 13, 1933, reported charges brought against a White barber in the the Central Square area of Cambridge for refusing to shave a Black man. On June 8, 1935, the same West Indian newspaper accused the famous Hi Hat Restaurant and Night Club owned by White Bostonian Julius Rosenberg of refusing Blacks entry and of "waiting on them in a lousy manner."

Such discrimination was exacerbated by racist verbal and physical harassment. The Irish and Italians called Jews "Christ killers" and Blacks "niggers." In retaliation Blacks and Jews described the Irish as "stupid drunkards."[26] By the late 1930s and the 1940s, when the whole country was experiencing heightened racial and ethnic tensions, Boston's Jews and Blacks were frequently ambushed and seriously beaten by gangs of Whites; Catholic Irish youths from South Boston and some districts of Dorchester figured prominently in such attacks.[27]

While most of the Black victims of these White racist gangs were simple, working-class people, successful middle-class and prominent blacks were also assaulted. The *Chronicle* reported on May 4, 1935, that renowned Boston tenor Roland Hayes was beaten when his home in Brookline Village was vandalized by a group of White youths in what Hayes and many others believed was a racially motivated attack. When William E. Harrison was ambushed and beaten severely only a few blocks from his home by what the *Chronicle* for April 26, 1947, called "black-hating white youths," West Indians especially understood that all Blacks were subject to racism. Harrison was a second-generation West Indian whose parents had migrated to Boston from Jamaica around World War I—a Harvard graduate, editor of the *Chronicle,* and leader of the Black community who, it was rumored, sometimes wrote speeches for Mayor Michael Curley.[28]

Boston's all-White police force was another major concern for the Black community. The two Black newspapers, the *Guardian* and the *Chronicle,* record many instances of the police mistreating Blacks under the pretext of enforcing law and order. One such incident occurred in 1934. On Sunday, July 8, Mr. Borden, a Black Bostonian, was with his family at his Copeland Street home when police burst in to arrest him on a misdemeanor charge. According to Borden, after the police started beating him, he ran out of the house, scared for his life. The police officers chased him and shot and wounded him, claiming that he resisted arrest and threatened them. Enraged at yet another police assault, the Black community appointed a lawyer to sue the police department, the *Chronicle* reported on July 21, 1934. Indeed, some of the *Chronicle*'s West Indian journalists were in the forefront of the crusade against Boston's police force. But the campaign eventually fizzled and the trial was abandoned, an outcome reminiscent of the 1910s and 1920s when Black leaders, including William Monroe Trotter of the *Guardian,* attempted unsuccessfully to have police officers prosecuted.[29]

U.S.-born children of the West Indian immigrants learned that a foreign identity could not protect them from the prejudice and discrimination experienced by Blacks in Boston and elsewhere in the United States. Low expectations greeted them in school, as when a White kindergarten director evaluating a second-generation Barbadian student concluded that "this bright precocious little Negro girl will, as is usual for members of her race, test at a much lower level as she gets older."[30] A second-generation Jamaican from a staunchly Catholic family could not attend parochial school in the 1940s because he was Black. As he explained: "The discrimination was de facto. Black Catholics were few to start with, and the few parochial schools that existed then were full of Irish Catholic kids who hated blacks."[31] A man whose parents were from Barbados and Guyana described the dilemma this way:

> I grew up on the one hand feeling positive about being a West Indian and Black; but on the other hand, I had to grapple with the negative imagery of being a Black child in the United States, not wanting to identify with people who were slaves and who behaved in a Stepin Fetchit/Rochester model. Every time one of those movies was shown we had to fight the next day in school, because someone would come up and mock you.
>
> As far as white teachers and white students were concerned, people who were black were considered Negro or Colored, but white people were of American or Italian or Irish descent. We resisted that by insisting that we were West Indians.[32]

The efforts of the families, the immigrant church, and the associations could not remove the children of West Indian migrants from the larger U.S. society in which they attended public schools and made friends with children of U.S.-born Blacks. The Hattie B. Cooper Community Center on Shawmut Avenue in the South End, for example, was, among other things, an after-school educational and recreational center for neighborhood children. The settlement houses created a certain cohesiveness that cut across family and cultural backgrounds: "After school and during vacations, we hung out there [the Cooper House]. I mean children whose parents were from Jamaica, Barbados, Cape Verde, Boston, North Carolina, Virginia, all over. At the Center we forgot our origins and just had a good time."[33]

At the same time that the children of West Indian immigrants were attending cricket matches and participating in the activities of the Sons and Daughters of the Associates and other such organizations that defined their identity as West Indians or British, they were also "hanging out" in Cooper House, attending public schools, and interacting with neighborhood children, aspects that defined their Black American identity. A Barbadian woman recalled the day in 1948 when she became, among other things, a Black American:

> My son, a well-brought-up boy, came home from school looking very rough. Some Irish kids had angered him by calling him a good-for-nothing nigger. This was not the first time, but this time it really got out of hand. I said, "Why don't you just make it clear to these

kids that you are not a Negro? You are a Bajan, a West Indian, a British." With tears running down his cheeks he replied, "But Ma, I am not completely those things. I am an American, a Black American. And you too, Ma, when most people around here see you, they see a Negro."[34]

Empathy with their children and their increasing awareness of discrimination encouraged the metamorphosis of the immigrants from foreigner to Black Bostonian. Some of the West Indian associations not only propagated West Indian identity and culture but also addressed prejudice against Blacks. West Indian community leaders advocated unity and cooperation with the larger Black community, encouraging membership in the NAACP and endorsing political candidates they considered "friends of the Negro."

In 1936, for example, Jamaica Associates invited Jamaican-born James S. Watson, a Municipal Court Judge of New York City, to give the keynote speech at a ceremony commemorating the second anniversary of the group's founding. Weeks before his arrival, some Jamaicans had begun to brag to U.S. Blacks and other West Indians about this symbol of the success of Jamaicans in America. Under the headline "Boston Jamaicans Fete Judge Watson," a *Boston Chronicle* article on February 15, 1935, described him as a "distinguished Jamaican, one of the most noteworthy colored men in America and one of the nation's ablest judges." But the judge's message, quoted in the February 22 *Chronicle*, was one of unity with U.S. Blacks: "You must spurn the specious arguments of those who would instill in you a sense of inferiority to those whose sojourn here in this land long antedated yours. Just as a fusion of Russian and Swede, Pole and Austrian, Irish and German made this great land an exemplary democracy, so must the admixture of Jamaican and North Carolinian, Barbadian and Pennsylvanian, Trinidadian and Georgian [work] to the common good of this buffeted race of ours."

Yet for Boston's West Indians, this race consciousness never translated to an ossified Black American identity. Instead, while acknowledging their status and identity as Blacks in Boston, they continued to develop and project their inherited identities.

"This country sure does a number on you," one Jamaican immigrant said in 1990. "It was only when I came to this country that I realized that I was a minority, a Black, a woman, a heterosexual, an alien, and even an undocumented."[35] All immigrants, as they become familiar with the complex racial, ethnic, and cultural tapestry of the United States, must reassess their identity. But for Black immigrants like the West Indians here, this issue is especially pressing, mainly because the mass of U.S. Blacks share a history and experiences largely defined by the struggle for freedom, equality, and advancement. Race consciousness, as the outcome of an awareness of a collective fate, is absent in most of the societies these immigrants come from. Until they arrive in the United States, few have been exposed to the history and plight of African-Americans.

Race consciousness evolves through a usually lengthy series of phases of detachment, denial, and awareness. Yet it does not prevent Black immigrants from adding their foreign identities and cultures to the diversity that enriches a pluralistic society such as that of the United States. The ultimate challenge for these immigrants is to develop the ability to move between race and ethnicity, to acknowledge and cope with their double status of Black and foreign.

Notes

1. Many of these questions were raised by students in my course "Race, Ethnicity and Immigration in the United States."

2. For more on the experience of double invisibility, see Simon Roy Bryce-Laporte, "Black Immigrants: The Experience of Invisibility and Inequality," *Journal of Black Studies* 3:29 (1972): 29–56.

3. Even blacks from racist South Africa tend to identify first with an ethnic group—Zulu, Shona, Xhosa, etc. Nigerians normally identify themselves first as Yoruba, Hausa, Igbo, or some other ethnic group. In Sierra Leone, people identify with their ethnic groups of Creole, Mende, Temne, etc., and Kenyans think of themselves as Kikuyu, Luo, Massai, etc. This extends to the Western Hemisphere in Black diasporic societies outside the United States and Canada: in the West Indies, for example, although the islanders share a history of slavery, colonialism, and endemic migration, collective identity is based on island or national affiliation. The islanders would refer to themselves as Barbadians, Jamaicans, Trinidadians, etc.

4. For good examples of such studies, see: Wilfred A. Domingo, "Gift of the Black Tropics," in *The New Negro,* ed. Alain Locke (New York: Albert and Charles Boni, 1925; reprint, New York: Arno, 1968); Edmund Haynes, *The Negro at Work in New York City* (New York: Columbia University Press, 1912; reprint, 1968); and Ira De Augustine Reid, *The Negro Immigrant, His Background, Characteristics, and Social Adjustment, 1899–1937* (New York: Columbia University Press, 1939; reprint, New York: Arno, 1969).

5. Marilyn Halter, *Between Race and Ethnicity: Cape Verdean American Immigrants, 1860–1965* (Urbana: University of Illinois Press, 1993), and Philip Kasinitz, *Caribbean New York: Black Immigrants and the Politics of Race* (Ithaca, N.Y.: Cornell University Press, 1992), are good examples of this new trend in Black immigration scholarship.

6. This composition was the result of economic and demographic conditions in the British West Indian colonies. Inhabitants of relatively prosperous colonies like Guyana and Trinidad tended to emigrate in insignificant numbers compared to those of overpopulated colonies with weak economies. Thus, while Trinidad and Guyana received migrants from other West Indian colonies, Barbadians, whose colony was perhaps the most economically and demographically troubled, migrated in large numbers to territories both within and outside of the Caribbean region. Monserrat, with similar problems, lost over one-third of its population in the first half of the twentieth century. Outmigration from Jamaica, one of the few colonies with plenty of arable land for independent small-scale farming, was propelled by higher off-island wages. The pattern of Boston's West Indian population was thus repeated in New York, Panama, Costa Rica, and other regions. For more on how economy and demography determined these patterns of emigration, see David Lowenthall, *West Indian Societies* (New York: Oxford University Press, 1972).

7. West Indian migration was not unique in this respect. Prior to 1930, migration flows to the United States, with a few exceptions such as the Irish, were male dominated. For more on gender and immigration, see Marion F. Houston, Roger G. Kramer, and Joan Mackin Barrett, "Female Predominance in Immigration to the United States since 1930: A First Look," *International Migration Review* 15:4 (1988): 908–59.

8. For more on the development of Boston's ethnic neighborhoods, see Thomas H. O'Connor, *Bibles, Brahmins, and Bosses: A Short History of Boston* (Boston: Boston Public Library, 1984), 119–52; and Andrew Buni and Alan Rogers, Boston, *City on the Hill* (Boston: Windsor Publications, 1984), 88–95.

9. In 1910, there were only a little over 11,000 blacks, 2 percent of the total population; in the 1930s, just over 20,000; in 1940, 23,000; in 1950, more than 40,000.

10. For details on the migration of southern blacks to Boston in the first half of the twenti-eth century, see J. Anthony Lukas, *Common Ground: A Turbulent Decade in the Lives of Three American Families* (New York: Knopf, 1985), 58–61.

11. John Bodnar, *The Transplanted: A History of Immigrants in Urban America* (Blooming-ton: Indiana University Press, 1985), 68–69.

12. Stephan Thernstrom's is still the most empirical investigation of Boston's ethnic groups; he reports the economic predicament of most of the Black population throughout much of the first half of the twentieth century in *The Other Bostonians* (Boston: Harvard University Press, 1973), 176–219.

13. In the nineteenth century, when the Black population was still concentrated in Beacon Hill, many Black women were domestic servants; they competed fiercely with Irish women by the end of the century. The *Boston Chronicle*, April 29, 1933, quotes George V. Goodman, executive sec-retary of the Boston Urban League: "Approximately 11,000 Negroes are gainfully employed, over 50 percent of this in the domestic and personal service, the lowest paid occupation."

14. Marcus Garvey, in a letter to Major R. R. Moton of Tuskegee Institute, February 1916, in *The Marcus Garvey and Universal Negro Improvement Association Papers,* ed. Robert Hill (Berkeley: University of California Press, 1983), 180. Garvey had founded the Universal Negro Improvement Association in Kingston, Jamaica, after his return from England in 1914. He was also an outspoken opponent of the injustices of racial stratification in the West Indies and other areas.

15. George Mikes, *Not by Sun Alone* (London: Andre Deutsch, 1967), 57.

16. The saying was familiar to many people interviewed for this study.

17. Hill, *Marcus Garvey and UNIA Papers,* 179.

18. Mr. and Mrs. Ira B. Williams, interview by Violet Johnson, Roxbury, Mass., June 15, 1990; Ira Williams, born in Bridgetown, Barbados, in 1920, came to Boston in 1938. Bajan is the term used to denote the ethnicity of Black Barbadians, who constitute over 80 percent of the island's total population.

19. Victor Bynoe, interview by Violet Johnson, Boston, Mass., August 6, 1990. George Com-missiong, interview by V. Johnson, Mattapan, Mass., November 20, 1989; and Elfreda E., inter-view by V. Johnson, Mattapan, Mass., June 7, 1987.

20. Many who contributed oral histories to this study explained that they were proud of their accent and clung to it largely because it drew attention to the fact that they were foreign.

21. William Sandiford, interview by V. Johnson, Boston, Mass., January 17, 1990.

22. For more on the history of St. Cyprian's, see Robert C. Hayden, *Faith, Culture and Lead-ership: A History of the Black Church in Boston* (Boston: Boston Branch of the NAACP, 1983), 50–53.

23. The Universal Negro Improvement Association was viewed by many as a West Indian organization. The ethnic character of the Garvey movement was a source of much controversy during its heyday. African American critics pointed to Garvey's shifting political strategies, which included berating U.S.-born Blacks, and labeled him a foreigner and his followers "ignorant West Indian Negroes." Federal and local government authorities exploited the UNIA leader's status as a foreigner, driving the wedge between the two Black groups deeper. Many in the U.S. Caribbean population, including many in Boston, claimed the local UNIA branch as their own ethnic asso-ciation. The tension between African Americans and Caribbean Blacks in the Garvey movement is addressed in Irma Watkins-Owens, *Blood Relations: Caribbean Immigrants and the Harlem Community, 1900–1930* (Bloomington: Indiana University Press, 1996), chap. 7.

24. For more on the socioeconomic ramifications of cricket, see "West Indian Cricket—A Socio-Historical Appraisal," *Caribbean Quarterly* 19 (1973): 7–27; C.L.R. James, *Beyond a*

Boundary (London: Hutchinson, 1969); and Michael Manley, *History of West Indies Cricket* (London: Andre Deutsch, 1988).

25. A group of investigative journalists, led by the Jamaican historian and *Chronicle* reporter J. A. Rogers, looked into allegations made repeatedly by Black passengers, the majority of whom were West Indians, of conditions in the steamers. The team concluded that "the worst cabins and eating areas were given to Negroes" (*Boston Chronicle,* May 13, 1934).

26. For vivid accounts of this ethnic strife, which often resulted in physical skirmishes, see Nat Hentoff, *Boston Boy* (New York: Knopf, 1986). Many anecdotal accounts in the oral history conducted for this study also speak to the volatile situation.

27. The racist ideologies of Nazism and Fascism were becoming increasingly apparent in the United States in that period. Father Charles E. Coughlin, a priest in Detroit whose weekly radio broadcasts reached thirty to forty-five million listeners, disseminated anti-Semitic and anti-Communist sentiments. For more on the violence against Blacks and Jews in Boston and the reaction of leaders from organizations like the NAACP and the Anti-Defamation League of B'nai B'rith, see Lance Carden, *Witness: An Oral History of Black Politics in Boston: 1920–1960* (Boston: Boston College Press, 1989); and Hillel Levine and Lawrence Harmon, *The Death of an American Jewish Community* (New York: Free Press, 1992), 21–23.

28. Victor Bynoe, interview by V. Johnson, South End, Mass., August 6, 1989; Carden, *Witness,* 53.

29. Carden, *Witness,* 5.

30. Evaluation in the report card of Elma Lewis, now a prominent educator and activist in Boston. Cited in ibid, 6.

31. David Nelson, interview by V. Johnson, Boston, Mass., December 6, 1990. Nelson's experiences in this area are also explored in Brian Doyle, "The Passion of Dave Nelson," *Boston College Magazine,* Fall 1988, p. 54.

32. Mel King, *Chain of Change: Struggles for Black Community Development* (Boston: South End, 1981), 10.

33. Bynoe interview, August 6, 1989.

34. Yvonne Mason, interview by V. Johnson, Roxbury, Mass., February 2, 1988. Mason was born in Bridgetown, Barbados, in 1920, came to New Bedford, Mass., in 1939, and moved to Boston in 1942. The son of whom she speaks was born in the West Indies and joined her in New Bedford in 1940 at the age of five.

35. Unidentified guest at the Symposium on the Caribbean American Family, Medgar Evers College, Brooklyn, N.Y., May 10, 1990.

*Cluny Macpherson and
La'avasa Macpherson*

5   The Children of Samoan Migrants in New Zealand

Expansion in some sectors of the New Zealand economy in the 1950s and 1960s rapidly exhausted the available supplies of local labor. The search for additional labor, which extended to New Zealand territories and former territories in the South Pacific, resulted in significant increases in the size of the Western Samoan, Cook Island, Tongan, Niuean, and Tokelauan populations in New Zealand in the 1960s and 1970s. The Samoan community grew dramatically, from 3,740 in 1956, with 79.1% born in Samoa, to 22,198 by 1971, with 55.6% born in Samoa.[1]

The rapid growth of migrant Polynesian populations generated considerable interest among social scientists, which in turn generated volumes of research.[2] The Samoans, as the largest non-Maori Polynesian group, were extensively studied by sociologists, social anthropologists, demographers, geographers, political scientists, economists and psychologists.[3]

Yet New Zealand's Samoan community has usually been represented as a socially homogeneous entity sharing social and economic traits. This representation not only fails to account for the complex of identities within the group, but when used as a basis for social decision making leads to ineffective social policy. For example, one finds policies designed to meet only the needs of "New Zealand–born Samoans."

Competent policy making requires the systematic mapping of ethnic identities among this population. We suggest basing such maps on central knowledges and competences that lie at the center of ethnicity—language, worldview, and life-style—and that distinguish members from nonmembers for *insiders* and *outsiders* alike.

Examining the factors that shape New Zealand–born Samoans' knowledge of Samoan culture and their orientation to it, we believe, sharpens the ways one conceptualizes, represents, and explains their ethnicity; in the course of our examination, we look at the diverse ways this community's children are constructing their ethnic identity in New Zealand.

The Migrant Generation

Samoan migrants showed little inclination to set aside their own values and institutions in favor of New Zealand's. They exhibited a strong sense of ethnic identity and pride, a commitment to the community of origin typical of sojourners, and a sense of being an extension of that community rather than a separate entity.[4] They were in frequent touch with their home communities, sending a flow of money to their families in Samoa.[5] They retained their language, values, and social institutions, that is, to the *fa'a samoa*, a word that can refer to any one or a combination of these three elements. This choice arose, not from an antipathy to their host culture's language, values, or institutions but from a preference for the familiar. As the migrants extended Samoan institutions to cope with the urban industrial environment and as they to some extent avoided participating in New Zealand's formal social institutions, a cultural and structural pluralism emerged.[6]

Samoan migrants retained their culture as a result of various structural factors. For instance, chain migration, which characterized their movement, typically produces residential and occupational concentrations.[7] Such concentrations make holding onto language, cultural values, and institutions easier and more likely. Furthermore, Samoan families sponsored the migration of those whose commitment to Samoan values and institutions would ensure a continuing loyalty and flow of remittances to the family back home.[8] Also, Samoan values and institutions that had evolved in a place where natural disasters and crop failures could suddenly render individuals dependent on each other were well suited to a group living in a vulnerable, marginal economic position. Extended kin groups and savings and loan associations, for example, provided some insurance for group members against the dangers that come with living at the edges of the economy.[9] It appeared that Samoan institutions and values would persist at least until upward social and economic mobility rendered them unnecessary in the eyes of their supporters.

New Zealanders too played a role in enhancing the awareness of a Samoan ethnic identity. Through the media, public attention was focused on ethnic boundaries and the significance of "being Samoan" by liberal groups who sought to advance the cause of Polynesian minorities through various political programs, as well as by racist groups who advocated limiting Polynesian migration and, in some cases, even promoted repatriation. New Zealanders' sentiments generally fell between the extremes of hostility and unreserved welcome, from high levels of intermarriage between non-Samoans and Samoans to a discrete social distance maintained by limiting contact with Samoans to prescribed social contexts and situations.[10] Eventually, New Zealanders' awareness of the presence of migrant Polynesians increased. The result was a stereotyped image that heightened the differences they perceived between themselves and immigrant groups.[11]

Samoans also retained institutions such as the extended family (*aiga*), savings and credit associations (*kalapu*), church-based welfare associations, village-based associations, and sporting and recreational associations because New Zealanders failed to accommodate their institutions to Samoan expectations.[12]

The combined effect of the migrant selection process, and the subsequent concentration of those committed to Samoan values and institutions, made the persistence of an ethnic community and identity in the immediate future a relatively safe proposition. It also supported the contention that pluralism would continue until changes occurred either in the host's counterpart institutions or in Samoans' expectations. These predictions of continuing cultural and institutional pluralism between the Samoan migrants and their non-Samoan hosts were shown to be accurate through the 1960s and 1970s.[13]

The New Zealand–Born Generation

A generation of children of Samoan descent born in New Zealand has recently come of age. By 1991, nearly half of all persons of Samoan descent in New Zealand had been born there.[14] Most of their parents, whose ethnic identity had been forged in villages of similar social, economic and political circumstance, had learned Samoan as a first, and in many cases only, language. For most, their individual and collective identities were founded in a Samoan life-style and worldview.

By contrast, New Zealand–born Samoans' ethnic identities have been forged in a variety of circumstances.[15] As a result, fluency in speaking the Samoan language varies considerably, as do the knowledge of a Samoan worldview and exposure to Samoan life-styles and social institutions. Differences in their home environments explain a great deal about the various ways in which ethnic identity is 'constructed' by New Zealand–born children.

A 1984 study showed that factors related to the home that shape a child's exposure to Samoan language, values, and practices include parents' attitudes toward these three elements; the number of adults of various generations in the home; use of the Samoan language at home; the household's kin-group, village, and church involvement; and the household's recreational choices.[16]

Representations of Samoan Culture

Whether or not children acquired a clear defined Samoan identity proved to be related not only to their opportunities to acquire key knowledge and skill in things Samoan but also to the encouragement for them to do so. The most influential force in this process was the attitudes and conduct of parents and other adults.[17] The attitudes emerged in both formal and informal contexts. Parents and other adults evaluated the relevance of Samoan identity and then represented this to their children quite formally and quite explicitly. But they also spoke informally about things Samoan in ways that reflected their attitudes. Both explicit and implicit representation influenced younger Samoans especially, who seemed to have a clear idea of how positively or negatively their parents viewed the fa'a samoa.[18]

The most positive evaluations of fa'a samoa tended to be formed by children living in households in which Samoan was the operating culture, the household was organized around Samoan principles, the Samoan language was heavily used, and involvement was great in kin-based, village, and Samoan church activity and their associated social affairs. This is hardly surprising. People who value these activities will participate in them and will generally represent them positively to their children.[19]

The promotion of Samoan culture in these households rested on several foundations. In some cases parents linked the culture with Christianity:

> The fa'a samoa is based on God's word. You know that the motto of Samoa is Samoa is founded on God. That is why you can find many parallels between the Lord's teaching and the ways in which Samoan custom works.

> Many Samoan proverbs are similar to the biblical proverbs.

Other parents emphasized the moral superiority of elements of the culture:

> The fa'a samoa is a loving culture. You know in the fa'a samoa everyone is looked after. There are no people who are excluded or who are left to fend for themselves like in Pālagi culture.

> You'll never see old people abandoned by Samoans. Old people are very important because it was their sweat and their support which got us where we are.

Mixed evaluations of fa'a samoa were formed by children in a group of households where Samoan was one of several operating cultures. In those households the use of the Samoan language values and practices was confined to certain sorts of events or parts of the household routine or occurred only when certain people were present. As a consequence, the fa'a samoa was seen to be context specific. It was one of several operating cultures that competed for attention. In these households, Samoan parents and other adults were committed to parts of Samoan culture but openly critical of others.

They did not present or promote fa'a samoa as the best or only way of comprehending the world. Parents would portray the Samoan culture as being "better" or more "useful" (aoga) in some respects and "worse" or less "useful" in others:

> Samoan culture is good. Even if you have nothing, you still have your family, and as long as you have the family you will always have a place to stay and food to eat. But you have to understand that because of the culture nobody will ever get very far.

Others argued that behavior was neither right nor wrong but rather more or less appropriate in various situations. Thus parents say:

> Behavior "x" is all right for Europeans because it's part of their custom. But don't ever do that in the presence of Samoans or you will make us ashamed, because it is very bad in Samoan custom. Samoans will think your family doesn't have any manners.

> You should know that sort of behavior is ok to me because I am a Samoan and I believe it is right. But don't do it around papālagi because they will think you don't know their ways and that you are ignorant.

Thus, these children come to experience a culture's relevance as situational because cultures are presented as alternatives. Language use is a case in point. Languages are presented as alternatives: parents are likely to use and encourage the use of Samoan in situations in which Samoans are present, and English in situations in which non-Samoans are present. Samoan is encouraged because it is the right language in the situation and only those who are *fia pālagi* would choose not to use it. Conversely, the use of English in other situations in encouraged because it is "polite," averts suspicion when papālagi are present, shows the all-important respect (*fa'aaloalo*), and demonstrates competence in English. Parents in this group lead by example, moving from one language to another as situations appear to demand. Thus, parents, by fiat and by example, present the languages as alternatives and discourage the exclusive use of one or the other in situations over which they have any control.

Negative evaluations of fa'a samoa were formed by children in a group of households in which Samoan was either deliberately marginalized or from which it was excluded. It was represented it as something of limited utility that would prevent children from acquiring more "useful" or more "relevant" knowledge and competences. In those households Samoan language was rarely used, and Samoan values and practices were either explicitly excluded or confined to a range of insignificant activities. It is, however, useful to distinguish between those parents whose decision is based solely on utility, and those whose decision is based on the supposed "inferiority" of Samoan culture.

The former argue that, as their children's future is in New Zealand, there is no use in their being familiar with the values and institutions of Samoa.

> It's more use to you to learn the pālagi language and ways. If you want a good position and a good future in the papālagi's country, you need to understand their customs because they are the people who can open the doors.

> Well, it's good to understand the fa's samoa, but that's not really going to help you get ahead in this country. It's not like Samoa either because there are not many Samoans in high positions who can give you some help to get up the ladder!

The latter argue that Samoan culture has little to commend it. In these households, parents were, either explicitly or implicitly, critical of the fa'a samoa. Its defects are "evident" in the behavior of Samoan migrants who come before the courts and in the material poverty among those who accept the obligations of Samoan culture.

> The fa'a samoa is the pathway to poverty and trouble. Look around and see what you get from following the custom. Look at all those lawyers who get a title and then steal from clients to pay for all the fa'a samoa. They end up in jail . . . and they're supposed to be smart, but the fa'a samoa can bring even them down.

> Look at the trouble that people get into following the fa'a samoa. That's the problem with fa'a samoa. People are too proud. They fight over this and fight over that. They fight over insignificant things like a little word which they should just ignore.

Parents may use Samoan in the home among themselves but speak English to their children and encourage its use. Cultivation of non-Samoan social networks that have English as a common language further limits opportunities to learn the Samoan language, as does their choice to settle in areas where there are few other Samoans. The schools in these areas have few Samoans, and these are frequently from homes in which little encouragement is given to use the language, and they typically have very limited fluency. These environments do not therefore provide language models that can be copied and in fact may confirm the belief that most other Samoans don't speak Samoan. Because most of their parents' contact with Samoans occurs away from the home, opportunities to hear the language spoken are further limited.

But if opportunity is a significant factor, lack of encouragement and deliberate discouragement may be even more so. Parents tell their children that the language has limited utility and a limited vocabulary and in the process may lead them to believe that the culture suffers the same "defects":

> Samoan is no use to you. You're not going to stay in Samoa, and besides all your friends are papālagi. They can't understand Samoan. If you want a good job, Samoan is no use. Where are the books written in Samoan? The teachers can't speak Samoan. . . . Why should children learn that language? It's no use for this country. It's got no words for all those things the papālagi have invented. Where is the Samoan word for computer? The Samoans' only computer is the hand! And the Samoan word for battery, *ma'a*, a stone—and there are more like that. It's just confusing.

Samoan migrants, then, reflect on their culture, its utility, and its role in their future plans. They then consciously and unconsciously construct environments in which their particular evaluation is reflected. The children born into and raised in these environments come, at least initially, to reflect them. The irony is that, despite the variety in their facility with and experience of Samoan culture, most of the children are persuaded to believe that they are Samoans: "real Samoans," "Samoans," and the "right kind of Samoans."

Breaking Out: The Reconstruction of Identity

Whether or not the children continue to accept their parents' assessment of the usefulness of Samoan culture is another issue. They are able to choose from increasingly broader information and experience to reassess the truth of their parents' claims about the fa'a samoa and do so. They reassess not only the general representations but the importance of various elements of ethnic identity for themselves. These lead to a series of *secondary orientations* to elements of cultural heritage. While their assessments may in many cases reflect their socialization and resemble those of their parents, this is not inevitably so. At any given time, an individual's decisions will reflect personal and political considerations and may lead to the repudiation of choices made on their behalf by their parents and guardians.[20] Samoan children may reject their parents' assessments partially or completely. In some cases they may be pushed away from a position taken in their childhood. In other cases they may be drawn away from a position.

In doing so they are in turn reflecting on the particular version of Samoanness they have inherited and continuing a process their parents initiated. Some will decide that the culture is of more significance than their environment, and adults within that environment, have led them to believe. Others may come to believe the reverse. Still others may continue to draw on two or more cultures without opting for one or the other. Thus children—or, more correctly, young adults—may revise their view of the significance and utility of Samoan language, worldview, and life-style, and when they do so they may use somewhat different bases for their decisions.

These comments by New Zealand–born Samoans reflect some of the things that shape the ways in which they have come to regard the Samoan language:

> I was pretty surprised when I went to university and joined the Samoan club. Some of the students from Samoa gave those of us who couldn't speak the language heaps. They asked us how we could call ourselves Samoans if we couldn't speak the language. At that time, I blamed my parents, whose attitude had been to study English because that was "useful" and had made no attempt to teach us Samoan because it was, in my mother's words, "no use for you kids." I know they were trying to do the right thing. Anyhow, I went to Samoa for a long vacation to learn the language and now we have started to speak the language at home and to attend a Samoan-language church. I am really happier now. I feel more like a Samoan and, funnily enough, my parents are rapt at my interest.

> My parents were heavily into the Samoan thing. We were sent to Samoan church and took part in all of the Samoan things like White Sunday. We spoke Samoan all the time at home and at church. But they always wanted us to be better than the other families' children. We had to speak better, look better, and behave better ... you know the sort of thing. They coached us in the language—they wanted us to speak like pastors, which just made us more nervous about it. One White Sunday I had had so much coaching and was so nervous that I wet myself standing in front of the whole congregation. As if that wasn't bad enough, I got a bollocking for it afterward and the whole thing became a family joke. That made me even more nervous about the language and I don't speak it much now if I can help it.

Similarly, New Zealand–born Samoans report discarding their parents' cultural values, whether they were pro- or anti-Samoan:

> My parents were reasonably well off. They were pretty critical of some of the Samoan beliefs. Like they said, you could give everything away to relations if you wanted to but you couldn't expect to get much back because the relations were always giving it away to other people to show how wealthy they were and would never have anything to give you when your time came and you needed it. I suppose I believed it until I went to stay with cousins in Wellington. They had nothing much, but when I needed things for school they would always give me anything they had. Even when they went to work with sneakers with holes in them all through the winter, they would work overtime and even borrow to make sure I could go on school trips. They were staunch people, man, and I love them for their generosity. I shouldn't say this, but I respect them more and feel closer to their values than to my own parents in many ways, because they live the Christian way and the Samoan way.

The early commitment to Samoan values in other cases led to their later rejection by children.

> My old man was a great church man and a *matai* [chief] in our family. He always did his duty in the church and in the family. He gave his money away as fast as he made it. There was always some sort of *fa'alavelave*: a family funeral, a wedding, a church opening, you know how it goes. Well, he was always at the front, leading by example, and he was greatly respected by the family and the congregation, as you know from his funeral. But he was always so busy worrying about what other people thought of him that he didn't really worry about us. He demanded obedience like most Samoan parents and wasn't too interested in what we had to say. We kept our thoughts pretty much to ourselves. He was really generous to us when he could afford to be and especially at Christmas. He'd spend his whole holiday pay on big presents and food. But I remember thinking I wish he had worried less

about what others thought of him and had thought more about what we needed and spent more time with us. I will be quite different as a parent.

The same rejection can occur in respect of particular cultural practices:

My parents were very much against Samoan healers and their work. My father was trained in Fiji at the School of Medicine and they were very committed to Western medicine. My father said there was little in Samoan medicine that was much value. We were always treated at home or at hospital and never taken to healers for illnesses like other kids. When my grandmother became ill, she was treated at the hospital but got worse and worse. She begged to be taken to a healer and my parents reluctantly agreed. Probably only because they knew there was not much else they could do. She was treated successfully. I started to think that there was a lot more to Samoan medicine than they were prepared to admit, and I know a lot of other educated people who now share that view.

My parents believed in Samoan medicine. In fact, my aunty was quite well known as a healer. I was usually taken to her for routine illnesses. She used to treat me with her medicine. Most of the medicines tasted terrible and had pretty drastic effects. The one that put me right off Samoan medicine was the one which she used to give me for my headaches. It involved purging the poisons in my stomach which were responsible for the headaches. It was oily, and used to purge you so thoroughly that you seemed to have diarrhea for days afterwards. It was terrible, especially at school. The cure was worse than the complaint. I prefer aspirin now.

What is interesting in these cases, and others like them, is that what seems to be causing children to reassess their early orientation to the Samoan language, values, and social institutions are their personal experiences as much as anything in the dominant culture to which they are exposed. But the external environment is not insignificant in determining the general importance of ethnicity and Samoan ethnicity in particular. Migrants and their children are aware of these new influences. Older people will claim that papālagi attitudes have changed in important ways and that it is easier to be a Samoan now because Samoans are viewed more positively.

When I first came, the Samoans were in the factories, in construction, or in businesses like cleaning. The pālagi hardly saw them except when they were in the papers, usually in trouble. But things have changed in the last ten or fifteen years. Now you can go into businesses all over town and you see Samoans in important positions and in front offices. Before, Samoans who wanted things had to ask the pālagi. Now, pālagi who want things have to ask the Samoans! People can see we're going somewhere.

If the general move into white-collar occupations has transformed the public's perceptions of Samoans, certain extremely prominent Samoans have had a disproportionate, and highly positive, influence on these views. Samoan ethnic identity is, as older migrant parents note, no longer the social liability it once was.

It's easier for our kids because some Samoans are doing really well now. Many of the top New Zealand sportspeople in many codes [sports] are Samoans and in a sport-crazy country like this that makes a big difference to the way the average papālagi sees us.... Some Samoan people are national heroes and are greatly respected for their ability. Look at Michael Jones. People respect him because he's a great loose forward and because he won't play on Sunday. They can see why other Samoans respect the Sabbath.[21]

Another parent noted that New Zealanders' passion for sport and their experience of being the underdog in international competitions with larger nations allowed them to admire and support Samoa's attempts to enter international sport.

> Our foreman and a lot of the other papālagi at work are really pleased when Manu Samoa [the Samoan national rugby side] wins in international competitions. They support the side because they say all us little countries should show those big countries a lesson.

But while prowess in sport may create a certain amount of social leverage in New Zealand society, Samoans are now becoming more prominent, and more visible, in the media and the arts, challenging the stereotype that Samoans are "great at sport but not much else." Their representation in the nation's most popular current long-running local television drama, *Shortland Street,* in a variety of semiprofessional roles in which they are portrayed as caring but upwardly mobile people has made a significant difference to the popular perception of the "Samoan." This is part of a general emergence of an increasingly visible middle class of Samoan descent which has produced a pool of well-placed, articulate advocates able to address prejudices of the dominant group in highly public contexts.

This may be the more credible because Samoan writers have proven willing to expose, probe, and criticize publicly areas of Samoan culture and social organization. One of New Zealand's more popular comedy series has a segment called "Milburn Place," written by two Samoan writers in which a mainly Samoan cast parodies supposedly "well-known" Samoan characters and practices on mainstream television. Alongside this is the more serious drama that explores, from the inside, such themes as family violence, spouse abuse, homosexuality, transgenderism, and the social distance that separates island- and New Zealand–born on mainstream television, in short films, and in live theater. It may be that the growing awareness, and emerging acceptance, of Samoan culture by the mainstream has created a space in which Samoans can celebrate a Samoan identity more openly because it does not provoke the same reactions among papālagi New Zealanders that it once did. This argument derives a certain amount of support from sociological theory, but there may be other factors at work in this situation.

Some young adults correctly note that the presence of new migrants from southeast Asia, and especially wealthy people who enter under the business immigration scheme, have replaced Pacific Islanders as the threat to the papālagi interest.

> When my parents' generation came in the 1950s they were welcome because the economy was booming and factories needed labor. Then in the 1970s the recession came and they were blamed for taking New Zealanders' jobs. Then when the restructuring of the economy took place and produced high levels of unemployment, they were blamed for being dependent on social welfare. Now the Chinese business immigrants have come and started to buy up the country. I think most Kiwis [New Zealanders] see them as a more serious threat than the PIs [Pacific Islanders] now. They've become the people who are blamed for all the problems. I think they look like a more serious threat to New Zealanders because they can make a big impact with their wealth and give wealthy papālagi a run for their money.

While all of these factors may have changed the dominant group's social attitudes to the Samoans, that change carries its own dangers, as younger people note:

The success of our people is great, but if people say, "Oh, the Samoans are doing ok now," it diverts attention from the very real problems our children are having in school and in the labor market. It becomes an excuse for doing nothing about the problems that are there. Not every Samoan is enjoying success in life.

Celebrating the successes of our people is great and it's a change from the old times when the only Samoans in the media were in court on their way to jail. It's great to see Samoan Miss New Zealands, Rhodes scholars, All Blacks, Warriors, musicians, actors, and all that, and I'm really proud. On the other hand this all leads people to overlook the very real tragedy of the social and economic consequences of restructuring and all the Samoans living on the edge.

Conclusion

Interesting changes are occurring in New Zealand Samoans' attitudes toward their language, values, and social institutions. The changes are complex and cannot be understood solely as individual choices or as responses to assimilative pressure exerted by the culture and social organization of the dominant group. Rather, it is essential to focus on ways Samoans assess the importance and relevance of their ethnicity and in turn adopt lifestyles that reflect their ethnic orientation. This requires an understanding both of the opportunity structure for acquiring knowledge of their cultural heritage and of the personal and political factors that determine individual and group evaluation of that heritage. We must also recognize that individual ethnic Samoan identities may change during what Melani Anae has called the ethnic identity journey. If, within one generation, such a variety of forms of Samoanness can be produced, the forms of Samoanness that may emerge within another generation should be even more interesting.

Notes

1. In 1991 some 85,743 persons resident in New Zealand claimed Samoan ethnicity. Of these some 42,000, or 49%, had been born in New Zealand. An unknown number of others had been brought to New Zealand as children and had spent a large part of their lives here. These groups may have been exposed to similar sets of influences during their childhood, and members of the latter group are similar in many ways to those born there. See P. Ongley, "Pacific Islands Migration and the New Zealand Labour Market," in *Nga Take: Ethnic Relations and Racism in Aotearoa/New Zealand,* ed. P. Spoonley, D. Pearson, and C. Macpherson (Palmerston North: The Dunmore Press, 1991); P. Ongley, "Immigration, Employment and Ethnic Relations," in *Nga Patai: Racism and Ethnic Relations in Aotearoa/New Zealand,* ed. P. Spoonley, C. Macpherson, and D. Pearson (Palmerston North: The Dunmore Press, 1996).

2. Paul Spoonley, K. A. Carwell-Cooke, and A. D. Trlin, *Immigration and Immigrants: A New Zealand Bibliography* (Wellington: Department of Labour, 1980).

3. Examples include: D. Pitt and Cluny Macpherson, *Emerging Pluralism: The Samoan Community in Urban New Zealand* (Auckland: Longman Paul, 1974); P. J. Kinloch, "Samoan Children in a New Zealand Secondary School: A Semiological Study of School Communication" (Ph.D. diss., Victoria University of Wellington, 1976); A. D. Trlin, "Residential Patterns and

Segregation of Racial Groups in the Auckland, Wellington and Hutt Urban Areas," in *Proceedings of the Sixth New Zealand Geographical Conference*, vol. 1, ed. R. J. Johnston and J. M. Soons (Christchurch, New Zealand Geographical Society, 1971), 244–251; A. D. Trlin, "Immigrants in the Cities" [chap. 15], *Urbanisation in New Zealand*, ed. R. J. Johnston (Wellington, New Zealand, Reed Education, 1973), 277–310; R. Bowman, "Factoring the Factors: Factorial Ecologies and Ethnic Research," *The Australian and New Zealand Journal of Sociology* 14, no. 2 (1978): 191–93; L. G. Hamilton, "The Political Integration of the Samoan Immigrants in New Zealand" (master's thesis, University of Canterbury, 1974); I. Fairbairn, "Samoan Migration to New Zealand," *Journal of the Polynesian Society* 70, 1 (1961): 18–30; N. B. Graves and T. C. Graves, *Culture Shock in Auckland: Pakeha Responses to Polynesian Migrants* (Auckland: South Pacific Research Institute, Report No. 3, 1973); T. D. Graves and N. B. Graves, *As Others See Us: New Zealanders' Images of Themselves and of Immigrant Groups* (Auckland: South Pacific Research Institute, 1974); N. B. Graves, *Egocentrism and Cultural Deprivation: Empirical Evidence for the Ethnocentric Bias of Piagetean Theory* (Auckland: South Pacific Research Institute, 1976); N. B. Graves and T. D. Graves, *Barroom Behavior in New Zealand: A Comparative Study* (Auckland: South Pacific Research Institute, 1976); N. B. Graves and T. D. Graves, *Preferred Adaptive Strategies: An Approach to Understanding New Zealand's Multicultural Workforce* (Auckland: South Pacific Research Institute, 1978); T. D. Graves and N. B. Graves, *Kinship Ties and Preferred Adaptive Strategies of Urban Migrants* (Auckland: South Pacific Research Institute, Research Report no. 19); I. Ah Sam, "Adjustment among Samoan Immigrants in New Zealand" (master's thesis, University of Auckland, 1977).

4. P. Schoeffel and M. Meleisea, "Conflicting Cultural Models of the Family and Approaches to Child Socialisation in New Zealand," paper presented to the Annual Conference of the Sociological Association of Aotearoa New Zealand (Palmerston North, November 1994).

5. Cluny Macpherson "Extended Kinship among Urban Samoans in New Zealand: Toward an Explanation of Its Persistence" (Ph.D. diss., University of Waikato, 1975).

6. Pitt and Macpherson, *Emerging Pluralism*.

7. Ibid.; Cluny Macpherson, "Migrant Polynesians and the New Zealand Factory: A Case for the Application of Human Relations Theory," paper presented to the New Zealand Sociological Association Conference (University of Auckland, 1974); Macpherson, "Extended Kinship"; Cluny Macpherson, "Polynesians in New Zealand: An Emerging Eth-class?" in *Social Class in New Zealand*, ed. D. Pitt (Auckland: Longman Paul, 1977).

8. Macpherson, "Extended Kinship"; Macpherson, "The Kalapu: A Samoan Migrant Approach to Insurance," paper presented to the Annual Conference of the Sociological Association of Australia and New Zealand (University of Waikato, 1975); Pitt and Macpherson, *Emerging Pluralism*; Paul Shankman, *Migration and Underdevelopment: The Case of Western Samoa* (Boulder, Colo.: Westview, 1976); Macpherson, "Extended Kinship"; Macpherson, "Guestworker Movements and Their Consequences for Donor and Recipient Countries," in *Population Mobility and Development*, ed. G. Jones and H. V. Richter (Australian National University, Development Studies Center, Monograph no. 27).

9. Macpherson, "Extended Kinship"; Macpherson, "Kalapu"; Macpherson, "Polynesians in New Zealand"; Graves and Graves, *As Others See Us*; Graves and Graves, *Kinship Ties*.

10. Trlin, "Residential Patterns and Segregation of Racial Groups"; Trlin, "Immigrants in the Cities"; A. D. Trlin, "Social Distance and Assimilation Orientation: A Survey of Attitudes towards Immigrants in New Zealand," *Pacific Viewpoint* 12, no. 2 (1971): 141–62; A. D. Trlin, "Attitudes toward West Samoan Immigrants in Auckland, New Zealand," *Australian Quarterly* 44, no. 3 (1972): 49–57; A. D. Trlin and R. J. Johnston, "Dimensionality of Attitudes towards Immigrants: A New Zealand Example," *Australian Journal of Psychology* 25, no. 3 (1973): 183–89.

11. Graves and Graves, *Culture Shock;* Graves and Graves, *As Others See Us;* Graves and Graves, *Barroom Behaviour.*

12. Pitt and Macpherson, *Emerging Pluralism.*

13. Ibid.

14. Forty-nine percent. Vasantha Krishnan, Penelope Schoeffel, and Julie Warren, *The Challenge of Change: Pacific Island Communities in New Zealand, 1986–1993* (Wellington: New Zealand Institute for Social Research & Development Ltd., 1994), 37.

15. This study depended primarily on the continuous observation of a group of some 250 kinspeople who regard themselves as family (*aiga*) and drew heavily on qualitative material on changes in the group over the past twenty years.

16. Cluny Macpherson, "On the Future of Samoan Ethnicity in New Zealand," in *Tauiwi. Racism and Ethnicity in New Zealand,* ed. P. Spoonley, C. Macpherson, D. Pearson, and C. Sedgwick (Palmerston North: The Dunmore Press, 1984), 107–27.

17. Schoeffel and Meleisea, "Conflicting Cultural Models."

18. Some also reflected on the inconsistency in parents' explicit, formal and implicit, informal representations of fa'a samoa. Children noted that while their parents were publicly committed and supportive, they were privately much less committed and more critical of fa'a samoa.

19. Schoeffel and Meleisea, "Conflicting Cultural Models."

20. Ibid.

21. An outstanding New Zealand–born rugby player who is arguably the best player in his particular position in the world.

Part III

Ethnicities of Dominated Indigenous Peoples

Phillip H. McArthur

6   Narrating to the Center of Power in the Marshall Islands

Tricky Identities and Culture

Tricksters are ambivalent characters. They have no respect for boundaries or for neat and tidy categories. In their destructive-regenerative capacity, they meet our apparent need for "a margin of mess, a category of inverted beings both to define and to question the order by which we live. Structure requires negation, things are by virtue and relation to what they are not; structure implies anti-structure and cannot exist without it."[1] This messiness and creative "free combination"[2] is very much at home in a postmodern environment, where ambiguity, fluidity, and multiplicity ignore rigid categorical boundaries.[3]

The struggle for identity in a postmodern world is much like a trickster; self-reflexivity is at times ambivalent[4] and at other times brilliantly creative. Identity formation, a modernist project, requires the construction of symbolic and cognitive boundaries—it suggests a boundedness—proposing that the content within is authentic and genuine to the individual or cultural self.[5] This boundary making and boundary maintenance require delineation and objectification of the content of the individual and collective self. Not that premoderns and the non-Western societies do not form identities, but the ideological forces that politicize such identities are part of modernity, in which social structures and relations of power are the by-products of mercantile and industrial capitalism, urbanization, the emergence of the nation state, a secular world view, and so forth.

Cultural identity, whether ethnic, national, or regional, necessitates a horizontal imagining of the collective self; it is, as Benedict Anderson contends, a rationalist model that can be transported globally.[6] I agree with Arjun Appadurai that we need to think beyond the nation state, beyond nationalism, beyond ethnicism,[7] not because people do not deserve their identities, but because such projects have led to systems of domination and subordination, and because such porous systems and constructs cannot be maintained in a postmodern world. Moreover, our theorizing and identification of national or ethnic groups is painfully too much like the processes of identity formation; it is a way of imbuing a group with social value and authority. In this we are not only at risk of privileging certain kinds of group formation (the ethnic over gender for example), but we naturalize the boundaries that define group membership, when in social practice identities may be nonexclusive, cross-cutting, and simultaneous. While such efforts may be undertaken with the best of intentions, we participate in the modernist project of empowering particular groups and their interests based upon our constructed categories.

Identities and their content are not received *sui generis,* they are constructed depending on the interests of a group at any point in history. Moreover, they are generated through institution building and shared discourses about and of culture.[8] They are flexible and contingent upon context. While identities are slippery and unstable, however, they are neither pure fictions nor purely spurious fabrications, as some have contended. To view these expressions of identity as simply the "invention of tradition"[9] is to neglect why the "stories we tell about ourselves"[10] are employed in the first place. They work because people find them experientially meaningful[11] and engaging, appropriate arenas to address issues of identity. The cultural meanings and narratives realized have a history. No doubt the meanings emerge and shift as narratives are recentered into new contexts. Nonetheless, creativity is not random. Even those who championed identification of the constructed nature of culture and identity regret the "[c]leavage ... [i]t asserts between custom and invented tradition" and essentializes the effect of colonialism and modernity.[12] It is more productive to view this dynamic cultural process as traditionalization (identifying aspects of the past as significant in present changing contexts) and as hybridization (mixing the traditional and the new). Both these processes occur where boundaries are disputed, appropriated, and negotiated.[13]

There is no set or absolute meaning to culture or the past; meaning is generated in the present, as human agents select and fashion the images of culture and history for the purpose of defining an identity.[14] These narratives are "equipment for living."[15] They function in times of social strain and "unquestionably where profound historical changes have taken place,"[16] "when elements of culture and politics are brought together in a jumble," and where there is a "struggle over the control of meanings."[17]

It is at such a moment of profound historical change that the Marshall Islanders explore the boundary of their collective identity through a narrative in which they imagine themselves at the center of the panglobal arena through identification with America. The power of this metaphorical play problematizes and challenges models that suggest a clear break between modernity and tradition, center and periphery, authenticity and the unauthentic, identity and difference, oppositions that have been at the heart of modernist discourses about ethnicity.[18]

Use and Abuse: Americans Thinking Small

Marshall Islander culture is significantly different from American: the Islanders live on resource-poor, low-lying coral atolls in the middle of the Pacific; theirs is a matrilineally oriented society with strong chiefdoms; they possess a rich heritage of sailing and fishing; power is genealogically ascribed.

Westerners see the Marshall Islands as small—small land, small population, a small place in the world. Perhaps for this reason, the U.S. government felt justified in removing some "small" populations from their home atolls in order to explode atomic bombs there "for the good of mankind."[19]

Marshall Islanders have been subjugated by a series of nations: first came the Germans, who made the islands a protectorate in 1888, followed by the Japanese with a mandate from the League of Nations in 1921, then by the United States, which was given a trusteeship over the islands by the United Nations in 1947. In February 1944, U.S. military forces invaded and took control of the primary Japanese fortifications, then pushed across Micronesia toward Japan. After the main forces moved on, some remained behind, bombing atolls where Japanese fortifications still stood. This was a very hard time for the Marshall Islanders as the Japanese, in their desperate condition, became brutal and demanded their food. After the war, the Marshalls were administered by the Navy Department until the mid-1950s, when the responsibility shifted to the Department of Interior. Nuclear bomb testing lasted into the 1960s with the Bravo experiments; its initial phases involved the forced removal and relocation of the Bikini and Enewetak islanders from their home atolls.[20] These tests not only decimated entire islets but made the atolls uninhabitable from the nuclear radiation. Only in recent years have some Islanders moved back into Enewetak Atoll. Fallout from the blasts drifted several hundred miles downwind, landing on atolls in the northern Railik and Ratak chains. The United States continues to occupy Kwajalein Atoll as a practice target for inactive missiles launched as far away as California. The rent paid on the atoll represents more than half the Marshalls' national budget, making the range a necessary problem for the modern nation state.

Not until 1979 and the ratification of the Republic of the Marshall Islands constitution did the Islanders gain some autonomy. In 1983 they entered into a "Compact of Free Association" with the United States and became semi-independent, and in 1987 fully independent (still with a compact), a status not recognized by the United Nations until December 1990. In 1991 the Republic became a full member of the United Nations and, while identified as a sovereign nation, the Marshalls remain profoundly dependent on U.S. aid. Despite these clear cases of abuse and control, most Marshall Islanders maintain a favorable impression of the United States and Americans, a sentiment that can be accounted for once one understands their assumptions and narratives about power.

Images of Power: The Islanders Making Sense of Americans at War

As is true in many Pacific societies, the Marshall Islanders possess a dualistic image of a chief and his power,[21] viewing him as both a kingly chief who is distant and untouchable (*utiej*), who has great knowledge (*meletlet*), and who is the fiercest of warriors (*lej*), and as a populist, approachable chief who maintains his power by taking care of his people, mainly in how he distributes (*ajej*) land (*bwidej*) and food (*mōñā*). A good and equitable chief is *joij* (kind) to his *Kajor ro* (people). *Kajor* is a polysemantic term that means people or commoners as well as power. Thus, a chief's power comes from being in possession of people. Nonetheless, the etymology of the term literally means "to cause to stand," and it is the chief's people who make him powerful, either through tribute (*ekan*) or war (*tarinae*).

The U.S. military impressed the Islanders by easily defeating the Japanese, who had spent years fortifying the islands. To the Islanders the Americans were brave, and their technological power revealed their intelligence. The Americans matched the Islanders' image of the great warrior chief, and once in occupation of the islands, the Americans maintained a chiefly distance. Whereas the Japanese had forced the Islanders to work within their system and had extracted their goods and services, the Americans simply moved the Islanders out of the way. The nuclear bomb testing over the next two decades only reinforced the image of the Americans as the most powerful and untouchable of chiefs. At dawn, having been shipped off an atoll a day's distance out to sea, one Islanderl said:

> Perhaps they had prearranged the time, for in just a little while we saw it. First like a cloud, white, but enlarging, up, away; then, as if they set ablaze the entire earth—colors; red, blue, purple, all colors of the rainbow, but stronger. Up higher and wider, until the entire sky to the north was filled with colors.
>
> And then they told us it was Enewetak, one of the bombs, and we began to be sad, for we knew it was gone. After some minutes, then we heard the sound, like thunder, but louder and it stayed. And we again saddened, for the sound revealed the truth: perhaps Enewetak was gone. And we did not hear talk of the atoll for many years, until now, and it only revealed to us our own thoughts, that island, the island of ours, was gone.[22]

In the populist image of the chief, not only did the occupying Americans not require anything from the Islanders, but they gave the Islanders food and clothing, gifts that kept coming even under the administration of the Trust Territory. For the Islanders, the Americans continue to display their wealth as a good chief should, but they also take care of people with it, as a good chief should. "The Americans," Islanders say, "are kind" (*joij*). On several occasions I was reprimanded for my less than "patriotic" leanings and critical approach to U.S. imperialism and abuses in the Islands. If, as many Islanders claim, the Americans are both great warriors and also take care of people, thus satisfying the dualistic image, then they are legitimate world rulers.

I have intentionally avoided a rehearsal of the American imagination of the Islanders, one that mixes eroticizing them with condemning them. Instead my interest is in the indigenous practice of sense making. Part of this strategy includes the Islanders' view of themselves in relation to the Americans and the outside world. The Islanders also see their atolls as small and recognize how geographically isolated they are from the continents and population centers of the world. But they still think big—they think outward. They see the interconnections of the world and their place within it.

One night in the Islands, I gave a ride home to an old man whose house was on my way.[23] As we drove, he said that there was too much sickness in the islands but that is just the way it always happens after a big event. I asked him what big event he was referring to, since many others had told me that the political tensions in the country were resulting in ill feelings and sickness. He responded that it was because of the bombs. I thought he was referring to the U.S. nuclear tests between the 1940s and the 1960s that continue to affect the Islanders with conditions that include thyroid problems and cancer. But he corrected me. It was not those bombs, but the ones that the Americans had used against the Iraqis during the Gulf War about seven months earlier. He explained that after the Americans had come to the Islands and defeated the Japanese during World War II, everyone had become ill. Since then, with every major war, all kinds of sicknesses had come to the Islands. Because this latest war had occurred on the opposite side of the earth, it had taken all these months for the sickness to reach the Marshall Islands. But now it had arrived. He said that it is not just that the bombs release "poison" in the air, but that American bombs and fighting shake up the heavens and the winds, putting everything out of order. Eventually, he said, we feel the effects of it. That conversation showed me just how large-scale the Islanders think.

Narrating to the Center:
The Islanders Thinking Big

While the Islanders have made sense of U.S. displays of power during and after World War II through local constructs about chiefs, they continue to make sense of American behavior and world events and to generate a transnational identity through a narrative about a trickster figure whose name is Letao, "the Sly One."

The Marshall Islanders enjoy the tales about the antics, subversion, and vulgarity of Letao more than any other tale cycle. Letao is like the archetypal trickster figures found around the world.[24] His most notable qualities are the ability to shape shift, an enormous libido, a power over nature, a cunning intelligence that enables him to outwit any opponent, and a penchant for subverting social authority. Of all the traditional narratives, stories about Letao are the best known, most often performed, and most widely distributed throughout the islands. It is through this trickster that Marshallese culture and the "other" (the Americans) are integrated in the most profound ways.

Letao is the youngest offspring of the youngest primal matriarch in the Marshall Islanders' cosmogony. Two key pan-Pacific motifs that recur through the tale cycle about Letao are usurping the power of those in authority, and men achieving heroic deeds after being granted cosmological power by women. This excerpt from a storytelling performance I recorded in the Marshall Islands represents only a single rendering of the narrative, and versions of this episode are told repeatedly all over the Islands. In episodes preceding this one, Letao engages in a series of tricks, subverting chiefs throughout the Islands. In later episodes he escapes to Kiribati, the islands just south of the Marshalls.[25]

He goes and then (reaches) Kiribati
He deceives a man there—the chief (of) Kiribati
He says
"Why DO WE NOT EAT—WHAT-IS-THERE-TO EAT?"
And he (the chief) says "There is no food"
"Crap!"
"LET'S (make) THAT EARTH-OVEN"

They lite a big fire
REALLY BIG
Then afterwards
he goes and lays in the earth-oven
"OKAY COVER IT"
Then they cover—cover—cover it with sand
And go to the house
They go to the house but uh—he—
is lagoon-side
clapping (his) hands *clapping slowly* and proceeds to land
"OKAY UNCOVER (IT)"
Then they uncover (it)
After (it's) uncovered it is full (of) fish and breadfruit *laughs* and preserved-breadfruit and
     all kinds of food
Then
Now
after he goes (to) lay with the women—
        |You see?
the women hate him
Since—because they only like the chief
Another day he does (it) again
Ah it is hungry—Kiribati is hungry—the people are hungry
He again makes food—starts the earth-oven again (and) does (it)
Then he says <"ME I AM LEAVING MAN MY FRIEND">
        |The word friend is big eeh it can be true it can be false *laughs hard*
<Then he says "OOO YOU GO (but) ME—WE WILL BE HUNGRY">
"OKAY *laughs* how-else-can-it-be I am leaving?"
"BUT (for) ME MAN HOW-WILL-IT-BE?"—he says—<"YOU SHOULD TEACH (it)">
The chief says
"OKAY—
LITE THE FIRE"
And then afterwards he says (to) the chief to jump and lie inside the fire
The chief jumps and lays-down
He lays (and) says "EKUK IT-IS-HOT"—he says "OOOO KNOW—" *laughs hard*
<He (Letao) says "COVER IT COVER IT">
Then they again cover-it-over
He goes (to) the house
and makes coconut-sennit-rope
Just-makes coconut-sennit-rope
Brings sennit and makes-sennit-rope
The women say "What man hasn't-it-been nearly a while since the man (has been) making
     food"?
He says "SSSh the man himself just greatly covets (it)"
"Eh-it is just many foods he is making no one can say (nearly) a thousand thousand" *laughs*
But (it) becomes night
Oohu
Goes (and) goes he does not come
The women say "Okay—"

"What now?"

He says "You-two go examine (it) please"

Uncover *laughs—inaudible words*

After uncovering the earth-oven he says "Kuhhuuhhu"—his face is turned red *wide-eyed*
  staring with mouth open—laughs hard

The women say *"EEKOK"* *laughs* the-two-of-them take-off *all laugh hard*

Takes-off and go and go and stay in the room

the room of the chief

But he—he-goes

goes and brings

brings the chief to the doorway of the woman and places (him) there

The women then look and "OH CRAP" *laughs* —the chief there by the door

THE TWO-OF-THEM TAKE OFF

TAKE OFF AND GO AND LAY WITH HIM

One is at one arm and the other— *we all laugh*

laughing and they (had) refused him

Oh (it is) day

They tell

The women (who) refused to lay with him laid with him *hard laughter again*

Ah he escapes

<Escapes and goes and does-more in the southern islands> (Polynesia)

And he goes (and) goes (and) goes (and) goes

A-America

And the man stays at the land of those Americans

    |But we don't know what he does

    |They say he is smart he makes (the) bomb

    |*laughter*

What may appear to be inconsequential detail in this narrative episode and to have very little to do with the Americans draws upon various meanings of Letao's power to comment on and make sense of them. Power derived from his ambiguity distinguishes him and makes it possible for him to become a metaphor for the Americans. Letao's getting into the earth oven and providing food for the famine-stricken Kiribati people appear as acts of chiefly kindness (*joij*). But with Letao, there are always ulterior motives; he wants to kill off the chief so that he can obtain sexual favors from his wives. Letao makes things appear to be something they are not, that is, he is the hero chief that brings bounty to the people and displays his kindness, but there are strings attached. To many, the Americans giving food has had strings attached: they tested bombs and continued to occupy the islands.

Letao's ability to get into the earth-oven, escape unnoticed, and bring forth bounteous food displays his power over nature and symbolizes his perpetually regenerative capacity. Letao appears to offer power that would figuratively represent the ultimate chiefly ability, to feed his people and thus have their support and consequent dominion over them. But the chief does not really obtain Letao's power and is tricked into cooking himself. This is not only subversion, but it inverts the meaning of food, kindness, and the sustaining of life, symbols of the populist chief. It is not food or life that is uncovered, but the grotesque nonfood (human flesh) and death. Following the war the Americans appeared to be providing bountifully for the Islanders, yet through nuclear testing they were subsequently "cooked," and many died.

The most poignant moment in this episode is when Letao calls the chief "my friend," and the narrator comments, "The word 'Friend' is big—eeh—it can be true, it can be false." Here the whole of Letao's deceptive capacity and power are presented, blurring what is true (*mol*) and false (*riab*). In this ambiguity we can see the Marshall Islander's vision of the Americans: they may act as your friend, but in the end, they will "burn you" figuratively and, for those who experienced nuclear fallout, literally. The Marshallese word for friend is *jera*. The word for luck, good fortune, and bless-ing is *jeramon*. Literally, the etymology of *jeramon* is *jera* (friend) + *mon* (good). Con-sequently, good fortune is a good friend. On the other hand, the meaning of the word *jerata* for bad luck or misfortune also derives from the meaning of friend. The literal etymology of *jerata* is *jera* (friend) + *ta* (what). Thus, misfortune is "what kind of friend?" meaning "none at all," a false friend, a liar. Accordingly a true friend is a blessing and good fortune; a false friend is misfortune and a liar. What kind of friend did Letao prove to be in the end? What kind of friend will the Americans prove to be?

Letao's trickery was at first productive: he fed people. Then he was destructive: he brought death to the chief, subverting the chief's status and the institutions over which he has power. But from death comes regeneration: Letao went on to engage in sexual relations with the chief's wives. Letao always gets what he wants (and the Americans do too). The Americans displayed their power over nature and brought death and destruction with the war, and they continue to do so elsewhere, but they also brought food, regenerating life, and therefore like a chief they accumulate power (*kajor*). In this episode, Letao goes on to Polynesia, and then on to America. On several occa-sions, performers of this narrative recalled how Letao struck a deal with the Ameri-cans because he coveted their wealth.

The metanarrative and interaction that concludes this part of the performance of the narrative connects Letao to the Americans, their "smarts," and their bombs. He is the source of their intelligence and thus the source of their military power. His power derives from his ambiguity, destructiveness, regenerative capacity, mobility, inversion of cultural rules, lies, and deceptions. He breaks boundaries wide open and, in doing so, brings to view the economic, political, and social transnational relations the Islanders have confronted and continue to confront. These relations are ambiguous, but as with Letao, ambiguity brings power. This ambiguity is also the target of laugh-ter, generated through the paradoxical trickster.

The meaning of Letao's power casts into relief the powerful "other" (the Americans). As an in-between character not only does he link the Islanders to the Americans, but he is the source of their ambiguous power. In this way the Islanders make sense of American power on their own terms, and in the process identify with the Americans. Letao's power is translated into American power through the narrative about Letao going to America, carrying with him all of the qualities that give him power. This narrative does not circulate at the level of the nation state, but in intimate storytelling sessions where local Islanders explore the meaning of their lives. It is within these inti-mate, small-scale scenes, where the narrative is situated in performance, that large-scale issues (global modernity and relations) are incorporated into the indigenous system of meanings about power.

Modern experience tells the Islanders that the Americans do not enact the perfect chiefly image. Letao's ambiguity and power do more than lead to a kinship with the destructive-regenerative power of the Americans; his qualities typify how the Islanders perceive him and the Americans. I was told on several occasions that Letao, as the "sly one," is the embodiment of extremes; he is at once good and bad, possesses all knowledge and all foolishness, all love and all hate, all kindness and all meanness, all truth and all lies. After recounting these qualities of the trickster, narrators such as the one recorded here have commented, "Isn't that just like the Americans?"

The Transnational Identity

The presence and wide use of this narrative provides a powerful resource for the construction of a transnational identity at a time when the Islanders are continually being pulled into global economic and political systems but remain peripheral to the centers of power. This is no simple task, since it involves identifying distinct cultural meanings about power at the local level, then refracting these meanings to identify similarities with the Americans at the transnational level. Instead of viewing this tale as a spurious fabrication, I prefer to approach it as a "representation of a general scheme of social life" and not a "rationalization of power."[26] Through the Letao narrative the Islanders do more than playfully imagine the Americans as enacting cosmological images of power, they imagine their own mythological character as the source of American power. In this way they see themselves connected to what they perceive to be the great figurative "world chief" not only by history (war and occupation), but cosmologically, thus giving meaning to their history and their modern lives. The Islanders recognize their geographic, economic, and political marginality on the international scene, but through the trickster narrative they imagine a new kind of social relation through identification with American power, viewing themselves not as peripheral but as profoundly central to the panglobal arena and world events.

This example of the Marshallese trickster presents a narrative that addresses quite meaningfully the social transformations the Islanders have experienced and continue to experience. Unlike most narratives that construct identities (national or ethnic and so forth) by differentiating "self" from the "other," the Marshall Islanders identify with the "other." This suggests that much may be missed when local cultures are viewed as purely dominated by larger structures such as the nation state or culture industry.

Some have argued that national and ethnic boundaries become meaningless as discourses pass in and out, carrying culture and ideologies and generating new forms of mediated relations.[27] Marshall McLuhan in 1970 spoke of the "global village," where communication media permit a simultaneity of culture.[28] Yet what some thought would lead to global homogeneity has yet to be realized, since cultures and ethnic groups respond differently to Western culture and the forces of modernity.

Apart from media linkages, transnationals are forming allegiances and multiple identities not restricted to one country[29] or localized ethnic group. Since the Cold War, the world has become both unipolar, with its centers of power in the West, and "multicentric,"[30] as "international and transnational organizations of every type proliferate" and "local politics and global process affect each other ... often outside the interactions of nation states."[31] In the process, people are often seen either as powerless and peripheral to these sweeping forces or as reactionary, reaffirming cultural differences only to assert some claim to power. By fragmentation, modern social life "constantly subdivides and reorganizes itself in ever-increasing complexity,"[32] and by centralizing, local structures are progressively incorporated into more centralized ones.[33]

Yet through narrative, the Marshall Islanders reverse the centralizing process by imagining themselves not at the periphery of global power but at its center. Their identification with America is a transnational identity and a comprehension of "the order of existence in the modern world in their own terms."[34] Through local methods of expression and local meanings, they narrate themselves to the centers of power at the most macrolevel: the world. Care should be taken not to restrict the meaning of power by ignoring the ability of such people to act purposefully, to create and recreate the meaning of their lives. Among the Marshall Islanders we see no rupture between modernity and tradition; they make sense of the modern through the traditional, which makes it truly postmodern.[35] Moreover, they gain power and identity not through the construction of difference and resistance, but by encompassing the "other" through local constructs. How they will reformulate their identity in the future is unpredictable, but at present, like the trickster who breaks and blurs boundaries, the Marshall Islanders reach beyond ethnic objectification and nationalism to explore a transnational identity.

Notes

1. Barbara A. Babcock, "'A Tolerated Margin of Mess': The Trickster and His Tales Reconsidered," *Journal of the Folklore Institute* 11 (1975): 147–86.

2. Victor Turner, *Drama, Fields, and Metaphors: Symbolic Action in Human Society* (Ithaca, N.Y.: Cornell University Press, 1974).

3. More than just decentering or deconstructing totalizing images and discourses, my use of the term "postmodern" follows Fredric Jameson's concept of periodization. Thus, this term marks a new kind of social life and economic order of late capitalism. This period is marked by postindustrial or consumer societies, globalization of media, spectacle and multinational capitalism. In this global environment new forms of social life are constituted as continuous rather than discrete formations, and as mixed and multiple. See Jameson, "Postmodernism, or the Cultural Logic of Late Capitalism," *New Left Review* 146 (1984): 53–92; Jameson, *Postmodernism or the Cultural Logic of Late Capitalism* (London: Verso, 1991); and "Postmodernism and Consumer Society," in *Postmodernism and its Discontents,* ed. E. Ann Kaplan (London: Verso, 1988), pp. 13–29. For recent surveys of postmodernity and postmodernism and their historical relationship to modernity, see Peter Brooker, "Introduction: Reconstructions," in *Modernism/Postmodernism,* ed. Peter Brooker (London: Longman, 1992); Lawrence Cahoone, "Introduction," in *From Modernism to Postmodernism: An Anthology,* ed. Lawrence Cahoone (Cambridge, Mass.: Blackwell, 1996).

4. For "ambivalence," I borrow from Homi K. Bhabba's discussion on cultural representation and signification of the sense of "nationness." Such representations, argues Bhabba, present

"conceptual indeterminacy" and "waver between vocabularies" as they attempt to articulate difference in formation of nation states. The use of these representations to delineate or look back on the collective self for the purpose of constructing a national identity are ambivalent; they are not fixed and are continually being constructed and reconstructed, most notably through narrative. See Bhabba, "Introduction: Narrating the Nation," in *Nation and Narration,* ed. Homi K. Bhabba (New York: Routledge, 1990).

5. See Frederick Barth, *Ethnic Groups and Boundaries: The Social Organization of Culture Difference* (Boston: Little, Brown, 1969). For a good example of the reconciliation of both content and boundaries, see, Anya Peterson Royce, *Ethnic Identity: Strategies and Diversity* (Bloomington: Indiana University Press, 1982).

6. On rationalist models as part of the modernist project, see Benedict Anderson, *Imagined Communities: Reflections on the Origin and Spread of Nationalism* (London: Verso, 1983).

7. Arjun Appadurai, "Patriotism and Its Futures," *Public Cultures* 5 (1993): 411–29.

8. The introduction to this book establishes well the institutional and cultural forces in the formation of ethnic groups.

9. Eric Hobsbawm and Terence Ranger, eds., *The Invention of Tradition* (Cambridge, UK: Cambridge University Press, 1983).

10. Clifford Geertz, "Deep Play: Notes on the Balinese Cockfight," in *Interpretation of Cultures* (New York: Basic, 1973), 412–53.

11. Pierre Bourdieu, *Outline of a Theory of Practice* (Cambridge, UK: Cambridge University Press, 1977).

12. Terence Ranger, "The Invention of Tradition Revisited: The Case of Colonial Africa," in *Legitimacy and the State in 20th Century Africa,* ed. Terence Ranger and Olufemi Vaughn (Hampshire, UK: MacMillan, 1993).

13. For a theoretical discussion on the processes of traditionalization, see Amy Shuman and Charles Briggs, "Introduction," in "Theorizing Folklore: Toward New Perspectives on the Politics of Culture," special issue, *Western Folklore* 52 (1993): 109–34. For a contemporary discussion and example of hybridization, see Deborah A. Kapchan, "Hybridization and the Marketplace: Emerging Paradigms in Folkloristics," *Western Folklore* 52 (1993): 303–26.

14. Jocelyn Linnekin argues that identities emerge and change historically in the contexts of social and political oppositions. Through the process of cultural objectification, or externalizing symbols, groups will invoke a model of the past to define a cultural identity in the present. The content of identities is not purely fabricated; rather, they are fashioned as members of the culture group select and condense meanings into "summarizing symbols" that evoke deeply rooted meanings and sentiments. See "The Politics of Culture in the Pacific," in *Cultural Identity and Ethnicity in the Pacific,* ed. Jocelyn Linnekin, and Lin Poyer (Honolulu: University of Hawaii Press, 1990).

15. Kenneth Burke, *The Philosophy of Literary Form: Studies in Symbolic Action* (Baton Rouge: Louisiana State University Press, 1941).

16. Bronislaw Malinowski, *Magic, Science, and Religion* (1948; reprint, Garden City, N.Y.: Doubleday, 1954).

17. Beverly J. Stoeltje, "Power and Ritual Genres: American Rodeo," *Western Folklore* 52 (1993): 157–72. For the foundation of Stoeltje's ideas, see V. N. Volosinov, *Marxism and the Philosophy of Language* (New York: Seminar Press, 1973).

18. See Shuman and Briggs, "Introduction"; Brooker, *Modernism/Postmodernism;* and Cahoone, *From Modernism to Postmodernism.*

19. American Military Governor, 1946. See *Marshall Islands: A Chronology: 1944–1983* (Honolulu: Micronesian Support Committee, 1983).

20. For exemplary studies on the Islanders' forced migration, see Robert C. Kiste, *The Bikinians: A Study of Forced Migration* (Menlo Park, Calif.: Cummings, 1974), and for a discussion on the *Enewetak* Islanders, see Laurence Marshall Carucci, "The Renewal of Life: A Ritual Encounter in the Marshall Islands" (Ph.D. diss., University of Chicago, 1980); Laurence Marshall Carucci, *Nuclear Nativity: Rituals of Renewal and Empowerment in the Marshall Islands* (DeKalb, Ill.: Northern Illinois University Press, 1997).

21. On the dual nature of Pacific Islands chiefs, see George E. Marcus, "Chieftainship," in *Developments in Polynesian Ethnology*, eds. Alan Howard and Robert Borofsky (Honolulu: University of Hawaii Press, 1989).

22. Quotation and translation provided by Laurence Marshall Carucci, "The Source of the Force in Marshallese Cosmology," in *The Pacific Theater: Island Representation of WWII*, ed. Gregory M. White and Lamont Lindstrom (Honolulu: University of Hawaii Press, 1989).

23. From August 1991 to July 1993 and May to August 1994 I conducted the primary portion of my field research in the Marshall Islands; see "The Social Life of Narrative: Marshall Islands" (Ph.D. diss., Indiana University, 1995). This research was made possible with grants from the Wenner Gren Foundation for Anthropological Research, Indiana Center on Global Change and World Peace, and Indiana University Graduate School, for which I am indeed grateful. I also lived in the islands for eighteen months as an LDS missionary (1982–1984).

24. The trickster figure plays a large part in oral traditions worldwide. Well-known tricksters include Coyote in Native America, Maui in Polynesia, Brer Rabbit/Fox in Black America, and Anansi the Spider in West Africa. See Paul Radin, ed., *The Trickster: A Study in American Indian Mythology* (New York: Schocken, 1956); Carl G. Jung, "The Psychology of the Trickster," in *The Trickster*, ed. Paul Radin; Claude Levi-Strauss, *Structural Anthropology* (New York: Basic Books, 1963); Babcock, "'A Tolerated Margin of Mess'"; Robert D. Pelton, *The Trickster in West Africa: A Study of Mythic Irony and Sacred Delight* (Berkeley: University of California Press, 1980).

25. I have attempted to retain the semantic and grammatical flavor of Marshallese without overwhelming the reader with an excessively literal translation. I also try to convey the nature of verbal art in the Marshall Islands and to make my transcriptions as information rich as possible.

Pause and transitional adverbs identify lines.

< >   Discourse within arrows is performed at a significantly faster tempo.

CAPS   Text in capitals registers discourse at a greater volume.

—   Dashes following a word indicate an immediate break-off from a word/idea/sentence or immediate transition into another word.

( )   Parentheses contain added discourse to clarify narration.

| plus a double indent   Identifies metanarrative asides when tellers break away from the narration to give explanation or comment on the story.

-    Hyphens register the connection of words that convey a single Marshallese word.

Italics   Text in italics records nonverbal gestures.

26. Marshall Sahlins, *Islands of History* (Chicago: University of Chicago Press, 1985).

27. On media and globalization, see Ien Ang, "Culture and Communication: Towards an Ethnographic Critique of Media Consumption in the Transnational Media System," *European Journal of Communication* 5 (1993): 239–60; Michael Curtin, "Electronic Imaginings: Collective Identities and the Global Reconfiguration" (in press).

28. Marshall McLuhan, *Counterblast* (London: Rapp and Whiting, 1970).

29. On transnationalism and the deterritorializing of identities, see Appadurai, "Patriotism and Its Futures."

30. James Rosenau, *Turbulence in World Politics: A Theory of Change and Continuity* (Princeton, N.J.: Princeton University Press, 1990).

31. Appadurai, "Patriotism and Its Futures."

32. Dean MacCannell, *The Tourist: A New Theory of the Leisure Class* (New York: Schocken, 1976).

33. Beverly J. Stoeltje and Richard Bauman, "Community Festival and the Enactment of Modernity," in *The Old Traditional Way of Life: Essays in Honor of Warren E. Roberts,* ed. Robert E. Walls and George H. Schoemaker (Bloomington: Indiana University Press, 1989).

34. Richard Bauman, "American Folklore Studies and Social Transformation: A Performance-Centered Perspective," *Text and Performance Quarterly* 9 (1989): 175–84.

35. Part of the postmodern discussion has been the breakdown of what was once seen as a categorically clear boundary between pre-modernity and modernity, and the free interplay between associated concepts of tradition and creativity. In the postmodern context the old and the new, as well as diverse genres and ideas are freely mixed. An outline of this discussion is provided by, Richard Schechner, *The End of Humanism* (New York: Performing Arts Journal Publications, 1982).

Stephen Cornell

---

7 Discovered Identities and American Indian Supratribalism

All collective identities contain an element of discovery. The process of identity formation itself is in part a process of discovery: persons or groups discover that they share something of importance to them—interests, experiences, social positions, a common fate, or something else of significance—with other persons or groups. If that perception of common ground endures for very long, one result is a growing sense of shared identity as well. The "we" expands to include relevant others, those who share the common ground. As the perception of commonality strengthens, so does the identity. Thus discovery and identity are linked, but in such cases it is not the identity that is "discovered." The identity is the gradually emerging precipitate of that perception of commonness, of the discovery of common ground. Discovery in this sense is simply part of the ordinary process of collective identification, the learning that people do all the time: discovering how the world around them works, how they fit into that world, and who else fits into it in similar ways.

By the term "discovered identities," however, I refer to something quite different. Calling an ethnic identity a discovered identity refers not to the discovery of shared positions, interests, experiences, practices, or the like, but to the discovery by a group of people that they constitute a category in the minds of others that has not previously existed in their own system of classification of groups in society, or that they have not previously recognized as including themselves. In this usage it *is* the identity that is discovered, an identity that other persons construct and assign to the group but that group members do not (yet) claim as their own.

The history of colonialism, immigration, and other intersocietal contact is replete with such cases. British colonial administrations in Uganda, for example, long read linguistic and other cultural similarities among some Ugandans as indicators of a degree of collective identity and groupness that in fact did not exist for those Ugandans—that is, they were not categories of group organization or identity among Ugandans themselves—and built administrative apparatuses to match the categories they thought they had found but in fact had invented. British colonial power turned these categories into effective bases of both administrative organization and social interaction and, eventually, of group consciousness. According to Crawford Young, British administrators thus "breathed life into quite novel categories of identity," categories Ugandans discovered largely through British eyes and assumptions.[1]

Immigration often produces similar effects. Italian immigrants to the United States, for example, generally had little sense of themselves as Italians. Their identities were primarily local or regional. But they discovered on their arrival that the receiving society perceived them not as Neapolitans or Sicilians or Lucanians but as Italians: this was the relevant category for both the U.S. state and the American public.[2] The critical discovery they made—at least for the purposes of this discussion—was not their shared position as immigrants or workers or residents of particular neighborhoods; it was the fact that they occupied an unanticipated place in the prevailing classification scheme of the receiving society. They discovered the category as a prevailing classification and discovered as well its application to them.

Panethnic Identities as Discovered Identities

Panethnic identities often are discovered identities in just this sense, occasioned by the classificatory schemes and actions of others. Someone else combines previously distinct groups in a new category. It may be the state, employers, organizational elites, or the public; it may be done out of ignorance, to facilitate administration, to reinforce and maintain group boundaries or statuses for economic, political, or other purposes, or just to make sense of a complex social world. The result is a revelation: the various members of the category discover that, in the eyes of others, they are something they have never been in their own.

This fact typically has consequences because the new category usually becomes an active component of the categorizers' worldview. It organizes their actions. Consequently, and especially if they have power over category members or over the world that such members encounter and inhabit, it begins to organize the experience of category members as well. In other words, the identity begins to matter not only to those who categorize but to those who are so categorized. The more it matters, the more likely category members are to respond to those who first articulate the identity in terms of the assigned category and even, in time, to adopt that category as an element in their own group classification scheme, in their own way of viewing the world. They move from being members of a category formed by others to being members of a self-conscious group, adopting the identity they discovered in someone else's understanding.

Thus, for example, in the history of the United States, not only did Sicilians and Neapolitans become Italians, but Wolof and Fulani eventually became Africans; Puerto Ricans and Mexican Americans became Hispanics or Latinos; Japanese, Koreans, and Vietnamese became Asians; immigrants from northern, central, and southern China, carrying disparate regional or local identities, arrived in Hawaii, discovered that they were viewed invariably as Chinese, and eventually began to see themselves the same way.[3] To be sure, in some of these cases group self-interest contributed significantly to the move from category to identity—a number of different logics may drive panethnic identity formation.[4] But in each of these examples the broader identity first gained salience in someone else's perceptions, needs, or interests. Category members discovered it there, encountered it not only as a perception but as an organizational principle of their daily life, and eventually adopted it as part of their own understanding of themselves. Their reasons for that adoption varied and often reflected their own interpretations of the situations they faced and the relative advantages of alternative bases of organization and identity, but the categorical identity they adopted was constructed first by others.

Discovery and Narrative

When the members of a category discover such an identity, what exactly do they discover? Among other things, they discover the category, its label, and its application to them. But more than that, eventually they discover the characteristics of that category: its logic, content, meaning. When they discover an unanticipated identity, they discover not only a category and label for their group but the significance of the label: the meaning and value attached to it. Ultimately, they discover the story behind the category, the story out of which meaning and value are conceived. In other words, they discover the narrative that others tell about them and out of which others construct them as a distinct group.

By narrative I refer here to an event-centered definition of the group that can be reduced, ultimately, to something along the following lines (here simplified and made generic): "They are the people who . . . ," followed variously by a set of events or acts: for example, came from there, did that, fled from so-and-so, took all our jobs, live off welfare, typically do the following, were outrageously abused, experienced such-and-such, are destroying Western civilization through this or that behavior, and so on. The narrative involves a selection of key events, a linking of these events to each other in causal or other ways, and their interpretation. The group forms the subject of the story, and the story, via selection, plotting, and interpretation, attaches value of some sort to the group: it carries a positive or negative moral charge.[5]

Discovered identities, then, involve in part the discovery of a narrative that gives meaning to the category and flesh to the bare bones of the label attached to the group. For those panethnic identities that begin as discovered identities, that—whatever their long-term logic—have their origins not in the calculus of group members but in the actions and assumptions of others, discovery involves learning the logic of the panethnic category to which the group is being assigned, a logic embedded in selected, plotted, and interpreted events.

Once the discovery is made, however, the critical question is, What happens next. Having discovered who they are in the eyes of others, what do groups then do with that discovery?

One option is to reject the category. Those so classified can insist on the identities they already claim and reject the one presented by others. But particularly where categorization and related action are carried out by the state or other powerful entities or forces, including massive public perception and behavior, rejection may be pointless: the world is being reorganized conceptually, and the consequences of that reorganization are very real. For example, the Mexican Americans and Puerto Ricans in Chicago whom Felix Padilla studied may not find a comprehensive Hispanic or Latino identity particularly congenial, but it is the operative category through which much of the surrounding world deals with them.[6] To reject it is to ignore a widely recognized and potentially useful basis of organization and action. This doesn't mean that they have to abandon the more exclusive identities they already carry, but it strongly encourages them to add the panethnic identity to their repertoire of self-concepts and bases of action.

The challenge then moves from category to content, from label to narrative. If, for whatever reason, the category cannot be rejected or ignored, then a new question emerges. To what does this new identity refer? What is the story that lies behind it? With what cargo is the vessel of identity—launched by outsiders—going to be filled, and by whom?

Here the panethnic situation is again distinctive. Those outsiders who first established the category already have a story to tell: the story that they attached to the category when they invented it or applied it to this particular population in the first place. Of course the category—the vessel of identity—may be virtually empty of meaning: the assigned identity may be largely a convenience for outsiders, a way of simplifying complex social life, in which case the story says little more than "they came from there," or "they speak that language," or "they all look alike but different from us." But in many cases it is loaded with meaning. Africans newly brought to North America discovered not only an unknown identity here, a label with no referent in their own identity schemes. They also discovered an elaborate story attached to that identity that not only highlighted physical differences between them and Europeans but proposed a distinctive set of origins for them, distinguished them as constituting a "race," placed them in categorical opposition to another, White "race," and consistently interpreted actions and events in ways that denied virtually any equality between the two "races."[7] Throughout U.S. history Whites have used narratives of difference to both account for and justify the situations of African Americans, and to sustain the notion that they constitute a distinct category of persons.

At one time or another, virtually all groups construct more or less elaborate narratives that give sense and meaning to their lives and situations, and many do so in opposition to the stories told by others. Typically, however, they begin with materials of their own, with existing stories that they alter to fit new circumstances or integrate new events. In contrast, panethnic groups often have relatively little of their own to start with. Their panethnic identities are discovered. Therefore, they often begin with stories told by others that in many cases both propose a new category and attach a negative value to it. The task for the group is not so much to rewrite its own story to fit new circumstances and agendas as to claim the story in the first place, to wrestle authorship away from outsiders, to construct a counternarrative on occupied and unfamiliar terrain. The alternative to rejecting the category, in other words, is to provide a new story that can fill the category with new meaning.

Thus the making of a discovered identity potentially has three parts: discovering the category or label; discovering the already existing narrative—good or bad—to which the label refers; and establishing the story or stories that the newly self-conscious group itself wishes to tell. Of course there remains a critical question: which of these narratives—that told by outsiders or the insiders' own tale—will gain dominance in the society at large and come to represent the group in those arenas where group fortunes are determined? Both the category and its meaning are not only significant but potentially contested matters, and the outcome will depend to a large degree on the openness of the public arena to group claims and on the resources the group can bring to bear in the telling of its own story.

This chapter considers "American Indian" or "Native American" identity as a discovered, panethnic identity of the sort outlined here, tracing the making of that identity in the hands of both outsiders and insiders and the contest between outsider and insider narratives for dominance in the society at large.[8]

Outsider Narratives and American Indian Identity

Once upon a time there were no "Indians" in the Americas. Then Europeans arrived and, miraculously, "Indians" appeared.

The category "Indian" existed first in the mind of the European, designating the indigenous peoples of the Americas, and only later became part of native self-concepts. At the time of the European arrival in North America, no comparable category was to be found in native discourse.[9] Indians in fact drew sharp distinctions among themselves, articulating their own identities most prominently at the national (tribal) or subnational (e.g., band, village, or kinship group) level. Only much later did changing circumstances and the long history of interaction between Indians and Whites gradually teach them, through hard experience, the overwhelming significance of the Indian-White distinction. Only then did that category and the label attached to it become significant parts of Native American self-concepts, organizing individual and collective behavior.[10] In a sense, Christoper Columbus was not the only one who discovered "Indians" in the Americas. In time, and through the impact of the European continental endeavor, Native Americans discovered themselves.[11]

The label, however, beginning with Columbus's geographically mistaken *los Indios,* was there from the beginning of European contact. As with other ethnic labels, it soon had a narrative attached to it: an emerging European (eventually, Euro-American) story about Indians. That narrative was thin at the start—for many Europeans, Indians were simply the people who already lived in the New World when Europeans appeared—but in time, as Europeans learned and imagined more about the peoples they had discovered, the narrative became more elaborate and detailed. It also began to divide and fragment over time, as more Europeans and Euro-Americans met and interacted with more Indians in more places, until there were a number of narratives attached to the Indian label at the same or different times, authored by different sets of outsiders, each telling the story of this category of persons. Often overlapping, they changed as time went on. Some have endured for centuries, others have disappeared, and new ones have taken shape, each capturing a different aspect of the Indian-European encounter, each focused on particular and not always the same events, all largely composed and read through outsiders' experience and imagination. Some were privately shared or little known, while others came to achieve a broad currency and even places of dominance in public discussion and debate about Native Americans, giving content to the category and identity that the label "Indian" merely named.

Columbus's own first impressions of Indians offered sketchy but highly suggestive materials for a narrative of Indian identity. According to the *Diario* account of his first voyage to America, he found the Indians to be in complete awe of the Spaniards, timorous, even terrified. "[T]hey are . . . so timid that a hundred of them flee from one of our men." And elsewhere: "They . . . are all naked, and of no skill in arms, and so very cowardly that a thousand would not stand against three." On Hispaniola, when Columbus's men discharged some firearms, the Indians "all fell to the ground."[12]

Apparently eager to please the Spaniards, the Indians "gave of what they had willingly"; "they brought us water in gourds and in clay jugs . . . and they brought us all that they had in the world . . . and all so bigheartedly and so happily that it was a wonder." To Columbus the Indians seemed childlike, innocent, and credulous. "Any little thing given to them, as well as our coming, they considered great marvels; and they believed that we had come from the heavens." On Hispaniola, the people "love their neighbors as themselves, and they have the sweetest speech in the world; and [they are] gentle and are always laughing. . . . They want to see everything and ask what it is and what it is for!" When Coumbus's ship ran onto a shoal at night, the people of Hispaniola came out in their canoes and helped "with care and diligence" to lighten the ship, and their king and the people wept on behalf of the now grounded Spaniards. The Indians, he believed, had no religion; "they do not know what evil is; nor do they kill others, nor steal."[13]

Their obedience impressed him. "All obey [the judge or lord who rules over them] so that it is a marvel." Indeed, their obedience, their timorousness, their eagerness to please, their apparent lack of skill in the use of weapons, all led Columbus to conclude that "they should be good and intelligent servants"; "they are fit to be ordered about and made to work, plant, and do everything else that may be needed."[14]

As he started back toward Spain, however, Columbus came across Indians he assumed to be Caribs. He had heard of the Caribs from Indians he had already met, who claimed they were fearsome cannibals. They attacked some of Columbus's men, who fought them off, wounding at least two. When Columbus heard about this, he expressed ambivalence but "was pleased because now the Indians would fear the Christians, since without doubt the people there . . . are evildoers and . . . would eat men."[15]

In Columbus's narrative account of his expedition, then, we find the beginnings of a narrative of Indian identity: a selection of events from all those that occurred or were heard about over a period of three months of almost continuous interaction with native peoples; an ordering of those events, a linking of them to each other in particular ways; and a process of interpretation leading to a set of conclusions about who these people were. The result is not entirely consistent. In particular, Columbus's encounter with the supposed Caribs suggests things very different from his earlier impressions, and as Stephen Greenblatt points out, his ideas about the Indians he met changed over time and with subsequent expeditions.[16] It is an inchoate, unfocused narrative, lacking structure and elaboration. But it is a beginning nonetheless: the translation of events into identity, the making of a first European conception of Native Americans as, among other things, simple, childlike, credulous, timid, and without God.

We can see also in Columbus's account elements of two opposed versions of who Indians were that would dominate European and Euro-American perceptions for the following five centuries. On the one hand, in his impressions of Indian simplicity, generosity, and innocence, there are nascent suggestions of key elements in the idea of the noble savage and the romantic, idealized variations upon it; on the other, in his encounter with those "evildoers," the Caribs, and in his acceptance of Indian accounts of cannibalism and of hideous and fearsome savages populating lands Columbus did not reach, there are early elements of the idea of the Indian as morally worthless in various ways—barbarian, wastrel, vermin, "evildoers"—an obstacle in the path of progress. These ideas are scarcely developed here, but in time, over the course of European contact and settlement, they took more coherent and focused form in response to real or imagined events and interpretations of them that frequently reflected the interests of the interpreters. Each of these ideas, in other words, has narrative substructures.[17]

Robert Berkhofer attributes much of the elaboration of the noble-savage idea to the French, and in particular to French Jesuits in Canada and the Great Lakes and their annual publication (through much of the seventeenth century) of the Jesuit *Relations,* a running history of their work in America, which "often provided flattering descriptions of Native Americans and their ways of life in order to gain contributions for missionary work from the faithful and to prove points against their Jansenist and atheistic opponents."[18] Montaigne and other French scholars also contributed to the elaboration of the noble-savage concept through their idealized comparisons of Indian societies with French, arguing that Europeans were corrupting Indian societies, which were little acquainted with avarice and inequality.[19] English conceptions of Indians as living in an exalted state of nature also played a part in the construction of a distinctive and assigned Indian identity. Berkhofer captures the essence of the idea: "Modest in attitude if not always in dress, the noble Indian exhibited great calm and dignity in bearing, conversation, and even under torture. Brave in combat, he was tender in love for family and children. Pride in himself and independence of other persons combined with a plain existence and wholesome enjoyment of nature's gifts . . . the Indian, in short, lived a life of liberty, simplicity, and innocence.[20]

The noble-savage narrative found its clearest expression in literature; one exemplar was Henry Wadsworth Longfellow's epic poem, *The Song of Hiawatha,* published in 1855.[21] Longfellow knew little about Native Americans, but using ethnographies, missionary accounts, and artistic representations of Indians, he produced in his tale of Hiawatha "the saga of a great culture hero: a George Washington of the primeval woods as it were, at one with nature and a devoted archetype of his people."[22] Among other things, Hiawatha establishes peace among his people, defends his mother's honor, struggles with the spirits of death and disease, converses with animals, and prophesies the coming of the Whites. Michael Kammen argues that the mid–nineteenth-century popularity of the poem "resulted, at least in part, from the solace it provided in assuaging the American conscience," troubled by moral issues attendant on the passage of Indians before the coercive thrust of emergent U.S. society.[23] Echoing Roy Harvey Pearce, Kammen argues that Longfellow's poem integrated Indians into America's own traditions. "Knowing and loving Hiawatha meant knowing the noble savage and perpetuating his traditions. Embarrassment (even shame) could be supplanted by vicarious pride via epic enchantment set in a remote and unknown place."[24] Thus the ennobled Indian became "an American hero."[25]

While the details vary widely, this fundamental perception of the Indian can be found in a broad array of literary and other creative works and through much of U.S. history up to the present day.[26] Berkhofer's description of the noble savage, just quoted, could easily describe the Sioux community portrayed in the enormously popular 1990 film *Dances with Wolves*. As Michael Dorris described the message of that film and others like it, "Indians may be poor, they may at first seem strange or forbidding or primitive, but, by golly, once you get to know them they have a thing or two to teach us about the Meaning of Life."[27]

The appeal of this general narrative can affect not only those who have little experience with Indians, but those who interact with them daily. More than a century after Longfellow's poem appeared, something of the same "vicarious pride" Kammen suggests was felt by Longfellow's readers was evident among Whites in a Canadian plains community. While they expressed little but contempt for their contemporary Indian neighbors, perceived as morally, physically, and spiritually degraded, they felt mostly nostalgia for those same Indians' nineteenth-century forebears, perceived as "brave but mysterious hunters of the buffalo, as great horsemen, and as persons of considerable dignity."[28] To these Whites, contemporary Indians were not "real" Indians; the "real" Indians were captured in tales of past behaviors and exploits. It would take a very different narrative, based on very different events, to capture their contemporary, degenerate progeny.

As these latter examples suggest, and as Berkhofer makes clear, over time the noble savage became more and more the romantic savage; the events in the narrative had less and less to do with Indian wisdom and the simplicity of Indian life and more and more to do with the passing of the Indian into history.[29] Gaining its broadest currency in the late nineteenth and early twentieth centuries, this more romantic notion flourished at a time when Euro-American society, secure in its control of both the American landscape and its original inhabitants, could afford a sentimental view in which tragic Indians, heads bowed in defeat, inevitably disappear into the western sunset. Wrote Joseph Dixon in 1913: "The door of the Indian's yesterdays opens to a new world—a world unpeopled with red men, but whose population fills the sky, the plains, with sad and spectre-like memories. . . . A land without the tall and sombre figure worshipping the Great Mystery; without suns and snows and storms—without the scars of battle, swinging war club, and flashing arrow—a strange, weird world, holding an unconquered race, vanquished before the tread of superior forces." Worshipping the Great Mystery, scars of battle, war club and flashing arrow—the events and practices that defined the Indian for many Americans are apparent in these few references. But now they were gone. "All serious students of Indian life and lore," wrote Dixon, "are deeply convinced of the insistent fact that the Indian, as a race, is fast losing its typical characters and is soon destined to pass completely away."[30] This passing became the central event in the romantic narrative of the vanishing Indian: an admirable race whose time was gone.

The heyday of "the vanishing Indian" coincided, not surprisingly, with the first great age of romantic Indian photography. Photographers like Edward S. Curtis and Dixon himself strove to convey something of both the mystical dimension of Indian life and the tragic aspect of Indian decline in their solemn, carefully posed, and typically touched-up pictures. Photographs such as Curtis's "The Vanishing Race—Navaho" and others of his works, and Dixon's "Skirting the Skyline," "War Memories," and "Sunset of a Dying Race" are extraordinarily evocative, but what they evoke is the already established romance of Indian freedom and decline. Defining events are captured or signified in the photographs; the titles tell us how to interpret those events. Together, they illuminate and invigorate the elaborate Euro-American narrative that already had constructed and identified the Indian subject. They present a people whose central activity now is the disappearing act itself. Only memories will be left behind, captured in these pictures.[31]

Nobility, dignity, and romance were keys to the first major efforts to bring tourists to Indian Country. It was not until early in the twentieth century that Indians became significant tourist attractions.[32] Among the pioneers in this nascent industry was the Santa Fe Railway, which used Indian motifs and tours of pueblos and cliff dwellings to promote its southwestern rail business. Indians may not have been vanishing in the railway's presentation of them, but they were clearly creatures of another time, relics of a distant American past. "The America of Coronado waits for you beside this motor trail," read one poster, under a painting of an Indian on horseback, promoting the railway's "Indian-detour."[33] This particular narrative was a pastiche: promotional art and photographs often showed Indians in buckskin and feathers, transporting to the Southwest the plains styles that were more familiar to many Americans. The events in this narrative were carefully chosen. For promotional purposes, Indians were frozen in time. They became the people who still lived in the old, "changeless" ways, far off the beaten track in lost corners of the Southwest. They were a connection to antiquity and the sacred, doing things they supposedly had done forever, living in their sun-splashed pueblos, engaged in mysterious ceremonies, connected to—even part of—nature, at one and the same time culturally distant and physically and emotionally accessible.[34] The attendant promotional paintings and pictures conveyed dignity and continuity and a certain sympathy for Indians themselves, but, like the narrative they illustrated, they ignored the turbulent events that, by early in the twentieth century, had transformed Native Americans' lives.

Thus, in what we might think of as the noble-savage narrative and variations upon it, Indians are the people who lived harmoniously with nature, who loved and fiercely defended community but treasured their individual freedom, who spoke wisely and well and understood things in ways the rest of us never will, who suffered defeat with tragic dignity, and who, in many versions of the narrative, have long since disappeared. Through the ways they ostensibly lived and through what happened to them, they occupy the moral high ground.

At the other extreme are the various versions of the Indian as morally degraded or worthless. The moral high ground in these narrative constructions is occupied by Euro-Americans; Indians are the obstacles that lie between them and their mission of nation building, or Christianity, or progress. In the classic versions of this conception, Indians demonstrate in their actions their own essential brutishness and depravity and inspire the most extreme solutions. This is a narrative of the frontier, composed not in nostalgia but in conflict. Berkhofer again captures the esssentials of this version of the Indian: "Nakedness and lechery, passion and vanity led to lives of polygamy and sexual promiscuity among themselves and constant warfare and fiendish revenge against their enemies. . . . Cannibalism and human sacrifice were the worst sins, but cruelty to captives and incessant warfare ranked not far behind in the estimation of Whites. . . . Indolence rather than industry, improvidence in the face of scarcity, thievery and treachery added to the list of traits."[35]

Among the clearest demonstrations of Indian barbarity were their methods of warfare. Indians disdained the more formal European approach to battle, meeting in massed ranks upon the field, in favor of guerilla tactics, a devious "skulking" that Europeans found contemptible.[36] Their raids on the outlying settlements of New England, erupting in a burst of sudden, intense violence, often at night, spread terror among White frontier settlers; for them, Indians were part of the chaotic disorder of the wilderness, a perilous world beyond society.

And Indians took captives. Captivity, in the Euro-American perception, presented Whites with the most profound challenges possible to their faith and their culture.[37] The physical trials were bad enough. Stories of captivity from the northeastern colonies and states include numerous accounts of the horrifying trek back to Canada or deeper into the western wilderness, often in winter, with Indians killing those who could not keep up. But the spiritual and moral trials were at least as difficult. Separated from their own society, living in savage circumstances, tormented in body and soul, and exposed to the barbaric practices of the Indians, White captives found themselves "figuratively in hell."[38] It was a hell filled, in the Euro-American mind, with devilish behavior, from gluttony, lust, cannibalism, and torture to paganism and idolatry. It was devilishly tempting as well—a significant number of captives were adopted into tribes and, when given the opportunity to return to their homes, chose to remain with the Indians—which was a key part of the horror Euro-Americans found in the captivity idea: the temptation to slip backward into a savage, precivilized life. Thus captivity tales made of the Indian "the consummate villain, the beast who hatcheted fathers, smashed the skulls of infants, and carried off mothers to make them into squaws," and who threatened to draw Whites back into ignorance and sin.[39]

While this view of the morally degraded Indian doubtless represented what many Whites truly believed, it also served a purpose. The practices and behaviors—the events—emphasized in these narratives of depravity presented a stark contrast to how most Euro-Americans perceived themselves. It encouraged the perception of White civilization as greatly superior to Indian cultures and thereby provided justification for the White advance.[40] A central part of that justification came not only from the reprehensible things that Indians did but from the far more respectable things they neglected to do. Governor John Winthrop of the Massachusetts Bay Colony argued in 1629 that the Indians "enclose no land, neither have they any settled habitation, nor any tame cattle to improve the land by." Whites, therefore, were justified in taking much of it. The Swiss jurist Vattel claimed that by moving their habitations through the countryside, Indians forfeited their legal right to the land, while President Andrew Jackson argued that Indians had no right to lands "on which they have neither dwelt nor made improvements."[41]

In its extreme version, this narrative made its racism explicit, and recommended commensurately extreme solutions. In 1866 the Kearny, Nebraska, *Herald* declared:

"Nothing is more absurd to the man who has studied the habits of the Indian savage than to talk of making permanent treaty negotiations with these heartless creatures. They are destitute of all the promptings of human nature.... The best and only way to reconcile the blood-washed animal will be to impose upon him a worse schooling than has ever befallen the inferior races."[42] Added the *News* of Emporia, Kansas, in 1870, "Extermination is a terrible word; but finally, we fear, they will come to know fully its bitter meaning, unless they subdue their wild restless natures and consent to engage in the peaceful pursuits of civilization."[43]

Instead of the noble or romantic savage, here we find the Indian as simply savage. Indians were variously those who not only engaged in but instigated "savage war,"[44] who demonstrated barbaric practices in every aspect of their lives, who failed to live up to the standards and values of Euro-Americans, and who, in their profligate and indolent ways, impeded the progress of civilization.

Of course there have been numerous variations on these two themes—the noble or romantic Indian and the morally worthless Indian—and some of the stories are more complex than these abstracted versions suggest.[45] Nor did every version of the Indian fit easily into one or the other of these. Somewhere in between, for example, was the Indian as presented by William F. Cody in "Buffalo Bill's Wild West," the extraordinarily successful commercial entertainment that from the early 1880s until World War I introduced hundreds of thousands of Americans and huge crowds overseas to the romance of the West and civilization's progress across it. Cody's program of reproduced scenes and episodes from the history of the West included Indian performers, among them some of the most famous figures of the day. Geronimo, Sitting Bull, Chief Joseph, and others appeared from time to time during the show's thirty years of touring. In the show, Indians did the things that fit Cody's vision of the West, reenacting the Custer fight, attacking the cabins of White settlers, hunting buffalo, and they were thus introduced to the public. Their actions in performance were central events in Cody's construction of Indians, part of the making of an Indian identity for public consumption. That identity in turn was part of Cody's larger enterprise, constructing his own narrative history of the American West. Cody's early shows took place before the last of the Indian wars had come to an end, and they presented the Indian as obstacle and threat. But in later years the point of the narrative changed. Bringing together veterans from each side in the Indian wars, Cody emphasized reconciliation and "the integration of the Indian into 'American' life as 'Former Foe—Present Friend.'"[46] Even as the Indians in his production theatrically abandoned the warpath for American civilization, they remained his invention. He simply added new events to indicate their new character.

Later voices transfigured these narratives in various ways. In the early decades of the twentieth century the destitute-Indian narrative emerged, in which those who had failed to vanish on cue were left to vegetate on dismal reservations under the negligent administration of the federal government.[47] In this account the critical events had become federal actions and policies that produced an Indian who did nothing at all. A descendant of that account is the contemporary welfare-dependent–Indian narrative, in which individual Indians soak up federal handouts and tribal governments grow like parasitic fungi, luxuriating in poverty. The federal government is again at fault in this more contemporary version, but Indians are hardly blameless. Once again, among the critical events in this narrative are the things Indians *don't* do: work, save for the future, take responsibility for themselves, and so on.

On the more approving side, in the 1960s—although it had earlier manifestations[48]—the environmental Indian narrative appeared, in which inherently ecological Indians nurtured and protected the wilderness. Eventually an Indian actor named Iron Eyes Cody, in a memorable television commercial, gathered the entire narrative into one symbolic tear, reflecting on how the world had changed. Among the generalized events—explicit or implicit—in this narrative were Indian ecological stewardship and conservation. This narrative and the Indian sensibility it described became central iconic themes in some parts of the environmental movement and the counterculture.[49] Along with it—and often connected to it—came the spiritual or New Age Indian narrative, focused variously on animist religious practices, prophecies of one kind or another, and an assortment of events in which individual Indians were believed to demonstrate extraordinary spiritual consciousness and insight. In both of these narratives, what Indians did, left to their own devices, was harmonize.

Although the details in these various narratives changed over time, some of the key elements remained very much the same. The environmental and New Age Indian narratives, for example, draw on noble-savage imagery, while key elements in the morally-worthless–Indian narrative have repeatedly appeared in White accounts of Indians.

Recurrent Features of Outsider Indian Narratives

These outsider narratives of Indian identity have varied in nature and over time, but they have tended to share certain characteristics or themes. First, like all identity narratives, they are simplifications. In their selection of events, in the linkages they draw among events, and in the interpretations they make, they simplify and generalize. They do so partly by necessity: the full story of any people is likely to be an unwieldy tale and more complex than most persons, insiders or outsiders, ultimately can know. They also do so by choice: events are selected in or out of such tales and are linked and interpreted in ways that construct particular kinds of identities, often to fit particular sets of interests. The life of virtually any people can supply material enough—factual or mythical—for a number of quite different identity narratives. Thus the worthless-Indian narrative takes certain real or imagined events as emblematic, places them at the center of the narrative, and ignores events that do not fit the meanings thus constructed. Similarly, the environmental-Indian narrative ignores the complexity of Indian/environment relations, both historically and today, in favor of a generalized and simplified version of those relations and a simplified version of Native Americans themselves.

Second, among the ways these narratives have been simplifications is in their tendency to assume a fundamental uniformity among Indian peoples. The diversity of native peoples was apparent to Europeans, who found it a curiosity, but it was vastly overshadowed in their perception by the differences they saw between Indians as a whole and themselves.[50] Today, that uniformity often continues to be assumed, supporting the supratribal identity it takes for granted. Euro-American narratives about Indians typically are just that: about Indians, not about distinct native peoples.

Third, a central theme in most Euro-American narratives well into the twentieth century has been the diametric opposition between Indians and Whites.[51] This was most apparent early on in the idea of Europe as civilization, order, and discipline, and Indians as savagery, disorder, and a dangerous kind of freedom. Indians had no society. As Stephen Greenblatt says, to the early Europeans Indians were "the people who live outside of all just order, apart from settled human community and hence from the very condition of the virtuous life."[52] Thus the story Europeans told about Indians was fundamentally opposed to the story they told about themselves.

The selection of events in each case made the point. The story of Europe was filled with achievement, a tale of progress toward both civilization and grace. The story of the Indian was frequently vacant.[53] Mistaking as knowledge their ignorance of Indian histories and cultures, Europeans often saw native peoples as ignorant, idle, and unaccomplished. Their narrative about Indians was composed of immediate events and behaviors—the generalized anecdotal trivia (albeit often horrifying) of everyday life. Their story about themselves, on the other hand, was a creation tale. Their project was society itself; building it was a grand endeavor.

Of course the noble-savage idea reversed these roles without abandoning the mirror image. In noble-savage narratives it was Indians who represented a finer state of being, Europeans who were corrupt. Some of the more recent outsider narratives—the environmental Indian, for example, or the Indian as victim[54]—likewise have transposed the content of the comparison, but the focus on difference remains: whatever the story, Indians are Other: they do things differently.

Fourth, the narratives of Indians told by others have tended to be embedded in larger narratives. For the most part, they are sideshows, while the main act goes on in a larger arena. Among the broader narratives of which the Indian story has been a part are what William Deverell calls "the super-narrative" of the American West, and beyond that the metanarrative of American identity and nation building as well as the narrative of Whiteness, the tale through which European Americans constructed themselves.[55] The differences between Indians and Whites that framed the Indian narrative were often crucial to these larger ones as well. William Cronon writes, for example, that "by making Indians the foil for its story of progress, the frontier plot made their conquest seem natural, commonsensical, inevitable."[56]

Fifth, the narratives have changed over time, and in so doing reflected the changing needs of the society that composed them. Thus during times of peace Indians were noble savages; in time of war, they were vermin; and so on.[57]

Through selection, plotting, and interpretation, these narratives have supplied variable content to the label "Indian" or "Native American" and thereby have given it meaning. They constructed a set of changing supratribal identities, assigned by others, that were more than labels; they were the highly selective story of a people (actually, although often ignored within the narratives themselves, of a set of peoples).[58] That story has a subject (Indians); it has action (events, the things Indians do or have done to them); it has attached to it—and typically attaches to Indians—a value (negative or positive in various ways). And it has dominance. For much of the history of Indian-White interaction, these are the stories that have prevailed, the narratives behind the identity. If there has been a struggle for preeminence, it has been a struggle among outsider narratives over which one will most powerfully shape the public consciousness of Native Americans. And those narratives, in turn, have been discovered by Indians as the larger society's conceptions of who they are and as the bases of that society's actions toward them.

American Indian Counternarratives

As noted at the start of this chapter, panethnic identities often begin as what I have called "discovered" identities: categories chosen and assigned by others and discovered, already formed and filled with content, by those they identify. As also noted, however, the groups they identify have choices. Their choices are limited by the power of the assigners to organize the lives of smaller, subordinate, or otherwise disadvantaged groups. Those groups can struggle to retain the identities they already carry in their own minds, and in favorable circumstances they may be able also to reject or ignore the identity they have been assigned. But they also can set out to alter the meaning of the new identity, in effect, to rewrite the narrative attached to it and fill the category with new meaning and content.

Indians do both. While they accept and eventually even adopt the supratribal category originally proposed by others, they also insist on its inadequacy, asserting the survival and diversity of tribal societies and, in some cases, narrating and producing their own tribal histories for a larger audience.[59] They also set out to change the content of the category "American Indian" or "Native American." They begin to fashion supratribal narratives of their own, "counternarratives"[60] of Indianness through which they claim authorship of their own story, and thereby make their own identity claims.

Of course Indian narratives are much more difficult to trace prior to the twentieth century than Euro-American ones are, owing to the sketchiness of the written record.[61] Native Americans always had stories to tell, including identity stories. In many Indian societies the public presentation of self was a narrative act explicitly linking identity and event.[62] It claimed, in essence, "Listen to what I have done, and it will tell you who I am." At the collective level, most indigenous societies in what is now the United States had their own origin or creation tales. In effect, these were identity narratives relating the events that created a people.[63] Beyond that, Indian leaders in negotiations with Whites often articulated tribal claims in terms of past actions, pointing out, for example, that they had hunted certain valleys for generations or had buried their grandfathers and grandmothers in certain places. For many Indians, both individually and collectively, stature, rights, and identity were embedded in acts, defined by events and their outcomes, which were told repeatedly within the community.

But Native Americans lacked the means to tell those stories in ways the larger society might hear. The dynamics of identity narratives, after all, are dynamics of power, having to do with authorship and dominance: whose voice will prevail?[64] Throughout much of the history of Indian-White relations, the prevailing voices were Euro-American ones. Indians had little access to the public or, much of the time, to policymakers, and few of the resources necessary to make their own voices widely heard. They were silenced also by certain of the dominant outsider narratives that claimed to provide a sufficient account of who Indians were and suggested that Indians themselves had little of interest to say. Those who heard Indian accounts often were unimpressed, for Indian acts, as bases of claims to rights or stature, frequently failed to measure up to White standards.[65]

Furthermore, as already noted, at least in the early stages of Indian-White relations, Indians themselves had no "Indian" story to tell. The identity itself was new to them, not only as a label but as a concept: they did not see themselves as a single population. Even the European arrival failed at first to suggest such a thing. To the Cherokees, for example, according to Cherokee anthropologist Robert Thomas, "Englishmen and Creeks were . . . simply different kinds of outsiders."[66] But Native Americans soon discovered that in the eyes of most Europeans they occupied (and shared) a category apart. They discovered as well the meanings attached to that category and began to attach to it meanings of their own.

Some of these meanings or understandings echo Euro-American ones. One could have found support for the vanishing Indian narrative, for example, among some Native Americans themselves. In 1889, faced with the end of Sioux freedom and angered by his tribespeople's agreement to cede yet more land to the United States, the great Hunkpapa leader Sitting Bull announced, "Indians! There are no Indians left now but me."[67] Two Leggings, a Crow, brought his own story to an abrupt end once the Crows had been confined on the reservation, late in the nineteenth century. "Nothing happened after that," he concluded. "We just lived. There were no more war parties, no capturing of horses from the Piegans and the Sioux, no buffalo to hunt. There is nothing more to tell."[68]

In the late nineteenth and early twentieth centuries, however, most Indian identity narratives, as well as being heard by few non-Indians, remained tribal in focus. Sitting Bull may have talked about Indians, but it was his own people he was angry with, while the "we" in the Two Leggings narrative refers to the Crows. Nonetheless, the beginnings of an explicitly supratribal narrative were emerging by the early part of the twentieth century, in particular among those Indians who were making their ways in the larger society. One version of that narrative can be found in the thinking of the Society of American Indians (SAI), the first supratribal, national Indian political organization, founded in 1911.[69] Made up largely of educated Indians who had pursued professional paths in the non-Indian world as doctors, ministers, bureaucrats, and the like, the SAI had an explicitly assimilationist orientation. One of its leaders, Arthur C. Parker, a Seneca, wrote in the society's journal, which he edited, "The future of the Indians is with the White race, and in a civilization derived from the old world." Elsewhere he argued that "the Indian should accustom himself to the culture that engulfs him and to the force that directs it, that he should become a factor of it, and that once a factor of it he should use his revitalized influence and more advantageous position in asserting and developing the great ideals of his race for the good of the greater race, which is all mankind."[70]

This was a narrative of the future. The imagined Indian in this narrative would proudly claim a great heritage but no longer practice it, while searching out a place as an active contributor to the further advance of Western civilization, doing things of value and importance. The great events in the past would still define Indians, but even greater events were yet to come. The members of the SAI had seen the possibilities in their own lives.

But Parker's was an isolated voice, one that found little resonance in the lives of most tribespeople.[71] Its isolation was a product not only of its assimilationist orientation, with which at least some tribal people of the time, faced with dependency and destitution, might have agreed, but of its supratribalism, which was at odds with the tribal frameworks that still organized most Indians' lives. A comprehensive Indian identity had yet to be built, and the SAI's nascent narrative of that identity was too far removed from most Indians' experience to play a central role in that building process.

It was not until well into the twentieth century that a supratribal voice began to emerge on a significant scale, and not until recent decades that it began to gain national exposure. Two developments were involved: the emergence of a broader, supratribal identity among Native Americans, and the opening of the public arena to Indian voices. These developments eventually allowed those voices to compete with—and to some extent displace—dominant, outsider narratives about Indians.

A supratribal identity had been a long time in the making, but it flourished in the mid–twentieth century in the aftermath of World War II (in which numerous Indians served), in the movement (often circular) of large numbers of Indians from reservations to U.S. cities, and in the growth in Indian education, particularly at the college level. As a result of these experiences, increasing numbers of Native Americans began to think and act in supratribal, Indian terms as well as in tribal terms, creating in the process a broad base for Indian political action.[72]

At much the same time, twentieth-century changes in the larger society were making it more likely that Indian voices would be heard. The dominant, Euro-American narratives of Indian identity served certain purposes and met certain needs; as those needs changed, the rationale for the narratives changed as well. Thus, for example, the decline in the demand for Indian land after the early 1920s made room for a different conception of Indians, one less dominated by differences between their supposedly ignorant and wasteful patterns of landholding and use and those of the larger society.[73] Less certain of what was most important about Indians, that society was more open to alternative interpretations. By then also, with the passing of the frontier, the United States had entered into that long period, not yet over, of romanticizing the American West. In this new emerging romance the Indian, disappearing down the sunset trail, became a glorious and tragic figure. Indians gained stature, as a general category, as they became a valued part of the American saga and no longer primarily an obstacle to its ultimate realization.

Such changes, in and of themselves, did not give Indians a voice in place of silence. But as the historical logic of interracial conflict began to fade and more romantic narratives prevailed, the Indian became a figure of growing interest to the nation.[74] By mid-century, Indian action had begun to lay the groundwork for a different narrative, particularly during and after World War II. Indian war heroes—the Navajo Code Talkers, for example, and Ira Hayes, the Pima Indian who was one of the Marines who raised the American flag over Iwo Jima, an event captured in the most famous photograph of the war—drew national attention and offered a new portrayal of Indians, although their stories were still told mostly by outsiders. Not until the 1960s did Indian voices begin to be widely heard, and a supratribal counternarrative begin to take shape. Changes in the audience certainly helped. By the 1960s, in the context of civil rights struggles and the war in Vietnam, there were growing doubts on the part of some sectors of the larger society about received versions of the grand narrative of U.S. history and life. At least as important were changes in Indians' own capabilities and resources. In the 1960s and 1970s, equipped with media savvy and organizational skills and facing a more interested audience, they began to tell their own stories.

The resultant narratives hardly form a well-integrated piece, or a finished one. Just as outsider narratives about Indians have varied, so have Indian accounts of themselves. There is no single Indian narrative but instead a number of stories, told by a variety of voices, in forms ranging from fiction and poetry to political statements and the work of Indian scholars. These stories emphasize different things and are occasionally in conflict with each other, and they change over time. But they share certain characteristics or themes that allow us to speak in general terms of an emergent counternarrative, an alternative version or set of versions of what it means to be Indian, rooted in Indians' own treatment of events, their selection, plotting, and interpretation.

Although it often focuses on the same events, this counternarrative tends to dispute the dominant narrative in both plotting and interpretation. A striking example is its treatment of Columbus. It acknowledges the centrality of Columbus's journey; indeed, it treats his first voyage as a world-altering event. But it takes that event not as an act of discovery but as an act of destruction, recasting Columbus not as discoverer of America but as destroyer of it, recasting Indian societies as victims of European invasion.[75] Similarly, the narrative reverses the larger society's colloquial version of the Indian wars, captured in midcentury television and movie images of Indians attacking wagon trains and army posts, focusing instead, for example, on savage White settler and military attacks on peaceful villages at Sand Creek in 1864 and the Washita River in 1868, and more generally on the Indian effort to defend their lands and communities before the Euro-American assault.

A small piece of this counternarrative-in-the-making was apparent during visits I made in the late 1980s to the Little Bighorn Battlefield in Montana, where in the summer of 1876 Lt. Col. George Armstrong Custer and his U.S. Seventh Cavalry attacked an enormous Sioux and Cheyenne village, and Custer and most of his command were killed. The traditional version of the battle, in which Sioux and Cheyenne warriors "massacred" Custer and his soldiers, was being replaced by a more complex account that situated the battle in the larger context of the federal effort that summer to drive the Sioux and Cheyennes once and for all from their traditional hunting grounds, force them onto reservations under federal control, and end their tribal ways of life and their extended and determined resistance. Individual Indians were among those presenting this revised official account on the battlefield. The specific events they discussed were not that different from those of the earlier narrative of Indian massacre, but the links among those events and their meanings, as presented in this new account, were very different.[76] Through their narrative of Indian practices and actions they also presented a very different Indian to the public—part victim, part defender of family and homeland, part skilled and enduring warrior. In renarrating the Custer fight, they reidentified themselves.

Among the recurrent themes in these counternarratives is the Indian as oppressed victim, not only historically but at the present time. In 1967 Clyde Warrior, president of the National Indian Youth Council (NIYC), testifying before the President's National Advisory Commission on Rural Poverty, said:

> Most members of the National Indian Youth Council can remember when we were children and spent many hours at the feet of our grandfathers listening to stories of the time when the Indians were a great people, when we were free, when we were rich, when we lived the good life . . . our people felt rich because they were free. They were rich in things of the spirit . . . we are poor in spirit because we are not free—free in the most basic sense of the word. We are not allowed to make those basic human choices and decisions about our personal life and about the destiny of our communities which is the mark of free mature people. We sit on our front porches or in our yards, and the world and our lives in it pass us by without our desires or aspirations having any effect.[77]

Two years later, William Pensoneau, another NIYC member, testifying at congressional hearings on Indian education, echoed Warrior: "We are totally administered. We can experience nothing directly but death. So we have turned to death . . . by drinking on railroad tracks in Ponca City and greeting our salvation train. We drown ourselves in wine and smother our brains in glue. The only time we are free is when we are drunk."[78]

The focus in these statements is as much on nonevents—what we cannot do—as on events—what we do instead, and what was done to us. At the collective level such victim narratives emphasize land loss, genocidal wars, repressive controls on cultural practice, and so on. They confront the "Indian as aggressor" theme of some dominant narratives with the "Indian as victim."

At the same time, while underlining the destructive impact of the European invasion and the strict administration of Indian communities, Indian counternarratives also emphasize survival. "We have endured. We are Indians," proclaimed the Pit River Indian Council in 1970, a narrative condensation of identity if ever there was one.[79] Contradicting the "poor in spirit" view presented by Warrior, this second theme focuses on events that show Indians not as vanishing or somehow decultured (as the dominant narratives typically held), but as enduring carriers of cultural and social continuities.[80] The "vanishing Indian" becomes the "enduring Indian."

A third recurrent theme is agency, in which the Indian as passive or incapacitated is replaced by the Indian as assertive actor. "The people are standing up," said Severt Young Bear during the 1973 occupation, by a group of Oglala traditionalists and Indian activists, of the village of Wounded Knee on South Dakota's Pine Ridge Sioux Reservation.[81] While his statement referred to the people of the Oglala Sioux tribe, protesting the heavy hand of the federal government and the actions of a tribal government that many Oglalas did not care for, he captured the sense of assertiveness that was pervading not only Indian country but emergent Indian counternarratives as well. Three books put together by Indians and published in the early 1970s gave voice and added dimension to Young Bear's sentiment. In 1972 an organization called Indians of All Tribes put together a book titled *Alcatraz Is Not an Island* that traced the Indian occupation of Alcatraz Island in San Francisco Bay in 1969–71.[82] In 1973, Akwesasne Notes published *Trail of Broken Treaties: B.I.A. I'm Not Your Indian Any More,* an account of a 1972 march on Washington, D.C., by Indians from around the country that culminated in the occupation of the headquarters of the Bureau of Indian Affairs. In 1974 the same organization published *Voices from Wounded Knee, 1973,* an account of the violent ten-week occupation and armed standoff at Wounded Knee.[83] Published at the height of the most radical phase of Indian activist politics and providing Indian accounts of three of the most dramatic incidents associated with the activist movement, these texts capture in words and photographs the reconstruction of Indian identity through action. What emerges in them is a reconstruction of Indians as people who challenge the federal government and the larger society, rise once again to the defense of community and culture, turn to their own traditions for strength and guidance, and seize the opportunity to make their own future.[84]

Other themes are also apparent in Indian counternarratives, but these three—the Indian as victim, survivor, and actor—appear repeatedly in various forms. They directly confront much of what the dominant narratives, which frequently constructed Indians as dangerous obstacles, vanishing peoples, or silent and impotent remnants of another time, had to say.

These counternarratives also have tended to privilege certain events that constitute what we might call *critical narrative sites:* they are events or sequences of events that carry rare emotional power for group members and, as critical moments in their version of their story, shape the tale that they tell. In many Indian counternarratives, such critical sites have included one or more of the following: ancient geographical occupancy, the dispossession of Indian lands (and key events such as decisive military actions or acts of organized deception that were involved in that process), treaty making, treaty breaking, and the subsequent denial of sovereignty to Indian nations. Narration often focuses on these sites; they are the events or sequences where—through selection, plotting, and interpretation—much of the construction of both narrative and identity takes place.[85]

In recent years, however, another Indian narrative has been emerging that pays much less attention to these sites. Significant numbers of Indians moving to U.S. cities—the majority of the Indian population has been urban for two decades now—have begun to piece together a very different set of stories. Often disconnected from reservation life and even from tribal networks, they are more acutely aware of the fuzziness of the boundaries that separate Indian from non-Indian in such multiethnic and multiracial settings. The events they focus on are less likely to be treaties, land loss, and the tribal past than dislocation, marginalization, and the continual negotiation of a culturally complicated present. This is an Indian identity very much in the making, its narrative structure uncertain and complex.[86]

The divergences in these counternarratives echo a common pattern in panethnic identity narratives. Having discovered a narrative that links them in a common identity, Indians set out to rewrite that narrative in their own way. But as they do so, the result reflects the diversity of their experiences, histories, interests, and perspectives—a diversity that the original narratives composed by outsiders often ignored. Thus panethnic counternarratives are often as diverse and contradictory as outsider narratives are—if not more so. They reflect the comprehensive category originally invented by outsiders but reflect as well the divergent realities that the category struggles to embrace.

As we make the transition from twentieth century to twenty-first, these diverse Indian counternarratives have gained voice, exposure, and in some cases acceptance. Some have gained not only currency in certain sectors of the wider society but even, in some cases, dominance, becoming the prevailing stories told about Native Americans.

Narrative and Counternarrative

Despite their many differences, narrative and counternarrative share certain features. Both are simplifications. Like outsiders' narratives of Indian identity, Indian counternarratives select their events carefully and link and interpret them in particular ways, making particular kinds of Indians in the process. They, too, generalize. Among the Indians who appear in counternarratives are ones familiar from outsider narratives as well. The environmental Indian, for example, familiar from recent Euro-American narratives, is as much a staple of contemporary Indian ones, which often ignore the ways that Indians, too, on occasion radically altered the landscape, fitting it to their purposes. The noble savage is no stranger to Indian counternarratives, some of which include a different but no less romantic vision of the past than Euro-American ones do.

There is another significant parallel between Euro-American narratives and Indian counternarratives. The dominant narratives typically saw Indians as what Whites were not (for example, bloodthirsty, amoral, pagan, ignorant, out of control). The counternarratives also tend to see Indians as what Whites are not (for example, at one with nature, communitarian, egalitarian, spiritual). These are narratives of difference, with each resultant identity mirroring the other. In each case, through their own narrative constructions, the authors assure themselves of their distinctiveness and, often, superiority.

By now, on the other hand, narrative and counternarrative have begun to converge.[87] It is a measure of the change in the Indian situation and in the arena of public discourse that the dominant narrative now often looks to the Indian narrative as a guide, and that the idea that Indians might have their own stories to tell, that they should be allowed to tell them, and that those stories have their own lessons to teach, no longer seems as startling as it once did. Although Indian identity narratives—insider and outsider—remain diverse, it is the Indian voice that in recent decades has been getting louder, claiming a discovered category as its own.

Notes

Acknowledgment: I am grateful to Joane Nagel and Paul Spickard for helpful commentary during the writing of this paper.

1. Crawford Young, "Ethnicity and the Colonial and Post-Colonial State in Africa," in *Ethnic Groups and the State,* ed. Paul Brass (Totowa, N.J.: Barnes and Noble, 1985), 74.

2. Richard Alba, *Italian Americans: Into the Twilight of Ethnicity* (Englewood Cliffs, N.J.: Prentice-Hall, 1985).

3. Alba, *Italian Americans;* Stephen Cornell, "Land, Labour, and Group Formation: Blacks and Indians in the United States," *Ethnic and Racial Studies* 13 (July 1990): 368–88; Laura

Gomez, "What's In a Name? The Politics of Hispanic identity" (B.A. thesis, Harvard College, 1986); Yen Le Espiritu, *Asian American Panethnicity: Bridging Institutions and Identities* (Philadelphia: Temple University Press, 1992); Clarence Glick, "The Relations between Position and Status in the Assimilation of Chinese in Hawaii," *American Journal of Sociology* 47 (1942): 667–79.

4. See, for example, Espiritu, *Asian American Panethnicity.*

5. For more detail, see Cornell, "That's the Story of Our Life," in this volume, and, for some more general treatments of narrative and identity that suggest some of these points, George Steinmetz, "Reflections on the Role of Social Narratives in Working-Class Formation: Narrative Theory in the Social Sciences," *Social Science History* 16 (Fall 1992): 489–516; Margaret R. Somers and Gloria D. Gibson, "Reclaiming the Epistemological 'Other': Narrative and the Social Construction of Identity," in *Social Theory and the Politics of Identity,* ed. Craig Calhoun (Oxford, UK: Blackwell, 1994), 37–99.

6. Felix M. Padilla, *Latino Ethnic Consciousness: The Case of Mexican Americans and Puerto Ricans in Chicago* (Notre Dame, Ind.: University of Notre Dame Press, 1985).

7. Winthrop D. Jordan, *White over Black: American Attitudes toward the Negro, 1550–1812* (Baltimore: Penguin, 1968).

8. The focus of this paper is on supratribal, American Indian or Native American identity. While the notion of discovered identities is less applicable, with some important exceptions (see, e.g., Stephen Cornell, "The Transformations of Tribe: Organization and Self-Concept in Native American Ethnicities," *Ethnic and Racial Studies* 11 [January 1988]: 27–47), to tribal identities, the narrative processes involved in their construction would be fundamentally similar.

9. There is some evidence, however, of a general category of outsiders or strangers; see, for example, Thomas (1968, p. 130).

10. Stephen Cornell, *The Return of the Native: American Indian Political Resurgence* (New York: Oxford University Press, 1988); Cornell, "Land, Labour, and Group Formation."

11. I am indebted to Joane Nagel for a remark along these lines.

12. Oliver Dunn and James E. Kelley, Jr., *The Diario of Christopher Columbus's First Voyage to America, 1492–1493* (Norman: University of Oklahoma Press, 1989), 143, 237, 287. Both Columbus's original *Diario* and the only known copy of it have long since disappeared. The material here is drawn from Bartolomé de las Casas's manuscript version—partly quoted, partly summarized—of Columbus's original. David Henige ("To Read Is to Misread, to Write Is to Miswrite: Las Casas as Transcriber," in *Amerindian Images and the Legacy of Columbus,* ed. René Jara and Nicholas Spadaccini [Minneapolis: University of Minnesota Press, 1992], 198–229) recently has challenged the accuracy of las Casas's transcription, but the issue is of little significance here, where what matters is what the transcription said, not its accuracy in representing Columbus's own words.

13. Ibid., 65, 255, 109, 281, 127, 143.

14. Ibid., 275, 65, 237.

15. Ibid., 333, 335.

16. Stephen Greenblatt, *Marvelous Possessions: The Wonder of the New World* (Chicago: University of Chicago Press, 1991).

17. These very different ideas of Indians have received much scholarly attention. The discussion here cannot pretend to be exhaustive; my purpose is simply to suggest the narrative form and derivation of these ideas and, in the process, to suggest how outsiders constructed and assigned to Indians different supratribal identities.

18. Robert F. Berkhofer, Jr., *The White Man's Indian: Images of the American Indian from Columbus to the Present* (New York: Random House, 1978), 74.

19. Ibid., 74–76.

20. Ibid., 28.

21. Henry Wadsworth Longfellow, "The Song of Hiawatha," in *The Writings of Henry Wadsworth Longfellow,* vol. 4 (1855; reprint, New York: Houghton Mifflin, 1886).

22. Michael Kammen, *Mystic Chords of Memory: The Transformation of Tradition in American Culture* (New York: Vintage, 1993), 83.

23. Ibid., 85.

24. Roy Harvey Pearce, *Savagism and Civilization: A Study of the Indian and the American Mind* (Baltimore: Johns Hopkins University Press, 1965), 191–92; Kammen, *Mystic Chords,* 85.

25. Richard Slotkin, *Regeneration through Violence: The Mythology of the American Frontier, 1600–1860* (Middletown, Conn.: Wesleyan University Press, 1973), 363.

26. On the noble-savage idea see, in addition to Berkhofer, *White Man's Indian;* Julie Schimmel, "Inventing 'the Indian,'" in *The West as America: Reinterpreting Images of the Frontier, 1820–1920,* ed. William H. Truettner (Washington: Smithsonian Institution Press, 1991), 149–89; and especially Pearce, *Savagism and Civilization,* chap. 5.

27. Michael Dorris, "Dances with Indians," in *Paper Trail: Essays* (New York: Harper Collins, 1994), 261.

28. Niels Winther Braroe, *Indian and White: Self-Image and Interaction in a Canadian Plains Community* (Stanford, Calif.: Stanford University Press, 1975), 136.

29. Berkhofer, *White Man's Indian,* 78–80.

30. Joseph K. Dixon, *The Vanishing Race: The Last Great Indian Council* (1913; reprint, New York: Popular Library, 1972), 4, 5.

31. These four photos and others can be found in Tom Robotham, *Native Americans in Early Photographs* (San Diego: Thunder Bay, 1994); also see Dixon, *Vanishing Indian,* and numerous collections of Curtis's work.

32. Earl Pomeroy, *In Search of the Golden West: The Tourist in Western America* (New York: Knopf, 1957).

33. T. C. McLuhan, *Dream Tracks: The Railroad and the American Indian, 1890–1930* (New York: Abrams, 1985), 22.

34. See McLuhan, *Dream Tracks;* also John A. Jakle, *The Tourist: Travel in Twentieth-Century North America* (Lincoln: University of Nebraska Press, 1985); Mark Neumann, "The Commercial Canyon: Culturally Constructing the 'Other' in the Theater of the West," in *Discovered Country: Tourism and Survival in the American West,* ed. Scott Norris (Albuquerque: Stone Ladder, 1994), 196–209.

35. Berkhofer, *White Man's Indian,* 28.

36. Patrick Malone, *The Skulking Way of War: Technology and Tactics among the New England Indians* (Lanham, Md.: Madison Books, 1991), 23–24.

37. On captivity narratives and Indian captivity itself, see Slotkin, *Regeneration through Violence,* chaps. 4 and 5, and John Demos, *The Unredeemed Captive: A Family Story from Early America* (New York: Knopf, 1994).

38. Slotkin, *Regeneration through Violence,* 109.

39. Pearce, *Savagism and Civilization,* 58. But see June Namias, *White Captives: Gender and Ethnicity on the American Frontier* (Chapel Hill: University of North Carolina Press, 1993), especially chap. 6, for evidence that at least some captivity narratives conveyed much more complex readings of Indian character.

40. The task of establishing and extinguishing Native American rights to land and, more generally, of justifying conquest preoccupied a good deal of European and early American legal and political thinking for several centuries, much of it having to do with just how Indians differed from Europeans. For a thorough discussion see Robert A. Williams, Jr., *The American Indian in Western Legal Thought: The Discourses of Conquest* (New York: Oxford University Press, 1990).

41. Winthrop is quoted in Berkhofer, *White Man's Indian,* 121. On Vattel, see Albert K. Weinberg, *Manifest Destiny: A Study of Nationalist Expansion in American History* (Chicago: Quandrangle, 1963), 78. Jackson is quoted in Ronald L. Satz, *American Indian Policy in the Jacksonian Era* (Lincoln: University of Nebraska Press, 1975), 19. Validity is not the issue here, where the focus is on what identity narratives claim, right or wrong. Nevertheless, it is perhaps worth pointing out that both the governor and the jurist had their facts mixed up. Most eastern Indians in the seventeenth century were both town dwellers and horticulturalists.

42. Quoted in Robert Winston Mardock, *The Reformers and the American Indian* (Columbia: University of Missouri Press, 1971), 86.

43. Quoted in H. Craig Miner, *The Corporation and the Indian: Tribal Sovereignty and Industrial Civilization in Indian Territory, 1865–1907* (Columbia: University of Missouri Press, 1976), 31.

44. "The premise of 'savage war' is that ineluctable political and social differences—rooted in some combination of 'blood' and culture—make coexistence between primitive natives and civilized Europeans impossible on any basis other than subjugation. Native resistance to European settlement therefore takes the form of a fight for survival; and because of the 'savage' and bloodthirsty propensity of the natives, such struggles inevitably become 'wars of extermination'.... In its most typical formulations, the myth of 'savage war' blames Native Americans as instigators." Richard Slotkin, *Gunfighter Nation: The Myth of the Frontier in Twentieth-Century America* (New York: Harper Collins, 1992), 12.

45. For one example, see Sherry L. Smith, *The View from Officers' Row: Army Perceptions of Western Indians* (Tucson: University of Arizona Press, 1990), who examines U.S. Army officers' perceptions of Native Americans in the nineteenth-century West. Diaries, memoirs, and other documents written by army officers and troops, many of whom spent years fighting Indians, negotiating with tribes, and administering reservations, reveal in the aggregate a fascinating mixture of admiration, contempt, subtle insight, and blatant stereotyping. They also show more explicitly than many documents the links between the narration of events and summary identity statements about Indians.

46. Slotkin, *Gunfighter Nation,* 81. On Cody and the Wild West show, see Slotkin's chapter 2, and, for a brief historical account of the show, along with photographs of Indians in performance in it, Joseph G. Rosa and Robin May, *Buffalo Bill and his Wild West: A Pictorial Biography* (Lawrence: University of Kansas Press, 1989).

47. For example, Lewis Meriam and associates, *The Problem of Indian Administration* (Baltimore: Johns Hopkins University Press, 1928); Richard Harding Davis, *The West from a Car Window* (New York: Harper and Brothers, 1892), chap. 6.

48. See, for example, O. Douglas Schwarz, "Plains Indian Influences on the American Environmental Movement: Ernest Thompson Seton and Ohiyesa," in *The Struggle for the Land: Indigenous Insight and Industrial Empire in the Semiarid World,* ed. Paul A. Olson (Lincoln: University of Nebraska Press, 1990), 273–88.

49. Like most identity narratives, this one mixes fact and fiction. For a useful discussion see J. Baird Callicott, "American Indian Land Wisdom," in *Struggle for the Land,* ed. Olson, 255–72. For an examination of the complex historical relations between Native Americans and the natural environment in one region of the country, see William Cronon, *Changes in the Land: Indians, Colonists, and the Ecology of New England* (New York: Hill and Wang, 1983).

50. Berkhofer, *White Man's Indian,* 26–27.

51. Pearce, *Savagism and Civilization;* Slotkin, *Regeneration through Violence.*

52. Greenblatt, *Marvelous Possessions,* 68.

53. Ibid., 104.

54. Slotkin, *Gunfighter Nation,* 590.

55. William Deverell, "Fighting Words: The Significance of the American West in the History of the United States," *Western Historical Quarterly,* 25 (Summer 1994): 192.

56. William Cronon, "A Place for Stories: Nature, History, and Narrative," *Journal of American History,* 78 (March 1992): 1352.

57. See, for example, Gary B. Nash, "Red, White, and Black: The Origins of Racism in Colonial America," in *The Origins of American Slavery and Racism,* ed. Donald L. Noel (Columbus, Ohio: Merrill, 1972).

58. These various narratives found ample illustration in artistic treatments of the Indian. For relevant, critical discussions that follow these diverse representations of Indians in painting and other graphic arts through the history of White settlement of the West and on into the twentieth century, see Alex Nemerov, "'Doing the "Old America"': The Image of the American West, 1880–1920," *The West as America,* ed. Truettner, 285–343; and Schimmel, "Inventing 'the Indian.'" And, for some useful skepticism regarding some of the essayists' conclusions, see Dell Hymes's review of the book in which these essays appear, "Indian Identities: What It Was and Is to Be a Native North American," *Times Literary Supplement,* August 7, 1992, pp. 3–4.

59. For example, N. Scott Momaday, *The Way to Rainy Mountain* (Albuquerque: University of New Mexico Press, 1969); Joe S. Sando, *The Pueblo Indians* (San Francisco: Indian Historian Press, 1976); Joseph Medicine Crow, *From the Heart of the Crow Country: The Crow Indians' Own Stories* (New York: Crown, 1992); George Weeks, *Mem-ka-weh: Dawning of the Grand Traverse Band of Ottawa and Chippewa Indians* (Sutton's Bay, Mich.: Grand Traverse Band of Ottawa and Chippewa Indians, 1992).

60. Personal Narratives Group, *Interpreting Women's Lives: Feminist Theory and Personal Narratives* (Bloomington: Indiana University Press, 1989), 11.

61. Owing to space and time constraints, my own tracing of those narratives here is necessarily sketchy as well.

62. Peter Nabokov, *Two Leggings: The Making of a Crow Warrior* (Lincoln: University of Nebraska Press, 1967); Bernard Mishkin, *Rank and Warfare among the Plains Indians* (1940; reprint, Lincoln: University of Nebraska Press, 1992).

63. See, for example, Christopher Vecsey, *Imagine Ourselves Richly: Mythic Narratives of North American Indians* (New York: Crossroads, 1988).

64. See Cornell, "Story of Our Life."

65. This has been a persistent complaint. A 1977 letter to the editors of *Time* magazine, for example, commenting on a story about Indian land claims and echoing earlier Euro-Americans like John Winthrop and Andrew Jackson, argued, "The Indians did not own the land in America; they simply used it much as animals do. Ownership comes with improvements, such as fences, trees, roads, buildings, etc." "Letters," *Time,* May 2, 1977, p. 7.

66. Robert K. Thomas, "Pan-Indianism," in *The American Indian Today,* ed. Stuart Levine and Nancy O. Lurie (Baltimore: Penguin, 1968), 130.

67. James Mooney, *The Ghost-Dance Religion and the Sioux Outbreak of 1890,* 14th Annual Report of the Bureau of Ethnology, 1892–93, Part 2 (Washington: Government Printing Office, 1896), 861.

68. Nabokov, *Two Leggings,* 197. Cf. Lucullus Virgil McWhorter, *Yellow Wolf: His Own Story* (1940; reprint, Caldwell, Idaho: Caxton, 1991), 229, on Yellow Wolf, a Nez Perce, who was convinced that anything that happened after the end of the Nez Perce War would be "of little moment to anyone." As Arnold Krupat comments, "Yellow Wolf attempted to adhere to the Plains sense of the *coup* story, the story of actions performed in war, as the central meaning of the request to 'tell his story.'" Kurpat, *For Those Who Come After: A Study of Native American Autobiography* (Berkeley: University of California Press, 1985), 123.

69. Hazel W. Hertzberg, *The Search for an American Indian Identity* (Syracuse, N.Y.: Syracuse University Press, 1971); Vine Deloria, Jr., "The Rise and Fall of the First Indian Movement: A Review Article," *Historian* 33 (August 1971): 656–64.

70. Quoted in Hertzberg, *American Indian Identity*, 63–64, 139–40.

71. Deloria, "First Indian Movement."

72. Stan Steiner, *The New Indians* (New York: Dell, 1968); Richard W. Trottier, "Charters of Panethnic Identity: Indigenous American Indians and Immigrant Asian-Americans," in *Ethnic Change*, ed. Charles F. Keyes (Seattle: University of Washington Press, 1981), 272–305; Cornell, *Return of the Native*.

73. Cornell, *Return of the Native*.

74. For example, see McLuhan, *Dream Tracks*; Marta Weigle, "From Desert to Disney World: The Santa Fe Railway and the Fred Harvey Company Display the Indian Southwest," *Journal of Anthropological Research* 45 (Spring 1989): 115–37; and Neumann, "Commercial Canyon," for discussions of the romanticization and commercialization of the Indian by the emergent tourist industry in the American Southwest at the turn of the century and after.

75. For example, United Nations' Working Group on Indigenous Populations, "Declaration of Indigenous Nations of the World in Respect to the 500 Year Anniversary of the Invasion of 'America,'" *Americans before Columbus* 18 (1990), 4; James Riding In, "The Politics of the Columbus Celebration: A Perspective of Myth and Reality in United States Society," *American Indian Culture and Research Journal* 17 (1993): 1–16.

76. See also the account of changing Little Bighorn narratives in Edward T. Linenthal, "From Shrine to Historic Site: The Little Bighorn Battlefield National Monument," in *Legacy: New Perspectives on the Battle of the Little Bighorn*, ed. Charles E. Rankin (Helena: Montana Historical Society Press, 1996), 307–17.

77. Clyde Warrior, "We Are Not Free," in *Red Power: The American Indians' Fight for Freedom*, ed. Alvin M. Josephy, Jr. (New York: McGraw-Hill, 1971), 72.

78. Quoted in Edgar S. Cahn and David W. Hearne, eds., *Our Brother's Keeper: The Indian in White America* (Washington: New Community Press, 1969), 139.

79. Pit River Indian Council, "We Have Endured. We Are Indians," in *Red Power*, ed. Josephy, 233.

80. For example, Gerald Vizenor, *Tribal Scenes and Ceremonies* (Minneapolis: Nodin, 1976); Paula Gunn Allen, *The Sacred Hoop: Recovering the Feminine in American Indian Tradition*, 2d ed. (Boston: Beacon, 1992); Duane Champagne, *American Indian Societies: Strategies and Conditions of Political and Cultural Survival* (Cambridge, Mass.: Cultural Survival, 1989).

81. *Trail of Broken Treaties: B. I. A. I'm Not Your Indian Anymore* (Mohawk Nation: Akwesasne Notes, 1973), 33.

82. Peter Blue Cloud, *Alcatraz Is Not an Island* (Berkeley: Wingbow Press, 1972).

83. *Trail of Broken Treaties; Voices from Wounded Knee, 1973* (Mohawk Nation: Akwesasne Notes, 1974).

84. Cornell, *Return of the Native*; Joane Nagel, *American Indian Ethnic Renewal: Red Power and the Resurgence of Identity and Culture* (New York: Oxford, 1996). See Nagel, *American Indian Ethnic Renewal*, and Nagel and Troy Johnson, eds., *Alcatraz Revisited: The 25th Anniversary of the Occupation, 1969–1971*, special issue, *American Indian Culture and Research Journal* 18 (1994), as well for the comments of Native Americans who were either directly involved in these and related events or were observers of them, interviewed or writing their own accounts twenty-five years later. They offer valuable perspective both on the events and, in some cases, on the ways those events affected their sense of themselves as Indians.

85. This is especially apparent in tribal identity narratives. For example, for some Indian nations, treaty signing holds enormous importance, even in contemporary times. The Yakama

Nation in Washington was created through the signing of an 1855 treaty with the United States that formally confederated fourteen separate tribes and bands. That treaty and its signing are featured prominently in the Yakama coat of arms and have been celebrated by Yakamas as the foundational event in their peoplehood. In memorial editions in 1978, the tribal paper claimed, in essence (here I paraphrase), that "we are the people who signed the treaty of 1855" ("1855 Yakima Treaty," *Yakima Nation Review,* February 5, 1978, p. 1; "1855 Yakima Treaty Chronicles," *Yakima Nation Review,* June 23, 1978, pp. 1–23). Treaties are not the only events treated as central to tribal identity. A critical feature of Hopi narrative and identity, for example, is their priority in the Southwest. In introducing the Hopi people to visitors, a Hopi newspaper emphasizes that "Hopis and our ancestors lived in these arid lands long before the coming of the Paiutes, Navajo, Apaches, Spanish, and Americans" (*Hopi Tutuveni* 1997, p. 11).

86. Some of the most vigorous identity making of this sort is taking place in the work of a new generation of Indian writers. For a brief discussion see Dinita Smith, "The Indian in Literature is Catching Up," *New York Times,* April 21, 1997, B1.

87. Which of these various narratives comes closest to "the truth" is of limited interest here. The issue is by no means irrelevant: although every identity narrative is at best a partial truth, and some clearly are systematic and destructive misrepresentations, such misrepresentations are understandably of concern to those who have to face the consequences of the stories told about them.

Patrick B. Miller

8   The Anatomy of Scientific Racism: Racialist Responses to Black Athletic Achievement

In the late 1940s, a highly regarded critic for the *New York Times* wrote that the modern dance revolution had opened the way for Black Americans to find themselves as "creative artists." The widespread embrace of new choreographic styles had enabled them, John Martin asserted, to "release in communicative essence the uninhibited qualities of the racial heritage, no matter what the immediate subject of any specific dance might be." Martin's survey text (republished in 1963 and in 1970) ranged over a large number of themes. But what stood out, from first version to last, was the chapter "The Negro Dance," with its persistent references to the "intrinsic" and the "innate." One feature of the Negro dancer, Martin insisted, "is his uniquely racial rhythm":

> Far more than just a beat, it includes a characteristic phrase, manifested throughout the entire body and originating sometimes so far from its eventual point of outlet as to have won the description of "lazy".... Closely allied to this pervasive rhythm is the wide dynamic range of his movement itself, with, at one extreme, vigor and an apparently inexhaustible energy (though, be it noted, a minimum of tension), and at the other extreme, a rich command of relaxation.[1]

For all their contributions to jazz and modern dance, Martin declared, African Americans had been "wise" not to take up academic ballet, "for its wholly European outlook, history and technical theory are alien to [them] culturally, temperamentally and anatomically." He went on:

> In practice there is a racial constant, so to speak, in the proportions of the limbs and torso and the conformation of the feet, all of which affect body placement; in addition, the deliberately maintained erectness of the European dancer's spine is in marked contrast to the fluidity of the Negro dancer's, and the latter's natural concentration of movement in the pelvic region is similarly at odds with European usage.[2]

A more expansive version of this article was published in *The Journal of Sport History* 25 (Spring 1998).

If other commentators have advanced less meticulous formulations than Martin's, they have unselfconsciously—but no less emphatically—stacked value judgments upon matters of "scientific" measurement without addressing either the segregation and racial prejudice that largely contributed to the development of distinctive social customs and expressive cultural practices or the hard work, discipline, and creativity that distinguish artistic innovations irrespective of color or culture.

Indeed, by underscoring "a minimum of tension" or "a rich command of relaxation" among Black performers, many White intellectuals like Martin have surveyed an enormous distance between what has been *studied,* which those image makers exalted for a particular conciseness, cleverness, and formality, and what they believed to *inhere* and thus could disparage as free or flowing or loose. At one level, references to the "pelvic region" derive from an expansive European and U.S. literature that has reduced racial and cultural difference to matters of sexuality. At another, the insistent contrast between mind and body within the Western tradition renders Black physicality as a kind of compensation for the absence of cerebral qualities and the traits of a purportedly advanced, or advancing, culture.[3]

Beginning in the early nineteenth century, the distinctions that eventually found their way into Martin's appraisals were becoming central elements of what was considered pioneering scholarship in anthropology as well as the "scientific" study of history, helping to define Western notions of civilization. Critically, an observation concerning the "*natural* concentration of movement" of African Americans, when contrasted to the ideal of "European *usage,*" was meant to reinforce a longstanding hierarchy of values and standards, with the cultural achievements of *the* Continent at its head. Long before Martin measured the "uniquely racial rhythm" of jazz dancers against the accomplishments of ballerinas, to differentiate was for many European American commentators to denigrate. When African American artists and athletes pursued excellence within the boundaries of Western aesthetic and agonistic traditions, they encountered more than customary biases and myriad discriminatory acts. They confronted a discourse of difference, which, inscribed as a set of "racial constants," effectively discounted the efforts of Black Americans or denied the cultural significance of their achievements.

Ultimately, this particular dimension of the politics of culture has engaged a vast scholarship that ranges far beyond the history of racial relations in the United States. Within one frame of analysis, the origins and development of the discourse of difference have been examined specifically with regard to the Nazi eugenic theories that finally marked Jews and gypsies, as well as homosexuals, for extermination. Such cultural boundary-marking has also been assessed with consideration of the linkages between gender and "race" in the construction of hierarchies of privilege and subordination over time. As scholars of postcolonial ideology and experience have demonstrated, furthermore, the ranking of "racial" traits—especially as it has elaborated the dichotomy between mind and body—continues to serve as a means of suppressing the claims of people of color around the world. What remains is the relationship between the pseudoscience of racial difference and the pernicious social policies it both inspires and informs.[4]

It is significant, then, that even those who endeavor to expose and thus dispose of the cultural hierarchies predicated on the tired old versions of ethnicity and race have lately become involved in earnest and extensive debates over Charles Murray and Richard Herrnstein's *The Bell Curve,* an elaborate ranking of so-called racial and ethnic groups in terms of IQ—with African Americans at the bottom of the list. Scholars have also felt compelled to address the claims made by Dinesh D'Souza, who in *The End of Racism,* has gone so far as to describe the civilizing and Christianizing effects of slavery on the majority of Blacks in the United States.[5] In such instances, progressive writers and educators must still regularly engage the persistent stereotypes concerning the "natural" physical abilities of Blacks, which are said to explain the "dominance" of African Americans in sports such as basketball and football.

To account for achievement in biologically essentialist terms effectively discounts the traits identified with "character": discipline, courage, sacrifice. And therein lies the significance of inquiries into racial science when they have been applied to athletics.[6] Ultimately, the questions of who can run faster or jump higher are simplistic, but they are pernicious as well as foolish if conceived as measures of innate racial difference. In light of this ongoing cultural dynamic, John Martin's observations not only help us understand the anatomy of racialist thinking in historical terms. Their similarity to more recent comments reminds us of the persistence of "academic" racism in contemporary U.S. society.

Since "race matters," as the title of one of Cornel West's recent books avows, we need to discuss not only why it should but when it should not—in judgments of individual abilities and accomplishments. With regard to the historical construction of racial categories, we ought to consider that the *body* continues to loom large in many people's thinking about difference. TV sports reports often provide the most obvious marker of distinctions associated with race and ethnicity. In basketball, the trope of the White point guard—court savvy, disciplined, and controlled—has stood in striking contrast to prevailing images of Black male athletes, able and all too willing to shatter backboards with their slam dunks. And if that juxtaposition appears too stark and simple—in light of the widespread recognition of what was Michael Jordan's mastery, not just of the mechanics of his game, but also of modern media techniques—we can turn to the lecture hall. "I don't know whether or not most white men can jump," the historian of science Stephen Jay Gould has written recently. "And I don't much care, although I suppose that the subject bears some interest and marginal legitimacy in an alternate framing that avoids such biologically meaningless categories as white and black. Yet I can never give a speech on the subject of human diversity without attracting some variant of this inquiry in the subsequent question period. I hear the 'sports version,' I suppose, as an acceptable surrogate for what really troubles people of good will (and bad, although for other reasons)."[7]

The "sports version" of human diversity, still placing population groups up and down a vertical axis of accomplishment, suggests another significant topic. Without discussing the economic and educational practices that mark "racial" distinctions in the United States, without examining the concepts of Whiteness and Blackness in cultural terms, and without recognizing the facts of mixed heritage, most racialist formulations have had as their objective the demonstration of African American inferiority, for example, on intelligence tests. But judgments about "culture" or ideologies of success also come in response to Black *achievement.* Frequently, in reaction to triumphs by African

Americans, we hear explanations that qualify excellence fashioned out of the notion of "natural ability."

When African Americans began to register an increasing number of victories on the playing fields during the first decades of the twentieth century, mainstream commentators abandoned the athletic creed that linked physical prowess, manly character, and the best features of U.S. civilization. Although many African Americans had subscribed to the ideal that achievement in sport constituted a proof of equality, a mechanism of assimilation, and a platform for social mobility, the recognition successful Black athletes actually received from many educators and journalists explained away their prowess by stressing Black anatomical and physiological "advantages" or legacies from a primitive African past.[8]

Many academicians, beginning in the mid–nineteenth century, thus turned away from the discourse of culture when interpreting the physical talents of Blacks—and other "Others." As they became engrossed in the "scientific" analysis of racial difference, various anthropologists and anthropometrists reached for the calipers and tape measure in search of a gastrocnemius muscle with a certain diameter or of an elongated heel bone in order to explain the success of certain sprinters or jumpers. In the dominant discourse, an individual's performance was bound to attributes ascribed to the group of his or her origin. Such a racialized view of excellence defined the physical accomplishments of Europeans in terms of diligence and forethought, the application of the mind to the movements of the body, while it framed the achievements of people of color with words such as "natural" and "innate." Ultimately, then, racialized responses to the athletic as well as the artistic accomplishments of Blacks have served both to shape and reinforce prevailing stereotypes. In so doing, they have also served to "rationalize" exclusionary social practices and discriminatory public policies.

The History of Racial Ranking

The construction of racial typologies can be traced in general terms to Aristotle's attempt to justify slavery. Pictorial representations of Africans dating back to Greek antiquity, as well as the patterns of thought that shaped the characterization of Caliban and Othello, for instance, undergird modern European racism. Such images speak to a lengthy history of racial boundary marking and the color coding of culture. Yet it is in the mid–nineteenth-century writings of Joseph-Arthur, Comte de Gobineau, that many scholars perceive the racist ideologies that first alluded to measurable distinctions and pretended to scientific objectivity. In *The Inequality of Human Races* (1853–55), Gobineau asked: "Is there an inequality in physical strength?" His answer, according to the intellectual historian Elazar Barkan "mixed aristocratic pessimism, romanticism, theology together with biology, all of which became part of a shared European value system based on racial differentiation":[9] "The American savages, like the Hindus, are certainly our inferiors in this respect, as are also the Australians. The Negroes, too, have less muscle power; and all these people are infinitely less able to bear fatigue."[10]

Gobineau's observations, which extended to three printed volumes, leapt from individual display to the characteristics defining a group, thus exposing powerful exceptions to exceedingly flimsy generalizations. This anthropology devoted to the ranking of peoples nevertheless had enormous influence, not despite but *because* of the inconsistencies in the criteria it used to render innate and immutable distinctions between population groups. What Gobineau implicitly promulgated was a bipartite notion of culture: the Western tradition involved social developments and creativity; the accomplishments of non-Western peoples derived from natural selection and genetics. If, for those who succeeded Gobineau as taxonomists of culture, Shakespeare and Beethoven illustrated European civilization, then Darwin and Galton explained all the rest. Ultimately, the African or the African American could not win within such a framework, even on the playing fields.[11]

Such assertions about European superiority, as strained as they were, also constituted arguments for White supremacy. The ideology of empire thus incorporated the so-called feeble races into elaborate systems of hard labor: the institution of slavery in the United States and colonial workforces elsewhere around the world. Stamina, therefore—as a kind of brutish endurance, the ability to "bear fatigue"—would ultimately be conceived as a trait characterizing subject peoples who would work on the plantations and in the mines that fed, clothed, and enriched imperialism. Yet, at the same time, persistence— the exaltation of hard work and steady accumulation—also stood as a key feature of nineteenth-century interpretations of the rise of modern civilization; bourgeois values and the doctrine of possessive individualism extolled toil over time above the heroic acts conventionally associated with generals and kings. To render this cruel paradox in somewhat different terms: the supposed hardihood characterizing people of color was used to justify the exploitation of their labor. Simultaneously, the cultivation of hardihood, as suggested by exhortations to the strenuous life from Theodore Roosevelt in the United States and his counterparts across the North Atlantic, was intended to (re)invigorate various imperial elites. Neither the ideologues like Gobineau nor the imperialists they informed ever addressed the illogic of these patterns of thought, which only begins to suggest the *contingency* and opportunism of such putatively "scientific" formulations.[12]

At the turn of the century, standard reference books continued to include broad generalizations about racial difference based on observations and measurements. Under the subject heading "Negro," the canonical *Encyclopaedia Britannica* of 1895 distinguished between cranial capacities (an average European, 45 ounces; Negro, 35; highest gorilla, 20) and underscored a differential development of the cranial sutures wherein the "premature ossification of the skull" was said to account for the intellectual limitations of Blacks. Significantly, such prematurity was said to be the result of "the inherent mental inferiority of the blacks, an inferiority which is even more marked than their physical differences."[13] Later versions of these notations would accentuate the so-called primitive features of the Negro physiognomy in order to explain the relative failure of African Americans—in the aggregate—on intelligence tests. Such references would also inform the doctrine of racial eugenics as it was elaborated on both sides of the Atlantic.[14]

By 1900, however, another dimension of scientific racism could be discerned. Rather than simply reinforce prevailing notions of Negro inferiority, experts felt compelled to account for the extraordinary achievements of some Black athletes. In the face of an increasing number of victories posted by African Americans, the mainstream culture began to "qualify" the meanings of excellence in sport. The *Encyclopaedia Britannica* had described "the abnormal length of the arm, which in the erect position sometimes reaches the knee-pan, and which on an average exceeds that of the Caucasian by about two inches," and "the low instep, divergent and somewhat prehensile great toe, and heel projection backwards ('lark heel')." Increasingly, these specifications would be advanced as reasons for Black success in sports. Thus, in 1901 the champion sprint cyclist Marshall "Major" Taylor was X-rayed, as well as measured up and down by a number of French medical anthropologists, in an effort to reveal the source of his triumphs in the velodrome. In similar terms, comment on the speed of the Black Olympian John Taylor, and on the prepossessing strength of the heavyweight champion boxer Jack Johnson a few years later, included "scientific" speculation.

Throughout the twentieth century, it would often be the accomplishments of people of color in the realm of sport that particularly vexed and intimidated those who endeavored to defend a longstanding racial hierarchy. The response would not be subtle. Indeed, the Western discourse of racial difference carefully juxtaposed Black athletic achievement—assessed in terms of compensation—to the supposed intellectual disabilities or cultural shortcomings of African Americans.

Critically, the initial forays into the anthropometry of athletic difference were expounded against the backdrop of increasing segregation in the United States, which involved—beyond the enforcement of Jim Crow in housing, transportation, and education—the exclusion of the vast majority of African American ballplayers, jockeys, and boxers from mainstream sporting competitions. The cyclist Major Taylor, for instance, competed when he could in Europe and Australia because of the hostility he encountered at home. Hypocrisy was piled upon paradox when those who spoke for the dominant culture began to contrast the alarming vitality of African Americans (as well as immigrant newcomers to the United States) to the alleged degeneration of Anglo-America. Such works as Madison Grant's *The Passing of the Great Race* and Lothrop Stoddard's *The Rising Tide of Color against White World Supremacy* reflected nearly hysterical feelings about the links between demography and democracy. Vaguely informed by statistical data, such discussions of the relative birthrates among the Mayflower descendants, the sons and daughters of the *shtetl*, and those who were moving from southern farms to northern cities revealed a deep fear about the claims Black Americans and "hyphenated" Americans might well make against hallowed ideals such as equality and opportunity.[15]

Indeed, Black leaders like W.E.B. Du Bois—alongside the guiding lights of the new immigrant groups—did indeed seek full participation in the social, economic, and political mainstream, though they demanded fairness not merely as a measure of their numbers but on the basis of their contributions to U.S. culture. And according to the "muscular assimilationists" among them, there was no better argument for inclusion than success in the "national" pastimes. Major Taylor and Jack Johnson were not the first African Americans to make their mark in sports, and it was clear to racial reformers that they would not be the last to tread "the hard road to glory." Well before the appearance of Joe Louis and Jesse Owens in the 1930s, and a decade later, of Jackie Robinson, Black leaders saw in athletics a platform for social change.[16]

Resistance to such assertions was formidable, however. Those who would maintain Jim Crow guarded the portals of the stadium just as they stood at the schoolhouse door.

Others reinforced racial hierarchy by constructing elaborate frameworks to distinguish between the laurels won by Whites and Blacks in sport. During the interwar period, anatomy and physiology were frequently invoked to explain the athletic success of African Americans, circumscribing declarations that prowess in contests of speed, strength, and stamina bespoke fitness for other realms of endeavor. In the idiom of sports, to deny the correspondence between athletics and other accomplishments (more profound and long-standing), numerous mainstream commentators "moved the goal posts."

By the 1930s, generalizations from individual performances to group characteristics dominated many descriptions of Black prizefighters, such as the heavyweight champion Joe Louis. Likewise, to account for the medals won by the sprinters Eddie Tolan and Ralph Metcalfe during the 1932 Olympics and by Jesse Owens, Metcalfe, and many other African American champions at the Berlin Games of 1936, White commentators insisted that Black success derived from innate biological advantages. Early in the decade, E. Albert Kinley—whose claim to expertise was that he was an X-ray special-ist—repeated the canard about the elongated heel bone, then predicted more world records for African Americans in events that depended on a certain kind of anatomi-cal leverage. Working from a similar premise, Eleanor Metheny, a well-known physi-cal educator, conducted a number of studies on body proportions. Though somewhat guarded in her conclusions, she asserted that kinesiological differences—in the move-ments generated by individuals with longer legs and narrower hips, for instance—could account for Black dominance in sport. Significantly, and ultimately ironically, Metheny would declare that a different, somehow deficient chest construction, as well as lower breathing capacity among Blacks, handicapped them in endurance events such as dis-tance running. In David Wiggins's apt phrase, "great speed but little stamina" became the watchword for many White commentators on Black athletics. In formulations repeated both in scholarly journals and the popular press, the science of sport further insinuated itself into the broader history of racism in the United States.[17]

If experiments like those conducted by Metheny were as flawed in their conception as in their conclusions, other writers appeared just as intent on defending myths of Anglo-Saxon or Aryan superiority. "It was not long ago," wrote the track-and-field coach Dean Cromwell in 1941, "that his [the Black athlete's] ability to sprint and jump was a life-and-death matter to him in the jungle. His muscles are pliable, and his easy-going disposition is a valuable aid to the mental and physical relaxation that a runner and jumper must have." The attempt thus to "historicize" racial difference in sport revealed a significant strand of popular thought. To invoke an African past, the prim-itive Other, a state-of-being predicated solely on physical prowess, was literally to den-igrate what flowed from it. By extension, it was also to exalt its presumed obverse—civilization, and the attributes of the dominant order.[18]

Cromwell's interpretation was a curious notion of nature and culture at odds. It imagined that when Blacks in Africa had been off running and hunting, the ancestors of White athletes were composing symphonies and building cathedrals, which placed their descendants at a substantial disadvantage at the modern-day Olympics. If the Black athlete's "easy-going disposition" lay at or near the center of his success, then again by contrast, White competitors may have been thwarted from starting blocks to finish line by their particular worries about the fate of Western civilization.

Such luridly imagined observations as Cromwell's never stood alone or without amplification. In the ensuing years, Black athleticism fell prey to the Harvard anthropologist Carleton S. Coon, who began his commentary on the inherited advantages of African Americans in sport with a depiction of their slender calves and loose jointedness. But what started with anatomy ended with a striking analogy, as was so often the case with racial scientists. The biological features that suited African Americans for certain sports, Coon declared, were characteristic of "living things (cheetahs, for instance) known for their speed and leaping ability." Two later chroniclers of the history of college football continued to rely on gross stereotype, though they had relocated their analogies from the African "jungle" to the American palladium. "Because of their tap-dancer sense of rhythm and distinctive leg conformation, Blacks excel as sprinters," John McCallum and Charles Pearson averred. "It follows *naturally* that on the football field they stand out as broken field runners."[19] The links between these comments and the discriminations advanced by the dance critic John Martin are unmistakable.

After midcentury, racial science often focused on the triumph of Black athletes in the track-and-field events of the Olympic Games. The stopwatch and the tape measure seemed to offer a certain validation to the claims of the hereditarians that significant and fixed anatomical and physiological differences accounted for the medals won by Black Americans in the sprints and jumps. But then, rather suddenly, racial commentators were confronted by the stellar efforts and world records of African distance runners. On the heels of successive gold medal performances in the marathon, steeplechase, and 10,000-meter race by competitors from Ethiopia and Kenya during the 1960s, the notion of fast-twitch and slow-twitch muscle fibers—which had for a time been used to distinguish between the speed of Blacks and the stamina of Whites—was displaced as a frame of analysis. Substituted for it were assertions that strove to mark differences between East African and West African physiques, long and lithe versus compact and muscular. From the vantage not so much of a later era but of a different ideological stance, such a shift in explanations suggests that the persistence of scientific racism lay not so much in the consistency of the science but in the constancy of its racism.

At odds with such racially essentialist notions, an increasing emphasis on cultural interpretations of African American success in sports characterized the social science of sport as well as mainstream journalism. A five-part series by Charles Maher in the *Los Angeles Times*, March 24–29, 1968, that surveyed current biological studies of black athletic performance concluded that hard training and motivational factors accounted for the increasing success of African American athletes. Mainstream sociological opinion had begun to yield the same conclusions.[20] These were noteworthy developments whose stress on Black struggle and triumph *within* the boundaries marked by the athletic establishment reflected the growing influence of the civil rights movement and its integrationist appeal.

Still, the (il)logic of athletic taxonomy remained largely in place. Indeed, it received its most thorough exposition in 1971 when *Sports Illustrated* published Martin Kane's "An Assessment of 'Black is Best,'" a survey of expert commentary on racial difference and athletic achievement intended to be impressive in its range. In fact, the findings of assorted anatomists and the observations of a number of successful athletes overwhelmed other perspectives. The article ignored historical and sociological considerations of discrimination on the playing fields and beyond. Conversely, it failed to discuss the notion that athletics offered a platform for social mobility or a move from margins to mainstream for many acutely aware of their outsider or "minority" status. Despite a slight qualification here and there, Kane's main point was ultimately that "physical differences in the races might well have enhanced the athletic potential of the Negro in certain events."[21]

Responses to the Racial "Scientists"

References to innate athletic differences between population groups persisted well beyond the era of desegregation in sport. But such ways of thinking have also provoked a variety of reactions, ofter passionate and profound, from Black Americans. From Du Bois at the turn of the century to educators and athletes such as Harry Edwards and Arthur Ashe in our own time, most African American commentators have objected to the use of stereotype and the misuse of science to distinguish the accomplishments of Black and White athletes. Urgently and insistently, many intellectuals and activists in the civil rights movement have asserted that the claims made by excellent Black athletes against the mainstream rhetoric of equality and opportunity have stood for the larger aspirations of Afro-America. They have also drawn upon the findings of numerous physical scientists and social scientists, who have disproved the allegations of biodeterminism and dismissed the idea of legacies from a primitive past.

During the early years of the century Du Bois enlisted a new generation of anthropologists led by Franz Boas to refute the tenets of scientific racism. In 1906, at the invitation of Du Bois, Boas delivered a paper titled "The Health and Physique of the Negro-American" at the eleventh annual Atlanta University Conference. Emphasizing the significance of culture in perceived racial differences, he was instrumental in prompting young African American scholars, such as Zora Neale Hurston, to undertake research in black folklore and culture. Through the first half of the century, Boasians were popular speakers on the campuses of historically black colleges. The environmentalism embraced by an increasing number of social scientists in the ensuing years seemed to remove Black athletic accomplishment from the shaky anthropometrical foundations first advanced by ideologues like Gobineau and to place excellence in sport, for instance, within the sturdier frames of analysis that address social circumstance and cultural innovation.[22]

At the same time, biological scientists also challenged the generalizations based on anthropometry. Few if any offered findings more emphatic or timely than the African American scholar W. Montague Cobb. Drawing on his experiments in physiology and anatomy, particularly his biopsies of the muscle tissue of Jesse Owens during the late 1930s, Cobb assailed the proposition that specific biological determinants could account for Black athletic success. With reference to the prevailing classification systems, the Howard University professor declared without equivocation that the "Negroid type of calf, foot, and heel bone" could not be found in the Olympic champion; if anything, Cobb asserted, the diameter of Owens's gastrocnemius conformed to "the caucasoid type rather than the negroid."[23]

In professional as well as popular journals, Cobb extended his analysis in important ways. He was neither the first scientist, nor the last, to underscore the salience of physical variations within population groups as well as between them. Nevertheless, he discussed that notion within the context of sporting accomplishment and thus engaged, at an early date, the athletic typologies then in place. What is more, Cobb indicated his clear sense that racial mixing subverted any assertion about fixed and isolated genetic determinants of muscular or mental prowess. Howard Drew had been a co–record holder in the 100-yard-dash and the first Black sprinter to be acclaimed "the world's fastest human," Cobb noted in 1936. But Drew was also light skinned and "usually taken for a white man by those not in the know." Edward Gourdin, the Harvard sprinter and former world-record holder in the broad jump, was similarly light skinned. "There is not one single physical feature, including skin color, which all our Negro champions have in common which would identify them as Negroes," Cobb asserted. A mixed heritage, he concluded, obviously removed such stellar athletes from consideration when rigid racial dichotomies were being cast, thus exposing as arbitrary and contrived the very principles of racial taxonomy.[24]

Cobb's scientific investigations stood among a host of scholarly articles and books that debunked biodeterminist assertions regarding athletic performance. Yet they have ultimately not been sufficient to counter prevailing speculation on Black success in sport. Neither, for the most part, have been the arguments of the sociologist Harry Edwards, whose stinging responses to the Kane article, in addition to his other writings and position statements, have both inspired and informed numerous critics of racism in sport and society. Nor have the appeals of such popular figures as Arthur Ashe, Jr., whose three-volume text, *The Hard Road to Glory,* documented a history of White hostility to Black effort and accomplishment in the realm of athletics. These commentaries might well have sent the innatists to the sidelines for good. Sadly, however, the muscular assimilationists—whether they positioned themselves as moderate or militant in the civil rights movement—have been largely unsuccessful in altering the terms of discourse from the natural to the cultural and social.[25]

The massive resistance to the efforts of the integrationists might begin to explain why other African American commentators have come to subscribe to essentialist considerations of physical hardihood and athletic prowess. The attempt to strategically appropriate the notion of racial difference—to turn it on its head, as it were—may have been born of frustration. It was clearly sustained by considerations of cultural nationalism and Black Power during the late 1960s and 1970s. But today such racialism is not only manifest in African-centered assertions regarding distinctive patterns of cultural development; it also makes its appeal through the notions of melanin theory, no less weird or pernicious than the pronouncements of coach Cromwell or the journalist Kane. Although the various tenets of Afrocentrism certainly speak to racial pride, it is important not to confuse such a sociological phenomenon with a solidly grounded school of critical analysis; while Afrocentrism may be good therapy, as one prominent scholar has noted, it is not good history.[26]

Like cultural nationalism, Black racial essentialism serves many purposes, though its separatist assertions and implications do much more than reinforce the notion of a fixed social identity and a consolidated political stance. They also divide persistent racial reformers from those who have attenuated their commitment to the civil rights crusade. The distinctions between integrationist appeals and essentialist formulations have not always been sharply drawn, however, just as the hazards of perpetuating athletic taxonomies have not always been apparent to some Black athletes and African American commentators. Edwin Bancroft Henderson, for example, for more than fifty years one of the leading chroniclers of Black sport and perhaps the foremost promoter of the ideal of "muscular assimilationism," devoted his career to civil rights activism. Yet in what seems a striking departure from his campaign to establish a level playing field of athletic competition, he embraced, at least in some measure, the prevailing discourse of difference. Specifically, in a 1936 article in *Opportunity,* the journal of the National Urban League, he alleged that it might have been the rigors of the Middle Passage that had winnowed the slave population, allowing only the fittest to survive. It was from this group, he suggested, that the great athletes descended.

> When one recalls that it is estimated that only one Negro slave in five was able to live through the rigors of the Middle Passage, and that the horrible conditions of slavery took a toll of many slaves who could not make biological adjustments in a hostile environment, one finds the Darwinian theory of survival of the fit operating among Negroes as rigorously as any selective process ever operated among human beings. There is just a likelihood that some very vital elements persist in the histological tissues of the glands or muscles of Negro athletes.[27]

Thirty-five years later, the Yale graduate and NFL star Calvin Hill echoed Henderson's peculiar notion. Black athletes were "the offspring of those who [were] physically and mentally tough enough to survive," Hill asserted. "We were simply bred for physical qualities." This explanation resonated for a number of African American commentators and athletes who had embraced certain elements of the Black Power movement.[28] Recast in a more positive way, such thinking drew attention to an African past and pride in physical accomplishment, which would eventually be manifest in many achievements by Black athletes. In telling counterpoint, the basketball player Isiah Thomas argued in 1987 against "the perpetuation of stereotypes about blacks": "When [Larry] Bird makes a great play, it's due to his thinking and his work habits. It's all planned out by him. It's not the case for blacks. All we do is run and jump. We never practice or give a thought to how we play. It's like I came dribbling out of my mother's womb."[29]

The most solid reaction to notions of White supremacy at the time, the construction of an idealized Black superhero in sports, also has played into a cultural taxonomy that ranks athletes as performers (with the line between the symbolic and substantive importance of their accomplishments still firmly drawn). Paradoxically, such assertions of a "strategic essentialism" have served to tighten the boundaries around the athletic ghetto. As the cultural historian and social critic John Hoberman argues passionately, when the foremost Black cultural heroes are the celebrities of the football field and basketball arena, and when they are held in esteem mainly for their innate abilities, the effect is to diminish the significance of other African American leaders and the years of dedication that lie behind their accomplishments.

Recent Developments

If racial essentialism was ever in retreat during the era of civil rights and national liberation, as some scholars maintain, its resurgence has been dramatically illustrated in recent years. Indeed, the emergence of melanism seems but a sidelight to other renderings of difference and dominance that reflect traditional patterns of thought within the mainstream culture. One of the most notorious episodes of "typing" occurred in the late 1980s when a major-league baseball official, Al Campanis, stated that Blacks performed well on the field but lacked "the necessities" to occupy managerial positions or places of responsibility and authority in the front offices of sports organizations. Another involved Jimmy "the Greek" Snyder, a football commentator on television, who linked the heritage of slavery to the modern playing field. "The slave owner would breed his big black with his big woman so that he could have a big black kid," Snyder maintained. The consternation evinced by their respective interviewers and the summary firing of both men indicated a shift of values and standards toward such public declarations and their racist underpinnings. Yet many Americans continue to mark racial differences in the athletic arena in terms both calculated and crude. Toward the end of the 1996–97 basketball season, a sportscaster was fined by the NBA for his retrograde appraisal of Black athletic ability. Commenting on a stellar play by one athlete, David Halberstam, who announces the games for the Miami Heat, remarked that "Thomas Jefferson would have been proud of that pass. When Thomas Jefferson was around basketball was not invented yet, but those slaves working at Thomas Jefferson's farm, I'm sure they would have made good basketball players."[30]

Clearly, such instances draw attention to the continuing prevalence of racialist thinking about athletic accomplishment. Other commentary has been less forthright in addressing the meaning of the success of Blacks in sport. In the aftermath of the firing of Jimmy the Greek, the syndicated columnist Richard Cohen vaguely suggested that civil rights activists would want to steer clear of any assessment of the racial dimension of physical attributes for fear of having to engage intellectual and psychological distinctions. Raising the issue of "political correctness," Cohen then shied away from further speculation about racial difference in sport or other endeavors.[31]

Cohen's comments nevertheless made their way into the much more purposive arguments of Dinesh D'Souza in *The End of Racism*, a book that deals with scientific racism principally by repeating its most atrocious pronouncements and ignoring its critics. Thus in a short section concerning athletics, intended to set up his selective digest of IQ statistics, D'Souza not only recapitulated the "categorical imperative" that has long prevailed among racial scientists, he also reiterated the notion of compensation. "It stands to reason that groups that are unlike each other in some respects may also differ in other respects," D'Souza contends offhandedly. "Why should groups with different skin color, head shape, and other visible characteristics prove identical in reasoning ability or the ability to construct an advanced civilization? If Blacks have certain inherited abilities, such as improvisational decision making, that could explain why they predominate in certain fields such as jazz, rap, and basketball, and not in other fields, such as classical music, chess, and astronomy." The end of racism indeed.[32]

The racial essentialism that continues to shadow much of the commentary on sport is confined neither to U.S. culture nor to considerations of the achievements of African Americans. A recent article from a popular New Zealand magazine, for example, titled "White Men Can't Jump"—how ironically it is hard to tell—documented the increasing prominence of native peoples in rugby, a sport long identified with British colonialism as a means of toughening those who administered the Empire. Amid a wide-ranging discussion of changing demographics in New Zealand as well as an analysis otherwise sensitive to Maori and Samoan cultural patterns, several White sports figures speculate, first, on the innate abilities vis-à-vis the acquired skills of Polynesian squads. "Polynesian players were naturally superior to us in talent," one former player declared, "but a lot of them aren't there now because they didn't have the discipline for physical conditioning. They lacked the right kind of mental attitude. They'd just turn up and play." Said another, it was once the case that "your typical Polynesian rugby team would have just lost their head in a pressure situation. It was almost as if it was the Polynesian way to do something really stupid that gave the game away." Another passage indicates the malleability of such typologies, however. Polynesians have come to excel at the sport because they are bigger now and play a "more physical and confrontational" brand of the game. Inevitably size will win out in such appraisals: "The Polynesian is basically mesomorphic, tending to be big-boned, muscular, of average height, wide shoulders, thin waist," one trainer asserts. "They have a higher proportion of fast twitch muscle fibre which is the source of their explosive style and the reason they are fast over short distances." Contrasting feats of character to mere physicality, the article offers yet another instance where innatist constructs can be placed in comparative perspective, encouraging us to generalize somewhat about the phenomenon of racial essentialism. In New Zealand as in the United States, athletic competition has offered a way for people of color to fashion significant emblems of identity and pride as well as to challenge the discriminatory practices of old. It is a critical commentary on both social systems that those initiatives are still contested, that racialist thinking continues to qualify such hallowed notions as sportsmanship and fair play, equality and opportunity.[33]

Conclusion

Significantly, taxonomic conventions in the representation of population groups have long stood as the predicate of social authority. That the dominant culture can employ them—and modify them when necessary—to maintain hierarchies of privilege and subordination means that "minority" cultures cannot use such typologies in the same ways. If the strategy of "muscular assimilationism"—a prominent element of the civil rights campaigns of the twentieth century—has not been entirely successful in creating a level playing field, it is more certain still that the separatism manifest in Afrocentrism and melanin theory is patently self-defeating in the long run. Moreover, to the extent that many African American youth exalt athletic heroes over other role models—spending their formative years in "hoop dreams"—the emphasis on athletic striving has been overplayed. What remains is yet another troubling fact. Even as sociological surveys and a new generation of biographies and memoirs tell us about the increasingly multiracial character of U.S. society, the discourse of innate and immutable racial difference still looms large in the popular consciousness.

Ultimately, for intellectual historians, cultural theorists, social scientists, as well as journalists who hope to engage entrenched modes of racialist thought and to create a more expansive conception of culture, it may be well as a first step to adopt a new perspective regarding the texts devoted to innatist thinking. Central to this undertaking would be the compilation of a roster of phrases and pronouncements that clearly links academic racism, past and present. To be sure, as we strive to move beyond category, the idea of an index of racialist literature involves a troubling dimension. Yet it is nevertheless crucial that progressive, or expansive, thinkers on the subject—rather than institute- and foundation-based conservative ideologues—become the cartographers of the contemporary discussion of "race." Better still, though from a different interpretive position, we might start erasing "racial" boundaries altogether.

With notions of history and collective memory in mind, perhaps it would be wise to evaluate such books as *The Bell Curve* and *The End of Racism,* deftly written as they might seem to some reviewers,[34] through the same lens that we would use to assess the essentialist observations of the dance critic John Martin, as contrived as they were and remain. From there we could examine the arguments still insisting on a broad-based anatomy of racial difference with an eye toward the ideological stance they share with those who spoke before, with the sportswriter Martin Kane, for instance, with the anthropologist Carleton Coon, and with Coach Cromwell. We could allude, then, to the polemics on White supremacy by Madison Grant and Lothrop Stoddard as well as to the pronouncements on European superiority by the Count de Gobineau. For, "essentially," de Gobineau and D'Souza are of a kind. To read such works together, indeed to draw the significant connections between nineteenth-century social theories and the most recent versions, would ultimately reveal the shared racism of their premises as well as of their prescriptions.

Notes

Acknowledgment: I am grateful to Paul Spickard, Elliott Gorn, David Wiggins, Peter Hoffenberg, Johanna Garvey, Steven Riess, June Sochen, Kirsten Fischer, and Ursula Bielski for their careful readings of earlier versions of this article.

1. *John Martin's Book of the Dance (The Dance,* 1947; reprint, New York: Tudor, 1963), 177–89.

2. Ibid., 178–79.

3. See, for example, Joyce Aschenbrenner, *Katherine Dunham: Reflections on the Social and Political Contexts of Afro-American Dance* (New York: Congress on Research in Dance, 1981), which quotes Martin on pp. 35–36.

4. See, for example, Stephen Jay Gould, *The Mismeasure of Man* (New York: Norton, 1981); Stepan, *The Idea of Race in Science: Great Britain, 1800–1960* (London: MacMillan, 1982); Nancy Leys Stepan and Sander Gilman, "Appropriating the Idioms of Science: The Rejection of Scientific Racism," in Dominick LaCapra, ed., *The Bounds of Race: Perspectives on Hegemony*

and Resistance (Ithaca: Cornell University Press, 1991), 72–103; Gilman, *Difference and Pathology: Stereotypes of Sexuality, Race, and Madness* (Ithaca: Cornell University Press, 1985); idem, *The Jew's Body* (New York: Routledge, 1991); idem, *Picturing Health and Illness: Images of Identity and Difference* (Baltimore: Johns Hopkins University Press, 1995); idem, *Smart Jews: The Construction of the Image of Jewish Superior Intelligence* (Lincoln: University of Nebraska Press, 1996); William H. Tucker, *The Science and Politics of Racial Research* (Urbana: University of Illinois Press, 1994). See also George Mosse, *Toward the Final Solution: A History of European Racism* (New York: Harper, 1980) and Michael Adas, *Machines as the Measure of Men: Science, Technology, and Ideologies of Western Dominance* (Ithaca: Cornell University Press, 1989); Laura Nader, ed., *Naked Science: Anthropological Inquiries into Boundaries, Power, and Knowledge* (New York: Routledge, 1996); Ivan Hannaford, *Race: The History of an Idea in the West* (Baltimore: Johns Hopkins University Press, 1996). See also William R. Stanton, *The Leopard's Spots: Scientific Attitudes Toward Race in America, 1815–1859* (Chicago: University of Chicago Press, 1960); Thomas Gossett, *Race: The History of an Idea in America* (New York: Schocken, 1965); John S. Haller, *Outcasts from Evolution: Scientific Attitudes of Racial Inferiority, 1859–1900* (Urbana: University of Illinois Press, 1971); and George Fredrickson, *The Black Image in the White Mind: The Debate on Afro-American Character and Destiny, 1817–1914* (New York, 1971).

5. See Charles Murray and Richard J. Herrnstein, *The Bell Curve: Intelligence and Class Structure in American Life* (New York: Free Press, 1994); idem, "Race and I.Q.," *The New Republic,* October 31, 1994, 10–37; Russell Jacoby and Naomi Glauberman, eds., *The Bell Curve Debate: History, Documents, Opinions* (New York: Times Books, 1995); Steven Fraser, *The Bell Curve Wars: Race, Intelligence, and the Future of America* (New York: Basic Books, 1995); Ashley Montagu, *Race and IQ* (New York: Oxford University Press, 1995); Robert Newby, ed., *The Bell Curve: Laying Bare the Resurgence of Scientific Racism,* special issue of *American Behavioral Scientist* 39 (October 1995); John L. Rury, "IQ Redux," *History of Education Quarterly* 35 (Winter 1995), 423–438; Leon J. Kamen, "Behind the Curve," *Scientific American* 272 (February 1995), 99–103; Claude S. Fischer, Michael Hout, Martín Sánchez Jankowski, Samuel R. Lucas, Ann Swidler, and Kim Voss, *Inequality by Design: Cracking the Bell Curve Myth* (Princeton, N.J.: Princeton University Press, 1996). See also Marek Kohn, *The Race Gallery: The Return of Racial Science* (London: Jonathan Cope, 1995) and Dinesh D'Souza, *The End of Racism: Principles for a Multiracial Society* (New York: Free Press, 1995).

6. See, for example, "The Black Athlete Revisited," *Sports Illustrated* August 5, 12, 19, 1991, pp. 38–77, 26–73, 40–51. The prevailing representation of black and white athletes had not changed significantly, the authors discovered, since 1968, when the magazine published its first expose of racism in the realm of U.S. sport.

7. Gould, "Ghosts of Bell Curves Past," *Natural History,* February 1995, p. 12.

8. See, for example, Patrick B. Miller, "'To Bring the Race along Rapidly': Sport, Student Culture, and Educational Mission at Historically Black Colleges during the Interwar Years," *History of Education Quarterly* 35 (Summer 1995): 111–34, and *The Playing Fields of American Culture: Athletics and Higher Education, 1850–1945* (New York: Oxford University Press, forthcoming).

9. Elazar Barkan, *The Retreat of Scientific Racism: Changing Concepts of Race in Britain and the United States between the World Wars* (Cambridge, UK: Cambridge University Press, 1992), 16. See Michael D. Biddiss, *Father of Racist Ideology: The Social and Political Thought of Count Gobineau* (London: Weidenfeld and Nicolson, 1970).

10. Gobineau, *The Inequality of Human Races* (London: William Heinemann, 1915), 151–53. I am indebted to Scott Haine for bringing this passage to my attention.

11. Gobineau also addressed racial mixing, referring to "tertiary" and "quaternary" races. In the paintbox formulation he advanced, Polynesians had "sprung from the mixture of black and yellow." Ibid., 148–49.

12. See, for example, Ronald Takaki, *Iron Cages: Race and Culture in Nineteenth-Century America* (New York: Knopf, 1979); Amy Kaplan and Donald Pease, eds., *Cultures of United States Imperialism* (Durham, N.C.: Duke University Press, 1993).

13. *Encyclopaedia Britannica,* American edition, vol. 17 (New York, 1895): 316–20.

14. See, for instance, Thurman B. Rice, *Racial Hygiene: A Practical Discussion of Eugenics and Race Culture* (New York: MacMillan, 1929). For historical assessments of eugenics, see Mark H. Haller, *Eugenics: Hereditarian Attitudes in American Thought* (New Brunswick, N.J.: Rutgers University Press, 1963); Gould, *The Mismeasure of Man;* Daniel J. Kevles, *In the Name of Eugenics: Genetics and the Uses of Human Heredity* (New York: Knopf, 1985); Troy Duster, *Backdoor to Eugenics* (New York: Routledge, 1990); Tucker, *The Science and Politics of Racial Research,* 54–137.

15. Madison Grant, *The Passing of the Great Race; or The Racial Basis of European History* (New York: Scribner, 1916); Lothrop Stoddard, *The Rising Tide of Color against White World Supremacy* (New York: Scribner, 1920).

16. The "contributionist" writings of George Washington Williams and Carter G. Woodson, for example, closely parallel those of immigrant U.S. authors. With respect to sport, see Edwin Bancroft Henderson, the foremost chronicler of Black achievements: *The Negro in Sports* (Washington: Associated Publishers, 1939) and *The Black Athlete: Emergence and Arrival* (New York: Publishers Co., 1968).

17. On Kinley, see the *New York World,* March 14, 1931. Eleanor Metheny, "Some Differences in Bodily Proportions between American Negro and White Male College Students as Related to Athletic Performance," *Research Quarterly* 10 (December 1939): 41–53; David K. Wiggins, "'Great Speed but Little Stamina': The Historical Debate over Black Athletic Superiority," *Journal of Sport History* 16 (Summer 1989):162–64.

18. Rice quoted in Chris Mead, *Champion: Joe Louis, Black Hero in White America* (New York: Scribner, 1985), 62–63, an especially helpful survey of the responses to Louis. Dean Cromwell and Al Wesson, *Championship Technique in Track and Field* (New York, London: McGraw-Hill, 1941), 6; Wiggins, "'Great Speed But Little Stamina,'" 161.

19. Coon quoted in Marshall Smith, "Giving the Olympics an Anthropological Once-Over," *Life,* October 23, 1964, p. 83. John McCallum and Charles H. Pearson, *College Football, USA, 1869–1973* (New York: Hall of Fame Publishers, 1973), 231.

20. See D. Stanley Eitzen and George Sage, *Sociology of American Sport* (Dubuque, Iowa: W. C. Brown, 1978), 300; Jay Coakley, *Sport in Society: Issues and Controversies* (St. Louis: Times Mirror/Mosby College, 1986), 146–50.

21. Kane, "An Assessment of 'Black is Best,'" *Sports Illustrated,* January 18, 1971, p. 74.

22. See David Levering Lewis, *W.E.B. Du Bois: Biography of a Race, 1868–1919* (New York: Holt, 1993), 351–52. See Boas, *The Real Race Problem from the Point of View of Anthropology* (New York: National Association for the Advancement of Colored People, 1912) and *Race and Nationality* (New York: American Association for International Conciliation, 1915).

23. W. Montague Cobb, "Race and Runners," *Journal of Health and Physical Education* 7 (January 1936): 3–7, 52–56.

24. Ibid. See also W. Montague Cobb, "The Physical Constitution of the American Negro," *Journal of Negro Education* 3 (1934): 340–88, and "Does Science Favor Negro Athletes?" *Negro Digest* 5 (May 1947): 74–77.

25. On his responses to the Kane article, see Harry Edwards, "The Sources of Black Athletic Superiority," *Black Scholar* 3 (November 1971): 32–41, "The Myth of the Racially Superior

Athlete" *Intellectual Digest* 2 (March 1972), 58–60, and "20th Century Gladiators for White America," *Psychology Today,* November 1973, pp. 43–52. Edwards's survey works include *The Revolt of the Black Athlete* (New York: Free Press, 1969) and *Sociology of Sport* (Homewood, Ill.: Dorsey, 1973). In the mode of Edwards's cultural critique, see Gary Sailes, "The Myth of Black Sports Supremacy," *Journal of Black Studies* 21 (June 1991): 480–87. See also Arthur Ashe, Jr., *A Hard Road to Glory: A History of the African-American Athlete* (New York: Warner Books, 1988).

26. On African-centered social commentary, see Molefi Kete Asante, *Afrocentricity: The Theory of Social Change* (Buffalo, N.Y.: Amulefi, 1980) and *The Afrocentric Idea* (Philadelphia: Temple University Press, 1987; rev. ed., 1997). See also Cheikh Anta Diop, *Civilization or Barbarism. An Authentic Anthropology* (Brooklyn, N.Y.: Lawrence Hill Books, 1991); Bernal, *Black Athena.* An impressive introduction to the mode of thought can be found in Carl Pedersen, "Between Racial Fundamentalism and Ultimate Reality: The Debate over Afrocentrism," *Odense American Studies International Series, Working Paper* no. 4 (1993). And, concerning its appeal, see Gerald Early, "Understanding Afrocentrism: Why Blacks Dream of a World Without Whites," *Civilization* (July/August 1995), 31–39. See also Clarence E. Walker, "You Can't Go Home Again: The Problem with Afrocentrism," *Prospects* 18 (1993), 535–43; on 'therapy' and 'history,' see Leon Litwack, "The Two-Edged Suspicion," American Historical Association *Perspectives* 31 (September 1993), 13–14. For a somewhat different view of this strand of black nationalism, see Bell Hooks, *Black Looks: Race and Representation* (Boston: South End Press, 1992), 30.

27. Edwin B. Henderson, "The Negro Athlete and Race Prejudice," *Opportunity* 14 (March 1936): 77–79. To read the large body of Henderson's works (as well as those of W. Montague Cobb) would be to understand their primary concerns as assimilationist or integrationist; the stray passages that speak to essentialist notions of Black excellence need to be read within this broader context. See David Wiggins, "Edwin Bancroft Henderson, African American Athletes, and the Writing of Sport History," in *Glory Bound: Black Athletes in White America* (Syracuse, N.Y.: Syracuse University Press, 1997). Miller, *The Playing Fields of American Culture,* chaps. 7 and 8.

28. Hill quoted in Kane, "An Assessment of 'Black is Best,'" 76, 79. See also David Zang, "Calvin Hill Interview," *Journal of Sport History* 15 (Winter 1988): 334–55. In a *Time* article, "Black Dominance," O. J. Simpson argued that blacks "were built a little differently . . . built for speed—skinny calves, long legs, high asses are all characteristics of blacks" (May 9, 1977, pp. 57–60); Wiggins, "'Great Speed But Little Stamina,'" 172–74.

29. Thomas quoted in David K. Wiggins, "The Notion of Double-Consciousness and the Involvement of Black Athletes in American Sport," in *Ethnicity and Sport in North American History and Culture,* ed. Wiggins and George Eisen (Westport, Conn.: Greenwood, 1994), 151.

30. On these episodes, see Wiggins, "'Great Speed but Little Stamina,'" 179–81; Phillip M. Hoose, *Necessities: Racial Barriers in American Sports* (New York: Random House, 1989); *New York Times,* March 27, 1997.

31. See Richard Cohen, "The Greek's Defense," *Washington Post,* January 19, 1988.

32. D'Souza, *The End of Racism,* 440–41.

33. Tom Hyde, "White Men Can't Jump," *Metro: Essentially Auckland,* September 1993, pp. 63–69. I am indebted to Charles Martin for pointing this work out to me. More recently still, the New Zealand anthropologist Phillip Houghton has spoken of the ways Polynesians, such as the great rugby player Jonah Lomu, have finally reached their "genetic potential." Houghton, *People of the Ocean: Aspects of Human Biology of the Early Pacific* (Cambridge, UK: Cambridge University Press, 1996). See also Iulia Leilua, "Lomu and the Polynesian Powerpacks," *New*

Zealand Fitness (February/March 1996), 24–27. I am grateful to Douglas Booth for sharing this article with me. In broader terms, Marek Kohn discusses the "race science system" directed at the control of the Romani (gypsy) population that has recently been established in parts of Southern and Eastern Europe; see Kohn, *The Race Gallery,* 178–252. On issues of classification and discrimination, see also Saul Dubow, *Scientific Racism in Modern South Africa* (Cambridge, UK: Cambridge University Press, 1995).

34. See, for example, Malcolm Browne, "What Is Intelligence, and Who Has It?" *New York Times Book Review,* October 16, 1994; George M. Fredrickson on D'Souza, "Demonizing the American Dilemma," *The New York Review of Books* 42 (October 19, 1995), 10–16.

Max E. Stanton

---

9 I'm Not a Chileno! Rapa Nui Identity

Easter Island is the smallest of Chile's fifty-one provinces in both population and area. Its 64 square miles lie as a remote outpost in the southeastern Pacific Ocean about 1,200 miles from its nearest inhabited neighbor (Pitcairn Island) and approximately 2,200 miles west of the Chilean continent. It is also the southeastern corner of the Polynesian Triangle, whose original inhabitants closely resemble the other eastern Polynesians (such as the Tahitians, Tuamotuans, Marquesans, Hawaiians, Rarotongans, and the New Zealand Maori) in language, social and material culture, and physical appearance. Except for a few outlying farmers, its 2,800 residents all live in the island's only community, Hanga Roa. The Polynesian inhabitants refer to themselves, their island, and their language as Rapa Nui.

Easter Island was annexed by the nation of Chile on September 9, 1888, when a Chilean naval expedition led by Captain Policarpo Toro Hurtado took formal possession of the island.[1] At the time of its annexation, there were scarcely more than 100 people left alive on Easter Island, a pitiful remnant of a population that probably exceeded 3,000 only twenty-five years before.[2] The consequences of the loss of the island's Polynesian residents are felt even today among the people of Easter Island,

Even before its annexation by Chile, a small number of persons of European origin lived on the island, including Roman Catholic clerics and two sheepherding families; then, some 250–300 Rapa Nui lived in Tahiti.[3] For the next eighty years Easter Island was, for all practical purposes, closed off from the rest of the world. There were no scheduled visits by steamships, and the only contact came through irregular and infrequent supply ships sent out to the island to service the sheep ranch, which grew to encompass nearly the whole island. The Polynesians were restricted to a two-square-mile plot of land on the southeastern portion of the island where the town of Hanga Roa stands today. This space was surrounded by a four-foot-high stone wall, still standing in most places.

The Chilean Navy took over direct rule of the island in 1953 to protect the interests of the sheep ranch and to establish a stronger overall presence in the region. "The Navy, however, began by administering the island as if it were a ship, with a commander as a governor; a second-in-command; a navy doctor; a paymaster three petty officers, four sergeants, three corporals, one seaman medical helper; and, a naval carpenter."[4] The navy began to strictly enforce the rule requiring the residents of the island to remain within the confines of the community of Hanga Roa except to work on the sheep ranch. They placed a barbed-wire fence on top of the rock wall and punished by flogging or jailing those who were caught outside of the walls without permission. The Rapa Nui were not allowed to leave the island except under extraordinary circumstances, such as the need for medical attention or marriage to a non–Rapa Nui.

The navy's rule proved so oppressive that between 1953 and 1966 thirteen small seven-meter fishing boats left the island in an attempt to reach Tahiti, where a sizeable Rapa Nui community persisted. It is remarkable that five of these escapee vessels made landfall—four in French Polynesia and one in the Cook Islands. In total, an estimated forty Rapa Nui attempted to escape from the island by open boat, and about half survived their voyage.[5] The navy maintained direct control over the island and its people until 1966, when the newly elected government headed by the reformist-minded Christian Democrat Chilean president Eduardo Frei established a locally elected municipality on the island.

The 1960s proved to be a time of rapid and, to the Rapa Nui, monumental change. A large contingent of Americans arrived in January 1967 to build a satellite tracking station and a paved landing strip on the island.[6] The first commercial flight arrived on the island in 1967 (bringing along sufficient tents for its adventurous occupants to stay in while they visited the island). In 1971 Easter Island began receiving twice-weekly scheduled airline flights from Santiago and became a stopover point on the Santiago to Tahiti route of the Chilean-owned LanChile (Lineas Áereas Nationales de Chile) airline. During this same time a number of young island men were sponsored by an international agency interested in the future of Easter Island to study on the Chilean mainland. About twenty lived with Chilean families and receive a quality of education still not available on their home island. Most have long since returned home and are now the educated elite among the Polynesians of the community, important in its political and economic affairs.

In spite of their loss of population in the eighteenth and nineteenth centuries, the Rapa Nui maintained their unique identity. They took on many of the technological aspects of the Latin American Chilean culture but continued to speak their own Polynesian language and thought of themselves as Polynesians. Their Polynesian identity has also been strongly affected by their experience with Tahiti. Between 1890 and 1930 a number of Rapa Nui who had been living in Tahiti returned to their home island, many with Tahitian and Tuamotuan spouses, Tahitian-born children, and a considerable affinity for the Polynesian culture of the Tahitians. They passed their Tahitian cultural experience on to the Rapa Nui at home. Even today, the Tahitian greeting, ¡Iaorana! is the most frequently used salutation by the Easter Islanders, and it is quite common for someone to express thanks with the Tahitian *maruru*. The Rapa Nui dances and songs are also heavily influenced by the Tahitians.

The 1960s also initiated large-scale migration to the island by non-Polynesian Chileans from the South American continent. Between 1960 and 1980, the island's population increased from 753 to nearly 2,000. Some of this increase can be accounted for among the Rapa Nui themselves, but many of them also took advantage of their newly gained freedom of movement to move to the Chilean mainland. In 1982, the last official census allowing ethnic classification found the distribution of the 1,931 people on the island to be: Easter Islanders, 923 (47.8 percent); Mestizos, 313 (16.2 percent); Continentals, 662 (34.3 percent); and Foreigners, 33 (1.7 percent).

The mestizos are, with few exceptions, the descendants of Easter Islander/Continental unions. Because of the draconian rule of the navy until the mid-1960s and also because of the lack of jobs and extreme isolation, it is reasonably safe to assume that, until the civilian government took over in 1967, few non–Rapa Nui elected voluntarily to live on Easter Island. Therefore, most of the 662 Continentals recorded in 1982 can be assumed to be recent arrivals. Also, because of a strict custom of preference among the Rapa Nui themselves, there are no marriages closer than the third cousin, so we can assume that the 313 mestizos are the children of mixed Rapa Nui/Continental marriages that occurred after the mid-1960s.

What drew continental Chileans to move to Easter Island are three closely related circumstances. First, with the exception of withholdings for the Chilean social services (welfare, medicine, and retirement), no taxes of any kind are collected on Easter Island. Since Chile granted tax haven status to its smallest province in the late 1960s, islanders have paid no income, sales, excise, property, or local taxes. All revenues needed to operate the twenty-nine publicly funded agencies on the island are paid directly by the regional or federal governments, including the island's national park system, hospital, school, navy, state bank, air force, national police, post office, national TV station, national petroleum distribution system, municipal and provincial governments, district court, office of public works, and office of public welfare.

The second attraction of Easter Island for the non–Rapa Nui is that most upper-level professionals and administrators live in homes either heavily or entirely subsidized by the agency that owns them. In some cases, the utilities are also subsidized. Also, all flights to and from the Chilean Mainland are available at half the regular fare to Chilean nationals who have lived on the island for more than six months previous to the purchase of the ticket.

A third important reason why Easter Island is attractive to non–Rapa Nui is that the government multiplies all incomes paid to the employees of the twenty-nine agencies just listed by 40 percent. This means that for every 1,000 Chilean pesos earned by a government-paid worker, the government adds 400 extra pesos to the salary.

The combination of no taxes, heavily subsidized housing, affordable return transportation to the continent, and a significantly higher wage has served to attract a number of younger emerging professionals to the island. They see Easter Island as a stepping-stone in their career plans. Jobs on the island are generally eagerly sought, and some of Chile's best and brightest have spent five years (the usual expected term of obligation for these positions) on the island. Most are either young married men with their wives and infant or school-age children, or, single persons, usually men, who enjoy spending their considerable extra cash and free time on a rather slow-paced island lifestyle. The two expected results of this demographic profile are a high attendance of unilingual Spanish-speaking children in the schools and a high rate of marriage between non-Polynesian men and Rapa Nui women.

The number—and influence—of Spanish-speaking children in the local school in Hanga Roa has been documented by Nancy and Roberto Weber.[7] In 1977, 77 percent of the children attending the local school reported that their first language of preference was Rapa Nui; by 1983, the number had dropped to 41 percent; and, by 1989, to 25 percent. In an interview with the Webers, I was told that these statistics pointed in two directions. First, there had been a substantial increase in the number of Spanish-speaking Continentals attending the school. (This agrees with the statistics available to me showing an increase of 662 Continentals in 1982 to nearly 900 in 1992.)[8] Second, there were more children born in mixed Rapa Nui/non–Rapa Nui families who speak Spanish in the home.

Another aspect of Spanish usage, which the Webers stated they were not able to document but which my wife, Margaret and I were able to later verify, was that a child who might enter the school as a Rapa Nui–speaker soon became uncomfortable with the use of the language in school and switched completely to Spanish, even at home. Only two of the teachers in the local school are Rapa Nui, and 31 of the 43 adults on the school payroll are from the continent. Surrounded by monolingual Spanish-speaking peers, teachers, and administrative staff it should not be a surprise that a young child would give in to the flow of discourse. This is strictly a personal choice and not the result of administrative policy. There are no longer any penalties imposed on children who speak Rapa Nui in school; in fact, the school requires all students to study the language in all grade levels. Many of the upper-level teenagers adopt Rapa Nui as their peer language, but they do not know or appreciate its deeper nuances and inner feeling.

The concentration of professional mainland Chileans in the twenty-nine governmental-funded agencies can prove a frustrating reality for the Rapa Nui. Because of the potential labor pool of more than thirteen million persons on the Chilean mainland—and because of the limited facilities and faculty at the local school—most of the upper-level administrative positions on the island are occupied by Continentals. Only five of the *jefes de servicio* (organization heads) of the government-sponsored agencies are local Rapa Nui. Also, the three major nonsponsored agencies—LanChile, Entel-Chile (the telephone system), and the U.S. NASA satellite receiver station—are all headed by non–Rapa Nui. None of the head administrators of the six local workers' unions are Rapa Nui. In fact, over half (256) of the 455 workers in the government-sponsored agencies are mainland Chileans. These facts take on special importance when we remember the generous perquisites that these agencies provide their employees. The Chilean government is aware of the discrepancies between so many of the Continentals (and their families) and the indigenous Rapa Nui. A number of steps have been taken to close the gap.

One major government-sponsored project has been the construction of nearly 500 subsidized homes (*subsidios*) on the island. The census of housing recorded 368 residential units on the island in 1970 and 530 in 1982, an expected increase considering the population growth during that period. Ten years later, there were 1,065 residences, an increase of over 100 percent. The construction of the *subsidios*, which began in 1985 and continued into the early 1990s, accounts for nearly all of the homes built between 1982 and 1992. This increase does not indicate that the population of the island doubled during this period of time. Many of the older homes on the island were of woefully substandard quality. The newly constructed homes with their running water, sliding windows, and electricity were occupied after their completion, and the older homes were either abandoned or torn down. The *subsidios* are not large and seem somewhat unattractive in their rectangular uniformity—but Easter Island has no large pockets of the cardboard and tar paper dwellings so painfully present throughout the Chilean mainland.

Another important aspect of the governmental concern over the economic condition of the people of Rapa Nui has been the nearly non-stop infusion of monies to improve public works, projects that provide a large number of employment opportunities: a multipurpose gymnasium, government office complex, state bank, museum, paved main thoroughfares on the island, airport terminal (to be replaced by an even newer terminal in the near future), breakwater for the harbor, resurfacing and strengthening of the airport runway, a proposed paved road across the island, and on and on. In a discussion with Sergio Rapu, the former governor of the island, I asked if anywhere else in the nation of Chile has received such a major per-capita infusion of public funds. Without hesitation he answered: "That would be impossible!"

For the Rapa Nui, a major negative consequence of the public works projects is that there are often more skilled and unskilled jobs available than there are individuals to fill them. Then Chileans from the mainland are given the opportunity to travel to the island to work. Once they have moved to the island, they often stay on to work on the next project and the next one after that, in direct competition with many of the Rapa Nui.

When these Chilean laborers from the continent find that their jobs on Easter Island are better paying, more stable, and less vulnerable to competition than equivalent positions on the continent, that they get a 40 percent cost-of-living increment and across-the-board tax relief, they often invite close relatives to the island to share in the benefits. Some from this group quickly adopt Rapa Nui behavior and a Polynesian outlook toward life and blend in with their Easter Island neighbors. Most, however, make little effort to try to accommodate themselves to the Rapa Nui way of living. Also, because they are not on the island through an agency-sponsored agreement, they often stay on long after the better-paid professionals have served their five years and moved on in their careers on the continent.

The economic position of the Polynesians on Rapa Nui is not fully dependent on the government-sponsored agencies. There are more than 100 privately owned stores and shops on the island, many of which are owned by the Rapa Nui. Also, many of the workers in the stores are Rapa Nui, even in stores owned by Continentals. In addition, thirty-six men are registered in the municipality as fishermen, most of them Polynesians, and a small number of Rapa Nui are cattle and horse ranchers. Another few families are full-time farmers. However, the single largest sector of the Rapa Nui economy, with the most local-born workers and a financial base that rivals those of the government-subsidized agencies, is tourism.

Sinice 1967, tourists have doubled in number about every ten years. Currently, about 8,000 tourists visit the island annually, approximately three times the total population of the island. The Rapa Nui are the primary group on the island who deal with the tourists. They own three largest hotels, six of the seven midsized hotels, twenty-five of the twenty-eight registered guest houses (*residenciales*), and five of the seven accredited travel agencies.

There are no automobile rental agencies on the island, and because of the absence of tax advantages, the government places no restriction on rentals. Anyone who owns a functioning automobile or motorcycle has the unrestricted legal right to rent it out to the tourists. Rates and terms vary with each prospective customer, often fluctuating wildly in time allotted for the rental, mileage charge, gasoline replacement, and so on, as the week-to-week tourist trade fluctuates. Many Rapa Nui rent out their vehicles for this purpose. Most of the hotels and guest houses will also arrange automobile and motorcycle rentals for their customers.

A number of restaurants and specialty shops in Hanga Roa (many of which are owned by Rapa Nui) cater almost exclusively to the tourist trade. Many Rapa Nui who are otherwise employed spend their leisure making wooden and stone replicas of the statues and other cultural phenomena for which Easter Island is world famous. These souvenirs and psuedoartifacts are sold in stores, in specialty shops, in market places designed for their display and sale, at the entrances of the most impressive archaeological sites on the island, at the airport, on tables along the main streets, in hotel shops and lobbies, at the fishing wharf, in people's front yards, at the entrance to the hospital, from tables set up at the beach, in front of and inside the gymnasium, in the leper colony, across office desks, and, from door to door. The items are generally well made and are eagerly sought after and appreciated by the tourists.

Tourism has helped to ignite a Rapa Nui culture renaissance. When the tourists began to arrive in the late 1960s, there were only a few people on the island who were skilled performers who could entertain these visitors. Most of the dances and songs that appealed to the tourists were of Tahitian origin or inspiration. It became apparent, as the tourists trade grew, that offerings with a more definite Rapa Nui flavor were called for.

There is now an annual song-and-dance fest in October that divides its entries into pre-1970 and post-1970 periods. The pre-1970 section enables the Rapa Nui to hearken back to their precommercial entertainment roots. The newer, post-1970–style performances often have a much more snappy look and sound. In early February comes *Tapati Rapa Nui,* a ten-day celebration of traditional culture that recreates portions of Rapa Nui tradition out of roots grown frightfully fragile and weak. Each *Tapati Rapa Nui* seems to grow stronger and more innovative. It is a splendid sight to see the otherwise conservative and somewhat reserved Rapa Nui painted in the bold yellow, ocher, red, orange, cream, mahogany, and jet black earth tones and adorned with feathers, fibers, woven leaves (and sometimes scarcely little more than their earth tone body paint), celebrating and dancing by torch light or at sunset. At no other time is there such an obvious outward affirmation that "Yes! I am Rapa Nui. I am a Polynesian."

Tourism has had its negative effect on Easter Island, as well. A successful travel agent of Rapa Nui ancestry told me that as tourism increased, so did the prices of commodities and services on the island. He was troubled by the high cost of living tourism had brought and concerned about the division of the Rapa Nui community caused by economic competition.

Twenty-three years ago when the first tourists came, the price for rice, potatoes, flour—everything you needed to eat—was exactly the same as on the continent. So local growers quit growing food because it was impossible to successfully compete with the prices of things from the continent. The local families opened their homes to the tourists. The government made the airlines lower their fares for the islanders. People would fly to Santiago just to see a soccer match. Now the price of the airline ticket for us [the Rapa Nui] is high. The price of food in the stores is high. Everything has gone up with the tourist trade except for our wages. We get a tax benefit and cost-of-living increment, but our wages are still fixed to the basic mainland rate. We can't afford to buy even small green tomatoes and most of us have given up farming. So what do we do? We raise our rental rates for our hotels and guest rooms and go into direct competition with each other. That's what we do!

The Rapa Nui have had a difficult time balancing their needs as a small, isolated, ethnically distinct community against the expectations of the larger Chilean nation. They celebrate the Chilean independence day and the day commemorating the overthrow of the government of Salvador Allende G. and the day of their annexation. They have also, however, created their own ethnic celebrations and have begun to revive their traditional cultural practices. Virtually all adult Rapa Nui speak their Polynesian language fluently and with impassioned animation, knowing full well what has happened to their sister languages in Tahiti, New Zealand, and Hawaii, and knowing equally well that their own children are growing up with Spanish as their language of preference and sociability. They know that theirs is the last generation in which on the street and in public gatherings the fluid vowels of Rapa Nui will drown out the rapid staccato of Chilean Spanish.

The Chilean government has shown a considerable degree of concern for the loss of language and culture amongst all of its ethnic minorities. There were times in the twentieth century when the goal of the central government was to eradicate all ethnic differences and mold all residents of their nation into loyal Chileans and nothing else. The current trend, however, is to recognize and respect these differences and allow the Aymara and Quecheuas of the north, the Mapuche of the Lake District, the Alacaluf and Yagán of the south, and the Rapa Nui of Easter Island a high degree of self-determination and freedom of ethnic expression and development.

In the past twenty years a number of laws and policies have been enacted to promote and preserve these ethnic identities. The most recent is the *Ley Indígena, Nº 19.253, Establece Normas sobre Protección, Formento y Desarrollo de los Indígenas* (the law establishing the rules with regards to the protection, promotion, and development of the indigenous peoples). When I first read the law in its thirty-eight–page entirety, I was impressed with the fairness and dignity it provided for the Rapa Nui and the eight other ethnic minority groups of Chile. I was, therefore, quite surprised when shortly after I had read the document, I was notified that there would be a parade and illegal demonstration (in which the outlawed *Rei Miro* flag of the Rapa Nui would be carried en masse) from the gymnasium to the Catholic church to protest the *Ley Indígena* and to demand its repeal. I hurried down to see just who would be there. There were dozens whom I had considered to be rational and loyal citizens of Chile.

I later asked a friend, one of the leaders of the protest, exactly what he disliked about this new law. He said that it seems on the surface to be beneficial, but that it was objectionable to him because it combines the Polynesian Rapa Nui with the Native American South American tribes. "*¡No somos Indios!*" (We are not Indians!) "We have our own province. We have our own governor. We have our own laws. We do not want to be more like the Indians—we want to be ourselves!" Following up on this line of thought, I later interviewed a man who was not at the protest rally, but who told me that he fully approved of what it represented. He told me that although he was born in his island land under the Chilean flag he was not a Chileno. He was Rapa Nui. "I am darker. I speak Rapa Nui. I have different customs. I have a name which is hard for them to pronounce." He then said, "Yes. I have served in the navy and have traveled the length of Chile. But this soil [pointing out the window] is not Chilean soil—it is the soil of Rapa Nui!"

The people of Easter Island are now extending their recognition of their Polynesian heritage to include a close identification with the rest of Polynesia. They frequently refer to themselves as *Tangata Maori,* a term that unifies them not only with the Maori of New Zealand but with all Eastern Polynesians, and by extension with all Polynesians. But their key identification is with Tahiti. The Rapa Nui have a deep love and attraction for Tahiti that extends into antiquity and that, in modern times, predates their annexation to Chile (at which time there were more Rapa Nui living in Tahiti than on Easter Island). They look to the Chilean continent for protection and financial support and then look to Tahiti—and their hearts lean toward Tahiti. One Rapa Nui expressed it simply: "The Tahitians are our cousins, they are us! They live in a modern, rich place governed by a first-rate developed nation. And what do we have? Chile! Can you blame us for how we feel?"

There is a rising sovereignty movement growing on Easter Island. It has yet to gain a powerful voice and is not yet fully focused on its ultimate goal. Islanders know what is happening elsewhere in Polynesia, however, and listen intently to what other Polynesians have said and are saying about their identity. Recently an impassioned Hawaiian, Lilikala Kame'elehiwa, expressed views that I believe many Rapa Nui hold but have not yet articulated:

Pehea la e ola ai? How shall we live and survive as Hawaiians in the western world? The answer perhaps is in the word ola, "life." We must regain our own 'olelo, "language," to firmly reestablish our link with the ancestors and their wisdom. Our *'olelo* shapes our identity and allows us to view the world through our ancestor's eyes. We must support the *Lahui,* our right to be a sovereign nation, and stubbornly work toward this goal, even for the next seven generations . . . we must have *'Aina* (land) upon which we can live, the *'Aina* that we can *malama* (care for; put in order). In the bosom of our *'Aina,* our earth-mother, we will create our own laws, according to our cultural beliefs, laws that we can understand and administer ourselves. Living in harmony with our beautiful and sacred *'Aina,* we will capture the *pono* (righteousness; state of perfect harmony) of our *Kupuna* (ancestors; elders). However, we must stand ever vigilant and ready to oppose those who would deny us the right to our *'olelo,* to our *Lahui,* or to our *'Aina,* for in doing so they deny us our life, our ola, and the time for genocide has passed.

Shortly after I arrived to conduct field research in Easter Island I asked a Continental working in the governor's office if she knew how many Chileans were presently living there. She thought that except for a few dozen Europeans and Americans like myself, they were all Chileans. Out of curiosity later that day I asked a Rapa Nui the same question. The answer was that about one-third of the people, perhaps 900 or 1,000, were Chileans. I then made a frequent habit of asking this question of both Continentals and Rapa Nui. Most of the time, the Continentals responded with a reply similar to that of the woman in the governor's office—they were all Chileans. Not once did a Rapa Nui give a response that included both Continentals and Rapa Nui as Chileans!

On February 7, 1994, my wife, Margaret, and I were attending the closing ceremony of the *Tapati Rapa Nui* in the gymnasium. It was near or shortly after midnight. A young man, a Rapa Nui, approached us and asked in English, "Why are you here?" I started to answer him in Spanish. He said, "Please, use English. I hate Spanish. I hate Spanish and Spanish-speaking people. I only want you to use Rapa Nui or English." He pointed to Margaret and myself and then swept his hand to point around the whole crowd and said: "You, them—you're all new Rapa Nui. I don't like new Rapa Nui and I don't want you to learn Rapa Nui because you will only learn to speak new Rapa Nui—and it is not good." He then went on to say how the Spanish (meaning, of course, the Chileans) had ruined his people, their language, their culture, the island itself. He raised his voice and said, "They think it's their island. You think it's their island. But it's not. It is my island. I am not a Chileno. I am a Rapa Nui. I am a *Tangata Maori!*"

Notes

Acknowledgment: Special thanks to Andrés Edmunds P. for his contribution to this chapter.

1. J. Douglas Porteous, *The Modernization of Easter Island* (Victoria, B.C.: University of Victoria Press, 1981), 23–24.

2. Paul Bahn and John Flenley, *Easter Island, Earth Island* (New York: Thames and Hudson, 1992).

3. Porteous, *Modernization of Easter Island*, 36–39; Grant McCall, *Rapa Nui: Tradition and Survival on Easter Island*, 2d ed. (Honolulu: University of Hawai'i Press, 1994), 143.

4. Porteous, *Modernization of Easter Island*, 168–70.

5. McCall, *Rapa Nui*, 147–49.

6. Porteous, *Modernization of Easter Island*, 172–73.

7. Robert Weber and Nancy Thiesen de Weber, "¿Podra Sobrevivir el Idoma Rapa Nui?" in *Revista Signos*, no. 28 (vol. 23), Instituto de Literatura y Ciencias del Leguaji: Universidad Católica de Valparaíso, 1990.

8. Claudio Cristino F., Andres Recasens S., Patricia Vargas C., Lilian Gonzales, and Edmundo Edwards, *Isla de Pascua: Proceso, Alcances y Efectos de la Aculturation* (Santiago: Universidad de Chile, Facultad de Arquitectura y Urbanismo, Instituto de Estudios de Pascua, 1984).

Part IV

Emerging Multiethnic Narratives

G. Reginald Daniel

---

10 Multiracial Identity in Brazil and the United States

The Dialectical Setting

Traditionally, Brazil has been contrasted with the United States in terms of its long history of racial and cultural blending. In addition, Brazil has differentiated its population into European Brazilians (*brancos*), multiracial individuals (*pardos*), and Blacks (*pretos*). This ternary model of race relations led to fluid racial/cultural markers and was accompanied by the absence of legalized barriers to equality in both the public and private spheres. It has been argued that in Brazil, not racial but class and cultural signifiers determined one's identity and status in the social hierarchy.

Brazil's racial democracy contrasted sharply with United States race relations. In the United States, European Americans have tried to preserve not only their cultural and racial "purity" but also their dominant status by relegating multiracial individuals to the subdominant group, for instance, by designating as Black everyone of African descent.[1] Furthermore, this binary model of race relations served as the underpinning for Jim Crow segregation: a generalized system of legal and informal exclusion that prevented individuals of African descent from having contact with Whites as equals in political, economic, educational, residential, associational, and interpersonal spheres.

During the 1950s and 1960s, Jim Crow segregation was dismantled in the United States and the myth of racial democracy began to erode in Brazil. Because of changes that have taken place since, the trajectories of race relations in these two countries began to converge. The Black consciousness movement in Brazil, which emerged in 1978 with the formation of the MNU (the Unified Black Movement), began challenging Brazil's ternary model. Part of its strategy was to get more individuals of blended African and European descent to identify themselves as African Brazilian rather than multiracial. During the same period, the multiracial consciousness movement in the United States emerged in 1979 with the founding of I-Pride (Interracial/Intercultural Pride). This educational and support organization for interracial couples and multiracial-identified individuals began challenging the United States' binary model of race relations. The objective was to make it possible for individuals who choose to embrace both their African and European backgrounds to identify themselves as multiracial.

By the 1990s, this debate had crystallized in both Brazil and the United States around procedures for collecting official data on race—particularly on the decennial census. In the United States, the multiracial consciousness movement has pushed to make it possible for multiracial-identified individuals to be enumerated as such; the Black consciousness movement in Brazil has sought to make it possible for Black (*preto*) and multiracial (*pardo*) individuals to be enumerated as a single African Brazilian (*negro*) group rather than as distinct categories. The net result of these new trends has been to move Brazil toward a greater emphasis on the Black/White, or *negro/branco*, dichotomy and to move the United States closer to recognizing three groups—White, multiracial, and Black.[2]

The Brazilian Path: Neither Black Nor White

Notions about the exceptional openness to miscegenation with people of African descent on the part of the Portuguese colonizers of Brazil, and the altruistic motives underlying their differentiation of mulattoes from Blacks, originated largely in Gilberto Freyre's monumental study of Brazilian race relations.[3] Such arguments, however, had more to do with racial romanticism than with reality. Throughout the Americas, and irrespective of the national and cultural origins of the colonizing Europeans, the quantity of miscegenation and the social distinctions made between individuals of varying degrees of African ancestry were motivated primarily by self-interest and closely related respectively to the ratio of European men to women and the ratio of Whites to Blacks.

In Brazil and other areas of Latin America, the colonizing Europeans were a minority and mostly single males. Africans comprised a majority of the colonial population. Rape, fleeting extramarital relations, extended concubinage, and common-law unions between White men and women of African descent were approved, if not encouraged, by an unwritten moral code. There were, however, legal barriers to interracial marriages during most of the colonial period, and formidable social prejudice against such relationships remained in place long afterwards.[4]

As slaves, the mulatto offspring of these unions were often assigned more exacting tasks that symbolized greater personal worth and required greater skill (e.g., as domestics and artisans). The pronounced scarcity of White women mitigated or prevented significant opposition from the legal wife and enhanced the likelihood that these offspring would be the recipients of socially tolerated demonstrations of affection, as well as economic and educational protection. Furthermore, mulattoes were given preferential liberation over Blacks, nearly all of whom were slaves. This made it possible for them early in the colonial period to enter the free classes, where they necessarily filled important interstitial, skilled roles in the economy due to a shortage of White labor.[5]

Free Colored urban artisans, long before abolition, readily advanced from these interstitial positions into the arts, letters, and liberal professions (including medicine, engineering, law, and the civil service), although they were barred from holding public office and entering high-status occupations in the clergy and governmental bureaucracy, and they experienced limitations on educational attainment and other rights. Free Coloreds did not achieve their vertical mobility through direct competition in the open market, but rather through the paternalistic support of patrons in the White elite.[6] It should come as no surprise, therefore, that these mulattoes feared that their position in the labor market would be threatened by the end of slavery. They were reticent to fight against slavery, tended to eschew alliance with slaves, and thus helped preserve the status quo. So reliable were mulattoes that the Portuguese monarchs viewed Free Colored militia as a balance wheel against independence-minded Whites. Both the Portuguese crown and Brazilian slaveholders relied on the Free Coloreds to help expel Dutch invaders. The planter class also used their services in local militia to protect their property, suppress slave uprisings, and catch and return fugitive slaves.[7]

The process of abolition made it possible for Whites to continue to rely on mulatto support long after slavery ended. As long as Blacks were retained in the least remunerative sectors of the secondary labor force as agricultural, industrial, and service laborers, mulattoes willingly settled for token integration into the skilled trades, the petty bourgeoisie, intelligentsia, and white-collar work force.

The paradoxical nature of the Brazilian model has thus assured that African Brazilians, collectively speaking, are denied the privileges of Whites, but mulattoes are rewarded in proportion to their cultural and phenotypical approximation to the European psychosomatic ideal. The inegalitarian nature of this integration is captured in Figure 1. Both the grey and black circles under **b** are in a subdominant position, yet the positioning of the grey circle is not only intermediate, and thus comparatively less subdominant than the black circle, but also linked with the dominant white circle due to its closer somatic approximation to the latter. This window of opportunity that Degler calls the "escape hatch" does not imply that the masses of mulattoes in Brazil gain access carte blanche to the ranks of Whites by virtue of their intermediate position. Rather the "escape hatch" is an informal social mechanism by which a select few multiracial individuals, for reasons of talent, culture, or education, have been allowed token mobility into the middle class and with it the rank of situational "Whiteness."[8] In its broadest sense, however, the escape hatch is an epistemological device that has fostered a collective state of amnesia and schizophrenia, making it possible for other millions of individuals whose ancestry has included African forbearers, but who are phenotypically near-White, to become legally White. This leads to socially sanctioned implicit passing, which sets Brazilian race relations apart from the explicit, but concealed and not so socially approved, passing that occurs in the United States.

Brazil's long history of miscegenation, and its absence of institutionalized White supremacy and legalized barriers to equality, should not, however, obscure the fact that "White" is synonymous with superiority, and inferiority is a general term that has as one of its synonyms the adjective "Black." The ruling elite is overwhelmingly of European descent and European in manners and has implemented forms of discrimination that have kept the majority of African Brazilians in a de facto subordinate status. Furthermore, racial and cultural blending were not posited on egalitarian integration. That is to say, there was not a random integration of European, African, and, by extension, Native American traits, seeking its own "natural" equilibrium, in which equal value was attached to each of these constituents through a reciprocal transracial/transcultural process. It was rather, a process of inegalitarian integration (or assimilation in disguise), an unnatural contest between unequal participants artificially manipulated in order to

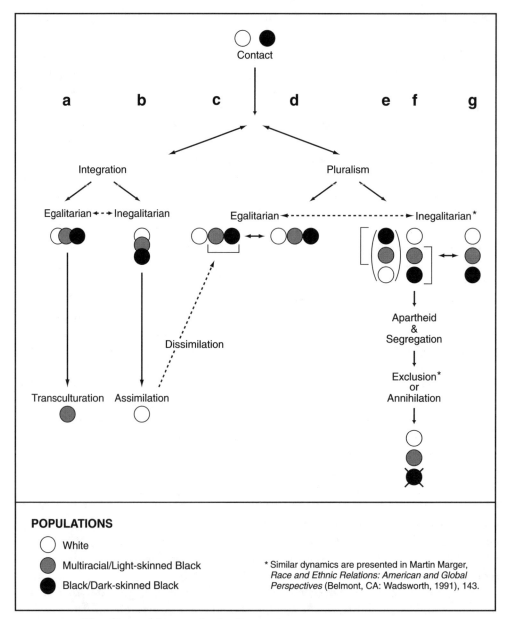

FIGURE I.   Pluralist and Integrationist Dynamics.

purify the Brazilian pedigree and culture of its vast accumulation of African (and Native American) traits with the goal of perpetuating only the European.[9]

These two types of integration are contrasted as **a** and **b** in Figure I. The integrative relationship is indicated by the fact that the circles are linked. However, the dynamic in **a** is horizontal (egalitarian) and therefore not premised on the dominance of any one circle. Also, the outcome of this dynamic is a blend of the white, grey, and black circles. Although this composite is similar to the intermediate grey circle, it is not in fact the result of its dominance. On the other hand, the integrative relationship in **b** is vertical (inegalitarian) and thus hierarchical. The goal of these dynamics is to perpetuate the norm image of the dominant white circle by eliminating the distinctiveness of the subdominant grey and black circles.

Some of these attitudes, of course, reflected toxins indigenous to Brazil's own racial ecology. We cannot, however, ignore the fact that this "whitening" ideology was part of Brazil's response to nineteenth-century Europeans and European Americans who preached the evils of miscegenation. By the latter half of the nineteenth century, most Brazilians, despite official claims to the contrary, were *"mulato claro"* (clear [light]-skinned mulatto), or *"claramente mulato"* (clearly mulatto) in terms of culture, ancestry, or phenotype.[10] Not even the most phenotypically and culturally European individuals of the elite could be certain that their family genealogy had remained free of African ancestry and, therefore, insulated from the stigma of slavery and miscegenation.

If miscegenation was the disease, however, whitening through miscegenation became the prescription for a cure. In order to achieve this, the Brazilian government encouraged the immigration of Europeans and passed waves of legislation restricting the immigration of Blacks. Many individuals sought spouses more apparently European in values, beliefs, and physical appearance than themselves; Brazilians exhibited a feverish desire to import everything from ideas to cultural artifacts that tasted of Europe and the United States. At the same time, informal inegalitarian pluralism was envisioned as the solution that eventually would eliminate the African Brazilian masses through the "laissez-faire genocide" of sharply lower levels of education and higher rates of poverty, malnutrition, disease, and infant mortality.[11] This type of pluralism is depicted in **f** in Figure 1. The pluralistic relationship is indicated by the fact that the circles are separated, not linked as they are in the integrationist half of the chart. The relationship not only is vertical (inegalitarian) and thus hierarchical, but results in the exclusion and, ultimately, annihilation of the grey and black circles by the white circle, due to their difference.

Pervasive miscegenation and the escape hatch, by blurring and softening the line between Whites and Blacks, indeed helped to diminish any collective problem in post-slavery Brazil stemming from race per se. They also served to maintain de facto White dominance and control by creating the illusion that whatever prejudice and discrimination exist in Brazil are not based on race but on acquired social, economic, and cultural characteristics subject to alteration by individual merit and achievement during one's lifetime. In fact, however, the privilege of first-class citizenship is awarded selectively in accordance with one's approximation to European phenotypical and cultural traits, working in combination with one's economic standing. Consequently, the polarization between haves and have-nots tends to follow the racial divide between White and Black.

Brazilian race relations are thus propelled by the same dichotomization and hierarchical valuation of "Blackness" and "Whiteness" that has characterized race relations in the United States, although these restrictions were not formalized. The escape hatch in Brazil, however, has historically brought with it the expectation, if not the actual achievement, of social advantages in the larger society and, more important, a psychological edge in the pursuit of those opportunities not historically available to light-skinned Blacks in the United States. The escape hatch has assured that most of those African Brazilians who benefit from this meritocracy are more multiracial than Black.

This dynamic has retarded political mobilization along racial lines, by guaranteeing that those individuals most likely to possess the cultural, intellectual, and social skills to unmask the myth of racial democracy, and speak for the African Brazilian masses, are coopted into silence.[12] Breaking through the hardened chrysalis of second-class citizenship, without also studiously avoiding the topic of racism, is a delicate balance that vertically mobile mulattoes find challenging. Not being White, yet aspiring to be treated as first-class citizens, multiracial individuals at any time could be classified as racial inferiors by Whites simply by being treated as second-class citizens racially, such that the escape hatch could easily become a trap door to the bottom of society.

The United States Path: Either Black or White

Race relations in the colonial United States—particularly in the North and upper South (North Carolina and the area northward and westward)—differed markedly from those in Brazil.[13] The early balance between European males and females precluded the permissive attitudes toward miscegenation and made the White family formed by legal marriage the standard social unit.[14]

If demographics in the United States made racial and cultural blending less pervasive than in Brazil, they did not prevent them from occurring. The existence of African and European centers of reference fostered an accommodation of and a melding of perceptions about time, aesthetics, approaches to ecstatic religious experience, an understanding of the Godhead, and ideas of the afterlife. Even the distinctive features of the southern dialect are a blend of West African and Old English speech patterns. Although Whites were generally unaware of their own transformation in this process, by the end of the colonial period, Blacks and Whites had forged a southern culture that in varying degrees was a transcultural blend.[15]

Also, during the early seventeenth century in the American South, the numbers of Blacks were comparatively small, and the distinction between White servant and Black slave was less precise than between bond and free. Consequently, a number of African-descent Americans were able to enjoy a measure of freedom in the public sphere and, in some cases, become independent landowners and employers of servants. In the private sphere, phenotypical differences were accommodated, and there were no laws prohibiting the commingling of ancestral lines—despite strong social prejudice against miscegenation. A small, but not insignificant, number of Blacks and Whites of both sexes intermarried or formed common-law unions of some duration and had legitimate offspring, alongside more widespread clandestine and fleeting liaisons that involved births outside of wedlock.[16]

Only with the increased presence of African slaves in the late seventeenth and early eighteenth centuries were codes promulgated to solidify the distinction between slave and free. At the same time, the southern colonies, and some northern colonies, began to enforce laws punishing sexual relations between Blacks and Whites and prohibiting intermarriages. Even in colonies where intermarriage was allowed, it carried painful social consequences. These legal restrictions, however, did not result in a marked decrease in miscegenation. The key change was a shift in public attitudes. Rape and extended concubinage involving White slave masters (or overseers) and women of African descent, whether slave or free, continued to be tolerated (and would become the source of most subsequent miscegenation). They conferred no legal status on the relationship and, thus, posed little threat to the slave system. Marriage, on the other hand, which reflected an assumption that the two parties were social equals, could not be allowed.

This change in attitudes toward miscegenation had a profound effect on attitudes regarding multiracial individuals. It was less racial and cultural blending than the challenge mulattoes implicitly presented to White domination that was feared. As the population of African descent expanded to meet labor needs, slavery and African ancestry became inextricably intertwined; it also became necessary to ensure White dominance over individuals of African descent. Lawmakers discovered that if legislation and public pronouncements against miscegenation were unsuccessful at controlling the sexual impulses of the European American male population, there was little harm done so long as White domination was preserved by disowning mulatto offspring. In fact, this practice had the dual advantage of divesting the offspring of White slave masters and slave women of privileges associated with paternity, as well as increasing the number of slaves.[17]

The early balance between European males and females in the United States, coupled with the numerical dominance of Whites diminished the White need for collaboration from multiracial individuals in protecting their dominant status. It precluded the pervasive miscegenation and the differentiation of multiracial individuals from Whites and Blacks in the social structure that occurred in Brazil. Although Free Coloreds in the United States also tended to be multiracial, there were always plenty of Whites.[18]

In the United States, the legal status of free mulattoes (and Free People of Color generally speaking) was ambiguous up to the time of the Revolution, although Whites had begun to chip away sporadically at their rights as early as the 1660s. In the early eighteenth century, when slaves began pouring into the colonies, however, their status rapidly deteriorated. Some southern legislatures began to make private emancipations by slave owners more difficult, to tax free mulatto women discriminatorily, and to deny equal rights to free mulattoes—including the right to vote and carry firearms. With the expanding numbers of Free Coloreds in the late eighteenth century, some states barred them from holding office, serving in the militia, and testifying against Whites; placed restrictions on their interstate travel and migration; and required them to carry passes giving proof of their free status or risk being fined, expelled from the state, or reenslaved.

The ancestral quantum defining legal Blackness varied from state to state. In most of the United States, any individual with up to one-eighth or one-sixteenth African ancestry would be subject to the laws regulating Free People of Color. Informally, however, any African ancestry—the one-drop rule of hypodescent—was used to classify a person as Black.[19] This device supported a generalized system of inegalitarian pluralism designed to exclude all individuals of African descent from having contact with Whites as equals, lest mulattoes slip into the ranks of Whites. This dynamic is captured in **f** in Figure 1. The pluralistic relationship is indicated by the fact that the circles are separated, not linked as they are in the integrationist half of the chart. The relationship is not only vertical (inegalitarian) and hierarchical, but more important, the grey and black circles are bracketed into one category. This results in the exclusion of both, despite the somewhat higher positioning of the grey circle in relationship to the white circle. Even those few individuals who have "passed" into the White population necessarily have been predominantly of European descent and carried very little African ancestry into the European American community. Consequently, only about 1 percent of the genes of European Americans is derived from West African ancestors, although the total of European Americans with West African forebears would number in the millions.[20]

Throughout the nineteenth and into the twentieth century, except for a brief retrenchment during Reconstruction (1865–1877), state after state enacted legislation not merely to prohibit interracial sex and marriage by imposing fines and penalties but also to void the marriages. This was accompanied by the universal acceptance of the one-drop rule. This was true even in those parts of the lower South that previously had exhibited a ternary model of race relations similar to Brazil.[21]

The Anglo-American patriarchy employed the one-drop rule as "the ideal answer to its labor needs, its extracurricular and inadmissible sexual desires, its compulsion to maintain its [culture and ancestral lines] purebred, and the problem of maintaining, at least in theory, absolute dominance, superiority and social control."[22] This device, by codifying the dichotomization and hierarchical valuation of "Blackness" and "Whiteness," underpinned a system of inegalitarian pluralism that restricted legal and informal contact as equals between individuals of African descent and Whites. At the end of the nineteenth century, these restrictions were ensured through Jim Crow segregation.

A New Brazilian Path: The Black Consciousness Movement

Despite the absence of institutionalized barriers to equality in Brazil, as compared to the United States, Brazil's image as a racial democracy began to erode under the weight of massive data compiled in the 1950s by Brazilian and foreign social scientists. These scholars revealed a complex web of correlations between phenotype, culture, and class in determining social stratification. Comprehensive data were lacking, some important regional variations existed, and researchers' opinions varied on how physical appearance might affect future social mobility. There was a consensus, however, that Brazilians who were phenotypically more African were disproportionately found at the bottom of society in terms of education and occupation.[23]

Journalists soon followed with anecdotal evidence of a pattern of subtle yet unmistakable racial discrimination. Discrimination was more complex than in the binary model of United States race relations and had never been codified after the colonial era. Furthermore, Brazilians could still tout the fact that they had avoided the United States' violent urban uprisings and its White supremacist ideology. The growing body of evidence nevertheless made the Brazilian elite cautious about discussing race relations. Paradoxically, the myth of racial democracy was systematically and staunchly defended by Brazil's ruling elite and reinforced by the military dictatorships that dominated Brazilian politics from 1964 to 1985.

During that time period, further research on racial inequality was censored by claims that no such problem existed. In 1969, this resulted in the "involuntary" retirement of university faculty who were branded subversives for researching race relations in Brazil. The machinery of the state also decreed that any efforts to mobilize along racial lines were "racist," "subversive," a threat to national security, and punishable by imprisonment. Individuals who organized to address a problem that the state declared did not exist were viewed as creating a problem and accused of having imported a contagion from the United States. Many individuals were imprisoned; others were exiled by self-imposition or government decree. In addition to the censorship of public discussion of race, no racial data were collected in the 1970 census. The principal reason given for the decision was that previous data had been notoriously unreliable, because definitions of racial category lacked uniformity. In actuality, officials were seeking to promote the notion that racial criteria were insignificant in determining the distribution of wealth, power, privilege, and prestige by depriving researchers (and therefore the public and politicians) of figures that would make it possible to verify how poorly African Brazilians fared in education, jobs, income, and health.[24]

The veil of silence cast over the discussion of racial inequality was not lifted until the 1970s during the gradual liberalization of the national sociopolitical ecology and the lifting of authoritarian rule. African Brazilians took advantage of the celebration of the abolition of slavery in 1978 to organize protests against police brutality, mistreatment by public agencies, and an overt act of discrimination in which three African Brazilian youth were barred from a yacht club. None of these events was unusual itself. But growing covert racial tension in Brazil in the early 1970s and the civil rights movement in the United States combined to set the stage for the Unified Black Movement, the MNU (*O Movimento Negro Unificado*).[25]

The MNU enjoyed some publicity in the late 1970s and early 1980s but gained greater attention from academics abroad than in Brazil. Since its inception, the MNU has been dominated by the urban bourgeoisie and plagued by class divisions. This has kept from it the broad support of other, particularly rural, sectors of the African Brazilian community, which remain largely unaware of its existence. Furthermore, the MNU's goal of mobilizing an African Brazilian plurality to challenge the dominant assimilationist ideology has met with hostility from the political and cultural establishment. At best, movement members have been termed "un-Brazilian" and mindless imitators of the U.S. civil rights movement. At worst, the MNU's egalitarian pluralism has been described as racist, reverse apartheid. The contrast between these two types of pluralism is captured in e and f in Figure 1. The pluralistic relationship is indicated by the circles being separated, not linked, as they are in the integrationist half of the chart. The relationship in e is not only vertical (inegalitarian) and thus hierarchical but reverses the positions of the previously subdominant black and dominant white circles in f. However, e and f differ from the Black consciousness movement, which is best reflected in c. The black and grey circles are bracketed by virtue of their shared dissimilarities to the white, yet the intention is neither to diminish the uniqueness of the grey circle nor to exclude the white circle. Rather, the goal is to establish a horizontal (as opposed to hierarchical) and thus egalitarian relationship that raises the positions of the two previously subdominant and excluded circles.

African Brazilian activists have received tentative support from intellectuals, students, progressive church people, and workers committed to political and social change.

Many of these individuals have socialist leanings and view African Brazilians as part of a larger transracial proletariat. They consider racism to be an epiphenomenon of class inequality and argue that by addressing the latter, one automatically addresses the former. Although they agree that the racial prejudice and discrimination directed against African Brazilians have led to gross inequalities in educational, socioeconomic, and political opportunities, they have focused their attention primarily on the poor, unemployed, and illiterate. They believe that singling out African Brazilians for special treatment as a racial plurality would deviate from the main course of social reform.

Notwithstanding the MNU's lack of mass support for a race-specific agenda, or its failure to organize a large race-based electorate in governmental politics, it is part of a larger Black consciousness movement encompassing a wide variety of social, cultural and political organizations and activities. This can be seen in the revitalization of African-derived religion and music, as well as a surge in the writing of African Brazilian literature. Militant African Brazilian action groups have gained the support of the leading national labor confederation and of domestic employees. Prominent Black and multiracial individuals have begun to speak out about their experiences with racial discrimination.[26]

The Black consciousness movement's efforts also have been aided by a new generation of social scientists. These researchers not only helped get the race question reinstated on the 1980 census but also provided a rigorous analysis of official data from earlier censuses and government surveys of the 1970s and 1980s. As a result, they documented glaring disparities in health, income, and education between Whites (54 percent of the population) and African Brazilians (46 percent).[27] These findings lifted the long veil of silence on race and its role in determining social inequality. More important, they showed that the racial divide, socioeconomically speaking, is primarily located between Whites and the African Brazilian masses and only secondarily between mulattoes and Blacks.

It is true that multiracial individuals have entered the petit bourgeoisie as teachers, journalists, artists, clerks, and low-level officials, are promoted more easily, and earn more than their Black counterparts. In fact, the most recent data indicate that mulattoes earn 42 percent more than Blacks.[28] It is equally true that rates of intermarriage and residential integration between multiracials and Whites are higher than between Whites and Blacks.[29] The presence of African ancestry in one's genealogy or some phenotypically African traits does not preclude a self-identification or social designation as White. Consequently, the credentials distinguishing someone who is White from someone who is multiracial are ambiguous.

Nevertheless, Whites earn another 98 percent more than mulattoes, and the intermediate positioning of the majority of those 40 percent of Brazilians who are considered multiracial is much closer to Blacks than to Whites. For the most part, they are excluded from the most prestigious professions, such as medicine, law, academia, upper-level government, and the officer and diplomatic corps. Even entry-level jobs in the primary labor force that require a "good appearance," such as receptionists and bank tellers, or jobs with even minimal authority, such as entry-level federal employees, are effectively closed to mulattoes. The multiracial population, along with the 6 percent of African Brazilians who are designated as Blacks, remains disproportionately concentrated at the bottom of society, as agricultural and industrial workers and service employees, or in the ranks of the unemployed.[30] Whites are not only seven times more likely than African Brazilians to be college graduates, but African Brazilian professionals also earn 20–25 percent less than their White counterparts. Blacks and multiracials have more difficulty breaking out of the proletariat and also suffer increasing disadvantages as their class mobility increases.[31]

A New United States Path:
The Multiracial Consciousness Movement

The dismantling of Jim Crow segregation and the implementation of civil rights laws over the last forty years dissolved the formal barriers to equality in the United States. More fluid intergroup relations have led to increased intermarriage. Approximately 98 percent of Blacks and Whites still marry within their respective communities, but there was a substantial increase nationally from 65,000 in 1970 to 246,000 by 1992.[32]

Although we do not yet have reliable data on the offspring from these marriages, children of African and European parentage are believed to number from 600,000 to several million.[33] This population received limited attention from scholars prior to the 1980s. Previous research is outdated, contradictory, or based on small-scale studies of clinical populations. Most stressed the importance for blended children to identify as African Americans, because society would view them as such. The children's mental health was defined by how successfully they achieved an African American identity. Many intermarried couples, however, are seeking to bring both Black and White backgrounds to the identity of their offspring. They use a variety of terms including "rainbow," "brown," "melange," "blended," "mixed," "mixed-race," "biracial," "interracial," and "multiracial." All these terms challenge policies and social attitudes that maintain the one-drop rule, which designates as Black everyone who is not "pure" White.[34]

In 1979, intermarried couples in Berkeley founded I-Pride (Interracial/Intercultural Pride) to provide general support for interracial families. Its specific aim (achieved in 1981) was to get the Berkeley Public Schools to include a multiracial classification on school forms. More than fifty similar organizations, with names such as Multiracial Americans of Southern California, the Biracial Family Network, and the Association of Multiethnic Americans (AMEA), have come into existence over the past decade. They are composed primarily of Black and White couples and their first-generation (or biracial) children but in some cases include other interracial couples and their offspring. Most organizations also include a smaller number of multigenerational individuals who have backgrounds that have been blended for several generations; they are viewed by the general society as Black, but have resisted identifying solely with the African American community.[35]

This new multiracial identity is not, however, indicative of someone who simply acknowledges, as do many Blacks, the presence of other ancestries besides African. This identity, therefore, differs from that of African Americans (who for the most part have multiple racial/cultural *backgrounds* but have a single racial/cultural *identity* as Black) in that it replaces this one-dimensional *identity* with a more multidimensional configuration. Nor is the new multiracial identity simply openness to multiculturalism;

a multicultural identity is applicable to anyone—including African American– and European American–identified individuals—who, irrespective of genealogy or ancestry, display a general temperamental openness and sensitivity to racial and cultural differences. These individuals, thus, have an affinity with more than one racial/cultural context, or blend aspects of these contexts into a new personal synthesis, *due to exposure to multiple racial/cultural groups.* However, the new multiracial identity is indicative of individuals who feel a sense of kinship with both the Black and White communities, directly in response to the *multiple racial/cultural backgrounds in their genealogy.* Exposure to these backgrounds enhances and helps concretize this feeling of kinship. Simple awareness of those backgrounds, however, can catalyze this sentiment, and lack of contact does not preclude its presence.[36]

The new multiracial individuals are neither totally dependent on the cultural predispositions of any one racial group nor completely free from the sociocultural conditioning of their racial backgrounds or contexts. The psychosocial configuration of their identity is premised, instead, on a style of self-consciousness that involves a continuous process of "incorporating here, discarding there, responding situationally."[37] Since contemporary multiracial individuals maintain no rigid boundaries between themselves and the various contexts within which they operate, their identity has no fixed or predictable parameters. They are liminal individuals whose identity has multiple points of reference and yet has no circumference, because it manifests itself *on* the boundary. Their marginality, however, neither precludes an affinity with both Blacks and Whites nor translates into the social dislocation and personal alienation traditionally ascribed to multiracial individuals.

Those traditional frameworks (particularly misinterpretations of sociologist Robert Park's theories), common before the 1970s, argued that marginality itself is necessarily pathological and the source of lifelong personal conflict, characterized by divided loyalties, ambivalence, and hypersensitivity as a result of the mutually exclusive natures of Black and White backgrounds. In support of racist hierarchy, they focused on the "psychological dysfunctioning" of multiracial offspring as a justification for discouraging miscegenation, rather than on the sociological forces that made psychological functioning problematic. These theorists not only distorted Park's actual theory of marginality, but also overshadowed other contemporary theorists who argued that marginality might imbue individuals with a broader vision and wider range of sympathies, due to their ability to identify with more than one racial reference group.[38]

Theories formulated since the 1970s and data collected since the 1980s have overturned this myth of negative marginality. There is a growing consensus that multiracial individuals may variously experience some of the ambiguities and strains that come with marginality in a society that views Black and White identities as mutually exclusive. Yet this is counterbalanced by increased tolerance of differences and appreciation of commonalities that derive from feeling kinship with both Blacks and Whites.[39]

The one-drop rule has become such an accepted part of the U.S. fabric that few are aware this device is uniquely applied to African-descent North Americans. All multiracial-identified individuals, therefore, must develop strategies for coping with societal pressures enforcing the one-drop rule. This mechanism challenges the legitimacy of their comfort with both racial backgrounds and their claim to membership in both communities. It also continually assigns them a racial identity that contradicts their personal identity.[40]

In the past there have been other, quite different manifestations of multiracial identity, including integration through "passing" and the formation of urban elites (e.g., blue-vein societies, Louisiana Creoles of Color) and rural enclaves (e.g., triracial isolates). These were responses to a system of segregation that sought to control the potential threat to White dominance posed by individuals of African descent (see **f** in Figure 1). They were less a response to the forced denial of one's European ancestry or cultural orientation than a reaction to being subordinated and having one's full ancestry denied. Those strategies maintained the hierarchical valuation attached to African American and European American racial/cultural differences. They operated out of inegalitarian integrationist and inegalitarian pluralist dynamics (depicted in Figure 1 as **b** and **g**). Those tactics were products of the Eurocentrism in the larger society and responsible for a pernicious colorism among African-descent Americans. This phenomenon has often resulted in the preferential treatment of individuals who more closely approximate Whites in consciousness, behavior.

In Figure 1, passing is illustrated in **b**; the Louisiana Creoles of Color, triracial isolates, and blue-vein societies are represented in **g**. Both are responses to **f**, in which the relationship between the circles is hierarchical and the grey and black circles are bracketed into one category. The circles are separated and excluded by virtue of their differences, despite a somewhat higher positioning of the subdominant grey circle in relationship to the black circle. The new multiracial identity is neither based on the desire to gain special privileges that would be precluded by identifying as Black nor is it synonymous with the psychosocial pathology of colorism. Whether it operates as an integrative identity, with both the Black and the White communities as reference groups; as a pluralistic and intermediate identity that blends aspects of both Black and White but is neither; or as an identity that operates more or less from both of these trends—this new identity resists both the dichotomization and hierarchical valuation of African American and European American cultural and racial differences. These dynamics are illustrated in Figure 1 as **a** and **d**. The relationship in both is egalitarian, so no circle dominates. In **d**, the relationship is pluralistic; mutual respect is accorded to the uniqueness of each circle. In **a**, a fusion emerges out of the three circles, in which mutual value is attached to the contribution each makes to the resulting blend. This composite is a melding of the three circles and similar to the intermediate grey circle but is not in fact the result of its dominance. The new multiracial identity thus not only recognizes the commonalities among Blacks and Whites (integration) and, at the same time, appreciates the differences (pluralism), but more important is posited on an egalitarian blending of pluralism and integration, in which Blacks and Whites are seen as relative, rather than absolute, extremes on a continuum of grays.

Data collected since the 1980s indicate that many individuals are navigating these challenging and uncharted waters of the new multiracial consciousness. Opponents, however, fear that the new multiracial identity, despite its egalitarian rhetoric, will actually sharpen intraracial stratification among African Americans, by widening the divide between the less privileged Black masses and the privileged few. The privileged historically have included more individuals who physically resembled Europeans and expressed less Black consciousness.[41]

Some scholars believe that the Black consciousness movement of the 1960s and 1970s significantly reduced color bias in the African American community. Recent studies found, however, that the gap between light- and dark-skinned African-descent Americans in terms of educational attainment, occupation, and income is as significant as the schism between all African Americans and European Americans. These studies, when compared to data compiled between 1950 and 1980, indicate that nothing has changed appreciably. These scholars do not, however, support the argument that the recent mobility of some African Americans is merely the result of accumulated benefits passed on by their families' higher socioeconomic status stemming back to preferential liberation during slavery. Scholars conclude, rather, that the primary factor is phenotype, particularly skin color, which continues to influence social stratification in the larger society.[42]

Other scholars argue that the discrediting of White supremacy and the dissolution of legalized inegalitarian pluralism have led to increased numbers, integration, and affluence of the Black bourgeoisie[43] and to an increase in the significance of culture and class as factors determining social stratification. Correspondingly, many European Americans and some privileged African-descent Americans have come to view continued government intervention in racial matters as no longer necessary, even pernicious.[44] Despite the legitimacy of pleas for race-neutral policies, this emergence in the United States of the myth of racial democracy—a belief that has been the cornerstone of Brazilian racial etiquette for most of the twentieth century and the greatest obstacle to eradicating racial inequality—originates largely from White fear of losing wealth, power, privilege, and prestige. The backlash against "racial preferences" undermines many of the gains in civil rights and obscures the fact that the attitudinal and behavioral bases of racism have merely gone underground, and that only a select few African-descent Americans have moved from the margin to the mainstream, while the Black proletariat has been pushed from the margin onto the periphery of society.[45]

Although most European Americans have repudiated notions of racial and cultural "purity" that supported the ideology of White supremacy, these trends do not indicate that the *hierarchical* relationship between Whiteness and Blackness that upholds White privilege has been dismantled. The achievement of comparatively greater integration by African-descent Americans indicates rather that the *dichotomization* of Blackness and Whiteness, originating in African American and European American racial and cultural differences, has been attenuated. The one-drop rule has ceased to be the primary, if not singular, factor determining the social location of African-descent Americans. This is due to an increase in the importance of *color* (phenotype), working in combination with shared values, beliefs, and customs associated with class, as an informal line of demarcation and stratification in the larger society.

This does not signal a decline in the significance of race per se, but rather that the adjectives in the *semantic distinction* between light- and dark-skinned African-descent Americans have gained significance in relation to the noun. Consequently, those individuals of African descent who display a more European phenotype and share similar sociocultural values with middle- and upper-class Whites have achieved greater wealth, power, privilege, and prestige in the larger society in a manner similar to their achievement in Brazil. This type of integration remains inegalitarian, in that it furthers the illusion of power sharing without European Americans actually giving up structural domination and control. It disguises the fact that the status accorded to race essentially remains unchanged, although the exact relationship between race and opportunity has been modified. For Whites—regardless of culture and class—race locates wealth, power, privilege, and prestige; for Blacks—irrespective of color, culture, or class—race identifies disadvantages and constraints.[46]

Given these insidious toxins in the racial ecology, African Americans have not sought complete integration in the private arena despite having challenged both the legal and informal inegalitarian pluralism barring them from integrating with Whites as equals—including intermarriage. Many Blacks argue that neither intermarriage nor a multiracial identification would result in the egalitarian blending of African American and European American racial/cultural differences into a more inclusive transracial/transcultural commonality (see **a** in Figure 1). Rather, they would lead to inegalitarian integration—assimilation, **b**—which would increase commonalities between Blacks and Whites by eliminating African American racial and cultural distinctiveness. Multiracial individuals would be coopted into the mainstream of society, **b**, while the Black masses would be further marginalized, **f**, much as in Brazil's "racial democracy."

What many Blacks envision instead is a mosaic of mutually respectful and differentiated African American and European American racial/cultural pluralities—egalitarian pluralism (see **c** in Figure 1). Both Whites and Blacks would have equal access to all aspects of the public sphere, with the option of integrating in the private sphere—egalitarian integration, **a**. In this case, the selective pattern would be voluntary, rather than mandated by Whites, such that if and when Blacks choose to integrate they do so as equals. If European Americans have become more willing to bend the one-drop rule, some African Americans, paradoxically, hold on to this device ever more tenaciously. They view it as necessary for maintaining a distinct but equal African American racial and cultural plurality, and for mobilizing Blacks in the continuing struggle against White privilege.[47]

Converging Paths

Brazil: Toward the Binary Model

Prior to fifteen years ago, discussion on Brazilian race relations was primarily expressed in historical and anthropological discourse. Historians focused on laws, traveler's accounts, memoirs, parliamentary debates, and newspaper articles; anecdotal accounts were their standard source of information. They generally neglected researching police and court records, health archives, personnel files, and other sources from which they might have constructed time series. And historians seldom studied race relations in contemporary society. Anthropologists generally studied African-derived religious and linguistic systems, and creative expression in the arts. When they did examine race relations, their focus was primarily on the ambiguity and situational nature of racial/cultural markers, and provided little analysis of larger structural issues of education, income, and occupation, etc., as they related to race.

The new generation of sociologists after the 1960s, however, has provided African Brazilian militants and White activists with quantitative data to wage their struggle for social change at the level of unions, courts, employers, and the media. Nevertheless, there is no comprehensive and in-depth overview of statistics after 1976. Much more information on race and health, housing, education, family structure, and so on, is needed, yet questions on census forms are designed to collect only the most basic information. Indeed, Census Bureau policies have been so obstructionist that most of the important information has never been published. The data that are available can only be obtained on tapes, and researchers were denied access to these sources for years.[48]

It would be premature to conclude that the Black consciousness movement's dissimilationist tactics for forging an egalitarian African Brazilian plurality have had a major impact on the prevailing assimilationist ideology. It is true that the 1988 Constitution, for the first time in Brazilian history, outlawed racism, declaring that "the practice of racism constitutes a crime that is unbailable and without statute of limitation and is subject to imprisonment according to the law." Yet, the antiracist article in the Constitution of 1988 is more rhetoric than societal commitment. Brazilian civil rights lawyers are finding it difficult in practice to establish a legal basis for criminal complaints.[49]

Although Geledés, a São Paulo based nongovernmental organization focusing on the problems of African Brazilian women, has pressed at least sixty-two cases of racial discrimination before the courts, by 1992 only four cases had been brought to trial. Governor Franco Montoro in São Paulo (and his successor, Orestes Quércia) and Leonel Brizola during his first term as mayor in Rio de Janiero initiated policies to move against racial discrimination. They placed African Brazilians in prominent positions and prohibited employers from requiring domestics to use separate stairwells and elevators, only to have their initiatives undermined by their successors. There has been some discussion of compensatory measures in the manner of affirmative action. Such tactics, however, are viewed with the suspicion that they would aggravate rather than resolve the problem of racial inequality.[50]

These trends suggest that the political and cultural establishment in Brazil has not been significantly affected by the new data about racial inequality. Although the myth of racial democracy has been largely discredited, it still dominates public discussion. There were no African Brazilians on the committee set up in 1984 by the Ministry of Justice to publish five books on the centennial of the abolition of slavery. Although African Brazilians mounted massive public demonstrations against racism during the centennial celebrations in the spring of 1988, their protests were overshadowed by a barrage of academic papers and civic ceremonies extolling Brazil's genius in having allegedly liquidated slavery without upheavals.[51]

African Brazilian activists, however, regard their battle as only in its preliminary stages. Since 1978, one of their prime goals has been to awaken more individuals to the reality of Brazil's racial democracy ideology. They have exposed this doctrine as a sinister myth that has translated into inegalitarian integration, or assimilation for a privileged few multiracial individuals (and some rare Blacks)—who are thus coopted into an alliance as "insiders." Simultaneously, it has perpetuated gross inequalities in the areas of education, jobs, income, and health between Whites and the African Brazilian masses through inegalitarian pluralism in the manner of de facto, if not de jure, apartheid. The complex relationship between these two inegalitarian dynamics is captured in Figure 1, **b** and **f**: the inegalitarian relationship between the white, grey, and black circles allows for a limited amount of linkage between the three circles contingent upon their approximation to the norm image of the dominant white circle. However, this trend operates simultaneously with another more pervasive one based not only on separation but, ultimately, on the exclusion of the grey and black circles.

The Brazilian Institute of Geography and Statistics (IBGE) documented these disparities between Whites (*brancos*) and the African Brazilian masses (*negros*) in 1980 when it begin analyzing and publishing racial data in dichotomous rather than trichotomous form. This change in procedure was no doubt a response in part to demands made by African Brazilian activists, and similar recommendations made by the new generation of social scientists. Although the IBGE had not completely abandoned the traditional three-category concept of race, it had moved toward a conceptualization of Brazilian race relations similar to the binary United States model.[52]

Black organizations and nine governmental agencies mounted a joint publicity campaign with funds from the Ford Foundation and Terra Nuova (an Italian agency for cooperation), directing all Brazilians to be more "conscientious" in filling out the racial question on the 1990 census. The campaign sought to explain the reality behind the myth of racial democracy. Its ultimate goal, however, was aimed at sensitizing African Brazilians to the concept *negro* as an affirmation of a politicized racial identity, rather than the color coding of *preto* and *pardo*.[53] The spirit of the campaign was captured in the slogan "Não Deixe sua Côr Passar em Branco. Responda com Bom C/Senso" (Don't let your color be passed off as White. Respond with good [census] sense). The campaign began in 1990, but the census was canceled that year because of problems between the Ministry of the Economy and the Census Bureau, and strikes the following year by census staff short-circuited discussions that might have completed the switch in terminology. Activists, however, hoped that African Brazilians would identify with the concept *negro* to such an extent that the Census Bureau would be forced to make this change by the year 2000 census.[54]

Although the Black consciousness movement was unsuccessful in getting the Census Bureau to use *negro* as an official overarching term in collecting data on the 1990 census, discussions on the topic for the 2000 census are ongoing. The IBGE is considering the option of keeping *pardo,* with a suboption that would allow Brazilians to claim "African ancestry." *Branco, preto, amarelo,* and *Indígena* (Indigenous Brazilians) would all remain. (Traditionally, the indigenous population was listed under *pardo.* However, beginning with the 1990 census it appeared as a separate racial category.) More important, Brazil's president, Fernando Henrique Cardoso, has called upon the IBGE to continue its policy of grouping *pretos* and *pardos* together. This grouping would likely happen not in actual tabulations, but in the presentation of data and certain of the cross-tabulation work with income, education, and so on. In other words, the IBGE would continue to count by four separate categories, but for the purposes of public presentation and certain statistical work, the relevant categories would be "White" and "non-White," if not *branco* and *negro*. It is unlikely that *negro* will be adopted as the all-encompassing term that Black activists would like. The term carries a particular political orientation that the government does not want to advance.[55]

Nevertheless, the Black consciousness movement has helped discredit the myth of racial democracy and awakened many African Brazilians to the fact that socioeconomic gains do not automatically outweigh one's phenotype. This in turn has furthered the political solidarity between Blacks and multiracial individuals and has led to a decrease in the social and official differentiation of *pardos* from Blacks (*pretos*), in a manner similar to that made between light- and dark-skinned African Americans in the United States. The net result of these trends has been to move Brazilian race relations closer to a binary model in which there is greater emphasis on the *branco/negro* designations, that is to say, Black/White dichotomy—if not the absolute enforcement of the one-drop rule—as has so long been the case in the United States.

The United States: Toward the Ternary Model

The furor over multiracial identity in the United States became intense in 1988 when a bill was proposed in the Rhode Island legislature to require application forms for state employment to include a box for "multiracial" in the race question. An African American legislator shot down the bill because he believed that racial categories are demeaning to begin with and this preoccupation with racial classification smacked of South African apartheid. That same year, the Office of Management and Budget (OMB), the branch of the government responsible for implementing changes in federal statistical surveys, published a notice soliciting public comment on a draft circular that would revise Directive No. 15, which was implemented in 1978 as guidance for conducting racial/ethnic surveys. These revisions would permit individuals to identify themselves as "other," if they believe they do not fall into one of the four basic official racial categories (Black; White; Asian/Pacific Islander; American Indian and Alaska Native) or in the "ethnic" category (Hispanic or not of Hispanic origin). Although a residual "other" category has been provided on each census since 1910 to increase the response rate to the race question, it has not been used as a standard category on all statistical surveys. Heretofore, the OMB advised that the category that most reflected the individual's recognition in his or her community should be used in cases where there was any uncertainty.[56]

Members of several support groups for interracial couples and multiracial-identified individuals requested that the category "multiracial" or "biracial," in lieu of "other," be added to the five standard categories. Public commentary on the original proposal was to end on April 19 but was extended through July 15 because of the large number of comments. While many multiracial individuals and interracial couples supported the addition of a biracial or multiracial category, the response was otherwise overwhelmingly negative. Of the ninety-five letters and 675 signatures that were received in response to the circular, approximately three-fourths opposed adding a multiracial identifier. This opposition included some of the federal agencies, such as the Civil Rights Division of the Department of Justice and several large corporations.[57]

Some of this opposition was based on logistical and financial concerns about an increase in paperwork, changes in the format of forms and computer programs for data analysis, and the data burden on respondents. Various Black leaders and organizations, aware that most African-descent Americans also have some European, and in many cases, Native American ancestry, feared the defection of a significant number of individuals, who, for reasons ranging from self-esteem to pragmatism, would designate themselves as "multiracial" rather than Black, if given the option.[58] Critics contended that for statistical reasons the one-drop rule must remain intact: it is necessary to prevent any decrease in the number of individuals who under the present system would be counted as Black. This would guard against any loss of prized slots in the already endangered affirmative action programs aimed at tracking historical and contemporary patterns of discrimination and in arriving at target goals for achieving social and economic equity.[59]

On November 12, 1988, the AMEA (Association of Multiethnic Americans) was formed in Berkeley to serve as a national network for the various independent support groups. Its overall goal was to promote healthy images of intermarried couples and multiracial individuals, as well as an awareness of the prejudice and discrimination directed at these individuals, but more specifically, to help galvanize people's consciousness about the multiracial category.[60]

Efforts by the AMEA and its affiliates to get the U.S. Census Bureau to make "multiracial" an acceptable means of official self-identification were unsuccessful for the 1990 census. Nevertheless, forms for the Operation Desert Shield/Storm Deployment Survey included "multiracial" as a designation for the offspring of returning intermarried veterans. Under the prodding of Project RACE (Reclassify All Children Equally), a Georgia-based organization, several states now include "multiracial" as an acceptable official means of self-identification.[61] A 1994 survey of 800 public school districts found that approximately 30 percent of them use a special separate category. Williams College now includes a multiracial identification on its official forms, and since 1989 reports prepared by the Center for Assessment and Demographic Studies at Gallaudet University have counted individuals who indicate identification with a multiracial background.[62] These local practices, nevertheless, conflicted with Directive No. 15, unless the data could be retrofitted at the federal level into one of the four official racial categories (and the "Hispanic" identifier, when it is given as an option); or into the figures for each of the single-race groups with which multiracial individuals identify.

Although multiracial was not universally accepted as a legitimate official means of self-identification during the early 1990s, the OMB began a comprehensive review process in 1993 to discuss possible changes in this direction on the 2000 census. Hearings before the House subcommittee on the census and joint meetings between the AMEA and Project RACE over the next four years were held to further this dialogue. Also, some activists began organizing a march to be held on July 20, 1996, in the nation's capital in order to make an even more public statement supporting this change.

After extensive cognitive research and field testing of sample households to measure the viability of allowing individuals to identify themselves as multiracial, the OMB on October 30, 1997, approved changes in federal standards that will allow multiracial individuals to identify themselves as such on official forms. Most activists had hoped for a combined format that included a separate multiracial box, and that also would allow individuals to check the boxes representing the various components of their background. This format had the advantage of both acknowledging and counting multiracial individuals as well as allowing for the data to be retrofitted into the existing official racial categories and providing figures for each of the single-race groups with which multiracial individuals identify. More important, it would allow for the continued enforcement and support of existing civil rights legislation and claims aimed at tracking historical and contemporary patterns of discrimination and in arriving at goals for achieving social and economic equity.

However, the OMB proposed a format that reads: "What is this person's race? Mark [X] one or more races to indiciate what this person considers herself/himself to be." This format, which appears on the form for the year 2000 census dress rehearsal scheduled for April 1998, was chosen partially in response to the unanimous support it received from the various federal agencies that require data on race and ethnicity. These agencies argued that, among other things, the mark-one-or-more alternative—unlike the combined format—would require fewer changes in formatting on existing forms, allow for data continuity, and take up less space. The mark-one-or-more format also received strong support from traditional African American civil rights organizations such as the NAACP and the Urban League, as well as the Congressional Black Caucus. They argued that a stand-alone multiracial identifier would lead to a loss of numbers, and considered as potentially divisive the appearance of a multiracial box even in combination with checking multiple boxes. Although these organizations support the mark-one-or-more format and feel that it addresses their concerns about the loss of numbers, they have expressed concerns about how the data will be tabulated.[63]

E Pluribus Unum

Discussion on this topic, however, should not center around multiracial identity, which in and of itself is not inherently problematic. The critical challenge is to alter the dynamics of race relations so that they operate horizontally, that is, in an egalitarian manner in which equal value is attached to differences, rather than vertically, that is, in an inegalitarian manner, in which differences serve as the basis for perpetuating inequalities. Part of this struggle for racial equality involves deconstructing the very basis of racism, which is its categories.[64] The Black consciousness movement in Brazil, which emerged in 1978 with the formation of the MNU, began seeking to get more multiracial individuals of African and European descent to identify themselves as African Brazilian. During the same time period, the multiracial consciousness movement in the United States, which emerged in 1979 with the founding of I-Pride, began seeking to make it possible for individuals who choose to embrace both their African and European backgrounds to identify themselves as multiracial.

Yet, considering that the infrastructure and superstructure of both Brazil and the United States remain profoundly racist, the multiracial consciousness movement and the Black consciousness movement must guard against becoming easy prey to larger social forces. Such racist forces could rearticulate new mutants: in the United States, in the form of inegalitarian integration like the Brazilian escape hatch; and in Brazil, in the form of inegalitarian pluralism like the United States one-drop rule. If that happened, blended individuals would be impelled to surrender the African aspect of their identity in the United States in order to achieve the first-class citizenship of Whites. In Brazil, they would be forced to renounce their European background for the sake of Black unity in the struggle against White privilege.

If the United States is to move closer to its longstanding image as a land of equal opportunity, and if Brazil is to move closer to the racial democracy on which it has prided itself, each nation would do well to learn from the other's past, by affirming egalitarian pluralism, while at the same time nurturing egalitarian integration. This system of pluralistic integration (or integrative pluralism) fosters racial and cultural pluralities that maintain relatively permanent centers of reference but also permeable boundaries that allow optimal autonomy for their individual constituents. Group pluralism based on racial and cultural specificity thus functions in tandem with individual pluralism, integrated under genuinely trans-American and trans-Brazilian identities that attaches equal value to their racial and cultural components. Taken to its logical conclusion, this would ensure that wealth, power, privilege, and prestige are more equitably distributed among the United States' and Brazil's varied citizenry. The African and European aspects of both societies would be seen as relative and complementary, rather than absolute and antithetical extremes, on a continuum of grey, which absorbs all colors, as does black— while at the same time reflecting them all, as does white.

Notes

Acknowledgment: Thanks to the UCLA Latin American Center for the support they provided me in the completion of this manuscript. Versions of this chapter were presented at the 1989 Winter Colloquium Series of the Center for African American Studies, UCLA, and at the Latin American Studies Association Meeting, Los Angeles, September 23–27, 1992.

1. See Jack D. Forbes, *Black Africans and Native Americans: Color, Race and Caste in the Evolution of Red-Black Peoples* (London: Blackwell, 1988), 131–50.

2. Thomas A. Skidmore, "Bi-Racial U.S.A. vs. Multi-Racial Brazil: Is the Contrast Still Valid?" *Journal of Latin American Studies* 25 (1993): 383–86; George Reid Andrews, *Blacks and Whites in São Paulo Brazil, 1888–1988* (Madison: University of Wisconsin Press, 1991), 249–54; I. K. Sundiata, "Late Twentieth-Century Patterns of Race Relations in Brazil and the United States," *Phylon* 47 (1987): 62–76; Howard Winant, *Racial Conditions: Politics, Theory, Comparisons* (Minneapolis: University of Minnesota Press, 1994), 111–70.

3. Gilberto Freyre, *The Masters and the Slaves: A Study in the Development of Brazilian Civilization,* trans. Harriet de Onís (New York: Knopf, 1963); Gilberto Freyre, *The Mansions and the Shanties: The Making of Modern Brazil,* trans. Harriet de Onís (New York: Knopf, 1963); Gilberto Freyre, *Order and Progress: Brazil from Monarchy to Republic,* trans. and ed. Rod W. Horton (New York: Knopf, 1970).

4. Carl N. Degler, *Neither Black nor White: Slavery and Race Relations in Brazil and the United States* (Madison: University of Wisconsin Press, 1986), 213–16, 226–38; G. Reginald Daniel, "Passers and Pluralists: Subverting the Racial Divide," in *Racially Mixed People in America,* ed. Maria P. P. Root (Newbury Park, Calif.: Sage, 1992), 91–107.

5. Maria Luisa Marcílio, "The Population of Colonial Brazil," in *The Cambridge History of Latin America*, vol. 2, ed. Leslie Bethell (New York: Cambridge University Press, 1984), 45–52; David W. Cohen and Jack P. Greene, "Introduction," 1–23, Herbert Klein, "Nineteenth-Century Brazil," 309–34, and A.J.R. Russell-Wood, "Colonial Brazil," 84–133," all in *Neither Slave nor Free*, ed. David Cohen and Jack P. Greene (Baltimore: Johns Hopkins University Press, 1972); Herbert S. Klein, *African Slavery in Latin America and the Caribbean* (New York: Oxford, 1986), 227–30; H. Hoetink, *Slavery and Race Relations in the Americas* (New York: Harper and Row, 1973), 108; John Burdick, "The Myth of Racial Democracy," *North American Congress on Latin America Report on the Americas* 25 (1992): 40–42.

6. Emilia Viotti da Costa, *The Brazilian Empire* (Chicago: University of Chicago Press, 1985), 239–43.

7. Russell-Wood, "Colonial Brazil"; Klein, "Nineteenth-Century Brazil"; Hoetink, *Slavery and Race Relations*, 37, 108; Burbick, "Myth of Racial Democracy," 40–42.

8. Degler, *Neither Black nor White*, 140, 196–99; Andrews, *Blacks and Whites*, 249–54.

9. Fernando Ortiz, *Cuban Counterpoint*, trans. Harriet de Onís (New York: Knopf: 1947), ix–xi; G. Reginald Daniel, "Black and White Identity in the New Millennium," in *The Multiracial Experience: Racial Borders as the New Frontier*, ed. Maria Root (Thousand Oaks, Calif.: Sage, 1996), 130–31; Anani Dzidzienyo, *The Position of Blacks in Brazilian Society* (London: Minority Rights Group, 1979), 2–11, 23–42; Abdias do Nascimento, *Mixture or Massacre?: Essays on the Genocide of a Black People*, trans. Elisa Larkin Nascimento (Buffalo: SUNY Buffalo Puerto Rican Studies and Research Center, 1979), 74–80; Thomas A. Skidmore, *Black into White: Race and Nationality in Brazilian Thought* (New York: Oxford University Press, 1974), 64–77.

10. Afrânio Coutinho, "El Fenómeno de Machado de Assis," *Brasil Kultura* 14 (1989): 8–12.

11. David T. Haberly, "Abolitionism in Brazil: Anti-Slavery and Anti-Slave," *Luso-Brazilian Review* 9 (1972): 30–46.

12. Degler, *Neither Black nor White*, 182–83; Rebecca Reichmann, "Brazil's Denial of Race," *North American Congress on Latin America Report on the Americas* 28 (1995): 35–42.

13. Colonial race relations in the United States lower South (South Carolina, the lower Mississippi Valley, and the Gulf Coast) differed somewhat from those in the North and upper South. That region was originally settled by the French and the Spanish. It followed the ternary model and originated in demographics similar to those that prevailed in Brazil.

14. Gary B. Nash, *Red, White, and Black: The Peoples of Early America*, 2d ed. (Englewood Cliffs, N.J.: Prentice-Hall, 1982), 162, 279; Marvin Harris, *Patterns of Race in the Americas* (New York: Norton, 1963), 79–94.

15. Mechal Sobel, *The World They Made Together: Black and White Values in Eighteenth-Century Virginia* (Princeton, N.J.: Princeton University Press, 1987), 3–20; Nash, *Red, White, and Black*, 141, 170–97; William D. Pierson, *Black Legacy* (Amherst: University of Massachusetts Press, 1993), 99–100.

16. Ira Berlin, *Slaves without Masters* (New York: Random House, 1974), 5, 10–11; Daniel, "Black and White Identity," 121–39; Paul R. Spickard, *Mixed Blood: Intermarriage and Ethnic Identity in Twentieth-Century America* (Madison: University of Wisconsin Press, 1989), 237–45; Laurence R. Tenzer, *A Completely New Look at Interracial Sexuality* (Manahawkin, N.J.: Scholar's, 1990), 56–68.

17. Winthrop D. Jordan, "American Chiaroscuro: The Status and Definition of Mulattoes in the British Colonies," *William and Mary Quarterly* 39 (1962): 183–200; F. James Davis, *Who Is Black?* (State University: Pennsylvania State University Press, 1991), 49, 54, 62–63; Naomi Zack, *Race and Mixed Race* (Philadelphia: Temple University Press, 1994), 33.

18. John G. Mencke, *Mulattoes and Race Mixture* (Ann Arbor: University of Michigan Institute of Research, 1979), 5; Joel Williamson, *New People: Mulattoes and Miscegenation in the United States* (New York: NYU Press, 1984), 8–11, 25; Berlin, *Slaves without Masters,* 7–9, 49, 90–97.

19. The rule of hypodescent has been variously extended to other Americans whose blended lineage includes a "background of color," along with European ancestry. Generally speaking, however, these individuals are not invariably designated exclusively, or even partially, as members of that group of color if the background is less than one-fourth of their lineage. Furthermore, self-identification with that background is more a matter of choice. The one-drop rule of hypodescent, on the other hand, guarantees that any amount of African ancestry ("one drop of blood") is passed on in perpetuity as a means of socially designating *all* future offspring as Black, and thus precludes any notion of choice in self-identification.

20. Berlin, *Slaves without Masters,* 98, 163–64; Mencke, *Mulattoes and Race Mixture,* 8–9; Davis, *Who Is Black?* 21, 29.

21. Tenzer, *A Completely New Look,* 65–66; Davis, *Who Is Black?* 51–58; Berlin, *Slaves without Masters,* 110, 216; Leonard Richard Lempel, "The Mulatto in United States Race Relations" (Ph.D. diss., Syracuse University, 1979), 43, 54–56, 247–99.

22. Nash, *Red, White, and Black,* 290.

23. Thomas A. Skidmore, "Race Relations in Brazil," *Camões Center Quarterly* 4 (1992–93): 49–57; Charles H. Wood and José Alberto Magno de Carvalho, *The Demography of Inequality in Brazil* (New York: Cambridge University Press, 1988), 135–53.

24. Peggy Lovell-Webster, "The Myth of Racial Equality: A Study of Race and Morality in Northeast Brazil," *Latinamericanist,* May 1987, pp. 1–6; Thomas A. Skidmore, "Race and Class in Brazil: A Historical Perspective," in *Race, Class, and Power in Brazil,* ed. Pierre-Michel Fontaine (Los Angeles: UCLA Center for Afro-American Studies, 1985), 24–41.

25. Andrews, *Blacks and Whites,* 146–56; M. G. Hanchard, *Orpheus and Power: The Movimento Negro of Rio de Janeiro and São Paulo, Brazil, 1945–1988* (Princeton, N.J.: Princeton University Press, 1994), 104–29; Michael Mitchell, "Blacks and the Abertura Democrática," in *Race, Class, and Power in Brazil,* ed. Fontaine, 95–119. For earlier, similar movements, see James Kennedy, "Luís Gama: Pioneer of Abolition in Brazil," *Journal of Negro History* 59 (1974): 255–67; Thomas Flory, "Race and Social Control in Independent Brazil," *Journal of Latin American Studies* 9 (1977): 199–224.

26. Skidmore, "Race Relations in Brazil," 49–57; Andrews, *Blacks and Whites in São Paulo,* 211–44; Lelia González, "The Unified Black Movement: A New Stage in Black Mobilization," in *Race, Class, and Power in Brazil,* ed. Fontaine, 120–34; Reichmann, "Brazil's Denial of Race," 35–42; John Burdick, "Brazil's Black Consciousness Movement," *North American Congress on Latin America Report on the Americas* 25: 23–27; Ana Lúcia E. F. Valente, *Política e Relações Raciais: Os Negros e As Eleições Paulistas de 1982* (São Paulo: Fundação de Amparo a Pesquisa do Estado de São Paulo, 1986), 25–33, 107–16; Luiz Silva, "The Black Stream in Brazilian Literature," *Conexões* 4 (1992): 12–13.

27. Mac Margolis, "The Invisible Issue: Race in Brazil," *Ford Foundation Report* 1 (1992): 3–7; Reichmann, "Brazil's Denial," 35–45; Regina Domingues, "The Color of a Majority without Citizenship," *Conexões* 4 (1993): 6–7; Carlos Hasenbalg, "Race and Socioeconomic Inequalities in Brazil," in *Race, Class, and Power in Brazil,* ed. Fontaine, 25–41; Peggy Lovell-Webster and Jeffery Dwyer, "The Cost of Not Being White in Brazil," *Sociology and Social Research* 72 (1988): 136–38; Nelson do Valle Silva, "Updating the Cost of Not Being White in Brazil," in *Race, Class, and Power in Brazil,* ed. Fontaine, 42–55; Anani Dzidzienho, "Brazil," in *International Handbook on Race and Race Relations,* ed. Jay A. Sigler (New York: Greenwood, 1987), 23–42.

28. Burdick, "Brazil's Black Consciousness Movement," 23–27; Silva, "Updating the Cost," 42–55.

29. Carlos A. Hasenbalg, Nelson do Valle Silva, and Luiz Claudio Bracelos, "Notas Sobre Miscegenação Racial no Brasil," *Estudos Afro-Asiáticos* 6 (1989): 189–97; Edward E. Telles, "Racial Distance and Region in Brazil: Intermarriage in Brazilian Urban Areas," *Latin American Research Review* (1992): 141–62.

30. Burdick, "Brazil's Black Consciousness Movement," 23–27; Silva, "Updating the Cost," 42–55.

31. Carlos A. Hasenbalg, "Race and Socioeconomic Inequalities in Brazil," in *Race, Class, and Power in Brazil,* ed. Fontaine, 25–41; Laurie Goering, "Beneath Utopian Facade, Brazilians Uncover Racism," *Chicago Tribune,* December 20, 1994; Marlise Simmons, "Brazil's Blacks Feel Prejudice 100 Years after Slavery's End," *New York Times,* May 14, 1988; Edward E. Telles, "Residential Segregation by Skin Color in Brazil," *American Sociological Review* 57 (1992): 186–97; Lovell-Webster and Dwyer, "The Cost of Being Nonwhite," 136–38; Silva, "Updating the Cost," 42–55.

32. Belinda M. Tucker and Claudia Mitchell Kernan, "New Trends in Black American Interracial Marriage: The Social Structural Context," *Journal of Marriage and the Family* 52 (1990): 209–19; Stanley Lieberson and Mary C. Waters, *From These Strands: Ethnic and Racial Groups in Contemporary America* (New York: Russell Sage, 1988), 162–246; Spickard, *Mixed Blood,* 278–83.

33. Lise Funderburg, *Black, White, Other* (New York: Morrow, 1994), 11–12; Jewelle Taylor Gibbs and Alice Hines, "Negotiating Ethnic Identity: Issues for Black-White Biracial Adolescents," in Root, *Racially Mixed People,* 223–38; Maria P. P. Root, ed., *The Multiracial Experience: Racial Borders as the New Frontier* (Newbury Park, Calif.: Sage, 1996), xiii–xvii.

34. Francis Wardle, "Are You Sensitive to Interracial Children's Special Identity Needs?" *Young Children,* January 1987, pp. 53–59.

35. Carlos Fernández, "Census Nonsense," *I-PRIDE Newsletter* 10 (1988): 1–4; Carlos Fernández, "Government Classification of Multiracial/Multiethnic People," in *Multiracial Experience,* ed. Root, 15–36; Nancy Brown and Ramona Douglas, "Making the Invisible Visible: The Growth of Community Network Organizations," in *Multiracial Experience,* ed. Root, 323–40.

36. Daniel, "Black and White Identity," 121–39; Manuel Ramirez, *Psychology of the Americas: Mestizo Perspectives on Personality and Mental Health* (New York: Pergamon, 1983), 55–62.

37. Peter S. Adler, "Beyond Cultural Identity: Reflections on Cultural and Multicultural Man," in *Topics in Cultural Learning,* ed. R. Brislin (Honolulu: East-West Center, 1974), 23–40.

38. Robert E. Park, "Human Migration and the Marginal Man," *American Journal of Sociology* 33 (1928): 881–93; Everett V. Stonequist, *The Marginal Man: A Study in Personality and Culture Conflict* (New York: Russell and Russell, 1937), 44–48, 139–58, 201–9.

39. Philip M. Brown, "Biracial Identity and Social Marginality," *Child Adolescent Social Work* 7 (August 1990): 319–37; Gloria Anzaldúa, *Borderlands: La Frontera—The New Mestiza* (San Francisco: Spinsters/Aunt Lute, 1987), 77–91; Maria P. P. Root, "Resolving 'Other' Status: Identity Development of Biracial Individuals," in *Complexity and Diversity in Feminist Therapy,* ed. Laura Brown and Maria P. P. Root (New York: Hayworth, 1990), 199–201; W. S. Carlos Poston, "The Biracial Identity Model: A Needed Addition," *Journal of Counseling and Development* 69 (1990): 152–55; Marvin C. Arnold, "The Effects of Racial Identity on Self-Concept in Interracial Children" (Ph.D. diss., St. Louis University, 1984), 1–12, 146–68; Agnetta Mitchell, "Cultural Identification, Racial Knowledge, and General Psychological Well-Being among Young Biracial Adults" (Ph.D. diss., California School of Professional Psychology, 1990), x–xii, 54–66;

Lynda Field, "Piecing Together the Puzzle: Self-Concept and Group Identity in Biracial Black/White Youth," in *Multiracial Experience,* ed. Root, 211–26.

40. Root, "Resolving 'Other' Status," 199–201; Davis, *Who Is Black?* 12, 14; Spickard, "The Illogic of American Racial Categories," in *Racially Mixed People,* ed. Root, 12–23; Zack, *Race and Mixed Race,* 1–50.

41. Michael Hughes and Bradley R. Hertel, "The Significance of Color Remains: A Study of Life Chances, Mate Selection, and Ethnic Consciousness among Black Americans," *Social Forces* 68 (1990): 1105–20; Verna M. Keith and Cedric Herring, "Skin Tone and Stratification in the Black Community," *American Journal of Sociology* 97 (1991): 760–78; Bart Landry, *The New Black Middle Class* (Berkeley: University of California Press, 1987), 23–35, 78–83, 216–33; Kathy Y. Russell, Midge Wilson, and Ronald Hall, *The Color Complex: The Politics of Skin Color Among African Americans* (New York: Harcourt Brace Jovanovich, 1990), 24–40.

42. Hughes and Hertel, "The Significance of Color Remains"; Keith and Herring, "Skin Tone and Stratification"; James H. Johnson, Jr., and Walter C. Farrell, Jr., "Race Still Matters," *Chronicle of Higher Education,* July 7, 1995, p. A48.

43. Reynolds Farley and Walter Allen, *The Color Line and the Quality of Life in America* (New York: Rowman & Littlefield, 1987), 209–361, 408–19; Joe Feagin and Melvin P. Sikes, *Living with Racism: The Black Middle-Class Experience* (Boston: Beacon, 1994), 26–28; Thomas D. Boston, *Race, Class, and Conservatism* (Boston: Unwin Hyman, 1988), 158–59.

44. Thomas Sowell, *Civil Rights: Rhetoric or Reality?* (New York: Morrow, 1984), 76–77, 139; William Julius Wilson, *The Declining Significance of Race,* 2d ed. (Chicago: University of Chicago Press, 1980), 19–23, 122–54.

45. Boston, *Race, Class, and Conservatism,* 8, 41–53; Howard Winant, *Racial Conditions: Politics, Theory Comparisons* (Minneapolis: University of Minnesota Press, 1994), 62–64, 166; Benjamin Ringer and Elinor Lawless, *Race-Ethnicity and Society* (New York: Routledge, Chapman and Hall, 1989), 168–69; William Julius Wilson, *The Truly Disadvantaged* (Chicago: University of Chicago Press, 1987), 3–19.

46. Lacayo, "Between Two Worlds," *Newsweek,* March 13, 1989, pp. 58–68; Robert Brent Toplin, *Freedom and Prejudice,* 91–109; Robert Allen, *Black Awakening in Capitalist America* (Trenton, N.J.: Africa World Press, 1990), 2–11, 18–20; Harold Cruse, *Plural but Equal: A Critical Study of Blacks and Minorities in America's Plural Society* (New York: Morrow, 1987), 201–3.

47. Rhett S. Jones, "The End of Africanity? The Bi-Racial Assault on Blackness," *Western Journal of Black Studies* 18 (1994): 201–10; Jack Sirica, "The Race Question," *Newsday,* January 16, 1995, pp. B4–5.

48. Reichmann, "Brazil's Denial of Race," 35–42; Skidmore, "Race Relations in Brazil," 49–57.

49. Skidmore, "Race Relations in Brazil," 49–57; Carlos Hasenbalg, "O Negro nas Vésperas do Centenário," *Estudos Afro-Asiáticos* 13 (1987): 79–86.

50. Skidmore, "Race Relations in Brazil," 49–57; Reichmann, "Brazil's Denial," 35–42; Margolis, "The Invisible Issue," 3–7.

51. Andrews, *Blacks and Whites,* 218–33.

52. Elvira Oliveira, "Dia Nacional da Consciencia Negra," *Nova Escola,* November 1993, pp. 23–25; Lori S. Robinson, "The Two Faces of Brazil: A Black Movement Gives Voice to an Invisible Majority," *Emerge,* October 1994, pp. 38–42.

53. Melissa Nobles, "'Responding with Good Sense': The Politics of Race and Censuses in Contemporary Brazil" (Ph.D. diss., Yale University, 1995), 133–75, 191–215; Domingues, "Color of a Majority"; Jerry Michael Turner, "Brown Into Black: Changing Attitudes of Afro-Brazilian University Students," in *Race, Class, and Power,* ed. Fontaine, 73–94.

54. Nobles, "'Responding with Good Sense,'" 133–75, 181–215.

55. Correspondence with Melissa Nobles, February 23, 1998.

56. Ramona Douglass, "Socio-political Consequences of Racial Classification in the U.S.," *Interracial/Intercultural Connection* (Biracial Family Network), November/December 1988, pp. 1–3; Elizabeth Radcliffe, "Round One Lost," *The Communiqué* (Interracial Family Alliance), Fall 1988, pp. 1–2; Yemi Tourér, "Census Bureau Stopped in Its Tracks," *Buffalo (N.Y.) Challenger,* August 31, 1988; Ira Lowry, "The Science and Politics of Ethnic Relations" (paper presented to American Association for the Advancement of Science, San Francisco, January 3–8, 1980), 15; Evelyn Thompson, "From the Editor," *Spectrum* (Multiracial Americans of Southern California), May 1988, pp. 1, 4; Sharon Lee, "Racial Classification in the U.S. Census: 1890–1990," *Ethnic and Racial Studies* 16, 1: 75–94.

57. John G. Brown, president, IFC [Interracial Family Circle, Atlanta], correspondence with MASC, March 26, 1988; Itabari Njeri, "A Sense of Identity," *Los Angeles Times,* June 5, 1988.

58. F. Finley MacRae, "Watson Fears Use of 'Mixed-Race' on Census Forms," *Los Angeles Sentinel,* September 22, 1988; Trudy S. Moore, "Black Lawmakers Oppose Michigan Bill That Makes New Multiracial Class," *Jet,* June 19, 1995, p. 46; Tom Morganthau, Susan Miller, Gregory Beals, and Regina Elam, "What Color Is Black?" *Newsweek,* February 13, 1993, pp. 63–65. In response to the ancestry question on the 1980 and 1990 censuses, most African-descent Americans (approximately ±95 percent), however, claimed only Black ancestry, and thus reaffirmed an African American identity, even with the knowledge of other ancestries in their background. Lieberson and Waters, *From Many Strands,* 16, 46, 48.

59. Ellis Cose, "One Drop of Bloody History," *Newsweek,* February 13, 1995, pp. 70–72; Itabari Njeri, "Call for Census Category Creates Interracial Debate," *Los Angeles Times,* January 13, 1991; Moore, "Black Lawmakers Oppose Michigan Bill," 46.

60. Douglas, "Socio-Political Consequences," 1–3; Steven Cheney-Rice, "Kaleidoscope: Annual Conference of MASC (Multiracial Americans of Southern California)," *Spectrum* (November–December 1988): 1–7; Njeri, "A Sense of Identity"; Njeri, "Call for Census Category"; Minutes, Founding Meeting of the AMEA (November 12, 1988); Fernández, "Government Classification"; Connie Leslie, Regina Elam, and Allison Samuels, "The Loving Generation," *Newsweek,* February 13, 1995, p. 72.

61. Susan Graham, *Project RACE (Reclassify All Children Equally),* personal communications, March 5, 1992; March 15, April 3, May 10, 1995; Susan Graham, "Grassroots Advocacy," in *American Mixed Race: The Culture of Microdiversity,* ed. Naomi Zack (Rowman & Littlefield, 1995), 185–90; Graham, "The Real World," in *Multiracial Experience,* ed. Root, 185–90.

62. *Review of Federal Measurements of Race and Ethnicity,* 28; UCLA School of Education Survey, 1991; Anim Steel, Williams College, Williamston, Massachusetts, personal communication, May 1995; *Annual Survey,* The Center for Assessment and Demographic Studies, Gallaudet University, Washington, D.C., Annual Survey, 1989.

63. Office of Management and Budget, *Federal Register* 62, 131 (July 9, 1997): 36937–39; William O'Hare, "Managing Multiple-Race Data," *American Demographics* (April 1998): 42–44; Christy Fisher, "It's All in the Details," *American Demographics* (April 1998): 45–47. The OMB officials indicated that they would make recommendations and provide additional guidance in fall 1998 with respect to this question after consulting with officials from various federal agencies, interested groups, demographers, planners, and social scientists. Whatever the outcome on the question of tabulations, these changes clearly indicate that the United States is shifting to a ternary model that would socially and officially recognize three racial identities—White, multiracial, and Black—as has so long been the case in Brazil.

64. Paul R. Spickard, Rowena Fong, and Patricia L. Ewalt, "Undermining the Very Basis of Racism—Its Categories," *Social Work* 4 (1995): 581–84.

Darby Li Po Price

11   Mixed Laughter

I am of Chinese descent from my mother, and Scots-Irish, Welsh, and Cherokee descent from my father, so in the United States that means I'm Latino to many people. I use this joke as my opener when I do stand-up comedy. The joke provides an example of how experiences that were previously alienating can be transformed through humor into an affirmation of multiethnicity.

As a doctoral candidate in ethnic studies at the University of California at Berkeley, I was encouraged, for the first time in my life, to research and write about issues relevant to my own heritage. My initial survey of literature on mixed race—tales of misfit mixed bloods, tragic mulattas, eugenic degeneracy, sociopsychological studies of marginalization—revealed a plentitude of socioscientific and literary materials that portray mixed-race identities with an overriding ethos of tragedy. Searching for representations that would affirm my identity as multiracial, I thought, "Why not explore constructions of mixed race as comic experiences?"

I am inspired by the way stand-up comedians confidently share life experiences and laugh about them with their audiences.[1] I also appreciate how they regularly subvert dominant expectations by expressing identities as multiplistic, shifting, transgressive, and socially constructed.[2] However—and this parallels dominant paradigms of race and ethnicity—most studies of humor treat ethnic identity in terms of separate and fixed group entities. Among the few studies of humor that refer to multiethnicity, most view multiethnic peoples as targets of humor rather than active creators of it.[3] In this chapter I analyze social contexts, joke texts, and identity development among multiethnic comedians, focusing on multiethnic subjectivity as central rather than peripheral. By "multiethnic" comedians, I mean people who say they are multiethnic, multiracial, or both, as part of their performance as well as personal identities.

No Laughing Matter: Contextual Constraints

What, as well as whom, is considered to be funny is greatly determined by dominant values, attitudes, and beliefs. Susan Purdie writes that dominant groups have historically dehumanized certain groups by making them the targets of derogatory jokes while simultaneously denying that they have a sense of humor. Whereas Purdie bases her observations on how German philosophers denied that Jews and women had a full sense of humor, in the United States the dominant culture stereotyped Native American, mixed-race, and Asian identities as bereft of humor.[4]

The simultaneous denial of a sense of humor and objectification of people of mixed descent as targets of humor is evident in dominant theories of ethnic humor. Interethnic marriages and offspring have been recognized as staples of ethnic humor.[5] Viewed as existing outside societal norms, however, multiethnic peoples are seen primarily as the targets of humor rather than its creators, as Christie Davies observes: the "ethnically ambiguous," those "peoples who cannot easily be fitted into the crude categories of 'insiders' and 'outsiders,' 'us' and 'them,'" are most likely to become the butts of ethnic jokes.[6]

Tragic and otherwise negative portrayals of people of mixed race spring from a monological racial system intolerant of racial ambiguities due to a perceived need to keep races separate. Naomi Zack refers to the tradition of negative cultural representations of mixed race people as "cultural genocide" that undermines any logical reason for people to assert mixed-race identities.[7]

Stigmatizing mixed-race people as tragic has been one way U.S. culture has suppressed mixed-race identity. For example, material identifying mixed-race identity as comic is absent from the tradition of blackface minstrelsy—the United States's most popular form of mass entertainment from the early nineteenth to the mid–twentieth century. As Eric Lott explains, blackface minstrel shows had two major themes: fear of Black uprising, and antimiscegenation.[8] Construed as threats to the separation of races as well as to the existence of the White race itself, mixed-race identity was no laughing matter. Mixed-race women were portrayed as tragic or melancholy figures of sexual desire. Mixed-race Black male identity was omitted from minstrel stages: "Even as a joke, an image of Black male sexual potency would prove too threatening, but the mulatto woman became a staple minstrel character."[9] Throughout the first half of the twentieth century, mixed-race Black men had to wear blackface if they wanted to be comedians. Bert Williams, known as the first great African American comedian, was a light-skinned mulatto of only one-sixteenth African ancestry who resented being forced to wear blackface to make his stage persona unquestionably Black.[10]

Mixed-race comedians of non-African ancestry have found it more acceptable to joke about their heritages. Partial Indian ancestry is less threatening to the dominant culture than African ancestry, especially when the Indian ancestors are a few generations removed.[11] While comedians of partial African ancestry such as Williams had to hide their heritage until the mid–nineteenth century, the exceptionally popular Will Rogers was able to claim his mixed European and Native American ancestry with jokes such as, "My father was one eighth Cherokee and my mother one fourth Cherokee, which I figure makes me about one eighth cigar-store injun'" and "My ancestors didn't come on the *Mayflower* but they met the boat."[12] Chicano comedians have asserted multiethnicity since the inception of Chicano comedy in 1848, but they have been viewed as cultural misfits—neither American nor Mexican—and "sinister clowns" from both Euro-American and Mexican cultural perspectives.[13]

Many of the sentiments that kept mixed-race identities out of minstrel shows still hinder multiethnic comedians today. When I asked an interethnic internet community in 1996 why there are so few comedians who express multiethnic/racial identities, e-mail respondents made statements such as this one I received from Charles My. Byrd: "Isn't it still somewhat in the realm of the taboo? ... I think it would be harder for a black/white multiracial/ethnic comedian to succeed than it would be for any other 'mixture,' The very thought of miscegenation or 'race mixing' is still so unsettling to many people, that this comedian would really be walking on thin ice."

Reflecting how "race mixing" is still unsettling to many people, many of the comedians I interviewed say they have been verbally and even physically harassed or attacked for expressing multiethnic identities or perspectives. Chicano comedian Jose Simon presents himself as both Mexican and American with jokes such as this one, which I heard him tell in a performance at the Ohanna Cultural Center in Oakland, California, in 1993: "I pronounce my name Jose Simon [Seemone] unless I'm looking for a job—then it's Joe Simon." Simon told me in an interview in Berkeley, California, that same year of an experience during a performance in Idaho. He was assailed with racial slurs such as "Spic" and "Beaner" and had a full shot of tequila smashed against his face—glass and all. After the show he was met in the parking lot by two guys with a shotgun who told him he "better get the hell outa' town" or else they would shoot him. Then the town sheriff showed up and told him to get in the police car so he could take him to his hotel to get his belongings and then drop him off at the airport, "'cause these guys mean business." Simon says he will never perform in Idaho again; "it's not worth it. ... I value my life too much."

The increased acceptability of "race mixing" also may be reflected in the amount of popularity today's multiethnic comedians enjoy. Nonetheless, disagreement exists over whether over the past few years it is has become an advantage to have a multiethnic identity as a comedian. Some comedians say that "political correctness" makes it an advantage to be from more than one ethnic group, since it is generally acceptable to make fun of groups that you belong to. The following excerpt from a televised dialogue about ethnic humor between moderator Lynn Waters (Caucasian) and Hawaiian comedians Mel Cabang (Filipino, Portuguese), Frank De Lima (Portuguese, Hawaiian), Billy Sage (Caucasian, Samoan), and Bo Irvine (Portuguese, Filipino, Hawaiian) reveals differences between dominant expectations and multiethnic perspectives in using multiethnicity as grounds for humor:

> LYNN WATERS: Start off by telling your favorite ethnic joke.
> MEL: Okay, one ethnic joke, but jeez, what is an ethnic joke, though?
> FRANK: I don't know.
> MEL: Pilipino ethnic?
> FRANK: You have the choice of Filipino or Portuguese, which one do you want?
> MEL: No mo' Chinese?
> FRANK: No, 'cause you're not—oh, but the mixture of Filipino and Portuguese makes Chinese.
> MEL: Okay, I finished my joke, your turn Billy.
> BILLY: How about Portapino?
> MEL: Portapino. Most people think that's a Pilipino you can take from one place to another place.
> LYNN: Okay, someone has to tell an ethnic joke.
> BO: Okay, I'm Portuguese and Hawaiian, so if you believe the stereotypes, I'm dumb but too lazy to find out why.[14]

Frank emphasizes that Mel has "the choice" of joking about "one" of his own ethnicities (politically correct) rather than telling a joke about an ethnicity "you're not" (politically incorrect). The witticism that mixing two groups—Filipino and Portuguese—"makes" a third entirely different entity such as "Chinese" or "Portapino" can serve as a premise for humor from a multiethnic perspective. However, as Lynn reveals, some people may not recognize such humor as "an ethnic joke," since it does not include stereotypical or disparaging references. Bo fulfills the dominant expectation that "an ethnic joke" about multiethnicity combines negative traits from each parent's ethnic group and thereby reduces multiethnic identity to a social absurdity.

Some people in the comedy business, such as Oakland comedy club manager Rick Sullivan, whom I interviewed in Berkeley in 1993, say we are starting to see more mixed-race comedy because society is starting to accept the idea that mixed-race people exist. Yet some comedians believe it has become more difficult to address mixed-race perspectives over the past few years, because mainstream comedy audiences have become more conservative. Reflecting on his experiences as a comedian over the previous ten years, Mike Moto told me in our 1994 interview in Berkeley that "the mixed race thing worked better a few years ago than now; now people are more reactionary due to increasing racial tension over the past few years. That means you have to step back in terms of racial issues. So I have to be the Asian guy, before the mixed-race thing, or the mongrel."[15]

Despite the constraints to multiethnic identities in comedy, many comedians say that at least in stand-up comedy you are allowed to go up as yourself, which is untrue in many other areas of performance, such as acting. Meeting the demands for easily recognizable characters, parts in mainstream movies and television are rarely multiethnic. Many comedians distastefully recount experiences as actors who were always given monoethnic roles but never multiethnic parts. Emphasizing the nonpersonal aspects of acting, in Berkeley in 1993 comedian Tessie Chua showed me her acting portfolio of glossy photos of herself dressed in costumes ranging from a white-faced nun to a giant black cockroach. Laughing at the ridiculousness of some of them, Chua exclaimed, "At least in stand-up I can go up as myself.... [A]pplause in stand-up gives me validation of who I am. That's me up there, not just a persona." In stand-up comedy multiethnic comedians have the opportunity to decide how they will portray themselves.

To go on stage as themselves, multiethnic comedians have to convey their identities, experiences, and observations in ways that will make audiences laugh. According to George Kitahara Kich, multiracial people go through three stages in the process of attaining a healthy biracial self-concept: awareness of differentness and dissonance, struggle for acceptance, and self-acceptance and assertion of an interracial identity.[16] While some comedians may joke only superficially about themselves in these terms, others employ comic narratives that express how their identity development includes these stages or processes. Their comedy thus becomes a window through which the development of multiethnic identity can be viewed.

Dissonance

Dissonance implies a negative judgment about differentness. Many jokes about being mixed race play upon dominant beliefs that people of mixed descent are strange or abnormal. Multiethnic comedians say that audiences expect them to joke about how being from multiple groups causes dissonance. Perhaps one of the most simple ways to joke about multiethnic identity is by creating intellectual incongruities by juxtaposing stereotypical qualities or by playing on language. Although such jokes are usually fairly superficial, they are potentially offensive. Comedians who use jokes based on juxtaposed stereotypes defend themselves by saying they are just trying to entertain people by making them laugh and that people shouldn't take them seriously.

Comedian Tessie Chua, for example, joked in a 1993 performance at San Francisco's Holy City Zoo that "Chua is a Chinese name. In addition to being Chinese, I'm Filipino and Irish. That means I eat dog, but only if I can wash it down with Guinness Stout!" Emphasizing that her main purpose is to entertain people, Chua told me in an interview after the performance that she's happy with her jokes as long as they make people laugh. When I asked whether different ethnic groups responded differently to her humor, she rolled her eyes and joked, "White people aren't offended, they love my jokes, but Asians sometimes get offended, they're like 'Oh, no, we don't eat dogs, only cats!'"

Another way to create jokes based on intellectual incongruities is by combining ethnic labels to create unique terms. For example, comedian Mike Moto introduced himself in a 1994 performance in Vallejo, California, by joking, "I come from a mixed marriage: I'm half Japanese and half Yugoslavian. Folks, you can't make up shit this weird. I'm a Japoslavian!" Moto's line about being a "Japoslavian" is potentially offensive because it says that being mixed is "weird." Another comedian (who asked to remain anonymous) told me in an interview in Boston that year, "I don't think being mixed should be described as 'weird' or 'abnormal' . . . instead of saying that it's 'weird' to be mixed, I would end the joke by saying something like 'while some people think it's strange, I think it's perfectly normal' or 'there's nothing wrong with being mixed.'" Moto defended himself in an interview in 1994 in Berkeley by saying that at least it makes it clear that he is of mixed descent.

Because of the stereotypical image of multiethnic people as psychologically torn or confused, many multiethnic comedians employ jokes that superficially play upon expectations that they are confused. While making references to psychological states, such jokes are often primarily based on the juxtaposition of stereotypical qualities of groups from the comedians' heritage.

For example, at a 1993 performance at Oakland's Ohanna Cultural Center, Mimi Freed joked, "It's a confusing combination being Italian and Cuban—I feel like one side of me throws the pizza up while the other side shoots it down." This joke juxtaposes stereotypes of Italians as pasta makers and Cubans as gangsters. Mimi addresses pressures to identify with one group: "I didn't know which side to side with in West Side Story—I sided with both." According to Freed she is not firmly rooted in either group but belongs to both. Intersecting multiethnicity with gender and sexuality, she jokes about how she has inherited male attributes such as facial hair and a deep voice from her Italian father and female attributes from her Cuban mother: "I feel like an Italian man trapped inside a Cuban woman's body and I wanna make a love to myself all a time. And I do because I'm that kinda guy/gal." This joke reflects Freed's belief that her gender and sexuality are just as important to her identity as her ethnicity.

Comedian Vernon Chatman says it has become almost a formula joke to talk about being from two groups, so he tries to put a different twist on it. In a 1993 performance at the Ohanna Cultural Center, Chatman started off with a joke based on the stereotypical juxtaposition of two groups: "I'm half Black and half White, which means I'm supposed to do a stereotypical joke—so here goes—when I'm driving to the store eating barbecued chicken, I pull myself over and beat myself with a police baton." Further playing upon the expectation that mixed-race people are torn between cultures, Chatman joked, "it's not about growing up with two different cultures, it's about growing up with two parents who force their child to dress up as a girl. Just kidding, they didn't force me to dress like a girl, I did it on my own." Chatman expands the dualistic concept of two opposing ethnic groups by emphasizing parental influences and cross dressing as nonessentialist variables in identity formation. Chatman's emphasis on his parents' influence on his identity parallels his own views from having grown up in the Bay Area, as he told me in an interview in Berkeley the same year: although "being racially mixed was not that big a deal for me ... people expect me to talk about it in my comedy."

Comedians who joke about their multiethnicity primarily in terms of dissonance tend to consider their ethnic identity a secondary issue. Many say their main agenda as comedians is to make people laugh and that they are trying to appeal to the widest audience possible. Some considered gender or sexuality more important to them than ethnicity. Comedians who consider their ethnicity an integral aspect of their performances tend to draw from experiences involving ethnicity.

Most comedians say the best way to come up with original material is to draw upon personal experiences or observations. Many say that rather than tell jokes, they merely tell stories about themselves or other people they have known. Multiethnic personal-identity joke narratives often begin by explaining how peoples' attempts to place them into easily recognizable dominant categories create dissonance.

Comedian Andy Bumatai, of Filipino, German, French, and Hawaiian descent, has a joke narrative about regional attitudes on race that addresses his belief that terms such as "White" and "non-White" are racist because they imply that "White" is the norm and "non-White" not the norm and because they don't allow a space for people who are both "White" and "non-White." Bumatai begins by explaining that when he was performing for a predominantly White audience in Georgia, a Hawaiian woman interrupted him to ask why he wasn't speaking in pidgin since he was from Hawaii and accused him of trying to be a haole. He notes the irony of being called White in Georgia as an insult with people in the audience not knowing what "haole" meant: "'What did she call him, a Harley?'" Emphasizing how attitudes about racial identity vary by region, Bumatai explains how in California he encountered a more subtle form of racism.

> During this film audition I looked down and this woman had a card on it with my name and "non-White" written next to it. I asked what this non-White meant and she got all defensive. She was like, "That's not official or anything, that's just my personal notes. So don't worry about it." I was trying to calm her down, but she was getting more upset and finally said, "Well, you're not White, so you might as well face it!" I was thinking how strange it is to identify someone by what they are not, because in Hawaii we try to so hard to identify

people by what they are. Imagine if we did it the other way: "Hey, you know Charlie, the guy who's not Hawaiian, Filipino, Portuguese, or Samoan?" "No, I don't think so, what else is he not?" And this woman is telling me I need to face it that I'm not White. Then back in Hawaii I go surfing with the guys I grew up with. They were like, "Hey Andy, how come you always goin' to the mainland, you trying to be White?" Yeah, I'm just trying to face it. You know those Escher drawings that start off like a bird and then wind up like a fish and in-between you can't tell what it is? That's like me living in the middle, going ahhhhhh!!!!![17]

Bumatai reveals how attempts to categorize multiethnic people such as himself merely as "non-White" or "White" are absurd. From a multiethnic perspective, a racial system that confines people to one racial category is a joke. Multiethnic identities exist and shift in between as well as at both ends of the White/non-White dichotomy.

Struggling for Acceptance

In attempts to overcome feelings of dissonance created by being perceived as different, many multiethnic people struggle to gain acceptance, often by trying to become the same as people around them. Perhaps the most sensational tales about people of mixed descent trying to find acceptance involve hiding one aspect of their ancestry in order to claim they are members of the dominant ethnic group. Whereas traditional "passing" tales involve the downfall of the passer, in comedy the passer lives on to joke about the ridiculousness of their attempts to pass.

Some multiethnic comedians have succumbed to pressures to perform as singular ethnic types to make themselves more acceptable to audiences. Many say that they initially felt pressures to identify according to the rules of hypodescent (with the ethnic group that has the lowest status in the racial hierarchy) by Whites and then reclaimed their multiethnicity after receiving negative feedback from members of the minority ethnic group they had presented themselves as.[18]

Tired of people regularly interrupting his performances to question him about his ethnicity, Japanese and Croatian comedian Michael Moto changed his name from Morgin to Moto to make clear his Japanese ancestry, he told me in 1994. He said that a readily Asian-identified stage name wasn't necessary when he began doing comedy in San Francisco but became necessary when he began performing on the East Coast. "Anyone who looks like some kind of non-Euro ethnic person has to explain what they are. As a guy who looks Native American, Filipino, Hawaiian, or East Indian, if I don't identify who I am they will sit there and wonder 'What is this guy?' to the point that it interferes with their ability to listen to the jokes."

Moto has mixed feelings over his name change. "When I first adopted the stage name, I felt like I was passing because I didn't have any mixed-race material. I felt like a fraud because I didn't mention both sides. I was presenting myself as a full-blooded Japanese. But the truth is I look more Hawaiian, or Native American, or Filipino, so Asians would call me on it." Moto said it was initially hard to discuss being mixed with no mixed-race identification base. "I learned to make it more personal rather than dance around the issue. I put the mixed-marriage issue right up front. But it is still difficult . . . the problem is it's difficult to find a group to identify with."

After introducing himself in the Vallejo, California, performance as the product of a mixed marriage, Moto told the audience, "I always lean toward my Japanese side. What's to be admired about Yugoslavia? The country is a whole rubble because they attacked themselves. And there are no more Yugo cars in the U.S. Try picking up a girl in a Yugo." This joke exemplifies how multiethnic peoples often attempt to gain acceptance by identifying themselves with their higher status heritage and disassociating themselves from their lower status heritage.

Boston comedian Gregory Carey draws upon his immigrant and multiracial experiences as a kid who was descended from a Black father and White mother in Jamaica, then had to struggle for acceptance when his family moved to New York City. He developed an ability to joke about himself and other kids as a way to keep from getting beat up. Because other kids as well as society in general gave him the message that being different was bad, Carey did everything he could to try to be the same as the other kids in the neighborhood. In a 1994 performance at Boston's Aku Aku Comedy Club, he joked about his desire be identified as African American:

> A lot of people hear me talkin' and they're like, "Hey, why don't you sound like the coconut man?" That's because after you've come to this country and you've been here a couple years and had your coconuts kicked a few times, you will tend to lose a foreign accent. In fact the first thing I did when we came to this country was to lose my accent. If INS came around I'd pretend I didn't know my parents. I'd be like, "Yo man, I'm African American. I don't know those immigrants. Send 'em back to Jamaica, they be takin' our jobs 'n' shit!"

Upon moving to New York, Carey disassociated with his Jamaican heritage in order to identify himself as Black in his personal life. However, when he began doing standup comedy he presented himself for some time as simply Jamaican. He told me in an interview in Boston in 1994 that he adopted a stereotypical Jamaican stage persona because other comedians and comedy club managers had told him it would allow him to market himself as a readily recognizable ethnic type. Carey says he never felt fully comfortable presenting himself as Jamaican, however, because he felt it didn't accurately represent who he is. An after-performance confrontation in which an irate Jamaican woman angrily charged him with performing a stereotype of Jamaicans caused him to seriously question the implications of his Jamaican stage persona enough to drop his Jamaican bit from being the whole show down to 15 percent of his show. Carey found it improved his confidence to go on stage as himself rather than as a stereotype: "It took me awhile to develop my courage. It's a matter of you letting yourself be yourself on stage. And that's why I didn't feel right going up as some Jamaican talking about coconuts—because that's not me. It's a matter of being comfortable with myself and feeling okay with myself . . . I'm not afraid of people anymore—I'm just who I am."

Accepting Self and Asserting Multiracial/Ethnic Identity

While multiethnicity may be incidental for some comedians, others have made their multiethnic heritages their central theme and have never considered presenting themselves as mono-ethnic. Comedian Teja Arboleda wrote me via electronic mail in 1994: "I have never thought it better to present myself as one ethnicity as a comedian. That would go against everything I'm doing." Arboleda says 90 percent of the motivation for his work comes from a desire to reveal the secrecy about race and ethnicity that he has observed in his family as well as in society. He believes that secrecy is a "powerful, painful, and sometimes necessary" aspect of all families. "My father is still living in this secrecy. It's to the point that one of my relatives has threatened to commit suicide because he can't deal with the secrecy. I think that secrecy exists in everyone's background in all families whether they think of themselves as mixed or not. It's always been a part of why people move far away, or stop communicating with relatives." According to Arboleda, "my performance is like undressing in public—there are no more secrets."

Asserting his multiethnicity as his central theme, Teja Arboleda opened a 1994 Boston show:

> My mother's mother is German, my mother's father is Danish. My father's mother is African/Native American, my father's father is Filipino/Chinese. I was born in Brooklyn and grew up in Japan, and that's why they call me Ethnic Man! ha, ha, ha: "There's that ethnic guy, doing that ethnic thing. Oh, isn't he so ethnic!" Yes, it's Ethnic Man. He can leap from race to race in a single bound. It's Ethnic Man. Not quite Black as Black, not quite White as White, but he's never green. Sort of brown, sort of in-between.

He then jokes about how despite their multiple heritages his father denies their multi-ethnic heritage:

> My friend Steve once told me that these scientists compiled a thousand faces from all over the world and put them into a computer to get the average face. And guess what? It looks like me! But my father always said [shaking finger], "You are German/Filipino period." I've spent what, two months in the Philippines. Does that make me a Filipino? I've spent a third of my life waiting in lines—does that make me a waiter?

Because his father denied their African American heritage, Arboleda wasn't sure what his ethnicity was. His ambiguous appearances caused dissonance when he and his brother were bussed to a predominantly Black school in New York City. "My brother and I are sitting there asking 'Am I Black, Am I Black?' and the other students were looking at us going 'Is he Black? Is he White?'"

Arboleda believes that "it would be dishonest to identify as anything other than multiracial or multiethnic." He has found it difficult to officially identify himself according to his mixed heritage, however, for his father had him classified as White on his birth certificate as part of an attempt to have the family identified as White. When Arboleda refused to comply with the 1990 census form that said "check one box only," a census taker wrote him down as Hispanic on the assumption that his last name and physical appearance are Hispanic. Ironically, of the five major ethnic/racial groups recognized by the census, Hispanic is the only one not part of his heritage. Arboleda jokes in his show: "So I was born legally White. Now I'm legally Hispanic. If I ever run for office, the media could hunt me down and splash newspapers with headlines that read 'Arboleda, candidate, falsified his race.'"

In his show, Arboleda explains what it was like when his family moved to Japan. He recalls Japanese girls trying to compliment him by telling him he looks like Michael

Jackson: "'Oh, you're so cute, you're so cute. You're an American—you look like Michael Jackson.' Michael Jackson?! If I went back now, they'd probably still think I look like Michael Jackson. I'd have to say, 'Michael Jackson doesn't even look like Michael Jackson!'"

Arboleda refers in his show to numerous incidents after his family moved back to the United States when people classified or mistreated him according to their racial misconceptions. For example, an irate person in a grocery store asked him, "Why don't you take your pita bread and go back to Mexico where you belong?" Annoyed by questions of "what are you" by people preoccupied with trying to classify him according to race, he emphasizes that we need to focus on multiethnicity because there is no such thing as race. To illustrate the transnational aspects of his identity, Arboleda jokes about being frisked by the Los Angeles police looking for Mexican suspects:

> So for two hours on the sidewalk I had to explain why I have an American passport, why my brother who was born in Germany has a German passport, why I live in Massachusetts, why my brother lives in Oregon, why I have an expired international driver's license, why we have six cameras between the two of us because we're both photographers, and why (get this) why, oh why . . . did we grow up in Japan?! Go figure!

After joking about a number of incidences of Americans harassing him because they thought he was a foreigner, Arboleda finishes his show with a strong statement against ethnocentrism: "We all want to preserve our heritages and our cultures—but we can't continue to isolate ourselves. America is not a melting pot. It never was, it never will be. Integration never worked. Diversity will. I know it, I'm living it. The Los Angeles riot, that's not a melting pot. If anything at all, the pot is melting! Ethnocentrism isolates and polarizes people into different groups. According to Arboleda, the melting-pot form of ethnocentrism, which attempts to culturally homogenize or "Americanize" diverse peoples, creates ethnic hatred and conflicts.

Comedian Amy Hill explains through comic narratives how the dominant society's negative attitudes about mixed-race identity made her feel bad about herself as a child of Japanese and Finnish descent growing up in Seattle. After joking about stereotypical traits of both of her parents, Hill explained to an audience in Boston in 1994 why she prefers the term "Hapa": "I'm happy. I'm a Happy Hapa. Hapa-Haole—that's Hawaiian. Better than half-breed, mongrel, or moral aberration." Hill then recounted incidents from her childhood. She joked about how she is often mistaken for Latina because of her ambiguous appearance:

> People see me walking down the sidewalk with my European friend and her daughter. People assume I'm the nanny or the housekeeper. I don't know where people think I'm from but it sure ain't here! . . . People do speak to me in Spanish all the time. I remember this Latina woman once told me I should speak Spanish. I told her "I'm sorry I don't speak Spanish." She seemed to think I was lying. She said, "You're ashamed, you're Latina, be proud!" It would be great if people could tell I was Japanese and Finnish right off the bat. But then I'd have to be dressed in a Kimono, pulling a reindeer.

Hill emphasizes in her show that there are many variables besides being multiethnic that greatly influence the lives of people of mixed descent. "I've got friends that are half Japanese and half African American that are dark. Half Chinese and half Puerto Rican that are overweight. Or half Filipino and half Mexican and shave their head and are really rich with a bad complexion, ha, ha. When they walk through the world I wonder what they feel, what voices they hear?"

Hill explains that she internalized societal beliefs that view difference negatively to the point that she sometimes has oppressive thoughts about other multiethnic people. "For me the voices never stop. Speak English! Like when I see someone is mixed race and I think, 'What the heck is that?' ha, ha." Hill ends her routine on an uplifting note: "I want to find my way back, walk back into that room and find like my mother did, find I am creating the voices, and I can make them stop until I can sing my song—Amy, Amy Crockett, King of the Wild Frontier!"

In offstage discussions that year, Hill told me it took her a long time before she felt comfortable enough to express her multiracial heritage. "Being multiracial, I always felt I was unacceptable. I grew up trying to please people. I didn't have a sense of who I was. It took awhile to say what I feel and what I am. It wasn't until my thirties that I felt like I had permission to talk about these things in a personal way." Hill uses comic identity narratives to transform her previous struggles for acceptance into affirmations and celebrations of difference.

Last Laughs

This guy once called me a mongrel and told me he could respect me more if I were full blooded. He said I was an aberration. I should have humped his leg.

—Mike Moto

Initially negative or traumatic incidents can be transformed through humor into positive narratives, often through role reversals whereby alienators are recast as the "other" and become the butt of the joke. Taken individually, many mixed-race joke narratives seem merely to recount negative experiences. Such narratives, however, can also be viewed as part of a necessary process of transforming a socially devalued identity into a healthy self-conception.[19] Most of the comedians I interviewed said their performances help them resolve negative experiences, give them a greater sense of who they are, allow them to express that sense of self, and increase their general happiness. Invoking a sense of shared identification through laughter, comic narratives about multiethnic identities can be appreciated not only as entertainment, but as a celebration of multiethnicity both among individuals and society at large.

Notes

1. Stand-up comedy is characterized by direct performer/audience interaction in which personal attributes of the performer—physical appearance, race, ethnicity, and gender—are often integral aspects of the performance that must be embraced or avoided.

2. Dwight Conquergood writes in "Poetics, Play, Process, and Power: The Performative Turn in Anthropology" (*Text and Performance Quarterly 1* [1989]: 82–88) that in the context of

performance "the idea of the person shifts from that of a fixed, autonomous self to a polysemic site of articulation for multiple identities and voices."

3. Christie Davies, *Ethnic Humor around the World: A Comparative Study* (Bloomington: Indiana University Press, 1990). Although Davies's work is based primarily on joke texts in isolation from their contexts and creators, Mohadev Apte calls it "the most authoritative crosscultural study of ethnic humor" (Review, *American Ethnologist* 19 [November 1992]: 832–33). Most studies of humor analyze joke texts, creators, and the contexts from which they arise apart from each other rather than as interrelated. Mohadev Apte, *Humor and Laughter: An Anthropological Approach* (Ithaca, N.Y.: Cornell University Press, 1985). Historically there have been three major theoretical approaches to the study of humor: intellectual, psychological, and functional. Intellectual approaches view humor in terms of the mental pleasures that arise from recognizing incongruities in language structures. Psychological approaches emphasize mental states, dilemmas, and problems of the users and receivers of humor. Functional approaches attempt to explain the role of humor in terms of larger societal purposes such as reinforcing or disrupting societal hierarchies. See Marcel Gutwirth, *Laughing Matter: An Essay on the Comic* (Ithaca, N.Y.: Cornell University Press, 1993).

4. Susan Purdie writes, "'Humour' . . . is crucially implicated in a construction of full personality. To be able to speak 'properly,' to be a 'proper' person" (*Comedy: The Mastery of Discourse* [Toronto: Toronto University Press, 1992], 138). In the United States, women have also historically had their sense of humor denied to a certain degree. As a group, however, women have been allowed to make inroads into U.S. comedy to a significantly greater degree than mixed race, Native American, and Asian American identities. See Regina Barreca, *They Used to Call Me Snow White . . . But I Drifted: Women's Strategic Use of Humor* (New York: Viking, 1991).

5. See John Lowe, "Theories of Ethnic Humor: How to Enter Laughing," *American Quarterly* 38 (1986): 439–60.

6. Davies, "Ethnic Humor," 314.

7. Naomi Zack, *Race and Mixed Race* (Philadelphia: Temple University, 1993), 113–27.

8. Eric Lott, *Love and Theft: Blackface Minstrelsy and the American Working Class* (New York: Oxford University Press, 1983).

9. Freda Scot Giles, "From Melodrama to the Movies: The Tragic Mulatto as a Type Character," in *American Mixed Race: The Culture of Microdiversity*, ed. Naomi Zack (Lanham, Md.: Rowman and Littlefield, 1995), 64. For a discussion of shifting portrayals of the mixed blood of Native American descent, see William J. Scheick, *The Half-Blood: A Cultural Symbol in 19th Century America* (Lexington: University of Kentucky Press, 1979).

10. Eric Ledell Smith, *Bert Williams: A Biography of the Pioneer Black Comedian* (Jefferson, N.C.: McFarland, 1992).

11. See Richard M. Ketchum, *Will Rogers: The Man and His Times* (New York: Simon and Schuster, 1973).

12. Bryan B. Sterling and Frances N. Sterling, *Will Rogers' World: America's Foremost Political Humorist Comments on the 20s and 30s—and 80s and 90s* (New York: Evans, 1989).

13. See Guillermo E. Hernandez, *Chicano Satire: A Study in Literary Culture* (Austin: University of Texas Press, 1991).

14. "Comedy in Hawaii: A Laugh A Minute," *Dialogue*, exec. prod. Edward Robello, Hawaii Public Television (Honolulu: Hawaii Public Broadcasting Authority, 1995).

15. Moto recalls performing in a club in Iowa and hearing an agitated man yell at him, "'Hey, the white man is a minority today!' I couldn't believe it because I was looking out at a sea of two hundred white faces and I could tell that they all believed it, even though I was the only nonwhite person there." Moto jokes, "It's getting harder, not easier to be mixed race. It's not time

to sit back and say everything is okay, it's time to get organized. What we need is a Hapa militia." (Personal interview with author, San Francisco, 1994.)

16. George Kitahara Kich, "The Developmental Process of Asserting a Biracial, Bicultural Identity," in *Racially Mixed People in America,* ed. Maria P. P. Root (Newbury Park, Calif.: Sage, 1992), 304–20.

17. Andy Bumatai, *Andy Bumatai: Standup Comic, 1984–1994,* compact disc digital audio recording (Honolulu: Tropical Jam, 1994).

18. Michael Omi and Howard Winant define the rule of hypodescent as when a person of mixed descent is affiliated with the subordinate group rather than the superordinate group to avoid racial ambiguity (*Racial Formation in the United States* [New York: Routledge, 1986], 60).

19. Studies suggest that joking about their lives serves for comedians many of the functions of psychotherapy by helping them overcome their emotional heritages, resolve personal traumas and alienation, and develop and assert a clearer sense of self (Glenn D. Wilson, *Psychology for Performing Artists: Butterflies and Bouquets* [London: Jessica Kingsley Publishers, 1994]). See Ann Brebner, *Setting the Actor Free: Overcoming Creative Blocks* (San Francisco: Mercury House, 1990). Psychotherapist Helena Jia Hershel explains that psychotherapy attempts to resolve pain within the patients's psyche through an interactive process that helps overcome feelings of isolation and helps people recognize faulty assumptions that cause internalized racial pathologies. "The therapist is useful by introducing perspective—cause and effect rather than self-blame; history—helping to understand the person within her own developmental process and particular "race" context; compassion—as an aid in helping a person toward more self-compassion; understanding—ending the isolation. The therapist reconnects the adult person with the renewed process of self-making and self-affirmation through the therapeutic relationship. . . . In-depth psychotherapy attempts to resolve internal conflicts and aid in the integration of the self . . . as part of a social process that includes belonging, identity, and alienation within the family and within the community." Hershel asserts the need for prevention, preparing responses to oppressive questions, and undoing internalized oppression through understanding history, ending bifurcation along race lines. Helena Jia Hershel "Therapeutic Perspectives on Biracial Identity Formation and Internalized Oppression," in *American Mixed Race: The Culture of Microdiversity,* ed. Naomi Zack (Lanham, Md.: Rowman and Littlefield, 1995), 169–81; quote on p. 81.

Karen Leonard

12   Punjabi Mexican American Experiences of Multiethnicity

Early in my research on the Punjabi Mexicans of California, I sat in a restaurant/bar with its owner, a large man in his early forties named Omar Deen. His last name indicated to me, a historian of South Asia, that his father, an immigrant from India's north-western Punjab province in the early twentieth century, had been a Muslim. As we talked, however, Omar stated emphatically, "My Dad was a Hindu; he came from the Punjab, back in India. And I'm a Hindu, too." Yet Omar's mother had been a Mexican American woman, and he and his wife were Catholics who spoke English and Spanish. In fact, the restaurant/bar was named Chavellas, after his wife, Isabella, and it served Mexican and American food. Was this an isolated instance of garbled cultural transmission, of confusion over one's "authentic" identity, or were there others like Omar? Was there a pattern here to be analyzed in the domain of multiethnicity?

I have argued, in *Making Ethnic Choices: California's Punjabi Mexican Americans*, for the historical contingency of ethnic identity and the authenticity of the identities constructed by the pioneer South Asian immigrants in the United States.[1] I want to argue here that these identities were essentially multiethnic even in the first generation, that the term "Hindu" itself referred to a multiethnic category in the United States, the category of immigrants from India or South Asia. Thus it was analogous to other terms indicating national origin (Italian, Swiss, German), and like those terms it brought together immigrants who may have differed with respect to religion, language, and other characteristics into a larger category in the American context. Further, members of the second and later generations are self-consciously multiethnic, and they are moving beyond their specific Punjabi and Mexican biethnic heritage to claim generalized multiethnic identities today.

As Stuart Hall says, all identity is constructed across difference,[2] and the configurations of sameness and difference in early twentieth-century British India and the western United States were quite different. I will focus on the U.S. context and the experiences of the earliest immigrants from South Asia to the United States, the Punjabi men who settled primarily in California in the 1910s and 1920s, and their descendants.[3]

Their construction of a multiethnic identity involved concepts of race, class, and ethnicity, as these concepts were understood and used by others and by the men themselves at the time.

Building a Multiethnic Community

It was almost inevitable that the experience of the Punjabi pioneers became a multiethnic one. Barred by changing immigration law from bringing their wives or other women from India, some of the men married in the United States, and their partners were primarily Mexican and Mexican American women. About three hundred of these biethnic couples settled in California's agricultural valleys and constructed a "Mexican-Hindu" or "Hindu" ethnic identity there.

The name "Hindu" was a misnomer from the South Asian point of view, since 90 percent of the men were Sikhs and 8 percent were Muslims, and to people familiar with South Asia today, particularly with Punjabi politics, calling members of the first generation "Hindus" seems strikingly inappropriate.[4] Yet back in India's Punjab at the turn of the century, Sikhs, Muslims, and Hindus were less differentiated than they are today, and the differences became even less important in the United States.[5] The sharp differences within the Punjab between the river-demarcated Doaba, Malwa, and Majha regions also became far less important in the United States. "Hindu" in those early decades of the twentieth century in the United States simply meant "from Hindustan, or India," and the men accepted the name; many of their descendants still use it.

To call members of the second generation "Hindus," people with names like Maria Juanita Singh, Jose Akbar Khan, and Roberto Chand, people who speak Spanish and English rather than Punjabi, seems to many even more inappropriate. The religious misnomer is even more obvious, for most of them are Catholic. (The immigrant men did not change their religions, but few practiced them rigorously; they were mostly illiterate, had no or few religious books with them, and worked too hard to teach their children. In any case socialization of children was the women's job and they encouraged their wives to see that the children got religious training; since the wives were Christian, the training was Christian.) Even though members of the second generation tended to "marry out," with Euro-Americans and Mexican Americans rather than with each other, most descendants of the early Punjabi immigrants still claim "Hindu" ethnicity. Clearly "Hindu" was an American ethnic label (and it still is in some rural areas), and for the second as for the first generation it is really a multiethnic category, although in different ways.

Race, Class, and Politics

Behind this constructed "Hindu" ethnicity lie laws, policies, and practices based on the contemporary understandings of race and class. U.S. immigration laws based on race and class began excluding Asians in the late nineteenth century: the 1882 Chinese

Exclusion Act (barring Chinese workers), the 1907 Gentleman's Agreement (barring Japanese workers), and the 1917 Barred Zone Act (designating most of Asia as a geographic zone from which immigrants were barred). U.S. citizenship, too, was based on race: one had to be "White" or of African descent, until the naturalization laws began changing in the 1940s.[6] The Punjabi immigrants arriving after 1900 were portrayed in newspapers and other contemporary sources as non-White and lower class; until they discarded them, the turbans and beards of the Sikhs earned them the derogatory name "ragheads."[7]

Since California, until 1951, like many other states, had on the books anti-miscegenation laws prohibiting marriages across racial lines, racism was also the chief reason the Punjabi men turned to women of Mexican ancestry when they decided to stay and settle down. Asian Indians might have been classified as Caucasian by anthropologists of the day, but they were not generally regarded as White and usually could not get licenses to marry White women. However, the Anglos or Euro-Americans who dominated California's agricultural development did not care if the Punjabis married black or brown women from the agricultural laborer class, and in California's southern Imperial County the flow of Mexican immigrants across the border increased just as the Punjabis began farming there. (The Mexican Civil War of 1910 sent many people across the international boundary from Texas to California for refuge and work.) Marriages between Punjabis and Hispanic women began in 1916 in Imperial County and became numerous. On the marriage licenses, the blank for "race" was filled in according to the county clerk's perception of the applicants. Some couples drove from county to county to get a license.

Racism threatened the livelihood of these Punjabi farmers in 1923, when a U.S. Supreme Court decision barred South Asians from citizenship on the grounds that, although Caucasian, they were not "White" in the popular meaning of the term. Declared "aliens" ineligible for U.S. citizenship, the Punjabis then fell under the "Alien Land Laws" passed in California and other western states to prevent the very successful Japanese immigrants from leasing and buying agricultural land.[8] This was a major blow to the Punjabis, most of them from farming castes (Jat Sikhs, Rajputs, and Arain Muslims) and working in agriculture in the United States, but they managed to continue farming in various ways.

The Punjabi men constituted themselves as a single "Hindu" category and put forward their own concepts of their racial and class status, insisting that they were Caucasian or Aryan and generally distancing themselves from other groups perceived to be non-White. Some fifty-nine men had asserted their status as Caucasians/Whites to become U.S. citizens before the 1923 Supreme Court decision.[9] Others, faced with de facto racial segregation in many of California's agricultural towns, argued that their children should not to be consigned to the "foreign section" schools (attended by predominantly Black, Mexican, and Asian children) but should go to the White schools. Blacks and Mexicans also worked as agricultural laborers in the California fields, but the Punjabi men did not ally themselves with these groups.

Most Punjabis were themselves prejudiced against Black or "colored" people. The 1918 Imperial Valley Hindustanees' Welfare and Reform Association pamphlet contained a clause warning the men not to marry "colored women."[10] While there were several respected Black spouses among the Muslim Punjabis in northern California, an Imperial Valley man who married a Black woman was reportedly run out of town (and the daughter of that marriage later changed her name from Singh and married out of the community). An old pioneer explained this avoidance by saying that the Punjabis recognized that they and the Blacks had similar problems, but they saw that Whites hated colored people, and they thought they could fight discrimination better on their own.[11]

The Punjabis' success in establishing a White or at least a distinctive and positively valued racial identity varied over time. An educated Hindu, one of the few among the immigrants, wrote that early ideas in the Imperial Valley about the "race inferiority" of the "heathen Hindus" had been overcome by 1924.[12] But prejudice and ignorance resurfaced in the 1930s as Anglo county officials and farmers used the Alien Land Laws against both Japanese and Punjabi farmers. In one grand-jury case against Anglo and Punjabi defendants (who had formed a corporation and were charged with conspiracy to evade the law), the Anglos requested a separate trial from their Punjabi codefendants on the grounds that "Hindus are not Caucasians or whites but are members of the Aryan race of India and ineligible to citizenship."[13] At the same time, both the Punjabi men and their Mexican intended spouses took to labeling themselves "Indian" and "Indian from Mexico" on the marriage license applications, indicating officials' attempts to prevent their marriages on the basis of difference.[14]

This move to emphasize a "sameness" between Punjabis and Mexicans was, in this instance, a response to prejudice from White officials. In other instances, Punjabis asserted a sameness between themselves and Mexicans with respect to language—Punjabi and Spanish are both Indo-European languages and share structural features and some specific words—and with respect to material culture, particularly household furnishings and food.[15] Yet despite their marriages, their shared "Caucasian but nonWhite" status, and intermittent claims of "sameness," the Punjabis generally distanced themselves from the growing community of Mexican Americans. Here class aspirations and male bonding prevailed over racial similarities and kinship ties. The Punjabis saw themselves as landowners, in both the Indian past and the American future, and they saw Mexicans as their employees, agricultural laborers. In addition to their farming backgrounds, many of the Punjabi men had first left the Punjab through military or police service with the British Raj, and their experiences with British colonial rule prepared them to move quickly into the Anglo-dominated agricultural system in California.[16] Listed as "ranchers" in the first Imperial Valley directories, the Punjabis also stood out as early telephone subscribers and senders of large money orders from the local post offices.[17] They hired Anglo lawyers, made gifts to Anglo judges, secured credit from the Anglo banks, and got Anglo storeowners and farmers to hold land for them.

Thus the Punjabis oriented themselves to the Anglo-dominated male world. Like others moving into the newly developing Imperial Irrigation District, they may have taken wives from Mexican families, but they did not take Mexican men as farming partners (I found one case), and they socialized almost entirely with other Punjabis. The Punjabi men's network was the basis of community life; a few of the Mexican women talked about "becoming Hindu," learning to cook Punjabi food, visiting the Sikh temple in Stockton (founded by the Sikhs in 1917, this served as a social and political center for all of the Punjabis), and socializing with the other Punjabi-fathered families.

While the women and the Catholic Church made the men godparents to each other's children through the *compadrazgo* system of fictive kinship, the Punjabi men were not incorporated into the larger Mexican American community.[18] In fact, Mexican men kidnapped and beat up some of the women who first married Punjabis.[19] The Mexican Hindu children experienced discrimination from Mexican children as fierce as or fiercer than that from Anglo children, being taunted as "Mexidus" or "half and halves" and having stones thrown at them on the way to school by the children of their fathers' workers. (Yet some Imperial Valley Anglos who were schooled with Spanish-speaking Singhs and Sandhus classify those names as Mexican.)[20]

The distance between Punjabis and Mexicans was a class issue, as became clear in the late 1920s and 1930s when violent conflicts erupted in California's agricultural valleys as agricultural workers attempted to organize. Mexican and Filipino workers fought hard against the Anglo power structure, and not one Punjabi farmer joined them. The Punjabis saw themselves as growers, or allies of the growers, in the struggle then and more recently (in 1978 it was on the ranch of Mario Saikhon, a Punjabi Mexican, that a Mexican striker was shot and killed). Even today, as Mexican Americans are finally moving up the agricultural ladder in California, some Punjabis remark on "bad Mexican blood" and decry the biethnic marriages of the early days.

Among the early "Hindu" immigrants to the western United States, it was the Punjabi Mexican families who were central to the Indian community. Most immigrants from India were in California, but their numbers were small (below 2,000 in California until the 1970s), and most remained bachelors in the United States.[21] Urban Indian men, many of them students or professional men married to Anglo women, may have outranked the rural Punjabis and their Mexican wives from some points of view. These more educated men provided leadership in both U.S. and Indian politics (lobbying for U.S. citizenship and fighting for India's independence from colonial rule), but they were few and scattered. The Punjabi Mexican families were the backbone of the immigrant community. Indian travelers and bachelors routinely visited them and gave gifts to the children; such "uncles" had many nieces and nephews. The wives cooked chicken curry, *roti* (bread), and other Punjabi dishes, and dinner guests were frequent. The families routinely visited the Stockton temple and took part in its activities. The Punjabi farmers and their families were the major providers of financial and political support to both the Ghadar party movement for India's independence from Great Britain and the efforts to gain U.S. citizenship.[22] The success of both these movements, independence for India and Pakistan in 1947 and the Luce-Celler bill making South Asians eligible for U.S. citizenship in 1946, dramatically altered the landscape for the pioneer families, ultimately challenging and expanding their concepts of themselves.

The Changing Political Landscape

These political changes of the late 1940s and the later changes in U.S. immigration policy in 1965, when a new Immigration and Nationality Act opened up immigration to large numbers of Asians,[23] have significantly affected the "Hindu" ethnic identity, pushing it even further in the direction of multiethnicity. A trickle of new immigrants from India and Pakistan began after the Luce-Celler bill, as the Punjabi pioneers sponsored a small number of relatives, resuming relationships they had thought sundered forever. (The 1924 National Origins Quota Act, applicable once Indians could become citizens, set an annual quota of 100 for India and then also for Pakistan.) The changed political context in South Asia had immediate repercussions in the United States. The British Indian Punjab province was split between the two new nations of India and Pakistan in 1947, something not really anticipated by the Punjabis in the United States and that tinged their patriotic pride with sadness. Although they experienced the partition and its bloody events only at a distance, ruptures occurred among California's "Hindus." A "Pakistani Queen" joined the "Hindu Queen" in the ethnic representations at county fairs, and many Muslim-fathered families of Punjabi Mexicans renamed themselves "Spanish Pakistani." The second generation was just reaching adulthood, and a few daughters married "real" Sikhs or Muslims from South Asia, while other young adults began to acquaint themselves with the Indian religions, tentatively calling themselves Catholic and Muslim, or Catholic and Sikh.

But the attempts to learn about and perhaps return to more "authentic" and narrower ethnic identities ceased as the trickle of new immigrants became a flood after 1965. These new immigrants from India and Pakistan did not readily grant legitimacy to the descendants of the "old Hindus." Confronted with newcomers from all over South Asia, the descendants are at a disadvantage. Their fathers and grandfathers had represented all of India to other Americans and to their own children, but the descendants often cannot locate themselves on a map of the Punjab, not knowing the correct pronunciation or spelling of their ancestral village; their disorientation with respect to the entire subcontinent is even worse. The new South Asian immigrants are overwhelming in terms of both numbers and diversity, speaking many different vernaculars and representing many caste and religious communities. They are primarily middle and upper class urban, highly educated, professional people, moving into U.S. society at high levels. Furthermore, they come as family units, married couples with children, and they strive anxiously to continue endogamous marriages and "preserve our culture" in the United States.[24]

Not continuities but rifts, then, have characterized the encounters between old and new South Asian immigrants. When few in number, the newcomers appreciated the hospitality of the Punjabi Mexican families, but as their numbers grew, even the new Punjabi immigrants in rural northern California no longer needed the "not really Indian" families. By example and comment, the newcomers make the Punjabi Mexican descendants feel their lack of experiential knowledge of Punjabi and South Asian culture.[25] Members of the second generation who had grown up visiting the Stockton temple, and who helped establish a new Sikh temple in Yuba City when new immigrants clustered there, no longer feel welcome at the temples. In some cases, the nephews, sons, or grandsons brought over by the aging pioneers after 1946 threaten the inheritances of the "American" sons. Attempts by self-identified "Hindus" to greet recently arrived South Asians sometimes meet with confused rejection. One example will suffice: a southern California farmer named Joe Mallobox (the surname an Americanized form of Moula Baksh, a Muslim name) went up to a family of recent immigrants from India at Disneyland, introduced himself as a Hindu, and offered to show them around.

But they did not believe him and turned away.[26] Frustrated, Joe and others like him increasingly represent themselves as "just plain Americans" and "multibreeds."

The descendants of the biethnic couples see themselves today as "choosing" situationally among the elements of their multiethnic identities. Admittedly it is difficult to reconstruct self-images in the past from oral evidence collected only over the last decade or so, and the descendants may seem oblivious of what social scientists have called the "historic inadequacy of assimilation in addressing racial difference," but the testimony is clear.[27] They are not merely biethnic, they say, but triethnic: Hindu, Mexican, and American. They take pride in "being Hindu," which, despite tensions between the fathers and children,[28] had many positive meanings for the wives and children of the Punjabis.

"Being Hindu" meant being a good farmer, working long hours to purchase land; it meant being political, fighting for India's freedom and U.S. citizenship. The Punjabi men were honest, tenacious, and fiercely loyal to each other, and those who stayed in the sometimes stormy marriages were strong fathers who transmitted their values of hard work, pride, and independence to their children. "Being Hindu" meant eating chicken curry and *roti*, lemon pickles and Punjabi vegetables, and having a reverence for the "holy book," whether the Granth Sahib of the Sikhs or the Quran of the Muslims. It meant attending Punjabi wrestling matches and Indian political speeches, and visiting the local "Hindu store" and perhaps the Stockton temple. And "being Hindu" had meant opening one's home to Punjabi bachelor uncles and other South Asians.

The American element has become emphasized as the "old Hindu" families defend themselves against the "new Hindus," but it was always present. The women saw themselves as marrying foreigners, men more different from Americans than they themselves were, and there was talk about "Americanizing" their husbands. The men had thought of themselves as permanently cut off from the Punjab and their relatives there, and many had explicitly discouraged their wives and children from learning about India or learning Punjabi, stating that they, and certainly their children, were now Americans. When they could become U.S. citizens after 1946, many aging Punjabis went through the daunting process, and they helped elect the first (and still, in 1995, the only) congressman from India, from the Imperial Valley in the 1950s.[29]

The members of the second generation, U.S. citizens by birth, are proud to be "Hindus" and Americans in rural California and, like their fathers, tend to distance themselves from "non-Whites." One daughter, giving birth in the early 1950s in Yuba City, California, was identified on the birth certificates of her three successive children as "Hindu," "Mexican Hindu," and "White." Descendants have been known to remark that the new South Asian immigrants are "smaller and darker" than the oldtimers, and much slower to "become American." They compare themselves to the Swiss and Italians, and very few identify primarily as Mexican Americans. They may watch Mexican novellas on TV, and the Mexican Hindu Christmas dance in Yuba City and the Spanish Pakistani reunions in Phoenix, Arizona, both feature mariachi bands and Mexican food, as I observed in the course of fieldwork. Yet most members of the second generation are still committed to the race, class, and ethnic claims staked by the "old Hindus."

The descendants have gone beyond the old meanings of their multiethnicity in some significant ways, however. It is clear that sometimes they mean not only that they can claim ethnic elements depending upon the situation or context, but that they are part of a larger generalized category of multiethnic people in the United States. At those same Yuba City and Phoenix dances, themes of multiculturalism and hybridity have appeared. The Yuba City Christmas dance theme was Hawaiian in 1988, with an invitation beginning "Hello/Ohio/Buenos Dias" and a banner above the stage saying "Aloha." One of the flyers about the 1990 reunion in Phoenix referred to the invitees as "multibreeds," and I think this was not only an attempt to make all members of the second and third generations and their diverse spouses welcome, but a valorization of the multiculturalism of the 1980s in the United States. (It also recognizes that the narrow and historically shallow label "Spanish Pakistani," unlike "Hindu," had no meaning to the wider community.)[30] These celebrations of multiculturalism also rebuke the parochialism of the new South Asian immigrants, who are very conspicuous in both localities. The associational and parental activities of the new immigrants, according to the descendants of the older immigrants, reinforce cultural values and practices that are not appropriate in the United States.

Here we see the descendants reaching for that "common ground" with the larger society, claiming and demonstrating sameness in social and ultimately political arenas and positioning themselves within the dominant culture in contrast to the newer immigrants.[31] I have argued elsewhere that they are probably among those "Americans" or "Whites" dropping ethnic specificities as they answer the recent census, to the dismay of some sociologists and demographers.[32] The Punjabi Mexicans have fought for a place in America, and why should they not situate themselves in the center of the sociocultural arena rather than at its margins?

The experiences of the Punjabi pioneers and their descendants show the need to see race, class, and ethnicity in dynamic relationship with time and place. Community boundaries constantly shift and are contested, and identities are always constructed relationally.[33] Mary John, in an essay on postcolonial feminists, states, "The very attempt to become such cultural representatives, the falterings of our memory, could lead to a different realization: the need for an examination of the historical, institutional, and social relations that have, in fact, produced subjects."[34] A close look at the local context in California and the Punjabi Mexican experience there clearly demonstrates the rootedness and authenticity of the early "Hindu" identity in the United States and its marked differences from Punjabi identity in India. When I first started doing research and talking about the early Punjabi immigrants and their families in 1980, the usual response of new South Asian immigrants was sharp criticism of the pioneers, pointing to "cultural loss" or betrayal of their religions by acceptance of the "Hindu" label; another response was to remain silent, essentially an erasure of this early immigrant history. More recently, there has been a greater appreciation of the harsh and difficult context in which the early immigrants found themselves and a growing interest in their historical experience, as the new immigrants locate themselves more confidently in the U.S. landscape and learn more about the flexibility and relational nature of culture and ethnic identity through their own children.

The case of the Punjabi pioneers in the United States helps us to better understand cultural transmission in general and multiethnicity in particular. It emphasizes the historical constitution of culture and identity, their flexibility and responsiveness to context. One can no longer write about "cultures" marching in bounded units through time and space—one must write about "connected social fields"[35] that can be moved, stretched, and interwoven in multiple ways. James Clifford talks about people migrating, "changed by their travel but marked by places of origin," and I have discussed elsewhere the need to look as carefully at the changes brought about by travel and settlement in new contexts as at the markings from the places of origin.[36] As Paul Gilroy puts it, "It ain't where you're from, it's where you're at."[37] To me, this means not only location in space but also in time, in terms of both historical periods and generations. Knowledges are "situated,"[38] and constructions of ethnicity and multiethnicity change significantly as people move through space and time.

Notes

1. Karen Leonard, *Making Ethnic Choices: California's Punjabi Mexican Americans* (Philadelphia: Temple University Press, 1992).

2. Stuart Hall, "Minimal Selves," in *Identity,* ed. Homi Bhabha (London: Institute of Contemporary Arts, 1987), 45.

3. More detailed material can be found in my book, where I talk about social relations in the Punjab and reproduce many more voices than can be cited in this article.

4. Some see this early migration as a Sikh one, despite a growing consensus that it was a Punjabi or "Hindu" diaspora. See Verne A. Dusenbery, "A Sikh Diaspora? Contested Identities and Constructed Realities," in *Nation and Migration: The Politics of Space in the South Asian Diaspora,* ed. Peter van der Veer (Philadelphia: University of Pennsylvania Press, 1994), 17–42.

5. In the Punjab at the turn of the century, relatively fluid pluralist paradigms were being replaced by more uniform and exclusive Sikh, Muslim, and Hindu paradigms. See Peter van der Veer, *Religious Nationalism: Hindus and Muslims in India* (Berkeley: University of California Press, 1994), chap. 2, which traces the formation of increasingly uniform Hindu, Muslim, and Sikh religious communities in nineteenth and early twentieth century India.

6. Harold S. Jacoby, "Administrative Restriction of Asian Immigration into the United States, 1907–1917," *Population Review* 25 (1982): 35–40, and "More Thind against than Sinning," *Pacific Historian* 11 (1958): 1–2, 8. The 1917 bill correlated physical with cultural distance and denied entry to immigrants from areas west of the 110th and east of the 50th meridian: U.S. Statutes at Large, 1915–1917, "An Act to Regulate the Immigration of Aliens to, and the Residence of Aliens in, the United States" 64th Congress, P.L. 876, 2d sess., vol. 39, pt. I, chap. 29, for the specific meridians.

7. For this early history, see Jane Singh, ed., *South Asians in North America: An Annotated and Selected Bibliography* (Berkeley: Center for South and Southeast Asia Studies, 1988); Bruce La Brack, *The Sikhs of Northern California 1904–1975: A Socio-Historical Study* (New York: AMS Press, 1985); Joan M. Jensen, *Passage from India: Asian Indian Immigrants in North America* (New Haven, Conn.: Yale University Press, 1988).

8. Karen Leonard, "Punjabi Farmers and California's Alien Land Law," *Agricultural History* 59 (1985): 549–62; Karen Leonard, "The Pakhar Singh Murders: A Punjabi Response to California's Alien Land Law," *Amerasia Journal* 11 (1984): 75–87.

9. Jacoby, "More Thind against Than Sinning."

10. The "Constitution and By-Laws of the Hindustanee's Welfare and Reform Society of America" (n.p. [Imperial]: Hindustanees' Welfare and Reform Society of America, n.d. [circa 1914–18]) for this clause.

11. Bagga Singh Sunga, interview by the author, El Centro, Calif., 1981.

12. Ram Chand, cited in "Survey of Race Relations," Hoover Institution Archives, Stanford, California, #232, Ram Chand, interview by W. C. Smith, June 1, 1924, El Centro, Calif.

13. Leonard, "Punjabi Farmers," 556–57.

14. Ibid.

15. Moola Singh (interview by the author, Selma, Calif., 1982) talked about the way benches were made and the level of material culture; many spoke of the resemblance between *rotis* and tortillas.

16. I have argued this in "Punjabi Pioneers in California: Political Skills on a New Frontier," *South Asia* 12 (1989): 69–81.

17. The local directories are in the Imperial Public Library, now relocated in El Centro. Early issues were titled *Imperial Valley Business and Resident Directory* (1912–13), *Thurston's Imperial Valley Directory* (1914–21), and *Imperial Valley Directory* (1924–26). For telephone subscribers, *Imperial County Pacific Telephone and Telegraph Company,* April 15, 1918 (in the Pioneers Museum, Imperial). U.S. Postmaster General, "Register of Money Orders Issued, Jan. 2, 1909 through Nov. 5, 1910, and July 16, 1912, through Dec. 18, 1913" (Joseph Anderholt directed me to these in the Holtville City Hall).

18. Non-Catholic Punjabi men seem to have been accepted as godfathers by Catholic churches throughout the Southwest; sometimes they were given Hispanic first names on official documents (for example, Arturo Gangara for Ganga Ram).

19. In 1918, the *El Centro Progress* headlined "Race Riot Is Staged," a fight between Mexicans and Punjabis in the cotton fields near Heber over a Punjabi's marriage to a Mexican woman: *Holtville Tribune* clipping dated the ninth of (month torn off), 1918. Four years later, two Mexican men abducted two Mexican women, sisters, who had married Punjabis: *Holtville Tribune,* March 9 and 10, 1922; confirmed by Janie Diwan Poonian, daughter of one of the women, Yuba City, Calif., 1982.

20. Information from Professors Duane Metzger (University of California, Irvine) and Ken Bryant (University of California, Berkeley).

21. See the tables in Leonard, *Making Ethnic Choices,* pp. 20, 77, and 175.

22. Harish K. Puri, *Ghadar Movement,* 2d ed. (Amritsar: Guru Nanak Dev University Press, 1992); see also Jensen, *Passage from India.*

23. Sucheng Chan, *Asian Americans: An Interpretive History* (Boston: Hall, 1991), chap. 8.

24. The South Asian ethnic press in the United States is filled with articles and letters testifying to this concern with transmission. For a perceptive posing of the issues involved, see R. Radhakrishnan, "Is the Ethnic 'Authentic' in the Diaspora?" in *The State of Asian America: Activism and Resistance in the 1990s,* ed. Karin Aguilar-San Juan (Boston: South End, 1994), 219–33.

25. Leonard, *Ethnic Choices,* chaps. 9 and 10.

26. Joe Mallobox, interview by the author, El Centro, Calif., 1982.

27. Michael Omi and Howard Winant, *Racial Formation in the United States: From the 1960s to the 1980s* (New York: Routledge, 1986). The phrase is Susan Koshy's, in "The Geography of Female Subjectivity: Ethnicity, Gender, and Diaspora," *Diaspora* 3 (1994): 81, n. 2.

28. Leonard, *Ethnic Choices,* chap. 8.

29. See his book, Dalip Singh Saund, *Congressman from India* (New York: Dutton, 1960).

30. And there is the fact that this label was designed to set the Muslim-headed families apart from the Sikh- and Hindu-headed ones, but members of the second generation generally did not

feel strongly about this separation and in fact all who had grown up in the Phoenix area were invited.

31. See R. Radhakrishnan, "Culture as Common Ground: Ethnicity and Beyond," in *Melus* 14 (1987): 5–19. See the discussions in Michael Keith and Steve Pile, eds., *Place and the Politics of Identity* (London: Routledge, 1993), especially David Harvey on the power relations embedded in "situatedness" (57–59).

32. Leonard, *Ethnic Choices*, 218. See Stanley Lieberson and Mary C. Waters, "The Rise of a New Ethnic Group: The 'Unhyphenated American,'" *Items* (Social Science Research Council) 43, no. 1 (1989): 7–10, and *From Many Strands: Ethnic and Racial Groups in Contemporary America* (New York: Sage Foundation, 1988), 249–50.

33. Gary Okihiro argues against the easy assumption of "community" in "The Idea of Community and a 'Particular Type of History,'" *Reflections on Shattered Windows*, ed. Gary Y. Okihiro, Shirley June, Arthur A. Hansen, and John M. Liu (Pullman: Washington State University Press, 1988), 175–182.

34. Mary E. John, "Postcolonial Feminists in the Western Intellectual Field: Anthropologists and Native Informants?" in *Traveling Theories, Traveling Theorists*, ed. James Clifford and Vivek Dhareshwar (Santa Cruz, Calif.: Center for Cultural Studies, 1989), 25–48.

35. The phrase is Sally Falk Moore's, in *Social Facts and Fabrications* (New York: Cambridge University Press, 1986), 4–5, and has been used by authors in *Towards a Transnational Perspective on Migration: Race, Class, Ethnicity, and Nationalism Reconsidered*, ed. Nina Glick Schiller, Linda Basch, and Cristina Blanc-Szanton (New York: New York Academy of Sciences, 1992); see also James Ferguson and Akhil Gupta, "Beyond 'Culture': Space, Identity, and the Politics of Difference," *Cultural Anthropology* 7 (February 1992): 6–23.

36. James Clifford, "Notes on Theory and Travel," in *Traveling Theory, Traveling Theorists*, ed. Clifford and Dhareshwar, 188.

37. Paul Gilroy, "It Ain't Where You're From, It's Where You're At . . . : The Dialectics of Diasporic Identification," *Third Text* (n.p. [UK], n.d. [c. 1987]).

38. For "situated knowledges," see Donna Haraway, "The Science Question in Feminism as a Site of Discourse on the Privilege of Partial Perspective," *Feminist Studies* 14 (1988): 575–99.

Part V

Theoretical Reflections

Maria P. P. Root

13   Rethinking Racial Identity Development

In 1989, with the good fortune of obtaining a one-year visiting professorship at the University of Hawai'i, I decided to use this year to compile an edited volume on racially mixed people. None had been produced in twenty years. During this elapsed time, the social context for racial mixing had changed, especially on the West Coast. Whereas I grew up with few other mixed people, there were young people of mixed descent everywhere now. Ironically, my excitement and drive to put together this book started to diminish once I arrived in Honolulu—I even wondered if the topic of racially mixed people was important. The people of Hawai'i have a different sentiment around race mixing—often celebratory. A few trips back to the mainland reoriented me to the country's limited ability to think, much less talk, about race. Silence and denial of the increasing presence of a mixed generation persisted. Convinced that for people of mixed racial heritage to become visible an accessible literature on them must be produced, I gathered contributors for the first contemporary edited volume on mixed heritage people.

Since the publication of that volume, *Racially Mixed People in America,* a number of cross-disciplinary anthologies and texts have explored the multiracial experience, the implications of this group's increasing size, and the delusions that abound around race.[1] Written primarily by multiracial people, these explorations relocate the marginalized multiracial experience as central to examining racial arrangements in this country. The essays and poetry call for abandoning delusions of racial purity and demand that this nation wake up to an impending identity crisis. The biracial boom is straining the monoracial framework for population counting.[2]

Racial identity is an issue in this country because the interpretation of phenotypical differences, real and imagined, has hierarchical meaning—some people are valued, others not, simply because of perceived social race. Social race does not always coincide with significant physical features. In fact, movies and trade books are emerging that deal with persons who are White discovering their African American heritage and vice versa.[3] This emergence suggests a permeability of racial boundaries on a conceptual level previously off limits.

In this chapter I discuss how the dialogue introduced by multiracial individuals and interracial families impacts current thinking about race and racial identity. For example: approximately a half dozen states have passed legislation to include a multiracial category on school and employment forms;[4] support groups are providing accurate information about interracial families to the media;[5] the U.S. Bureau of the Census is grappling with increasing numbers of persons choosing to identify themselves as multiracial;[6] and for the first time in sixty years, multiple racial classification will be an option on census forms for the year 2000.

I also critique contemporary racial identity theories based in an exclusively monoracial framework, which, from the multiracial perspective, implicitly reproduce the conventional assumptions about race and racial classification.

Positive and Negative Differentiation of the Other

This country has persecuted the very people it has used to toil, mine, and construct its contemporary wealth. Various nineteenth-century racial theories justified policing the boundary between White and not White and in effect made people of color the "other" to limit access to material wealth and resources.[7] Promoting theories of infertile hybrids, science was used as an unsuccessful birth control method between the races. The products of miscegenation were relegated to the margins, removed from the dialogue about race and turned into objects of curiosity or pity.

Defining self in relation to the other seems to be a basic human pattern. French philosopher Jean-Paul Sartre suggested that human nature leads us not only to observe the other, but to define ourselves in contrast to the other.[8] Critical aspects of social status are regularly defined in binary terms: male versus female; White versus not-White; able-bodied versus disabled; same-sex orientation versus opposite-sex orientation. In all these locations of the self, there is a primary, preferred reference group as part of each binary: male, White, able-bodied, heterosexual orientation. The other position is a marginal or secondary one with inherently less ascribed power. For example, the use of the pronoun "he" to reference all persons relegates women to "other than he." Newspaper stories let us know with racial signifiers that a person is other than the assumed White person. Discussions of romantic relationships assume heterosexual partnering.

Identifying the other and deriving a sense of one's place or self in relationship to that person or group sets in motion a process of differentiation, either *constructive differentiation* or *destructive differentiation*.

Constructive Differentiation

Constructive differentiation requires both tolerance for ambiguity and the ability to operate fearlessly in the face of difference. When we tolerate ambiguity we can suspend our urge to apply conceptual frameworks that are irrational or rigid. For example, can one tolerate the racial ambiguity of a person of mixed descent when introduced for the first time and listen to what that person has to say? Or is one distracted by trying to figure out what the person's race is? Does one's ambiguity raise anxiety and the urge to fit the new person into a category? When we operate fearlessly, we are less compelled to judge and are open to new information. For example, a young child may ask why people are different colors. This question seeks information to help make meaning out of the difference. Differences remain merely differences, some of which the child might like more than others, but not ranked superior to inferior. When we resist applying a hierarchical schema to difference we can constructively ignore the superficial differences and see universalities between people, characteristics, and things. New frameworks for understanding self and relationships between and among people become possible through constructive differentiation, which creates the opportunity to broaden our worldview. This ability to differentiate constructively, however, can be facilitated or stifled by external input.

Destructive Differentiation

Responding to fear, eliminating ambiguity, constructing difference within hierarchical matrices of power, and employing ill-fitting frameworks are all defensive strategies of *destructive differentiation*. Unfortunately, by seven or eight years of age this process may have already been assimilated. In the film *South Pacific,* set during World War II, Lieutenant Cable, a White naval officer, tries to make sense of prejudices that prevent him from marrying the Polynesian woman with whom he has been infatuated. He breaks into a well-known song, declaring that prejudices and hatred are learned rather than innate. Furthermore, the evidence of this learning occurs early, before seven or eight.[9] The underlying teachings here are to arrange physical differences hierarchically and to overgeneralize.

In destructive differentiation, one oversimplifies, generalizes, stereotypes, and employs many of the binary modes of evaluating difference that create hierarchies. Racial epithets, for example, are overtly hostile acts of destructive differentiation that declare the target the less desirable person; name calling is a dehumanizing process that allows the name caller to construct a self superior in contrast to the other.[10] A false sense of confidence allows name callers to avoid thinking about how life is experienced from the perspective of those with secondary status. Many racially mixed individuals have each been called the entire range of racial epithets. Name calling repeatedly defines who persons in power perceive as the other and exposes the anxiety or fear raised by racial ambiguity.

Ultimately, negative differentiation results in defining oneself by *what one is not*—a distancing from feared association with the other—with a less complex understanding of what one is. For example, a person may have ideas about what he or she is not, as in, "not like Filipino Americans, not like African Americans," but still not have constructively defined who she or he is as a White person.[11] Racially mixed persons, socially located as other, have had to struggle to create self-definitions of who they are in the face of being told what they are not.

Destructive differentiation also results in unresolved conflict that regenerates itself. Sometimes, those very people who have been the target of oppressive, destructive differentiation internalize this process and inflict it upon those they view as on a lower rung of the ladder of racial value. For example, given that race is constructed along the lines of pure race, in many places mixed-race people occupy a marginal, bottom rung on the ladder of race. Racial authenticity challenges further remind these individuals of their marginality. For example, multiple allegiances and affiliations may be construed as making a person an inauthentic African American or Native American.

The history of race in the United States limits our cognitive ability to critically think about race and the social fluidity by which people negotiate its borders.[12] Centuries of unresolved racial trauma, displaced feelings of anger, resentment, and fear have led us to build defenses that we manifest as reactivity, depression, anger, addiction, and anxiety.[13] In this context, our society's defenses against the racial ambiguity of people of mixed descent remain primitive. Treating people as if they do not exist, excluding their physical presence or personal reality (i.e., marginalizing a person) to reduce our internal anxiety are hallmark primitive psychological defenses. Because human beings want to belong and be accepted, the other wants inclusion. The processes of denial or marginalization have effectively coerced the other to conform to the conventional rules of race, which include affiliating with only one race. In the contemporary monoracial and monoethnic schemas, the individual who refuses to subscribe to a single racial group is marginalized. So are revolutionaries, people who refuse to perpetuate adversarial attitudes between racial groups.

Ironically, political consciousness of racial and ethnic identity development in this country derives from negative differentiation. Being the other simultaneously confers negative meaning and invisibility. Hurtado and Gurin discuss three interrelated influences that raise the political consciousness of individuals with Mexican heritage that relate to the racial and ethnic identity process for all multiracial and multiethnic individuals.[14] First, there is indignation about the lack of power experienced by the group, for example, receiving lower wages than other ethnic groups in the same work environment performing the same work. Second, there is acknowledgment of suffering brought about by structural constraints rather than by individual or group characteristics, for instance, inadequate housing caused by lack of access to resources for adequate housing. Lastly, there is an assertion that it takes collective action to improve the social standing of the group; for example, striking farm workers, garment workers, and machinists have had an impact on the labor force because certain ethnic groups sometime occupy niches of wage work that can stop production.

The Importance of a Multiracial Identification

The significance of race in this country makes personal racial identification political—whether one intends it or not. One outcome of self-definition is empowerment.[15] The racial pride movements of the 1960s and 1970s claimed one's right and authority to determine labels for one's own reference group. Similarly, today, many multiracial people proudly declare their existence without succumbing to external pressures to choose sides or prove racial authenticity. Issues of empowerment and legitimacy are particularly important, given that biracial children are stereotyped as products of inappropriate sexual liaisons or of unwanted pregnancies. Furthermore, in this race-based society, with much of our class structure embedded in this politic, either an unrecognized or an undeclared racial identity may jeopardize one's civil rights in specific situations.[16]

Declaring a multiracial identity also inspires and informs a different dialogue on the social, psychological, economic, and political construction and irrationality of race in this country. Rather than accusing one group of oppressing another, the new dialogue may deal with the toxicity of oppression and how it affects individuals, families, communities, and the nation at large.

A multiracial movement in its various forms—community support groups, student groups, journal clubs—accomplishes two central social support functions. First, it legitimizes a previously denied status, thus creating a reference group for support against toxic racial rules that give rise to racial authenticity tests and intrusive questions. Second, it provides a place for positive social recognition of multiracial people. Positive role models and shared experience facilitate esteem and counter negative attitudes toward multiracial people and interracial interactions.

Blurring the boundaries and borders between racial groups is another step toward deconstructing our current racial system.[17] Dialogue on multiraciality continues to reveal the inadequacies of the government's arbitrary "five-race" framework.[18] Such deconstruction may lead us to more fluid systems of racial construction and the use of less destructive differentiation to evaluate the meaning of these differences.

Finally, multiraciality brings into question the degree to which race has been central, implicit, and confounded in the definition of ethnicity. By identifying themselves as multiracial, people are challenging parochial attitudes about the exclusivity of ethnic group categories; for example, one might be *both* African American and Korean American. The ability to choose a dual heritage and affiliation and the right to belong to both groups or communities is not only a matter of individual well-being but also a step toward redefining ethnicity and group membership.

Opposition to multiracial and multiethnic identification arises from a variety of sources and is rooted in an unquestioning acceptance of the monoracial framework that until recently has dominated discussion of identity. Those who patrol the borders of racial identity come in all colors and ages. I have distilled their opposition into four questions and commented on each one.

- *Doesn't this identification reify the problematic concept of race?* In this society race is currently used as a divisive force that affects lives adversely: it restricts an individual's choice of identity, group affiliation, and even partners. A multiracial identification uses the familiar term "race" to change the rules about how race is applied. Increasing the options for identity—opening the borders—is a way of deconstructing an oppressive system. Given that race is so embedded in the institutions and attitudes that have formed policy and social interaction in this country, to eliminate any racial terms is too big a cognitive, and political, challenge.
- *Aren't the multiracial movement and the recognition of multiracial people creating an insidious new class structure?* In this country's history of racial mixing, particularly between Blacks and Whites,[19] the sexual exploitation of Black women by White men and prejudice directed at African heritage and skin color stand out. Some uninformed stereotypes suggest that multiracial people view themselves as superior

physically or intellectually through their European heritage. For White people, it historically reinforced the superiority of whiteness. For Black Americans, it provided a defense against rejection and marginalization by kin. Within multiracial support groups, there is a concerted effort not to replicate this oppressive process of negative differentiation. However, much of the past history was instigated not by persons of mixed origin but by the unresolved tensions between Black and White in which the mixed person was used as a warring ground.

- *Isn't this dual identification racial hatred in disguise?* The subversive strategy that a multiracial identity provides is misunderstood in a monoracial framework. Identifying oneself as a biracial or a multiracial person resists fragmenting individuals and society, a process that has weakened our social structure.[20] Dual loyalties, multiple affiliations, contextually driven declarations of identity, and successful, creative integration of values challenge the conventional wisdom that a child cannot be loyal to parents who have different personalities and different values. If countries grant dual citizenship, can we not permit multiple identities? The lack of understanding that dual affection, pride, and loyalty can coexist within an individual reflects on the dysfunctional way in which race has been constructed in our society.

- *Won't the recognition of multiracial people disenfranchise some political groups?* The current monoracial model for talking about race cannot account for a growing number of Americans.[21] The U.S. Bureau of the Census will allow people to check more than one racial category for the 2000 decennial population count. This change will still allow implementation of federal policies and programs without disenfranchising the people these policies were designed to assist.[22] Field tests have ascertained that the multiple "check-off" will not jeopardize the numbers for political population accounting.

Models of Identity

Racial identity models document the ravaging damages of our country's racial politic upon individuals. These models summarize how the insidious trauma of racism holds hostage many individuals of color who either believe in White superiority or disbelieve that racism is purely race-based until it happens to them.[23] These models outline the process of moving from the psychological damages of our racism to the reparative work on the individual psyche made possible by civil rights guarantees in the political system.

All widely used monoracial identity models are linear, stage models that suggest one should progress toward valuing one's racial status, in the meanwhile growing in political consciousness about race relations.[24] In psychological models of racial identity, this progression is theoretically correlated with positive self-esteem and positive general well-being.

Every theory develops in the context of history, politics, and the life experience of the theorist or researcher. Monoracial and multiracial theories of identity therefore differ. Initial research on psychological models of monoracial identity emerged in the late 1960s and 1970s, consequent to the racial and ethnic pride movements, which allowed the theorists, many in their late twenties and their thirties, for the first time to assert pride in being persons of color. The struggle personally and politically was for civil rights. Life experience and historical influences on identity development have recently been incorporated into Cross's model of nigrescence.[25] I observe five similarities across the most eminent models.

- In from three to five stages, persons move from lack of awareness of race, conformity to White norms, or disenfranchisement because of race, to transcending race, aware of how it affects their life. This transcendence results from working through anger and hurt, asserting constructive strategies for personal and political empowerment, and understanding differences with greater cognitive complexity.
- Positive identification as a person of color comes with immersion in the worldview and status that has been denigrated by Euro-American values. For example, a Chinese American suddenly goes only to Asian-owned restaurants, associates almost exclusively with Asian people, perhaps mostly with other Chinese, and intensely studies Chinese American history. This insular process creates a physical, social, and psychological refuge that helps increase pride for one's heritage and the sense of belonging to a particular group, and provides definitive strategies to counter the process of destructive differentiation that occurs daily around race. Pride comes via both constructive and destructive differentiation.
- In each stage, persons progress toward racial pride and mental health; these are thus linear, hierarchical models.
- Existential crises catalyze movement through the stages, resulting in increased political consciousness.
- The stages are the same, regardless of gender or any other secondary status.

More recent theorists emphasize that stages may overlap. Thus Parham's model, for example, while still a stage model, becomes more complex, for it accommodates situationally circumscribed identities, different identities that have saliency in different contexts.[26]

The 1980s witnessed the emergence of a small cohort of multiracial researchers who started systematically to explore multiracial identity in contemporary context and from a life experience perspective.[27] Almost uniformly, these researchers' results challenged the existing models of racial identity formation.

Following the trend of monoracial identity development models, stage models account for the evolution of a biracial identity.[28] Kerwin suggests that biracial identity development mirrors developmental life stages around psychological separation and individuation, from preschool to adulthood. Both Kich and Jacobs define stages of biracial identity development by the cognitive ability to understand the political concept of race and to develop a multiracial schema for integrating the individual's different racial backgrounds and their political meanings.[29] Acquiring a biracial label for self is seen as evidence of the emergence of a multiracial schema. Poston more recently translates and adapts one of the well-known monoracial identity models of African American identity development to a multiracial identity model for Black-White multiracial people.[30]

Some research has focused on qualitative descriptions of the racially mixed experience.[31] Hall, Stephan, and Williams, for example, find simultaneous identities present in one individual, a finding that should dissuade subsequent researchers from trying to use subtractive or additive models of identity. For example, applying an additive model to persons of African American and Japanese American heritage might predict that being highly identified with being African American would correlate negatively with endorsing one's Japanese American ethnic identification. However, this is not the case. Researchers have found no reliable method of extrapolating the core or breadth of one's identity from one context of identity or from a response to one question.[32] Many multiracial people strongly claim both or multiple heritages, as these researchers found, or identify simply as multiracial.

Another observation is that multiracial people typically shift identities, depending on the context. For example, a Cherokee White Scottish young woman may declare herself to be Cherokee in one situation, Indian in another, mixed heritage in still another, and Scottish at a clan gathering. Her shifts in identity should simply be taken as a warning against reductive conclusions, yet it is often mistaken for diffused or confused identity.

Although monoracial identity development models seem reliable for many monoracial people, they do not account for the developmental process among many multiracially identified people, even though political consciousness[33] and a search for belonging or acceptance,[34] important features of their lives, remain. I suggest that more fluid, interactive models that combine qualitative and quantitative data may be necessary for describing the experience of all people, particularly persons possessing multiple secondary statuses.[35] Significant historical events and social changes that could alter the content and process of racial identity struggles have intervened since the first racial identity development models were proposed.

Current and new models must take recent events and social changes into account. To understand how people make meaning out of their racial experience, they must recognize generational differences in the experience of race and the context within which it is defined and brought to awareness. Young people who are coming of age now are beneficiaries of the civil rights struggles of the 1950s through 1970s. They have not experienced the political and sometimes violent struggles salient in the lives of the original researchers and their age cohorts. The younger generation is coming of age in the context of increases in multiracial births, organized support groups for multiracial families and individuals, and changes in population counting by the U.S. Census Bureau.[36] Together, these changes challenge current models of ethnic and racial identity in several ways, raising new research questions.

- Monoracial identity models assume that a retreat from White society's denigration and refuge in the community of color results in an affirmation that increases well-being. Instead of refuge, however, biracial people may find themselves subjected to racial or ethnic authenticity tests. For example, a Black Chinese individual may be required to denounce her or his Chinese heritage in order to be accepted as Black. In Chinese American contexts, she or he may be required to demonstrate more knowledge of the culture than monoracial Chinese American peers. These experiences add to the unique phenomenology of the multiracial experience. *How do these experiences and the lack of refuge in monoracial groups inform the identity process?*

- Identity development models have not considered the simultaneous influence of other secondary statuses on identity development, such as gender, sexual orientation, or even class or nationality. *How do multiple secondary statuses within society or within a group inform the identity process?*
- Stage models do not explain the easy exchange of aspects of identity as background or foreground, for example, gender and race, race and class, sexual orientation and race. In a pilot study, I have been asking participants to tell me what is important about their identity in five different contexts: home, work/school, with friends, in the community, and in a community in which no one knows them. Sometimes the most salient aspect of identity is race, sometimes it is health or talents, often it is a combination of identity statuses. For example, many women of racially mixed heritage are aware that in a party setting where few people know them, their gender interacts with the meaning placed on their racial features, and they are viewed, perhaps, as exotic or the object of sexual fantasies. *What regulates this contextual changing foreground and background?*
- Models have been implicitly generation specific. Most beneficiaries of the civil rights movement have not experienced the kinds and degree of racial injustice that prevailed prior to the last quarter of this century. In my undergraduate classes, students of color are often stumped when I ask them to talk about racism in their lives. Undoubtedly their generation, growing up in the Northwest, and growing up middle class accounts for this. It would seem that identity is constructed differently when individuals and groups are not subjected to tremendous amounts of accumulated psychological trauma. *What contextual factors of history, class changes, and political climates inform the identity process, and how?*
- Physical appearance is a less reliable marker of race and ethnicity as racial mixing increases. For example, while my brothers are darker skinned than I, they have tended to identify as White by *race* though acknowledging their Filipino *ethnic* heritage. *To what extent does the incongruity between one's self-perception and others' perception of self create stress?* Physical appearance has always been a more poignant issue for women and girls than men and boys. *What role does physical appearance play in ethnic identification of the self and external perceptions of ethnic belonging?*
- Negative differentiation from "Whiteness," implicitly part of the racial immersion experience, may no longer be the process by which one comes to an integrated, proud meaning about one's racial identification. Again, constructive differentiation results in a more solid perception of self than negative differentiation. Furthermore, many multiracial people lead multicultural lives; many people of color have had to become bicultural in order to survive in this country. *How might models account for the bicultural existence of most people of color in this country and the ability of many persons of mixed heritage of European origins to construct a positive racial identification without denigrating Whiteness?*
- These questions lead to yet another question: *Might there be an underlying general process of identity development that guides gender development, ethnic identity, racial identity, and so on?* If there is, would understanding this process facilitate our exploration of multiple, overlapping identities as they potentially interact and mutually influence each other?

Toward More Complex Models of Racial Identity

Current models do not account for the range of ways in which people construct their core identities and determine the importance of race in them. In order to change the ways in which race is approached and conceptualized in this country, racial identity models must accommodate both monoracial and multiracial experience. Models with more cognitive complexity would allow us to explore multiple identities and a multiracial experience that may mirror real life more closely than we currently do. New models must accommodate the observations that follow. Figure 1 provides an ecological, interactive model of identity development that accommodates these observations and data; each box is a lens that can change its position in terms of influence and importance.[37]

- *Contextual factors govern the need for racial identity and the way it emerges and resolves.*[38] Generational, regional, gender, and class differences are important to the meaning that is made of race. People are driven to adapt to the environment.
- *No identity is necessarily better than another.*[39] Without knowing the individuals, no significant conclusions can be reached about an individual of multiracial heritage who identifies as such versus a multiracial individual who identifies monoracially. The resolution of identity reflects a balance between the needs of the environment and the needs of the individual.
- *Identity can change over a lifetime.*[40] Lifespan development issues and experience may catalyze changes in identity. For example, in the broader culture of "Americanness," one's need for individuality may be replaced by a need to find meaning to one's life. A need to compete may give way to a need to deal with one's mortality. Developmental life goals may influence which aspects of identity are foreground versus background to one's awareness of self.
- *A racial immersion experience may be less necessary to the process of racial identity since the civil rights era has created more positive role models for racially diverse youth.* History and regional histories influence race relations and the formation of identity. Furthermore, racial immersion that requires the denigration of others different from self replicates an oppressive process that reinforces social fragmentation.
- *Physical appearance is neither a necessary nor a sufficient variable for certainty about one's racial or ethnic orientation in this world.*[41] Phenotypes within racial groups and ethnic groups are increasingly diverse. One's internal experience is influenced by contextual factors and interactions of which phenotype is only a part.
- *Gender interacts with how one makes meaning out of life experience and race.*[42] Because physical appearance has been a marker of both race and value for women, it is likely to make this experience significantly different for women than men.[43] Furthermore, regardless of their race, many women experience constricted roles and parochial definitions of femininity by men. Nurturing the development of self in the context of this secondary status may involve a process that informs racial identity development, particularly when accurate gender identification of others occurs earlier than accurate racial identification.

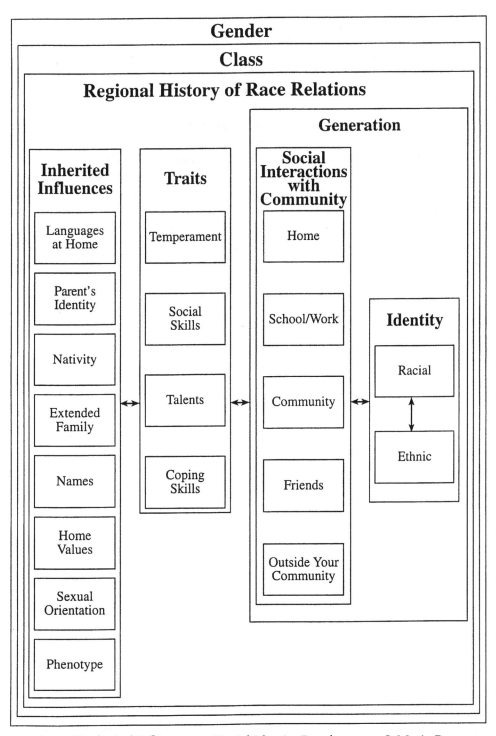

FIGURE I.   Ecological Influences on Racial Identity Development. © Maria Root.

- *Sexual orientation interacts with how we make meaning out of our life experiences and racial orientation.*[44] All racial and ethnic groups have denigrated persons with same-sex orientations, who may feel more oppressed for their sexual choices than by racism. There may be contexts within which sexual identity prevails over racial identity, although they are possibly coconstructed.[45]

- *Class and race remain confounded in this country.*[46] People of color in this country have not had the same access to class mobility as Whites; when they do move up in class, that accomplishment is not recognized. Antimiscegenist attitudes were based on preventing class mobility. Socially, markers of race are confounded with phenotype. Despite multiple generations in this country, Asian Americans continue to be thought of as immigrants and even sojourners, a status that is a class marker in that it justifies some of the invisibility to which Asians Americans are relegated. Accents, particularly from Mexico, Central America, South America, and various Asian countries, are variously associated with intelligence and class standing. Skin color, despite one's capital assets, is a class marker in this country.

- *Race, class, and gender influence each other.*[47] In the matrix of power in which race and gender are the independent variables, Whiteness and maleness are the privileged positions, indices of class standing. (White women have been able to use beauty as a ticket for upward social mobility.) The men of a racial or ethnic group are the indicators of the group's class standing; the women's class standing is defined by the male positions in a patriarchal society. For example, White women achieve positions of status over women of color through White men. Women of color achieve status through men of color. However, because these men occupy a secondary status because of color, women of color have secondary status by gender *and* color.

- *European heritage must be acknowledged.* We need to understand how this heritage may influence and change the process of racial identity formation. How does the social location and process of identity vary for persons who construct a minority-minority identity versus an identity with heritage from majority-minority influence?

Learning how we define ourselves through constructive differentiation may help us understand the shifts in our self-identity over time. This approach has been taken by researchers on adolescent identity development, primarily from a psychodynamic orientation.[48] I suggest that three processes are involved in identity exploration and integration throughout one's life, and that they mirror life stage processes that may occur simultaneously or sequentially. They are *exposure/absorption,* which corresponds to our earlier years and involves orienting to new information; *intellectual competition,* which corresponds to the independence associated with adolescence and later years; and *reflective appraisal,* which requires the hindsight associated with accumulated experience in living. I believe that we repeat these processes as we acquire information about ourselves in relationship to our larger communities, and that not participating in them may stunt our psychosocial identity development.

Exposure/absorption may be passive or active. The process allows one to take the world in by observing differences, accepting others' interpretations of meanings of differences, and organizing information into existing schemas. In this interactive process, significant others and influences direct the interpretation of differences through constructive or destructive differentiation. One notices this process frequently in children; they encounter new information about the world with wonder and curiosity. They are sometimes brutally honest because they still see clearly. Fortunately, some adults retain the ability to suspend judgment and can absorb new information or notice differences with constructive differentiation.

Intellectual competition leads to reorganizing information and reformulating meaning while positioning one's "self" in a most favorable light. I believe this to be a more prevalent process in societies that emphasize individualism. Characteristics of this process are competition, interpretation of the meaning of differences with hierarchical schemata typical of destructive differentiation, and advancing one's organizing schemata and agendas over others. Ambiguity is to be resolved as quickly as possibly. This lack of tolerance for ambiguity can make this process very vulnerable to negative differentiation, particularly if negative differentiation has been modeled for resolving conflict.

Reflective appraisal fosters connection to humanity and to the needs of the collective. Requiring hindsight, it leads us to evaluate priorities, attempt to resolve regrets, and move toward simple (though not necessarily reductionistic) theories for understanding human beings. Often this process is apparent when people are older and reappraising the decisions they have made in life.

I think these three processes provide one way of understanding identity development as an interactive and dynamic, spiraling process; we revisit issues through different content over the course of our lifetime. This model recognizes the importance of learning constructive versus destructive means of construing differences between people. Because the three processes are neither equally weighted nor sequential, one can take into account gender differences in socialization. For example, many girls and women have not been as highly socialized as men to competition and an individualistic orientation. This may influence how they understand multiplicity and simultaneousness—or even multiraciality. Cultural orientations to individualism rather than collectivism may also help us understand the salience of processes and variables in the ecological model for different cultures. Entitled positions exist in every culture and will influence the matrix of power and the subsequent lenses through which one construct a positive identity for a secondary status.

W.E.B. Du Bois noted almost a century ago that the color line would preoccupy social relations in the twentieth century.[49] The boundaries set by the multiracial experience seem to be the new context for tackling race and its construction in this country as we contemplate the twenty-first century. This experience and new theories of identify may help change some of the rigidity and negative differentiation around race practiced by those who subscribe to monoracial frameworks.

When university students of multiracial descent filled the room for a poetry reading at UC Santa Cruz in 1995, laughter, tears, talent, and humor flowed. Something revolutionary took place. The students' comments on race and race relations reflected a reality and dialogue that went far beyond the Black-White racial discourse of talk shows, newspaper columns, and textbooks. These students beckoned the dawning of a new era. Sitting and listening, I wondered if the nation would be able to join in the dialogue that these students offered that spring day of 1995.

Notes

1. Popular literature includes Carol Camper, ed., *Miscegenation Blues: Voices of Mixed Race Women* (Toronto: Sister Vision, 1994); Lise Funderburg, *Black, White, Other: Biracial Americans Talk about Race and Identity* (New York: Morrow, 1994); Lisa Jones, *Bulletproof Diva: Tales of Race, Sex, and Hair* (New York: Doubleday, 1994); and Cherie Moraga, *The Last Generation: Prose and Poetry* (Boston: South End, 1993). Academic texts and anthologies include Naomi Zack, *Race and Mixed Race* (Philadelphia: Temple University Press, 1993), and *American Mixed Race: The Culture of Microdiversity* (Lanham, Md.: Rowman and Littlefield, 1995), and Maria P. P. Root, *Racially Mixed People in America* (Thousand Oaks, Calif.: Sage, 1992), and *The Multiracial Experience: Racial Borders as the New Frontier* (Thousand Oaks, Calif.: Sage, 1996).

2. Maria P. P. Root, "The Multiracial Experience: Racial Borders as a Significant Frontier in Race Relations," in Root, *The Multiracial Experience.*

3. Gregory Howard Williams, *Life on the Color Line* (New York: Dutton, 1995); Shirlee Taylor Haizlip *Sweeter the Juice* (New York: Simon and Schuster, 1994); and a 1996 film, *A Family Thing.*

4. Susan Graham, "The Real World," in Root, *The Multiracial Experience.*

5. Nancy Brown and Ramona Douglass, "Making the Invisible Visible: The Growth of Community Network Organizations," in Root, *The Multiracial Experience.*

6. M. Anderson and S. E. Feinberg, "Black, White, and Shades of Gray (and Brown and Yellow)," *Chance* 8 (1995): 15–18; Suzanne Evinger, "How Shall We Measure Our Nation's Diversity?" *Chance* 8 (1995): 7–14.

7. An excellent review of this literature is provided by Robert J. C. Young, *Colonial Desire: Hybridity in Theory, Culture, and Race* (New York: Routledge, 1995); Gary B. Nash, "The Hidden History of Mestizo America," *Journal of American History* (December 1995): 941–62. Paul Spickard reviews some of the history of racial classification as it affects people of mixed descent in "The Illogic of American Racial Categories," in Root, *Racially Mixed People in America.*

8. Jean-Paul Sartre, trans. A. Sheridan-Smith, *Critique of Dialectical Reasoning: Theory of Practical Ensembles* (London: New Left Books, 1976).

9. Richard Rodgers and Oscar Hammerstein, *South Pacific* (1958).

10. See Whillock for an excellent discussion of the process and production of hate speech in *Hate Speech,* ed. Rita K. Whillock and David Slayden (Thousand Oaks, Calif.: Sage, 1995), 28–54.

11. Ruth Frankenberg, *The Social Construction of Whiteness: White Women, Race Matters* (Minneapolis: University of Minnesota Press, 1993); Janet E. Helms, *Black and White Racial Identity: Theory, Research, and Practice* (New York: Greenwood, 1990).

12. Root, *The Multiracial Experience.*

13. Maria P. P. Root, "The Impact of Trauma on Personality: The Second Reconstruction," in *Theories of Personality and Psychopathology: Feminist Reappraisals,* ed. Mary Ballou and Laura S. Brown (New York: Guilford, 1992). On racial traumatization, see Root, "The Biracial Baby Boom: Understanding Ecological Constructions of Racial Identity in the Twenty-First Century," in *Racial, Ethnic, and Cultural Identity and Human Development: Implications for Education,* ed. Rosa H. Sheets and Etta Hollins (Mahwah, N.J.: Erlbaum, in press).

14. Aida Hurtado and Paul Gurin, "Ethnic Identity and Bilingualism Attitudes," in *Hispanic Psychology: Critical Issues in Theory and Research,* ed., Amado M. Padilla (Thousand Oaks, Calif.: Sage, 1995), 89–103.

15. Helms, *Black and White Racial Identity.*

16. Carlos A. Fernandez, "Government Classification of Multiracial/Multiethnic People," and Deborah A. Ramirez, "Multiracial Identity in a Color-Conscious World," in Root, *The Multiracial Experience.*

17. Root, *The Multiracial Experience.*

18. Roger Sanjek, "Intermarriage and the Future of Races in the United States," in *Race,* ed. Steven Gregory and Roger Sanjek (New Brunswick, N.J.: Rutgers University Press, 1994), 103–30.

19. G. Reginald Daniel, "Passers and Pluralists: Subverting the Racial Divide," in *Racially Mixed People in America,* ed. Root; bell hooks, *Ain't I a Woman? Black Women and Feminism* (Boston: South End, 1981).

20. Christine M. Chao, "A Bridge over Troubled Waters: Being Eurasian in the U. S. of A.," in *Racism in the Lives of Women: Testimony, Theory, and Guides to Antiracist Practice,* ed. Jeanne Adleman and Gloria Enguidanos (New York: Harrington Park, 1995), 33–44; Maria P. P. Root, "A Bill of Rights for Racially Mixed People," in *The Multiracial Experience,* ed. Root, chap. 2.

21. Root, "The Multiracial Experience"; Mary C. Waters, "The Social Construction of Race and Ethnicity: Some Examples from Demography," paper presented at "American Diversity: A Demographic Challenge for the Twenty-First Century," Center for Social and Demographic Analsysis Conference (SUNY, Albany, April 1994).

22. Anderson and Feinberg, "Black, White"; and Evinger, "How Shall We Measure?"

23. Root, "The Impact of Trauma on Personality."

24. Donald R. Atkinson, George Morten, and Derald W. Sue, "A Minority Identity Development Model," in *Counseling American Minorities,* ed. Donald R. Atkinson, George Morten, and Derald W. Sue (Dubuque, Iowa: Brown, 1989), 35–52; William E. Cross, Jr., "The Negro-to-Black Conversion Experience," *Black World* 20 (1971): 13–26; William E. Cross, Jr., *Shades of Black: Diversity in African American Identity* (Philadelphia: Temple University Press, 1991); Helms, *Black and White Racial Identity;* James Milliones, "Construction of a Black Consciousness Measure: Psychotherapeutic Implications," *Psychotherapy: Theory, Research, and Practice* 17 (1980): 175–82.

25. William E. Cross, Jr., and Peony Fhagen-Smith, "Nigrescence and Ego Identity Development: Accounting for Differential Black Identity Patterns," in *Counseling across Cultures,* ed. Paul B. Pedersen, et al. (Thousand Oaks, Calif.: Sage, 1996); Cross, *Shades of Black.*

26. Thomas A. Parham, "Cycles of Nigrescence, *The Counseling Psychologist* 17 (1989): 187–226.

27. Christine C. I. Hall, "The Ethnic Identity of Racially Mixed People: A Study of Black-Japanese" (Ph.D. diss., University of California at Los Angeles, 1980); George Kitahara Kich, "Eurasians: Ethnic/Racial Identity Development of Biracial Japanese/White Adults" (Ph.D. diss., Wright Institute of Professional Psychology, 1982); Stephen L. Murphy-Shigematsu, "The Voices of Amerasians: Ethnicity, Identity, and Empowerment in Interracial Japanese Americans" (Ph.D. diss., Harvard University, 1987); Michael C. Thornton, "A Social History of a Multi-ethnic Identity: The Case of Black Japanese Americans (Ph.D. diss., University of Michigan, 1983).

28. James Jacobs, "Identity Development in Biracial Children," in *Racially Mixed People in America,* ed. Root; Christin Kerwin, "Racial Identity Development in Biracial Children of Black/White Racial Heritage" (Ph.D. diss., Fordham University, 1991); George Kitahara Kich, "The Developmental Process of Asserting a Biracial, Bicultural Identity," in *Racially Mixed People in America,* ed. Root.

29. Kich, "Eurasians"; Kich, "Developmental Process"; J. H. Jacobs, "Black/White Interracial Families, Marital Process and Identity Development in Young Children" (Ph.D. diss., Wright Institute of Professional Psychology, 1977); Jacobs, "Identity Development."

30. William S. C. Poston, "The Biracial Identity Development Model: A Needed Addition," *Journal of Counseling and Development* 69 (1990): 152–55; Cross, *Shades of Black*.

31. Lynda D. Field, "Piecing Together the Puzzle: Self-Concept and Group Identity in Biracial Black/White Youth," in *The Multiracial Experience*, ed. Root; Hall, "Ethnic Identity"; Murphy-Shigematsu, "Voices of Amerasians"; Thornton, "Social History of a Multiethnic Identity"; Teresa Kay Williams, "Prism Lives: Identity of Binational Amerasians," in *Racially Mixed People in America*, ed. Root; Cookie White Stephan, "Mixed-Heritage Individuals: Ethnic Identity and Trait Characteristics," *Racially Mixed People in America*, ed. Root.

32. Hall, "Ethnic Identity"; Amy Iwasaki Mass, "Interracial Japanese Americans: The Best of Both Worlds or the End of the Japanese American Community?" in *Racially Mixed People in America*, ed. Root; Stephan, "Mixed-Heritage Individuals"; Williams, "Prism Lives."

33. Hurtado and Gurin, "Ethnic Identity and Bilingualism."

34. Jewelle T. Gibbs and Alice Hines, "Negotiating Ethnic Identity: Issues for Black-White Biracial Adolescents," in *Racially Mixed People in America*, ed. Root.

35. Maria P. P. Root, "Resolving 'Other' Status: Identity Development of Biracial Individuals," in *Diversity and Complexity in Feminist Therapy*, ed. Laura S. Brown and Maria P. P. Root (New York: Haworth, 1990), 185–206. Also see Root, "Biracial Baby Boom."

42. Nancy Brown and Ramona Douglass, "Making the Invisible Visible."

37. A detailed explanation of this interactive model is found in Root, "Biracial Baby Boom."

38. Root, "Resolving 'Other' Status."

39. Ibid.

40. Ibid.

41. Hall, "Ethnic Identity."

42. Patricia H. Collins, *Black Feminist Thought: Knowledge, Consciousness, and the Politics of Empowerment* (New York: Routledge, 1991); Jones, *Bulletproof Diva*; Gerda Lerner, *The Creation of Patriarchy* (New York: Oxford University Press, 1986); Streeter, "Ambiguous Bodies"; Wilkinson, "Gender and Social Inequality."

43. Root, "Mixed Race Women."

44. Karen M. Allman, "(Un)Natural Boundaries: Mixed Race, Gender, and Sexuality," in *The Multiracial Experience*, ed. Root; and George Kitahara Kich, in *The Multiracial Experience*, ed. Root.

45. Root, "Biracial Baby Boom," discusses this further, highlighting the coconstructive process around multiple secondary statuses.

46. Michael Omi and Howard Winant, *Racial Formation in the United States from the 1960s to the 1990s* (New York: Routledge, 1994); Cornel West, *Race Matters* (Boston: Beacon, 1993).

47. M. L. Andersen and Patricia H. Collins, eds., *Race, Class, and Gender* (Belmont, Calif.: Wadsworth, 1992); Collins, *Black Feminist Thought*; Ellen C. DuBois and Vickie L. Ruiz, eds., *Unequal Sisters: A Multicultural Reader in U.S. Women's History* (New York: Routledge, 1990); Cherie Moraga and Gloria Anzaldua, *This Bridge Called My Back: Writings by Radical Women of Color* (New York: Kitchen Table: Women of Color Press, 1981); Cherie Moraga, *The Last Generation* (Boston: South End, 1993).

48. James Marcia focuses on adolescent identity, e.g., in "Ego Identity Status: Relationship to Change in Self-Esteem, 'General Maladjustment,' and Authoritarianism," *Journal of Personality* 35 (1967): 119–33; Mary F. Belenky, Blythe M. Clinchy, Nancy R. Goldberger, and Jill M. Tarule, *Women's Ways of Knowing* (New York: Basic Books, 1986); Jean S. Phinney extends Erikson's and Marcia's work on identity and uses process to identify primary conflicts that must be resolved and extends the work of identity to race in "Stages of Ethnic Identity Development in Minority Group Adolescents," *Journal of Early Adolescence* 9 (1989): 34–49.

49. W. E. B. DuBois, *The Souls of Black Folk* (New York: Vintage Books, 1990, reissue).

Lori Pierce

---

14   The Continuing Significance of Race

Every Black person I know has a story about the day they became Black. Some are famous. Some are funny. All reveal an ironic self-consciousness. W.E.B. Du Bois made his journey of Black self-identification the subject of his extended meditation on the state of Black America at the turn of the twentieth century in *The Souls of Black Folk*. He recalled the numerous incidents that reinforced his Black identity: having his calling card rejected by a White classmate; riding on Jim Crow train cars in the South; having bystanders hurl racial epithets at him and his wife while they walked behind the casket of their first-born son.[1] In several speeches Malcolm X addressed the issue in the form of a joke: What do you call a Black person with a Ph.D.? Nigger. Henry Louis Gates, the head of Harvard's Afro-American studies program, tells a story on himself. Leaving the Schomburg Library in New York after a highly intellectual discussion on the subject of race as a "trope of irreducible difference," he and his Black colleague are stranded uptown, unable to hail a cab. As he grows angry by his invisibility to cab drivers, his friend reminds him, "But sir, it is only a trope."[2]

My own story is not so much about a day (though I do remember being asked by the White girls in my Brownie troop if I preferred "brown brownies or white brownies"), as a growing awareness over many years. I am a child of the integration era, and like Du Bois I was frequently one of only a few Black children in my classes in grade school, high school, and college. It never felt odd or strange or wrong to me. I had White and Black friends; I don't ever remember not being allowed to play in my White friends' homes. I grew up with the sense of privilege and confidence that comes with a middle-class American life-style. Nothing would be denied me; if I worked hard or desired something, I was, of course, entitled to it.

I was out of college a year or so and working in a social service agency in San Francisco when I suddenly decided to leave California and move to Maine. I was speaking with an administrator in the office, a middle-class Black woman, filling her in on the details of my new life—10 × 12 cabin, no running water, twenty-five miles from the nearest large town—when her eyebrows lifted in disbelief. She looked at me intently for a few seconds and then said, "But *we* don't do that kind of thing!"

That "we" bothered me for a long time. Who was this "we," and why was she so sure I belonged to it? Upon what was "we" predicated? If moving to Maine and living in the woods wasn't a "Black thing" to do, was it because it was not a shared cultural value? Or because I would be an obvious target for racial assaults by choosing to live in isolation from other Blacks? What I gradually came to realize was that no matter what my relationship to my Black *ethnicity*—those shared cultural values—I would always be a part of that we, a part of the Black *race*. What is the difference between these two things? Ethnic identity can be stronger or weaker, depending on my economic and social circumstances. But racial identity is perpetuated by racial and racist incidents that are an inevitable part of the lives of Blacks and other minorities in the United States. No amount of success or intellectual tap dancing can mitigate the effect of being reminded, as Professor Gates was in Harlem, that race is more than "just a trope."

The purpose of this chapter is to discuss the necessity of race as a category of analysis within theories of ethnicity and multi-ethnicity. Mired as we are in centuries of misunderstandings about the ideology of race, the temptation is almost overwhelming to dispense with the term altogether in favor of something that more accurately reflects how human populations and cultures function and interact. Those who study human populations have known for decades that race is a discredited concept that reflects seventeenth- and eighteenth-century scientistic thinking. Why, then, the persistent use of race and racial reasoning by historians, sociologists, and political scientists? And of what possible use can race be in attempting to map out a theory of ethnicity for the twenty-first century?

Discrimination based on the perception of racial (i.e., essential) differences has been a central (though by no means the only) force in the construction of ethnic group identity for African Americans, Hispanics, Native American Indians, and Asians in the United States. This same racism has also been a primary force in the construction of Euro-American ethnic identity, not as the result of discrimination but as the result of the privileges associated with being "White." Racist discrimination based on the perceived reality of race has, in the United States, created a self-perpetuating system of privilege *for* Whites and discrimination *against* non-Whites. It is my contention that ethnicity theorists will fail in their efforts to address problems of ethnic group formation and interethnic conflict without an adequate understanding of race, racism, and the process of racialization. Racism and its effects necessitate our continuing to use race as a category of analysis and understanding of the history of ethnic groups in the United States.[3]

In chapter 1 of this volume, Paul Spickard and Jeffrey Burroughs assert that a race "is a particular kind of ethnic group. The mechanisms that divide races from each other are the same mechanisms that divide ethnic groups from one another. The processes that bind a race together are the same processes that bind an ethnic group together. . . . [W]e propose to use 'ethnic group' as the generic term." They also take issue with racialization theorists, who, they feel, rely too heavily on the outdated concept of race in order to fight racism. This is, they believe, a self-defeating position. "There is no long-term good to be served by maintaining false and oppressive categories such as 'race.' To adopt the rhetorical posture of our racializationist colleagues is . . . to give in to the pseudo-scientific racists." In their reading of racializationists, race is the mark of the oppressed in opposition to the oppressor. "'Race' becomes then an all-purpose synonym for 'oppressed group' and loses its specifically ethnic character." The tendency among racialization theorists is to overemphasize racial oppression to the exclusion of other cultural traits that bind an ethnic group together. We certainly see this in reference to African Americans in the United States; we rarely, if ever, talk about "Black ethnicity."

Spickard and Burroughs's argument is worthy of careful consideration. They are attempting to move away from any hint of racist thinking by abandoning the terminology altogether. The differences between Italian Americans and African Americans are not genetic, biological, or in any way essential. Therefore we ought not talk about them as if they are. Thinking in terms of ethnic groups and not as races reiterates their antiracist stance. Their argument as presented here, however, fails to address a number of issues: first, by using terms such as "adopt" and "choose" in referring to the persistent use of racial terminology by racializationists, they suggest that we are at liberty to speak or not speak of race. Even the most cursory reading of the history of the United States would reveal the depth to which racial ideologies have permeated our cultural, political, and social institutions. One of the first legislative acts passed by the U.S. Congress in 1790 limited naturalized citizenship to "White persons."[4] The Dred Scott decision of 1856 established as legal precedent what had been common knowledge: that the descendants of enslaved Africans had no rights of citizenship the law was bound to respect. They "were not intended to be included, under the word 'citizens' in the Constitution, and can therefore claim none of the rights and privileges which that instrument provides for and secures to citizens of the United States."[5] I do not mean to suggest that our history has robbed us of our free will. But steeped as we are in racism as a driving force in the course of our history, how can we speak otherwise? How can we make sense of racism, which is at the core of our being as a nation and a culture, without speaking of race and racial ideology? How do we make sense of the internment of Japanese Americans during World War II without speaking about the reality of "race" as it was applied to them? How can we speak about how Negroes "became" African Americans without understanding and speaking about race? We cannot understand the state of ethnic groups in the present without understanding the historical processes that made racial objects out of ethnic subjects. Many ethnic groups became ethnic groups only after passing through the crucible of race.

Second, by proposing the use of the term "ethnicity" as the generic referent for all groups, it seems as if Spickard and Burroughs are attempting to level the playing field. The potential for serious misunderstanding exists here because of the nature of racism in U.S. culture. It may well be true that all ethnic groups are the same in the ways in which they function, but racism has played a significant role in the group funtioning of ethnic minorities in the United States. And while most immigrant groups were subjected to years of discrimination and exclusion upon arrival in the United States, ethnic groups to whom racist ideologies were applied suffered not only individual acts of discrimination but wholesale exclusion from the body politic and therefore did not have redress within the legal system.

Spickard and Burroughs, of course, are not unaware of the force and importance of racism in the lives of ethnic groups in the United States, and they acknowledge the importance of antiracist work by racialization theorists. Our disagreement is a matter of emphasis: by highlighting the ways in which their argument can be seen to overlook racism as a critical factor in ethnic group formation, I mean to draw attention to the attempt of racialization theory, in my reading of it, to place racism in the forefront of our understanding of ethnicity.

We would do well to have a better understanding of just what is meant by "racialization" before we overburden it with unintended meanings and implications. Racialization theorists attempt to account for the disparity in income, education, and opportunity for non-White minority populations as well as the persistence of racism by conceiving of race as a process. Though racialization is not a fully formed or consistently applied theoretical model, by examining how the term has come to be used and defined, we can see that it has the potential to offer race and ethnicity theorists a way of bridging the gap between fictive biology and lived experience of certain ethnic groups.

Most race theorists would agree that the use of the term "racialization" has its roots in the work of British race relations theorists. Though David Theo Goldberg attributes the coining of the term to Frantz Fanon in *Black Skin White Masks,*[6] the scholarly use of the term to describe race relations begins quite a bit later, in the early 1980s. Most of the theoretical explorations of racialization are the work of or at least in response to the work of British Marxists. Sociologists and cultural theorists from the University of Birmingham's Centre for Contemporary Cultural Studies began rethinking the traditional Marxist vision of race as merely a function of class relations in light of the so-called "race relations" crisis related to increased Black immigration to Great Britain in the 1960s and 1970s. The British Marxist sociologist Robert Miles is generally credited with first defining racialization, in part as a linguistic maneuver around the term race.[7] Miles argued that "'race' cannot be the object of analysis in itself, since it is a social construction which requires explanation ... [and] the object of analysis should be the process of 'racialisation' or 'racial categorisation' which takes place within the context of specific economic, political and ideological relations."[8] In other words, races do not exist in isolation or in any objective reality, but are part of the social and political life of nations. Miles, then, is attempting to deal with the dual nature of race, bracketing it (literally, within quotation marks) as an object of serious inquiry while simultaneously retaining it within the formulation of the process of racialization. Racialization is the creation of racial groups to serve specific political purposes. Miles's definition draws our attention away from race as an essential reality and toward the political and social function of race.

Other writers have borrowed from and expanded upon Miles's formulations; what they all have in common is an emphasis on race as a process. John Stanfield refers to race making as a social process common to modern industrial societies and defines it as "premised on the ascription of moral, social and symbolic and intellectual characteristics to real or manufactured phenotypical features which justifies and gives normality to the institutional and societal dominance of one people over other populations."[9]

Marci Green and Bob Carter elaborate on this definition, stressing the role of power relations in the process of racialization.[10] Like Miles, they reject the notion that "race" refers to any essential reality, but they are unwilling to dispense with the term entirely because of the political weight it still carries. Racism and discrimination, they argue, against those to whom race has been ascribed needs to be explored and explained.

Racism is not the result of the "presence of races." "Race-ism and discrimination are historical solutions to particular structural and ideological 'problems.' 'Race' is a powerful concept, both for those who have employed it to justify oppression and exploitation and for those who have resisted these things. None the less it is a concept whose referent has been constructed. The means and manner of its construction are illuminated by the ideal of 'racialization.'"[11]

Floya Anthias and Nira Yuval-Davis follow this same logic of retaining race, though it has been "totally discredited.... None the less, from a sociological point of view, 'race' denotes a particular way in which communal differences come to be constructed and therefore it cannot be erased from the analytical map."[12] They argue that race is one way of constructing an ethnic boundary, but the term "ethnicity" too often implies a certain "voluntarism" of affiliation that is not accessible to "races." They borrow their concept of racialization from Miles, arguing that it "retains the notion of race as a social construction which is at the heart of the racialization process, and which is converted to racism when it is imbued with negative valuation."[13]

Michael Omi and Howard Winant put a slightly different spin on racialization. Theirs was the first attempt to translate the theory of racialization into a U.S. context. In *Racial Formation in the United States,* they reinvent racialization as "racial formation" defining it as "a sociohistorical process by which racial categories are created, inhabited, transformed, and destroyed.... [R]acial formation is a process of historically situated projects in which human bodies and social structures are represented and organized.... [W]e link racial formation to the evolution of hegemony, the way in which society is organized and ruled.... From a racial formation perspective, race is a matter of both social structure and cultural representation."[14] Once they have elaborated a theory of racial formation, they attempt to show how racial projects have worked in the United States since the 1960s. Whereas the Marxist race relations theorists have been focused more on positioning race within the axes of political power relations and understanding whether race or class should have primacy in theoretical analyses of social relations, Omi and Winant produced a model that accounts for the persistence of racism and identifiable racialized groups within which historians could understand and elaborate on the histories of minority groups in the United States.

Stephen Small elaborates on these themes and notes that the concept of racialization moves the debate "from an analysis of 'race,' race relations and Black people, to one of racism, racialised relations and white people.... The problem with a focus on black people alone is that it conceives the Black population as a 'cause' of racialised antagonism, rather than it being a consequence of white attitudes and actions.... [T]he problem is not 'race' but 'racisms', not relations between 'races' but relations which have become racialised, not the physical attributes of Blacks or their presumed inferiority, but the motivations of non-Blacks, and the obstacles they impose."[15]

Small's contribution to the discussion brings us back around to Spickard and Burroughs's criticism of racialization. Examining theories of racialization proposed by Carter and Green, Anthias and Davis, and Omi and Winant, the reader is certainly left with the impression that Spickard and Burroughs were left with: race is ethnicity plus oppression. But if we keep in mind that racialization theories are not an attempt to explain race but to explain racism and if we look more carefully at the way the theories have been deployed, we begin to see that racialization is not necessarily limited to the United States, indeed even to White or Euro-American–dominated societies or the West. I would propose that we can distill the most salient elements of these racialization theories into one simple sentence: racialization is the essentialist politicization of ethnic identity for any reason. Though it is most clearly seen in the oppression of non-White minorities in White-dominated societies, the process of racialization can be applied to any group for a variety of political purposes. Racialization then could be seen at work in the African American community as it reacts to racist incursions and assaults by drawing upon an externally imposed group identity to resist racism. It can also be seen at work in the shifts and changes in U.S. immigration laws as the court struggled to define who counts as "White."[16]

Such a wide-open definition allows us to see racialization at work in a growing body of work on White racial formation in the United States. David Roediger, Noel Ignatiev, George Lipsitz, Theodore Allen, Ruth Frankenberg, Vron Ware, and others have opened up historical and cultural studies through their examinations of the effect of White racial identity on White Americans.[17] The critical insight here was that articulated by Stephen Small: racism is not just a "Black thang." By turning our historical attention to not just White racism but the constructed nature of White racial identity, we begin to see the reverse side of racism and discrimination: privilege and endowment. Racialized societies, cultures where everyone's ethnic identity is politicized to some degree or another, create not just wrack and ruin for minorities but the invisible shield of privilege for the majority. This privilege shields the majority from ever having to reflect upon their identity as politicized. As the majority population, their lives, their values, their histories are the norm against which all others are measured. Examining the process of racialization helps reveal this invisible map of privilege. In a White-dominated society, the privilege associated with coming as close as possible to the White norm—in looks, speech, behavior, or values—pays off for non-Whites in educational, economic, or social advancement. Racialization is the process of reading race back into our histories and understanding how it was deliberately and consciously used by the government, labor and civic leaders, ministers, and business people at all levels of society to promote one group's advantage over another.

I think this broader understanding of racialization as the politicization of ethnic identity can be widely applied. And because racialization is not dependent upon the existence of "races," we can see how it might be at work even in situations such as those described by Spickard and Burroughs. The Han Chinese and Tibetans may at one time have been relegated to the same "racial" category, but the Han Chinese are relying on racial formulations to justify their hegemony over Tibet. The same is true of Muslims and Croats who, in an archaic and entirely irrelevant racial schema left over from the eighteenth century, are Caucasians. But the "ethnic cleansing" practiced by the Serbs against their Croat neighbors had all the signs of the racialization of a group of people. Racialization is the process of making a specific group of people fit into a rigidly defined social construct based on discredited "racial" categories. It is valid whether races exist or not.

Race is still of some strategic use in ethnic studies. There is certainly some good to come from a universal understanding of ethnic group processes. But retaining the category of race, especially by way of theories of racialization, gives ethnicity theorists a way of understanding and accounting for the political forces that create and transform ethnic groups.

Notes

1. W.E.B. Du Bois, *The Souls of Black Folk* (New York: Bantam, 1989).

2. Henry Louis Gates, Jr. "What's in a Name: Some Meanings of Blackness," in *Loose Canons: Some Notes on the Culture Wars* (New York: Oxford University Press, 1992), 147.

3. As a student of U.S. history and culture I do not feel qualified to make statements about the functioning of race and ethnicity outside the United States. Though the contributors to this volume attempt to create some sense of the universal functioning of ethnic theory, I will refrain from attempting to apply my own insights beyond what I know to be the case in the United States. I do believe that racialization theories can be applied to other parts of the world, but I will leave that to scholars more worthy of the effort than myself.

4. Ian Haney Lopez, "White by Law," in *Critical Race Theory: The Cutting Edge*, ed. Richard Delgado (Philadelphia: Temple University Press, 1995), 542.

5. "Dred Scot v. Sandford," U.S. Reports, 1856 Opinion of the Supreme Court. Reprinted in *Race and Ethnic Relations 94/95*, ed. John Kromkowski (Guilford, Conn.: Dushkin, 1994), 8.

6. See David Theo Goldberg, "The Semantics of Race," in *Ethnic and Racial Studies* 15 (1992): 543–69. Footnote 11 makes this reference, though I have not been able to substantiate it through my own reading of *Black Skin White Masks*. Fanon does use the term (with no definition) in *The Wretched of the Earth* (which predated *Black Skin White Masks*) while referring to emergent "Negro Culture" in colonized African socieites. It seems clear that Miles and others borrowed the term from Fanon and elaborated on its meaning. See Frantz Fanon, *The Wretched of the Earth*, trans. Constance Farrington (New York: Grove, 1966), 171.

7. An excellent introduction to/review of British Marxist sociological theories of race relations is to be found in John Solomos's article, "Varieties of Marxist Conceptions of 'Race,' Class, and the State: A Critical Analysis," in *Theories of Race and Ethnic Relations*, ed. John Rex and David Mason (London: Cambridge University Press, 1986), See also E. San Juan, *Racial Formations/Critical Transformations: Articulations of Power in Ethnic and Racial Studies in the U.S.* (Atlantic Highlands, N.J.: Humanities Press, 1992).

8. Solomos, "Varieties," 99.

9. John H. Stanfield, "Theoretical and Ideological Barriers to the Study of Race-Making," in *Research in Race and Ethnic Relations* 4 (1985): 161.

10. Interestingly, Carter and Green give two slightly different definitions of racialization in their article, one in the text and another in a footnote. The definition in the text, quoted in Spickard and Burroughs's article, assumes but does not mention political power relations. The definition in footnote 13, which is an elaboration of the connection between racialization and "race-ism," makes the role of power relations explicit, defining racialization as: "the process by which attributes are transformed into identities, and people come to be treated as members of 'race' groups; it is a structurally determined, politically organized and ideologically inflected process occurring within and re-presenting relations of domination and subordination." See Marci Green and Bob Carter, "'Races' and 'Race-makers': The Politics of Racialization," *Sage Race Relations Abstracts* 13 (1988): 4–29.

11. Carter and Green, "'Races' and 'Race Makers,'" 6.

12. Floya Anthias and Nira Yuval-Davis, *Racialized Boundaries: Race, Nation, Gender, Colour, and Class and the Anti-Racist Struggle* (New York: Routledge, 1992), 1–2.

13. Anthias and Yuval-Davis, *Racialized Boundaries,* 11.

14. Michal Omi and Howard Winant, *Racial Formation in the United States from the 1960s to the 1990s,* 2d ed. (New York: Routledge, 1994), 56.

15. Stephen Small, *Racialised Barriers: The Black Experience in the United States and England in the 1980's* (New York: Routledge, 1994), 30.

16. See Ian Haney Lopez, "The Social Construction of Race" and "White by Law" in *Critical Race Theory: The Cutting Edge,* ed. Richard Delgado (Philadelphia: Temple University Press, 1995).

17. See Shelley Fisher Fishkin "Interrogating 'Whiteness,' Complicating 'Blackness': Remapping American Culture," *American Quarterly* 47 (1995): 428–66, for a review of the literature. See also George Lipsitz, "The Possessive Investment of Whiteness: Racialized Social Democracy and the 'White' Problem in American Studies," *American Quarterly* 47 (1995): 369–87; David Roediger, *The Wages of Whiteness: Race and the Making of the American Working Class* (New York: Verso, 1991), and *Toward the Abolition of Whiteness* (New York: Verso, 1994); Theodore Allen, *The Invention of the White Race,* vol. 1, *Racial Oppression and Social Control* (New York: Verso, 1994); Vron Ware, *Beyond the Pale: White Women, Racism, and History* (London: Verso, 1992); Ruth Frankenberg, *White Women Race Matters: The Social Construction of Whiteness* (Minneapolis: University of Minnesota Press, 1993); and Noel Ignatiev and John Garvey, eds., *Race Traitor* (New York: Routledge, 1996).

Cookie White Stephan and
Walter G. Stephan

15   What Are the Functions
of Ethnic Identity?

The multidisciplinary study of ethnic identity has shown it to be subjective, unstable, and reciprocal.[1] Ethnic identity is subjective because it is not simply the consequence of cultural exposure or biological heritage: one can identify with a group in the absence of in-depth information regarding the group or experience with the group. An individual's biological heritage may thus not be strongly associated with ethnic identity; individuals may be biological members of a group without identifying themselves or being identified by others as members of the group. It has been argued, for example, that being acknowledged as an American Indian by other Indians is achieved by continuously acting like an Indian, not by merely demonstrating biological ancestry in a tribe.[2] For example, in Osage society, Indianness involves consistently presenting oneself as an Indian in appearance, interaction, personality characteristics, and behavior, as well as not displaying non-Indian identifiers (e.g., chattiness, braided hair, bragging, speaking for others, claiming considerable cultural knowledge).[3]

Similarly, individuals may be biological members of a group without identifying themselves as members due to lack of cultural exposure. In our interviews of mixed-heritage college students in Hawaii and New Mexico, we heard a variety of reasons for not identifying with the group, including lack of information due to low levels of contact with family members from the group, minimal cultural presence of the group in the community, a desire to assimilate, and perceptions of a group as relatively low in status.[4] In addition, beliefs regarding biological heritage may shift to coincide with ethnic identity.[5] We have found that college students' reports of their ethnic identity often match not their reports of their parents' biological heritage, but their own feelings of identity, so that they overemphasize groups with which they identify and underemphasize groups with which they do not identify.

Individuals may also adopt a common identity despite being biologically diverse. For some groups, choice of identity is not even based on factors of ethnicity. For instance, a number of Jews from many different biological and cultural backgrounds identify themselves as ethnically Jewish, despite being linked only through religion.[6]

Ethnic identity is situational because it may vary from situation to situation and with events across the life cycle, for example, leaving the family of birth, marriage, changes in levels of prejudice and discrimination against minority group members, and changes in geographic location.[7]

Ethnic identity is reciprocal, for it depends on both the individual's and others' identification of the individual as a member of an ethnic group. Prejudice and discrimination have imposed minority identities on mixed-heritage people, for example, through the legal and social pressures on mixed-heritage African Americans in the United States to identify themselves as African American.[8]

The research on ethnic identity reflects its multidisciplinary origins. Anthropologists have studied the process by which ethnic identity occurs, particularly at the boundaries of ethnicity; psychologists have focused on mental health and other indicators of the well-being of members of a variety of ethnic groups; and sociologists have studied the definition and continuing subjective importance of ethnic identity. In our own work we have tried to combine these traditions by exploring the causes and consequences of ethnic identity for mixed-heritage individuals.[9] In this essay, we look at how such an identity is constructed and suggest a new direction for its study. We move from the characteristics of ethnic identity to the prevalence and experience of multiple ethnic identities. We explore the antecedents of ethnic identity, discuss problems associated with its prediction, and argue for focusing on its functions.

The Prevalence of Multiple Ethnic Identities

Sociological models tend to assume that mixed-heritage individuals will adopt a single ethnic identity, either through assimilation or through selection of a single identity among several available options.[10] Mixed-heritage individuals often are pressured to select a single identity, as they are on U.S. Census forms, which allow individuals to list themselves as a member of one of a limited number of ethnic groups (not including Hispanic) or as an "other"; selecting more than one box is treated as an error in later data analysis. In fact, the right of mixed-heritage individuals to specify a multiple ethnic identity is a relatively new phenomenon, an option still effectively denied to African Americans.[11] Another barrier to the selection of multiple ethnic identities has been the charge by single-heritage group members that individuals with multiple ethnic identities are "sellouts" or "traitors."[12]

Despite these pressures to adopt single-heritage identities, we have found considerable multiple ethnic identity among mixed-heritage Hispanics in New Mexico, Japanese Americans in Hawaii, and among a sample of all types of mixed heritage individuals in Hawaii (44 percent, 73 percent, and 89 percent, respectively), when individuals were given the opportunity to express more than one ethnic identity.[13] Both joint ethnic identities (e.g., consistently identifying oneself as Japanese-Chinese) and situational identities (e.g., Japanese in one setting and Chinese in another) were common. The participants with situational identities consciously associated their identities with family, student, friendship, academic, occupational, and artistic roles, for example: "I'm Portuguese, but in my singing I feel Hawaiian"; and "When I'm with my mom's side of the family I tend to identify with them more. . . . But when I went to my Japanese grand-father, my dad's family, I get so involved in it. You know, you're there. . . . I guess when I'm with my different families I fall back into whatever comes out." Individuals with joint ethnic identities reported routinely feeling like members of more than one group. Said one, "I combine things from Chinese and I combine things from Japanese just to get what I am." Even when asked to name the group with which they most identified, 25 percent of part Japanese Americans, 6 percent of part Hispanics, and 47 percent of the mixed-heritage sample in Hawaii gave multiple identity responses.

The Experience of Multiple Ethnic Identities

The subjective experience of having multiple identities varies. Some individuals iden-tify with the group with which they are interacting. As one part-Japanese interviewee in Hawaii said, "When I'm with Japanese people, I guess I feel Japanese, and when I'm with Haole [Caucasian] people, I'm Haole." For others, group differences are pre-dominant in such settings and they report typically feeling like a member of the other group or groups with which they identify, but with which they are not currently inter-acting. One Hawaii interviewee stated, "When I was with one group I always felt like the other because I noticed the differences." Still others report feeling a part of all of their identity groups at all times. Racial composition of the community, the school, and the neighborhood can be associated with these subjective experiences.[14] For example, in a school setting in which most of the students belonged to one of their identity groups, some mixed-heritage individuals felt a part of that group, and others felt dif-ferent from the dominant group.

Society's assumption that mixed-heritage individuals will have only one ethnic iden-tity and its insistence that individuals select only one may be related to the common view that mixed-heritage individuals are at considerable psychological risk. An exten-sive literature based on qualitative data has suggested that intermarriage can have a number of negative effects for the mixed-heritage children of these marriages. These predicted negative effects include anxiety, insecurity, guilt, anger, depression, and identity conflicts.[15] Such consequences are alleged to be created by bicultural socialization that is inconsistent, frustrating, and difficult to comprehend; ambivalence and confusion over ethnicity; and rejection by their extended families and the larger society. Consistent with this view, stories in U.S. literature typically present mixed-heritage individuals as com-ing to tragic or horrifying ends.[16]

Yet in Hawaii and New Mexico we have found no negative psychological effects of multiple ethnic identity, and some benefits of bicultural socialization as manifested in favorable intergroup relations.[17] For example, Hispanics and mixed-heritage Hispan-ics had higher levels of contact with Hispanics than Anglos, and Anglos and mixed-heritage Hispanics had higher levels of contact with Anglos than Hispanics.

These positive results are mirrored in other recent literature exploring the self-concept, psychological adjustment, and personality characteristics of mixed-heritage individu-als.[18] Since intergroup and intragroup discrimination and prejudice against mixed-heritage individuals appear to be declining,[19] these positive results may in part be the result of a decrease in the tension and marginality mixed-heritage individuals face in the United States.

Because mixed-heritage individuals can have single- and multiple-group ethnic identities, an interesting possibility arises. Does the ethnic identity of mixed-heritage individuals have the same association with personality, adjustment, and intergroup relations variables as does ethnicity? For example, do mixed-heritage Hispanics whose ethnic identity is Hispanic have personality, adjustment, and intergroup relations characteristics similar to those of single-heritage Hispanics?

To explore this idea, we reexamined the personality, adjustment, and intergroup relations characteristics of the sixty-seven mixed-heritage part-Anglo, part-Hispanic college students from New Mexico mentioned earlier. We found that Hispanics had more favorable attitudes toward Hispanics, higher levels of enjoyment of Hispanic culture, and greater facility in Spanish than Anglos. Hispanics had higher levels of contact with Hispanics than with Anglos, and Anglos had higher levels of contact with Anglos than with Hispanics. Further, the Hispanics scored higher on measures of dogmatism and xenophobia than Anglos.

The mixed-heritage Hispanics' ethnic identity with these intergroup relations, personality, and adjustment variables shows a similar pattern. That is, mixed-heritage Hispanics with a strong Hispanic ethnic identity had psychological and behavioral characteristics very much like those of the single-heritage Hispanic sample, and mixed-heritage Hispanics with an Anglo ethnic identity had characteristics very much like those of the single-heritage Anglo sample. These findings suggest that the ethnic identity of mixed-heritage individuals may be a product of the same cultural, socialization, and other practices that are associated with single ethnicities.[20]

The Antecedents of Ethnic Identity

The question then becomes, What are the antecedent conditions of ethnic identity? Empirical work supports the importance of various aspects of culture, including language, religion, religious or cultural ceremonies, group rituals and rites of passage, and food customs in the acquisition of ethnic identity.[21] Investigation has shown that the influence of these elements of culture is more easily observed when the extended family is strongly embedded in the culture, lives nearby, has extensive contact with the individual, and accepts the individual, and where internal group pressures to maintain group identity are high.[22] As one mixed-heritage Japanese American reported of her single identity as Japanese, "Our family is more Japanese culturally. I was sent to Japanese [language] school and . . . I like Japanese food. All the time we went to Bon dances. I still enjoy dancing [at these festivals]. . . . We did a lot of traditional Japanese things, like on New Years Eve, my mom made the traditional Japanese soup and the rice cakes. Even the types of paintings we had in our house were Japanese." Another said, "My father is very Chinese culture–minded and really wanted us to learn Chinese. We do the Chinese New Year celebration, and then there's a time when you worship the dead."[23]

Family events such as death, divorce, and quarrels can create loss of cultural information leading to loss of identity with a particular group, as can misinformation or hidden information. In answer to a question regarding lack of identity with Japanese Americans, a Portuguese-identified individual of mixed heritage stated, "I haven't had that good of relations with my father's side of the family. My grandmother treated my mother badly and I resented that."[24] A Japanese-identified mixed-heritage individual said, "Only my grandfather was Portuguese, and he himself didn't follow the Portuguese ways."[25]

However, cultural exposure is not a necessary condition for developing ethnic identity. In our work on the ethnic identity of mixed-heritage Japanese Americans in Hawaii, we found a minority (15 percent) who did not have cultural exposure to one or more of the heritage groups with which they identified. Identity with a heritage group in the absence of cultural exposure occurred for a variety of reasons, such as becoming interested in the group on one's own, identifying with a group because of a friend, perceiving the group to be high in status, or identifying with the group because the identity was viewed as biologically accurate.[26] Thus, while lack of exposure to the culture of a group typically results in identity being lost for later generations,[27] some exceptions occur. One part-Japanese American explained his part-Portuguese identity in this way: "I think it was more my friends that I hung out with and the things their families did." Another individual said, "It just being my largest ethnic group and it coming directly from father to son, I figured the lineage was there to identify myself as Portuguese."

Cultural exposure does not necessarily cause ethnic identity to occur. In the same study we found that around 25 percent of the participants reported no identification with one or more groups to which they had at least some cultural exposure. Cultural exposure experienced as negative tended to weaken, rather than strengthen, identity with a group. One woman described the Chinese side of her family: "I never felt comfortable. You always have to be so proper. I can never be myself around them. Since I grew up with my Portuguese side of the family, I was very loud." Another part-Portuguese individual said, "In my family we've always had a negative thing about Portuguese people." In the absence of family members, friends, or a cultural community to which one has direct and extensive access, cultural learning is virtually impossible. As one part-Caucasian participant stated, "I don't even know how Haoles live." Another part-Portuguese participant said, "I don't know what Portuguese are like, except that people say they talk too much."

A second antecedent widely linked to ethnic identity by both theory and empirical data is physical appearance, although our work on mixed-heritage Japanese Americans and Hispanics suggests that such a link does not always exist. When it does, it may in part be a case of identity leading to perceived physical resemblance, rather than the reverse.[28] The practice of giving children the father's surname may make identification with the maternal side of the family more difficult. Several mixed-heritage Asian participants in Hawaii who were not clearly Chinese, Korean, or Japanese in appearance mentioned that their ethnic last names not only guided others' presumptions about their ethnicity but had a cumulative effect on their ethnic self-identity. Because they were consistently identified and treated as Japanese, Chinese or Korean, they had come to think of themselves as such. Other indicators of societal patriarchy may have the same effect: women who take their husband's surname may be then mistaken for a member of the husband's group.

In addition, theory and research suggest that the advantages or disadvantages of identifying with a specific group vary with economic and political events.[29] Other intergroup relations factors linked to ethnic identity include the history of the groups, the valence of the group's stereotypes, and the degree to which identification with a group provides access to valued occupational and family roles. For example, some of the mixed-heritage participants in our studies were quick to exploit any ethnic advantage and to hide disadvantages. One part-Caucasian said she listed herself as Caucasian when applying for jobs: "There are situations where you can't use Chinese and Hawaiian. . . . I just put it down for status." One part-Hawaiian explained that he wanted to be Hawaiian when he was young but now that he was at the university he saw the negative stereotype of Hawaiians. He further explained that as he had begun to want to "get ahead," he had begun to feel more Causasian. With respect to access to family roles, a number of Hawaii participants mentioned rejection from a branch of their families. One man explained his ethnic identity by saying, "My Hawaiian family accepted me." Additional intergroup relations factors include the coerciveness of the labeling system and group size, with identity increasing as the size and thus recognition of the group increases.

While also important, individual-level variables associated with identities, such as educational level and similarity of the groups, are somewhat offset by the homogenizing effects of technology and mass communication systems.[30] Opportunity variables such as exposure to other groups, including spatial proximity, are also positively associated with ethnic identity. One woman in Hawaii with many Spanish relatives explained her identity as Filipino "because there's not too many Spanish people here. There's not much Spanish culture."

The Antecedents of the Importance of Ethnic Identity

Ethnic identity may hold a central place in an individual's self-conception or may be completely ignored. We have found that mixed-heritage Japanese Americans and Hispanics with multiple ethnic identities perceived ethnic identity to be as important as did those with single-heritage ethnic identities.[31] One Laotian-Chinese participant who answered "Caucasian, Laotian, Chinese" to the question, "With which group do you identify most closely?" and who indicated that ethnic identity was extremely important to her, explained her answer by talking about living in the same house with a large extended Laotian family, her close relationship with her Chinese father, and the importance of her high school friends and classmates, virtually all of whom were Caucasian. A Chinese- and Japanese-identified woman who rated ethnic identity as very important to her said, "I always thought it would be good to stay half way." Researchers studying other ethnic groups have also found no differences in the importance of ethnic identity between individuals with single and multiple ethnic identities.[32]

One factor that is clearly necessary for ethnic identity to assume importance is the opportunity to express it; typically one must be able to affirm and reaffirm an identity in order to hold it.[33] Ethnicity can be either coercively enforced or denied by the state.

If ethnic sentiments are perceived to be a threat to the concept of nationalism, a state may use violence to suppress ethnic dissidence and often try to eliminate the minority groups.[34] The recent history of the Hutu-Tutsi conflict in Burundi and Rwanda and the flight of the Hutu refugees to Tanzania provide a case in point. Where ethnic identity determines critical roles in the social, political, or economic realms, it assumes greater importance. The size, visibility, and status of the group are obvious factors in the process of affirming identity, as is access to information regarding it. One cannot "act like" a group member in the absence of any knowledge regarding the group. The literature on ethnogenesis provides clues regarding the structural origins of these conditions (e.g., historical time, geographic location).[35]

Further, intergroup relations factors such as recent patterns of contact and conflict should prove important to ethnic identity. Claims to ethnicity are often activated by enforced acculturation.[36] In addition, broad historical and political factors (e.g., war, revolution, colonization, immigration history, reception of the immigrants), and the interaction of state and ethnicity at the societal, state, and global levels play critical roles. The ongoing upheavals in the former Yugoslavia and USSR dramatically demonstrate the importance of ethnicity and the structural processes that make some ethnic identities more possible and others less so. For example, many Croatians have moved from Serbia to Croatia; those who have been unable to move have found their ethnic identity increasingly socially and culturally problematic.

At the individual level, ethnic identity is minimized if social or economic interests are served by avoiding identity with certain groups; similarly, ethnicity is likely to be emphasized where one's interests are better served by identity with particular groups. Moreover, an ethnic identity can increase feelings of self-worth by providing a sense of belonging, both to kin and to a broader community.[37]

Finally, researchers have found that interest in ethnic identity varies across the life cycle.[38] Ethnic identity often becomes a concern of young people at the time they first leave their family home because they often mix more with people from other groups and are thus primed to think about ethnicity and the differences between groups. This process may lead these young people to simplify their ancestry at this time. In addition, during old age the focus may return to issues of ethnicity. One goal of future research should be to understand how all of these factors determine the importance of ethnic identity within specific groups, situations, historical contexts, and geographic locations.

Theoretical Problems

In our work in Hawaii and New Mexico on the ethnic identity of mixed-heritage individuals we have found the antecedents of ethnic identity as Japanese American and as Hispanic to be quite different from one another. Only degree of cultural exposure to the group in question was significantly associated with ethnic identity in both groups. Other factors were significant predictors of ethnic identity for one but not for the other. For Hispanics, these were physical resemblance to Hispanics, psychological identification with the Hispanic parent, and percent of father's Hispanic heritage; for Japanese Americans, they were relative status of the group and involvement in Eastern religion.

We have previously argued that three factors account for these differences.[39] First, variables are significantly associated with ethnic identity if they distinguish the group in question from other ethnic groups in the same geographic location. Second, the relative status of the groups is positively associated with ethnic identity only when the status of the group is high. Third, socialization practices are important, and these may be associated with factors such as the relative status of the group, so that efforts to socialize the child within a group are more likely if the group is high in status.

Although the predictors of mixed-heritage Hispanic New Mexicans' and Hawaii-located Japanese Americans' ethnic identity represent important information about these particular groups, obviously many of these predictors will not generalize to other groups. As we have seen, the predictors of ethnic identity do not always transcend situations within even a single group. Not only do antecedents of identity vary by situation and ethnic group, ethnic identity also depends on other structural and contextual factors. Thus, a set of general antecedents of overall ethnic identity seems not to exist. Even such defining characteristics as skin color may not be important to ethnic identity in some contexts. For example, we found that physical appearance was not predictive of ethnic identity as Japanese in Hawaii, but it did predict ethnic identity as Hispanic in New Mexico, perhaps because it is often distinctive in that setting.

Similarly, it seems fruitless to attempt to compile a list of the antecedents of ethnic identity by ethnic group. First, an ethnic designation often contains many groups within it. As an example, Latinos in the United States are derived from countries with diverse histories and cultures, and people of Puerto Rican, Mexican, and Cuban descent have surprisingly little cultural commonality.[40] Even within a subgroup, such as Mexican Americans, class and legal-residence differences create substantial diversity. The life of a Mexican American socialite bears little resemblance to that of her Mexican American housekeeper; even on the border, the difference between a Mexican national and a Mexican American is often as great or greater than that between Mexican American and Causasian. Predictors of the identities of a subgroup may also vary due to such factors as religion and geographic location.[41] In fact, ethnic self-labels of the subgroup itself vary on these dimensions (e.g., Chicano, a label used throughout Texas, is rarely used on the New Mexico border; Spanish American, a common ethnic identity throughout New Mexico, is virtually never used in Texas).

Despite the assumption of researchers that ethnic identity findings generalize broadly, it now seems clear that the factors associated with ethnic identity often do not generalize across groups, situations, historical contexts, and geographic locations, much less across individuals within these categories. Although specifying the correlates of ethnic identity by group, situational, historical, and geographic context does produce more accuracy than earlier overgeneralizations regarding ethnic identity, the understanding and prediction of ethnic identity has not been greatly advanced by the compilation of dozens of specific lists of antecedents.

The Functions of Ethnic Identity

Because the focus on ethnic identity has produced little in the way of generalizable correlates, it may be time to turn our attention from the content of ethnic identity to the purposes for which ethnic identity is created. We believe that one promising way of attempting to understand this process is to examine the underlying functions of ethnic identity. In our previous work, participants from Hawaii spontaneously mentioned many specific functions of their ethnic identities, such as increasing prestige, increasing perceived wealth, avoiding censure, being accepted, identifying with important others, avoiding identification with a disliked individual or group, avoiding ambiguity associated with not having an identity niche, minimizing discrimination, getting a job, filling other family members' needs to have an ethnicity represented in the family that is not claimed by other siblings, acting out other's perceptions of oneself as like or unlike a specific relative, trying to fit in, being distinct from one's friends or family, getting dates, increasing self-esteem, expressing artistic or cultural interests, expressing perceived inner characteristics, avoiding the difficulty of not accepting others' assumptions regarding one's ethnicity, and fulfilling a duty or debt to the family.[42] An analysis of ethnic identity in terms of the functions it serves may create a greater understanding of the roles of context (e.g., historical time, situation, and geographic location) and individual needs by reducing a large list of antecedents to a manageable number of constructs.

A functional perspective has the value of being consistent with a narrative analysis of ethnic identity. We have argued that individuals do not experience the selection of an ethnic identity or identities but instead experience being a member of a group or groups. As we have noted before, when asked to explain their ethnic identities, individuals render accounts of their identities; they construct justifications for their identities on the basis of their past experiences. As one of our interviewees said, when speaking of the importance of ethnic identity, "It helps you know who you are." In our previous work we have used narrative accounts to identify antecedents of ethnic identity. We now propose that narratives of individuals' identities should be used for a different purpose: to examine the functions of these ethnic identities. An analysis of the functions of ethnic identity provides information about the purposes such narratives serve. Like Stephen Cornell in chapter 3 of this volume, we believe that issues of order and power are intertwined with ethnic identity. Our exploration of ethnic identity at the individual level complements his analysis at the group level.

A simple economic or exchange analysis can provide a useful starting point for assessing the functions of ethnic identity. Exchange theorists begin with the argument that people are motivated to obtain rewards and avoid costs. Exchange relationships are relationships in which interacting individuals are dependent on one another to some degree. Such relationships endure when the interacting individuals provide reciprocal benefits to each other, either through increased rewards or costs avoided.[43]

It seems likely that the implicit calculus at the heart of exchange theory is performed by actors when determining their identities. The rewards and costs of various potential identities are likely to be weighed when selecting an ethnic identity among the available options in a particular interaction. This calculation is likely to be largely nonconscious, especially when the identities have become routine in particular contexts.

One issue that requires clarification is the functions served by situational ethnic identities compared to ethnic identities that are stable across contexts. In some instances, the stability of ethnic identity may be related to the degree to which the function of the ethnic identity endures. When the function the identity serves persists (e.g., providing status), the identity may be more stable than when the function it serves is transitory (e.g., feeling similar to a particular group of friends).

Another issue that should be addressed in an analysis of the functions of ethnic identity is that of multiple identities. Although many mixed-heritage individuals have single ethnic identities (e.g., Japanese), many others have multiple ethnic identities (e.g., Japanese-Chinese). It seems likely that the separate identities that comprise multiple ethnic identities may serve separate functions. For example, in one of our studies a man with a Portuguese-Chinese identity stated that his identity as Portuguese was based on his lifelong participation in Portuguese dance performances, and his Chinese identity represented his desire to fulfill his Chinese father's need for a first-born son to carry on the family line. Of course, even a single ethnic identity may have more than one function. One woman felt that her identity as Hawaiian suited her life-style, recreational interests, and political viewpoints, and brought acceptance among her closest friends.

In a functional analysis, it may be useful to distinguish ethnic identities that increase rewards (e.g., "At school the kids with the nice clothes and things were Japanese") from those that avoid costs (e.g., "There's a lot of stereotypes where they say Hawaiians are lazy"). Perceptions of the magnitude of the increased rewards or avoided costs may help explain the stability and importance of ethnic identity, with more positive outcomes being associated with greater stability and importance. Within these basic functions of rewards gained and costs avoided, numerous other distinctions could be drawn (e.g., social vs. economic functions, self-initiated vs. other-initiated functions) that might prove to be useful tools for prediction.

Recent work links exchange theory to social networks and explores the ways in which interactions, commitments to individuals, normative constraints, and affective ties influence the terms and consequences of exchange.[44] Linking exchange theory with existing theories of the self and identity seems an especially promising direction for the analysis of ethnic identity. To frame issues with respect to ethnic identity and its functions, we will refer to work on self schemata, especially as they differ by sex and culture and by social identity and social categorization, and to theories of role-linked identities, such as identity salience, roles as resources, and situated identities.

The Self and the Functions of Ethnic Identity

The argument that roles constitute resources is consistent with an examination of the functions of ethnic identity. Callero argues that instead of viewing roles as a set of expectations pertaining to a status, roles should be viewed as resources.[45] In this view, roles (e.g., ethnicity) are resources that create unique positions in the social structure (e.g., Hawaiian-Chinese) and also aid in establishing access to other resources (e.g., a sense of being the valid residents of Hawaii for Hawaiian; access to high status for Chinese). That is, roles often function to create rewards and avoid costs. When asked to list the ethnic group she identified with most closely, one participant wrote, "Depending on the situation I claim either Hawaiian or Caucasian"; she explained, "If I'm around Hawaiians, then Hawaiian and Caucasians, Caucasian. If I'm around Orientals it depends on whichever one is more benefit to myself."

Both social identity theory and social categorization theory emphasize only one overriding function for social identities. According to these theories, the process of categorizing oneself as an ingroup member and others as outgroup members creates and maintains attitudinal and behavioral distinctions favoring the ingroup. Social identity theorists argue that the function of this ingroup favoritism is maintenance or enhancement of self-esteem. Thus, these two theories suggest that the ethnic identity chosen from the available options should be the identity that maximizes self-esteem (e.g., identity with a powerful, high-status, or large group). As a Hawaiian-identified participant explained his identity, "Most of the people respect Hawaiians more than they do the Portuguese."

Situational Ethnicity

Work on self schemata suggests that cognitive factors can influence which aspects of the self are salient at a given time. For example, priming a particular aspect of the self can result in that aspect becoming situationally salient. For example, an anxiety-provoking social setting may prime ethnic identities associated with fitting in or being accepted. One's cultural background may, in fact, determine the outcome of such priming. For instance, a mixed-heritage Vietnamese-Caucasian is likely to have group-oriented aspects of identity primed through interaction with her Vietnamese family members, but individualistic aspects of identity primed by interaction with her Caucasian family members. Thus, when ethnic identity varies by situation, the function served by the identity may be primed by some characteristic of the situation. As one participant explained, "I can relate to Caucasians and I can relate to Orientals, but they don't mix together. It's one or the other, depending on the situation."

Another approach to situational changes in ethnic identity is to think of these ethnic identities as situated identities. Situated identities define the relationship between the actor and others in the environment at a given moment. Individuals use their knowledge of these identities to predict others' behaviors and determine their own behaviors. One implication is that, in situations in which ethnic identity is salient, the individual and others will monitor the situation for information regarding ethnicity and its behavioral correlates. Others' situated identities may then serve to determine one's own. The identity selected should depend on the function it serves. For example, if the ethnic identity fulfills a need for uniqueness, the individual will probably select an identity that distinguishes him or her from the other interactants. One way of demonstrating distinctiveness among mixed-heritage individuals may be to adopt a multiple ethnic identity. In Hawaii individuals who can claim many different backgrounds are often proud of their unique mix. One such participant stated he was "part Hawaiian, Chinese, and Irish and so many other things I can't even divide them up."

The Importance of Ethnic Identity

According to identity theory, the self is composed of a series of identities, each of which corresponds to a role played by the individual. Identities form a salience hierarchy, with highly salient identities being those to which the individual is most committed. Commitment, and thus salience, is a function of the degree to which members of one's social network are associated with the identity and the congruence of role expectations associated with the identity. Identities such as sex and ethnicity are referred to as master statuses because they are important transituational determinants of others' responses to the individual.

Identity theory has several implications for ethnic identity. First, because of the weight others give to an individual's ethnic identity, ethnic identity is likely to be important to most people's sense of self, regardless of the specific function it serves at any given time. Second, since others tend to place great emphasis on ethnicity, the importance of an individual's ethnic identity may be associated with the degree to which the ethnic identity is readily ascertained on the basis of appearance. Third, because ethnicity is a master status, ethnic identity is particularly likely to influence the conception and performance of many of the individual's other roles. Finally, the reverse may also be true: since ethnic identity is only one of a number of possibly salient identities, in some instances an individual's ethnic identity and its functions may complement other salient identities and their functions.

Focusing on the functions of ethnic identity and attempting to apply existing theories of the self to ethnic identity may make it possible to devise a model in which the myriad of known factors associated with ethnic identity begin to fit. If the known individual-level and societal-level antecedents of ethnic identity can be linked to various functions of ethnic identity, it should be possible to predict the conditions under which specific antecedents will become important to the selection of ethnic identity in particular contexts.

Notes

1. Fredrik Barth, *Ethnic Groups and Boundaries: The Social Organization of Culture Difference* (London: Allen and Unwin, 1969); Judith A. Nagata, "What Is a Malay? Situational Selection of Ethnic Identity in a Plural Society," *American Ethnologist* 1 (1974): 331–50; Pierre L. van den Berghe and George P. Primov, *Inequality in the Peruvian Andes: Class and Ethnicity in Cuzco* (Columbia: University of Missouri Press, 1974).

2. J. D. Forbes, "The Manipulation of Race, Caste, and Identity: Classifying Afroamericans, Native Americans, and Red-Black People," *Journal of Ethnic Studies* 17 (1990): 1–51; D. L. Wieder and S. Pratt, "On Being a Recognizable Indian among Indians," in *Cultural Communication and Intercultural Contact,* ed. D. Caubaugh (New York: Erlbaum, 1990); Terry P. Wilson, "Blood Quantum: Native American Mixed Bloods," in *Racially Mixed People in America,* ed. Maria P. P. Root (Newbury Park, Calif.: Sage, 1992).

3. Wieder and Pratt, "Recognizable Indian."

4. Cookie White Stephan and Walter G. Stephan, "After Intermarriage: Ethnic Identity among Mixed Heritage Japanese-Americans and Hispanics," *Journal of Marriage and the Family* 51

(1989): 507–19; Cookie White Stephan, "Ethnic Identity among Mixed-Heritage People in Hawaii," *Symbolic Interaction* 14 (1991): 261–77.

5. Stanley Lieberson, "Unhyphenated Whites in the United States," *Ethnic and Racial Studies* 8 (1985): 159–80; Stephan and Stephan, "After Intermarriage."

6. W. P. Zenner, "Jewishness in America," in *Ethnicity and Race in the U.S.A.,* ed. Richard D. Alba (London: Routledge and Kegan Paul, 1985).

7. Ruby Jo Reeves Kennedy, "Single or Triple Melting Pot? Intermarriage Trends in New Haven, 1870–1950," *American Journal of Sociology* 58 (1952): 56–59; Lieberson, "Unhyphenated Whites in the United States"; Paul R. Spickard, *Mixed Blood: Intermarriage and Ethnic Identity in Twentieth-Century America* (Madison: University of Wisconsin Press, 1989); Stephan and Stephan, "After Intermarriage."

8. M. Harris, *Patterns of Race in the Americas* (New York: Walker, 1964); Pierre L. van den Berghe, *The Ethnic Phenomenon* (New York: Elsevier, 1981).

9. Stephan, "Mixed-Heritage People in Hawaii"; Cookie White Stephan, "Mixed-Heritage Individuals: Ethnic Identity and Trait Characteristics," in *Racially Mixed People,* ed. Root, 50–63; Stephan and Stephan, "After Intermarriage"; Walter G. Stephan and Cookie White Stephan, "Intermarriage: Effects on Personality, Adjustment and Intergroup Relations in Two Samples of Students," *Journal of Marriage and the Family* 53 (1991): 241–50.

10. Albert I. Gordon, *Intermarriage* (Boston: Beacon, 1964); Andrew Greeley, *Why Can't They Be Like Us? America's White Ethnic Groups* (New York: Dutton, 1971).

11. Spickard, *Mixed Blood;* Forbes, "Manipulation of Race"; G. Reginald Daniel, "Passers and Pluralists: Subverting the Racial Divide," in *Racially Mixed People,* ed. Root, 91–107.

12. Cynthia L. Nakashima, "An Invisible Monster: The Creation and Denial of Mixed-Race People in America," and Teresa K. Williams, "Prism Lives: Identity of Binational Amerasians," both in *Racially Mixed People,* ed. Root, 162–80 and 280–303.

13. Stephan and Stephan, "After Intermarriage"; Stephan, "Mixed-Heritage People in Hawaii."

14. Ronald C. Johnson, "Offspring of Cross-Race and Cross-Ethnic Marriages in Hawaii," and Amy Iwasaki Mass, "Interracial Japanese Americans: The Best of Both Worlds or the End of the Japanese American Community?" both in *Racially Mixed People,* ed. Root, 239–49 and 265–80.

15. For example, Gordon, *Intermarriage;* F. Henriques, *Children of Conflict: A Study of Interracial Sex and Marriage* (New York: Dutton, 1974); J. F. McDermott and C. Fukunaga, "Intercultural Family Interaction Patterns," in *Adjustment to Intercultural Marriage,* ed. W. Tseng, J. F. McDermott, and T. W. Maretzk (Honolulu: University Press of Hawaii, 1977); V. Piskacek and M. Golub, "Children of Interracial Marriage," in *Interracial Marriage: Expectations and Reality,* ed. I. R. Stuart and L. E. Abt (New York: Grossman, 1973).

16. W. Sollars, *Beyond Ethnicity: Consent and Descent in American Culture* (New York: Oxford University Press, 1986).

17. Stephan and Stephan, "Intermarriage."

18. Ana Mari Cauce, Yumi Hiraga, Craig Mason, Tanya Aguilar, Nydia Ordonez, and Nancy Gonzales, "Between a Rock and a Hard Place: Social Adjustment of Biracial Youth," and James H. Jacobs, "Identity Development in Biracial Children," both in *Racially Mixed People,* ed. Root, 207–22 and 190–206; Johnson, "Offspring of Marriages in Hawaii"; Mass, "Interracial Japanese Americans."

19. G. Reginald Daniel, "Beyond Black and White: The New Multiracial Consciousness," and Christine C. Iijima Hall, "Coloring outside the Lines," both in *Racially Mixed People,* ed. Root, 333–41 and 326–29; Spickard, *Mixed Blood.*

20. We assessed the degree to which the sixty-seven students identified with various ethnic groups in five different situations. We classified the responses to each situation into five categories: sole identity as Hispanic, identity as Hispanic-Anglo, identity as both, identity as Anglo-Hispanic, and sole identity as Anglo. We next summed the responses to create an identity scale ranging from twenty-five (consistent sole identity as Hispanic) to zero (consistent sole identity as Anglo). Then we correlated this identity scale with the personality, adjustment, and intergroup relations variables mentioned previously. We compared these correlations to single-heritage Hispanics' and Anglos' mean scores on these variables to see if mixed-heritage people who identified themselves as Hispanic responded similarly to single-heritage Hispanics and if mixed-heritage people who identified themselves as Anglo responded similarly to single-heritage Anglos.

Ethnic identity as Hispanic among the mixed-heritage Hispanics was significantly positively associated with enjoyment of Hispanic culture ($r = .47$, $p < .001$) and Spanish language facility ($r = .43$, $p < .001$), marginally significantly positively associated with contact with Hispanics ($r = .22$, $p < .09$), and significantly negatively associated with contact with Anglos ($r = -.32$, $p < .05$). Hispanic ethnic identity among the mixed-heritage Hispanics was also significantly positively associated with dogmatism ($r = .31$, $p < .05$) and marginally significantly negatively associated with xenophobia ($r = -.25$, $p < .06$).

21. Frederick Elkin, "Family, Socialization, and Ethnic Identity," in *The Canadian Family*, ed. K. Ishwaran (Beverly Hills, Calif.: Sage, 1983), 145–58; Max Weber, "Ethnic Groups," in *Theories of Society*, ed. Talcot Parsons et al. (New York: Free Press, 1960); Harold R. Isaacs, *Idols of the Tribe: Group Identity and Political Change* (New York: Harper, 1975); Alejandro Portes, "The Rise of Ethnicity," *American Sociological Review* 49 (1984): 383–97; G. Stevens and G. Swicegood, "The Linguistic Context of Ethnic Endogamy," *American Sociological Review* 52 (1987): 73–82; Pierre L. van den Berghe and George P. Primov, *Inequality in the Peruvian Andes*; Nagata, "What Is a Malay?"; Abner Cohen, *Urban Ethnicity* (London: Tavistock, 1974); Lieberson, "Unhyphenated Whites in the United States"; Michael Novak, "Pluralism in Humanistic Perspective," in *Concepts in Ethnicity*, ed. William Peterson, Michael Novak, and Philip Gleason (London: Belknap, 1982); Richard D. Alba, *Ethnic Identity: The Transformation of White America* (New Haven, Conn.: Yale University Press, 1990).

22. Christine C. Iijima Hall, "Please Choose One: Ethnic Identity Choices for Biracial Individuals," in *Racially Mixed People*, ed. Root, 250–264; Don Handleman, "The Organization of Ethnicity," *Ethnic Groups* 1 (1977): 187–200; Johnson, "Offspring of Marriages in Hawaii"; Nagata, "What Is a Malay?"; Elkin, "Family, Socialization, and Ethnic Identity"; Portes, "The Rise of Ethnicity"; Stephan, "Mixed-Heritage People in Hawaii"; Stephan and Stephan, "After Intermarriage"; Lieberson, "Unhyphenated Whites in the United States."

23. Stephan, "Mixed-Heritage People in Hawaii."

24. Ibid.

25. Ibid.

26. Stephan and Stephan, "After Intermarriage."

27. Lieberson, "Unhyphenated Whites in the United States."

28. Stephan and Stephan, "After Intermarriage"; Isaacs, *Idols of the Tribe*; Mary C. Waters, *Ethnic Options* (Berkeley: University of California Press, 1990).

29. O. P. Dickason, "From 'One Nation' in the Northeast to 'New Nation' in the Northwest: A Look at the Emergence of the Metis," in *New Peoples: Being and Becoming Metis in North America*, ed. J. Peterson and J. S. H. Brown (Lincoln: University of Nebraska Press, 1985); Lieberson, "Unhyphenated Whites in the United States."

30. Michael Novak, "Pluralism in Humanistic Perspective."

31. Stephan and Stephan, "Mixed-Heritage Individuals."

32. K. Parsonson, "Intermarriages: Effects on the Ethnic Identity of the Offspring," *Journal of Cross-Cultural Psychology* 18 (1987): 363–71; N. Salgado de Snyder, C. M. Lopez, and A. M. Padilla, "Ethnic Identity and Cultural Awareness among the Offspring of Mexican Interethnic Marriages," *Journal of Early Adolescence* 3 (1982): 277–82; but see Mass, "Interracial Japanese Americans."

33. Anya P. Royce, *Ethnic Identity: Strategies of Diversity* (Bloomington: Indiana University Press, 1982).

34. Pierre L. van den Berghe, "Introduction," in *State Violence and Ethnicity*, ed. Pierre L. van den Berghe (Boulder: University of Colorado Press, 1985).

35. Peterson and Brown, *New Peoples*.

36. E. E. Roosens, *Creating Ethnicity: The Process of Ethnogenesis* (Newbury Park, Calif.: Sage, 1989).

37. Barth, *Ethnic Groups and Boundaries*; L. A. Despres, *Ethnicity and Resource Competition in Plural Societies* (Chicago: Aldine, 1975); Lieberson, "Unhyphenated Whites in the United States"; Alba, *Ethnic Identity*; A. L. Epstein, *Ethos and Identity: Three Studies in Ethnicity* (London: Tavistock, 1978); Henri Tajfel, *Social Identity and Intergroup Relations* (Cambridge, UK: Cambridge University Press, 1982).

38. Stanley Lieberson and Mary C. Waters, "Ethnic Groups in Flux: The Changing Ethnic Responses of American Whites," *Annals of the American Academy of Political and Social Science* 487 (September 1986), 79–91.

39. Stephan and Stephan, "Mixed-Heritage Individuals."

40. For example, Margarita B. Melville, "Hispanics: Race, Class, or Ethnicity?" *Journal of Ethnic Studies* 16 (Spring 1988): 67–84; C. Nelson and M. Tienda, "The Structuring of Hispanic Ethnicity: Historical and Contemporary Perspectives," in *Ethnicity and Race in the U.S.A.*, ed. Alba.

41. William L. Yancey, Eugene P. Ericksen, and G. H. Leon, "The Structure of Pluralism: 'We're all Italian around here, aren't we, Mrs. O'Brien?'" in *Ethnicity and Race in the U.S.A.*, ed. Alba.

42. Stephan, "Mixed-Heritage People in Hawaii."

43. Peter M. Blau, *Exchange and Power in Social Life* (New York: Wiley, 1961); George C. Homans, *Social Behavior: Its Elementary Forms* (New York: Harcourt Brace and World, 1961); L. D. Molm and K. S. Cook, "Social Exchange and Social Networks," in *Sociological Perspectives on Social Psychology*, ed. K. S. Cook, G. A. Fine, and J. S. House (Boston: Allyn and Bacon, 1995); John W. Thibaut and Harold H. Kelley, *The Social Psychology of Groups* (New York: Wiley, 1959).

44. Linda D. Molm, "Dependence and Risk: Transforming the Structure of Social Exchange," *Social Psychology Quarterly* 57 (1994): 163–76; Molm and Cook, "Social Exchange and Social Networks."

45. Peter L. Callero, "From Role-Playing to Role-Using: Understanding Role as Resource," *Social Psychology Quarterly* 57 (1994): 228–43.

W. Jeffrey Burroughs and
Paul Spickard

16   Ethnicity, Multiplicity, and Narrative: Problems and Possibilities

The essays that make up this book rotate around three axes. First, they emphasize the constructed quality of ethnicity, both for groups and in the lives of individuals. This constructive quality has implications for the distinction between race and ethnicity. The second theme of this collection is an examination of ethnic multiplicity. A major international change in ethnic studies is a focus on the rise of multiethnic identities. This volume gives abundant testimony to this shift, with a number of authors documenting multiple identities at both the individual and the group levels. The third theme, and perhaps the major contribution of this collection, is its emphasis on narrative as a key to understanding ethnic phenomena. Each of these themes contributes importantly to our understanding of ethnic processes in individuals and groups. However, each theme may also present a problem of misunderstanding if it is misinterpreted or misapplied.

Constructedness

The consensus of scholars today is that ethnicity is a socially and politically constructed identity, not a biological entity.[1] Yet it is possible that some people may willfully or unwittingly misuse the insight that ethnicity is constructed to argue that, because ethnicity is not biological, it is not real. Of course ethnicity is real: people kill people because of it—one need look no further than Bosnia or Howard Beach. But it is a social and political reality and thus subject to social and political manipulation. Nonetheless, such people may attempt to argue that racism is not real, because it is not founded on biology, as they had originally supposed. The danger then is to minimize racism, when it is a very real problem that shows no signs of going away.

The classic case here is a book by Dinesh D'Souza, *The End of Racism*. D'Souza's arguments are labyrinthine, ever feinting left before going right. He employs nearly every conceivable rhetorical gambit from every point of the political compass and every methodological angle in his search for a justification of his belief that the reason for the problems of African Americans is African American culture. In his grudging correction of Richard Herrnstein and Charles Murray's *Bell Curve* (IQ is cultural, he argues, not biological in origin, but it is nonetheless a legitimate basis for discrimination by Whites against Blacks), D'Souza follows the racial constructionist line for a while: "Apparently [according to liberals] race is a dubious concept while racism is real enough." But then D'Souza goes one step further: "Race may indeed be a social construct.... [In fact] 'Racism' is a social construct." By the end, D'Souza has built a rhetorical edifice that allows him to conclude that racism may or may not be real, but it is trivial; African Americans and their pathological culture are to blame for disadvantages they experience; and, in policy terms, "What we need is a long-term strategy that holds the government to a rigorous standard of race neutrality, while allowing private actors to be free to discriminate as they wish."[2]

This way lies madness—and thoroughly irresponsible social policy. It is far better to admit the constructed quality of ethnicity and at the same time take with utmost seriousness the causes, courses, and consequences of racism.[3]

In viewing ethnicity as a social construct we have asserted that racial processes and ethnic processes are similar. We believe it is incontrovertible that, if one looks around the globe and considers the constructed nature of ethnic identities, one cannot sustain the old, pseudoscientific, racist division of humankind into four or five big "races," with each of those subdivided into smaller "ethnic groups." Rather, there are many peoples, which the present authors choose to call ethnic groups, but for which we might well choose another name if we could all agree on one.

Yet, as has been pointed out by Lori Pierce in this volume and by Michael Omi, Howard Winant, Robert Miles, and others elsewhere, the danger exists that some people may misuse our insight to de-emphasize the enduring oppressions of racism. Omi and Winant rightly credit scholars of the first half of the twentieth century such as Franz Boas and Robert Ezra Park with using the generic term "ethnicity" to de-emphasize the biological pretensions of the pseudoscientific racists who promoted eugenics and Nazism. They also note the role of mid-century liberals like Gunnar Myrdal, who made "ethnicity" the conceptual term of choice: "In its elevation to theoretical dominance with the Myrdal study, ethnicity theory derived its agenda from the political imperatives of the period: to condemn in the liberal terms of the war years the phenomenon of racial inequality.... [T]he ethnicity-based theoretical tradition, derived from the experiences of European immigrants, was extended in the conclusions of *An American Dilemma* so that it might apply as well to nonwhites, especially blacks." They argue that later, in the 1970s, neoconservatives led by Nathan Glazer twisted the egalitarian ideals of their predecessors when peoples of color, especially African Americans, became strident in demanding group rights and recognition. "[B]eginning around 1970, ethnicity theorists developed a conservative egalitarian perspective which emphasized the dangerous radicalism and (in their view) antidemocratic character of 'positive' or 'affirmative' antidiscrimination policies. State activities should be restricted, they argued, to guarantees of equality for individuals."[4]

There is merit to the criticism of Omi, Winant, and their colleagues. Glazer's 1975 diatribe, *Affirmative Discrimination,* and similar pieces by neoconservatives picture

American society as effectively a common social escalator: each immigrant group (and they like to picture Blacks as a recent immigrant group) gets on at the bottom and then rides blithely to the top over a couple of generations.[5] The message is: If you haven't gotten yours yet, you soon will, but you will have to give up your ethnic distinctiveness. There are no structural impediments to keep you on the bottom long. If, like African Americans or Native Americans you have been on the lower steps for many generations, it is your own fault, and ultimately the American ethnic pot will melt everyone together into one happy people.[6]

Such a position is, in our view, a perversion of the egalitarianism of Boas, Park, and Myrdal and a refusal to admit the continuing impact of racism (and its partner, colonialism). Nonetheless, we think it is still important to seek terminology that allows scholars to compare the experiences of peoples over the entire globe—individual identities, group processes, and intergroup relationships—and we believe that "ethnicity" is the term that best fills that bill.

Multiplicity

The problem that accompanies our second contention regarding the rising consciousness of multiple ethnic identities is that individual identity expressions may win out over group needs. As several authors have demonstrated in this volume, the claiming of a multiethnic identity serves the interest of psychological wholeness for most people of mixed ancestry. It also makes conceptual sense in an era when we are coming to acknowledge the constructedness of ethnic identities, and when growing numbers of people are cognizant of the fact that they possess multiple ancestries.

Yet there are potential group costs to wholesale societal embrace of the multiethnic idea. Most multiracialists speak the language of individual expression and empowerment. Carlos Fernández writes from an individualist perspective, "Anyone whose 'racial' or ethnic identification encompasses more than one of the classifications currently employed by government ... is well aquainted with the absurdity and insult of rules requiring a monoracial response on government forms."[7] Maria Root's emphasis in "A Bill of Rights for Racially Mixed People" is equally individualistic:

I have the right not to justify my existence in this world.
I have the right not to keep the races separate within me.
I have the right not to be responsible for people's discomfort with my physical
    ambiguity.
I have the right to identify myself differently than strangers expect me to identify.
I have the right to identify myself differently than how my parents identify me.
I have the right to identify myself differently than my brothers and sisters.
I have the right to identify myself differently in different situations.
I have the right to create a vocabulary to communicate about being multiracial.
I have the right to change my identity over my lifetime—and more than once.
I have the right to have loyalties with more than one group of people.
I have the right to freely choose whom I befriend and love.[8]

Such expressions are heartfelt and logical, but they speak to individual yearnings, not to group needs.

There are those who express monoethnic group imperatives with equal fervor. Some Black leaders point out that most if not all African Americans could legitimately check a multiracial box on the census, because they have some Native American or European ancestry. Similar mixednesses characterize most Hispanic and Native American populations. But, if a significant number were to identify themselves as multiethnic, then the government counts of African Americans, Latinos, and Native Americans would be drastically reduced, and hence the political power of each of their groups and their share in government programs would also be reduced. Raul Yzaguirre writes: "Many civil rights laws rely on race and ethnic data to ensure effective enforcement in such key areas as education, voting, employment and housing. This data gathering is now imperiled by a new 'multiracial' category.... 98 percent of respondents who classified themselves as 'other race' in the 1990 Census were Hispanic.... Latinos already are the most undercounted group in the U.S. If a multiracial question were added, many Latinos might select 'multiracial' as their identifier, and never get to the Hispanic question."[9] Some may argue that Yzaguirre does not have his facts quite right, and that if he read Mary Waters's essay in this volume he might find his fears fading. Yet there are leaders of various groups, most prominently monoracially defined African Americans, who voice similar fears.

Some decry multiracialists as people who would abandon their "real" racial group and seek to be White. Ed Vaughn, a Black member of the Michigan House of Representatives, told *Jet,* "I can see all kinds of Negroes who don't want to be Black jumping off the ship because they feel they can get more out of the system. They wouldn't be supporting Black people and the issues that Black people have fought for."[10] A few monoracialist African Americans go so far as to predict that tolerance of a multiracial identity will create a third racial caste, like the Coloured population of South Africa, and that this will be the beginning of a descent into apartheid-like racial oppression, with Multiracials siding with Whites against Blacks. *Emerge* magazine notes, "Privately, some Black leaders contend the multiracial families pushing this movement are pawns for racists, whose real goal is to eliminate racial categories altogether, pushing the nation toward this delusion of a colorblind society. Such a move towards this fraud would dissolve the safeguards the government constructed to promote equal opportunities for Blacks."[11] No one has made a credible case that advocates of a multiethnic identity support abolishing race or ignoring the oppressions of racism. But it gives pause to more than a few leaders—Blacks, Latinos, Asians, and others—that White hegemonists from former California Governor Pete Wilson to former House Speaker Newt Gingerich seem to want to do away with all talk of race and racism.

There is a real split, then, as yet unsolved, between the compelling logic of multiethnicity and its promise for mixed individuals on the one hand, and the practical political imperatives of monoethnically defined groups on the other, in an age that has not yet wholly given up monoethnic definitions.

There is also a further question: Is there a groupness to mixedness? That is, are there common interests, institutions, or culture that hold all or a substantial part of the mixed population together as a group? Are mixed people beginning to form something like an ethnic group of their own? Or are their stories of mixedness inevitably individual stories, and their ethnic ties only to those groups that make up their ancestry? It is too early to come up with a definitive answer to this question, but there are some signs that such a multiethnic group may be forming. Certainly, there are multiethnic institutions. Colleges coast to coast have multiethnic student organizations, from the University of California's Hapa Issues Forum to Harvard Hapa. The Association for Multi-Ethnic Americans lobbies Congress on behalf of a multiracial census category. And groups that were formed originally as support networks for intermarrying couples, such as Multiracial Americans of Southern California and Chicago's Biracial Family Network, now have large and increasingly separate multiethnic caucuses. There are multiethnic list-serves on the Internet and periodicals such as *New People* devoted to multiethnic issues.

Multiethnic interests exist. Multiracial historian Laurie Mengel asks several pertinent questions: "[I]s there an actual affiliation shared between mixed race people, regardless of their particular racial makeup? Are mixed race people not 'halves' or 'doubles,' but a third category: possessing a third consciousness which stands on its own, qualifying mixed race identity as not one thing or another, not both or fractions, but as a distinct and encompassing awareness, possessing a collective memory through shared experiences?" She writes of "mixedness as a racial link between people which is different from linkages between mixed and monoracials who share a common ancestry … a legitimate and viable *panethnicity*—a group response to a collective racial categorization."[12] She draws parallels between the ways such panethnicities as Asian Americans and Hispanic Americans were created and the census debate's impact on multiethnics.

It is not yet clear that much mixed-ethnic culture has built up, aside from the common appropriation of the Hawaiian word *hapa*. But Mengel may be right that there is "a commonality, a level of comfortability, a place where one does not have to codeswitch, a level of unspoken understanding, that is experienced by people of mixed race that is not found within their experiences as monoracials."[13] If she is correct, then we may be seeing the birth of a multiethnic group.

Questions remain regarding the issue of multiethnicity. Nonetheless, whether or not all the practical political and conceptual issues have been solved, it seems clear that the die has been cast. Multiethnicity is a vivid feature of today's and tomorrow's ethnic world. We cannot go back to monoethnic definitions even if we would.

Narrative

Finally, this volume's emphasis on narrative as a key to understanding ethnicity, both group and individual, might lead some investigators down the path toward inaccurate or incomplete representation of people's lives. This is not just a potential shortcoming to the focus on narrative here. It is a general problem with the literary turn in social and cultural studies of recent decades. When one concentrates on a text—a narrative—one may lose sight of the lives it illuminates and the context within which those lives are meaningful.

We would do well here to remember the old Buddhist proverb that asks us not to mistake the finger pointing at the moon for the moon itself. The finger, the narrative, points us toward the human experience of ethnicity. But the narrative is not itself that experience. The human lives that lie behind the narrative and the social and historical contexts of those lives are the subject of our study. The narrative is a means by which we may gain considerable understanding of those lives and contexts, but that is all. The text is the messenger, not the message; it is the finger, not the moon.

Beyond this, not all texts are equal in their ability to direct us toward our proverbial moon. Ethel Merman was a charismatic singer, but when she sang Irving Berlin's "I'm An Indian Too" she was not singing a Native American ethnic narrative.

Like the Seminole, Navajo, Kickapoo,
Like those Indians, I'm an Indian too.
A Sioux, ooh-ooh! A Sioux, ooh-ooh!
Just like Battle Axe, Hatchet Face, Eagle Nose,
Like those Indians, I'm an Indian too.
A Sioux, ooh-ooh! A Sioux, ooh-ooh!
Some Indian summer's day without a sound
I may hide away with Big Chief Hole In The Ground
and I'll have totem poles, tomahawks, small papoose,
which will go to prove I'm an Indian too.
A Sioux, ooh-ooh! A Sioux, ooh-ooh!
With my chief in his tepee, we'll raise an Indian family,
and I'll be busy night and day.
Looking like a flour sack with two papooses on my back,
And three papooses on the way....
I'm an Indian too.[14]

Berlin's words and Merman's interpretation may tell us some ethnic things: about the life patterns, values, and aspirations of New York Jews of the middle third of the twentieth century; about White Americans' stereotypes regarding Native Americans. But they tell us nothing at all about Native American lives and cultures themselves.

It is easy to see the flaw in Merman's assertion of Indianness. It may be harder for us to see the problem with the treatment of other, more recent texts. One of the editors of this volume attended an international African-American studies conference in the mid-1990s where there were multiple panels on female genital mutilation in the fiction of Alice Walker. Walker is one of the late twentieth century's most honored writers, and her treatment of female genital mutilation in *Possessing the Secret of Joy* is an important literary and political milestone. Yet would it not have been a worthy activity at a conference of this sort, which had many African participants along with Europeans and North Americans, to hold some discussion of female genital mutilation itself—its incidence, its cultural role, its tragic effects for human lives, attempts to discourage the practice, counterattempts to assert it as a cultural symbol, and so forth? Alas, all we did at that conference was discuss, intelligently—even subtly—the contours of the finger (Walker's writing); we never addressed the moon, the tangible human problem of female genital mutilation.[15]

In a related way, a focus on narrative accounts may lead us away from the social context of ethnic behavior. The metaphor upon which much research in narrative is based stems from written journals. In this situation a narrative is externalized in a concrete form. Such activities have been generalized so that all people are thought to keep a sort of virtual journal as a result of normal cognitive processing. Following the journal metaphor, individuals are thought to retrieve their virtual journals and work in them so that over time, an extensive life account is built up. The journal metaphor may lead us, to use a computer expression, to expect what we might call a "narrative in residence" in the memory of each individual. Although memory for life events would surely be a well-established part of one's episodic memory,[16] the particular processes of selection, emplotment, and interpretation that are essential for narrative creation may not be automatic. We assert that the "narrative in residence" virtual journal is a misleading metaphor that causes us to ignore the process of narrative creation and the circumstances within which narratives come to be.

Cornell's attention to power issues such as "who gets to narrate whom" and "whose version of an identity narrative gains currency where"[17] provides a starting point for an alternative view of narrative. Power relations in narrative construction make us realize that the process of narrative construction is inherently social: all narratives are the result of social interaction, and such interactions form contexts that are inherently part of narratives. As a result, narratives do not arise in a vacuum but rather are constructed in particular social situations. An interesting example is Wallace's[18] account of his efforts to draw life reviews from elderly individuals. Although every effort was made to allow respondents to structure their own life accounts, Wallace found that spontaneous talk about the past was the exception in his respondents and that prompts were typically required to aid individuals in structuring their responses. Wallace's conclusion is that life stories are social constructions that arise in particular social situations. Narratives are then shaped through social interaction with an audience—the audience constitutes a context that is intrinsic to the narrative.

A lack of consideration of both individual and context is evident in Robin Kelley's remarkable book, *Race Rebels*. Chapter 7 is titled "The Riddle of the Zoot: Malcolm Little and Black Cultural Politics During World War II." A reader may expect that Kelley will explain the social and cultural dynamics that gave rise to and were expressed by a group of young African American men some called zoot-suiters, who adopted what many others regarded as outlandish dress and styles of communication and who were much persecuted in the early 1940s. One might even hope the author would lay out for us the similarities and differences in background, culture, motivation, and behavior between zoots in New York and Chicago, between Black zoots and Chicano zoots and Japanese American zoots (yes, there were some), between male zoots and their female companions.[19]

Alas, Kelley is brilliant in his interpretations, but he has only one zoot: Malcolm Little. And he has not Malcolm Little the zoot describing his life, nor others describing Malcolm Little. Rather, he has Malcolm X the former zoot describing his past life with politically tinged disdain. Thus, through a single glass very darkly, we see a very small part of the zoot-suit phenomenon, and we are expected to take that part uncritically for the whole. That Malcom X's self-narrative was presented to a particular audience for a particular purpose never enters the analysis of the text. Kelley's interpretation is wonderfully inventive. He concludes, powerfully but at the level of almost naked assertion:

> While the suit itself was not meant as a direct political statement, the social context in which it was created and worn rendered it so. The language and culture of zoot suiters represented a subversive refusal to be subservient. . . . [T]he conk [w]as part of a larger process [no pun, apparently, intended] by which black youth appropriated, transformed, and reinscribed coded oppositional meanings onto styles derived from the dominant culture [and imitated palely by middle-class blacks]. . . . [T]hey represented the negation of black bourgeois culture and a reaffirmation of a subaltern culture that emphasized pleasure, rejected work, and celebrated a working-class racial identity. . . . presenting a public challenge to the dominant stereotypes of the black body, and reinforcing a sense of dignity that was perpetually being assaulted.[20]

This was surely true for some zoots, perhaps for Malcolm Little, maybe even for his friends. But will it do as a reliable interpretation of the zoot-suit experience at large? We cannot know unless we consult more than this single text. The exclusive consideration of a text draws us away from a contextualized understanding of Malcom X.

We conclude with a positive example from this collection. Cluny and La'avasa Macpherson provide a description of the construction of Samoan ethnicity among second-generation Samoan migrants to New Zealand. They are able to focus on both the narrative and on individuals and their context. In their work they demonstrate that the high degree of homogeneity among first-generation Samoan migrants was and is replaced by significant variability in the second generation. Different opportunities lead to different experiences generally and the selection of different experiences for narrative use in particular. For example, the narrative story "Samoans are great at sports but not at much else" has given way to a more inclusive narrative of Samoan success as Samoans have moved into white collar occupations and as certain prominent Samoans have attained highly visible success. This change in narrative has effected public perceptions of both Samoans and larger society. Individuals also interpret their experiences differently. For example, the Macphersons provide an example of two individuals who do and who do not speak Samoan as a result of their upbringing. The subsequent experiences of these individuals caused them to feel that Samoan was of little value in one case or to desire and then gain a knowledge of Samoan in another. Experiences and opportunities caused each of these individuals to interpret and value their cultural knowledge differently. In general, the narrative developed by the Macphersons is sophisticated because it provides a contextualized understanding of the development of ethnic identity in the children of Samoan migrants to New Zealand.

These, then, are some of the limitations and advantages to the use of narrative as a key for understanding ethnic formation and processes. Understanding of narrative, whether it be the collective narrative of a people such as African Americans reciting the history of slavery, or the individual narrative of a Samoan chanting his genealogy, is a powerful tool in the search to unlock the meaning of ethnicity. As Stuart Hall informs us, "identities are the names we give to the different ways we are positioned by, and position ourselves in, the narratives of the past."[21]

So, too, the other main contentions of this volume—that ethnicity is constructed and that it is fraught with multiplicity—have both advantages and limitations. Nonetheless, we believe these general insights, and the more detailed accounts of various ethnic situations that are presented in this volume, will advance collective understanding of ethnicity.

Notes

1. Chapter 3, this volume.

2. Neo-pseudoscientific racists need not detain us here, For examples, see J. Philippe Rushton, *Race, Evolution and Behavior* (New Brunswick, N.J.: Transaction, 1995); Richard J. Hernnstein and Charles Murray, *The Bell Curve: Intelligence and Class Structure in American Life* (New York: Free Press, 1994). For correctives, see Steven Fraser, ed., *The Bell Curve Wars: Race Intelligence, and the Future of America* (New York: Basic Books, 1995); William H. Tucker, *The Science and Politics of Racial Research* (Urbana: University of Illinois Press, 1994).

3. Dinesh D'Souza, *The End of Racism* (New York: Free Press, 1995), 448, 544.

4. Andrew Hacker, *Two Nations: Black and White, Separate, Hostile, Unequal,* rev. ed. (New York: Ballantine, 1995). It should be noted that the present authors disagree strongly with some of Hacker's assumptions, preoccupations, and conclusions; to take just one example, we think he is dead wrong when he writes that "second and subsequent generations of Hispanics and Asians are merging onto the 'white' category, partly through intermarriage and also by personal achievement and adaptation" (p. 19). Nonetheless, he does deal responsibly with both the constructed quality of ethnicity and the desperate reality of racism.

5. Michael Omi and Howard Winant, *Racial Formation in the United States,* 2d ed. (New York: Routledge, 1994), 16–20. See also Robert Miles, especially *Racism After Race Relations* (New York: Routledge, 1993). The Myrdal study was *An American Dilemma: The Negro Problem and Modern Democracy* (many editions, beginning 1944).

6. Nathan Glazer, *Affirmative Discrimination: Ethnic Inequality and Public Policy* (New York: Basic Books, 1975).

7. See also Thomas Sowell, *Ethnic America: A History* (New York: Basic Books, 1981); Thomas Sowell, *Race and Culture: A World View* (New York: Basic Books, 1994).

8. Glazer's advice on this last score is that, despite cultural variety and ethnic oppression, "We should still engage in the work of the creation of a single, distinct, and unique nation, and this requires that our main attention be centered on the common culture"; "The Problem of Ethnic Studies," in *Ethnic Dilemmas,* Nathan Glazer (Cambridge, Mass.: Harvard University Press, 1983), 124.

9. Carlos Fernandez, "Government Classification of Multiracial/Multiethnic People," in *The Multiracial Experience,* ed. Maria P. P. Root (Thousand Oaks, Calif.: Sage, 1996), 16.

10. Maria P. P. Root, "A Bill of Rights for Racially Mixed People," in *The Multiracial Experience,* ed. Root, 7.

11. Raul Yzaguirre, comment in Internet chat group (November 1996).

12. Laurie M. Mengel, "Triples: The Social Evolution of a Multiracial Panethnicity," in *Rethinking "Mixed Race,"* ed. David Parker and Miri Song (London: Pluto Press, forthcoming).

13. Ibid.

14. Irving Berlin, *Annie Get Your Gun,* vocal score (New York: Irving Berlin Music Corporation, 1967), 121–24. Copyright 1946 by Irving Berlin. Used by permission.

15. Alice Walker, *Possessing the Secret of Joy* (New York: Harcourt Brace Jovanovich, 1992). See also the reviews reprinted in Henry Louis Gates, Jr., and K. A. Appiah, eds., *Alice Walker* (New York: Amistad, 1993), 27–34. Scholarly treatments of female genital mutilation in Africa and the diaspora are legion; some recent examples: L. Bishop Tammi, "Female Genital Mutilation," *Journal of the National Medical Association* 89 (1997): 233ff.; L. M. Bashir, "Female Genital Mutilation: Balancing Intolerance of the Practice with Tolerance of Culture," *Journal of Women's Health* 6 (1997), 11ff.; Lori Ann Larson, "Female Genital Mutilation in the United States: Child Abuse or Constitutional Freedom," *Woman's Rights Law Reporter* 17 (1996), 237ff.

16. E. Tulving and D. L. Schacter, "Priming and Human Memory Systems," *Science* 247 (1990): 301–06; E. Tulving and D. L. Schacter, *Memory Systems* (Cambridge, Mass.: MIT Press, 1994).

17. Chapter 3, this volume.

18. J. B. Wallace, "Reconsidering the Life Review: The Social Construction of Talk About the Past," *Gerontologist* 32 (1992): 120–25.

19. For Japanese American zoots see Paul Spickard, "Not Just the Quiet People: The Nisei Underclass," *Pacific Historical Review* 68 (1999): 78–94. For Chicanos, see Mauricio Mazon, *The Zoot-Suit Riot* (Austin: University of Texas Press, 1984).

20. Robin D. G. Kelly, *Race Rebels: Culture, Politics, and the Black Working Class* (New York: Free Press, 1994), 166–69.

21. Henry Louis Gates, Jr., "Black London," *New Yorker* (April 28 and May 5, 1997), 203.

Contributors

W. JEFFREY BURROUGHS is Professor of Psychology and Associate Dean of the College of Arts and Sciences at Brigham Young University–Hawai'i. He is the editor of *Applied Psychology* (1989) and the author of many articles and papers on topics in social perception and consumption symbolism.

STEPHEN CORNELL is Professor of Sociology and Director of the Udall Center for Studies in Public Policy at the University of Arizona. He is the author of *The Return of the Native: American Indian Political Resurgence* (1988), co-editor of *What Can Tribes Do? Strategies and Institutions in American Indian Economic Development* (1992), and co-author of *Ethnicity and Race* (1997).

G. REGINALD DANIEL is Assistant Professor of Sociology at the University of California, Santa Barbara. He is the author of many articles and papers on multiethnicity in the United States and Brazil, as well as three forthcoming books, including *Multiracial Identity and the New Millenium: Black No More or More Than Black?*

VIOLET JOHNSON is Associate Professor of History and Director of Africana Studies at Agnes Scott College and author of several articles on the migratory populations of the African diaspora. She is completing a book on the history of Boston's West Indian community.

KAREN I. LEONARD is Professor of Anthropology at the University of California, Irvine. She is the author of many articles and several books on ethnicity and social structure in India and the Indian diaspora, including *Making Ethnic Choices: California's Punjabi Mexican Americans* (1992) and *The South Asian Americans* (1998).

CLUNY MACPHERSON is a professor in the Department of Sociology at the University of Auckland. He is currently working and writing on social and economic development and migration and settlement in the Pacific. He has written widely on Samoan matters and is co-author of *Emerging Pluralism: Samoans in Urban New Zealand* (1976), *Nga Take: Ethnic Relations and Racism in Aotearoa/New Zealand* (1991), and *Samoan Medical Belief and Practice* (1991).

LA'AVASA MACPHERSON is a research assistant in the Department of Sociology at the University of Auckland. She has written on migration and settlement and Samoan medicine. She is co-author of *Samoan Medical Belief and Practice* (1991) and several articles on Samoan culture in the diaspora.

PHILLIP H. MCARTHUR is Associate Professor of Humanities at Brigham Young University–Hawai'i and a specialist on folklore and identity in the Marshall Islands.

PATRICK MILLER is Associate Professor of History at Northeastern Illinois State University. He is the author of *The Playing Fields of American Culture* (forthcoming) and many articles and papers on American cultural and racial history.

LORI PIERCE is a Ph.D. candidate in American Studies at the University of Hawai'i and author of several publications on race, culture, and religion in Hawai'i.

DARBY LI PO PRICE, holder of a Ph.D. in Ethnic Studies from the University of California, Berkeley, is the author of many articles on ethnic humor. He has taught at Vassar College and at the University of California campuses in Berkeley and Davis. His current project is a book on Asian American, Latino, African American, Native American, Hawai'ian, and multiracial comedians, performance artists, and writers.

MARIA P. P. ROOT, a clinical psychologist in Seattle, is an authority on the developmental and social issues raised by the biracial baby boom. She has written extensively on identity development, and has published two award-winning books, *Racially Mixed People in America* (1992) and *The Multiracial Experience* (1995).

PAUL SPICKARD is Professor of History at the University of California, Santa Barbara. He is the author of many articles and papers on ethnic questions, and the author or editor of seven books, including *Mixed Blood: Intermarriage and Ethnic Identity in Twentieth-Century America* (1989), *Pacific Island Peoples in Hawai'i* (1994), and *Japanese Americans* (1996).

MAX E. STANTON is the author of many articles and papers on Pacific Islanders in the Pacific and in the diaspora, as well as on Hutterites and on Native Americans. He is Professor and Chair of Anthropology and Sociology at Brigham Young University–Hawai'i.

COOKIE WHITE STEPHAN is Professor of Sociology at New Mexico State University. She is the author or co-author of many articles and papers on ethnicity and social psychology, as well as five books, including *Intergroup Relations* (1995) and *The Future of Social Psychology* (1991). Her current work is on the psychology and sociology of racism and related issues such as sex prejudice, prejudice against the disabled, and homophobia.

WALTER G. STEPHAN is Professor of Psychology at New Mexico State University. He is the author or co-author of many articles and papers on attribution processes, cognition and affect, intergroup relations, and intercultural relations, as well as five books, including *Intergroup Relations* (1995), *The Future of Social Psychology* (1991), and *Reducing Prejudice and Stereotyping in the Schools* (1998).

MARY C. WATERS is Harvard College Professor of Sociology at Harvard University. She is the author of three books: *Ethnic Options* (1990), *From Many Strands: Ethnic and Racial Groups in Contemporary America* (1988), and *Black Identities: West Indian Immigrant Dreams and American Realities* (1999). Her current work is on patterns of assimilation among second-generation immigrants and patterns of racial intermarriage and identity formation.